Roswell D. Hitchcock

Carmina Sanctorum

A selection of hymns and songs of praise with tunes

Roswell D. Hitchcock

Carmina Sanctorum
A selection of hymns and songs of praise with tunes

ISBN/EAN: 9783744781749

Printed in Europe, USA, Canada, Australia, Japan

Cover: Foto ©Thomas Meinert / pixelio.de

More available books at **www.hansebooks.com**

Carmina Sanctorum

A SELECTION OF

HYMNS AND SONGS OF PRAISE

WITH TUNES

EDITED BY

ROSWELL DWIGHT HITCHCOCK, ZACHARY EDDY

LEWIS WARD MUDGE

————

A. S. BARNES & CO

NEW YORK AND CHICAGO

PREFACE.

THIS Book may, for the most part, be left to speak for itself. It aims to provide expression for every variety of healthy Christian experience, emphasizing especially the more jubilant, hopeful, and courageous graces and virtues. It represents the great Communion of Saints of all ages and nations.

Some who use the Book are likely to miss here and there a familiar Hymn. Further reflection may possibly convince them that the omitted Hymns are mostly inferior echoes and duplicates, which can well be spared. Where three or four really fine Hymns adequately embody some Christian feeling or purpose, three or four other inferior Hymns, striving to embody the same feeling or purpose, only lower the tone of worship.

The musical adaptations have been very carefully studied. Valuable assistance has been kindly rendered by Mr. Howard E. Parkhurst, organist of the Madison Square Presbyterian Church in this city, and by the Rev. James Carter, a recent graduate of the Union Theological Seminary. Great pains have been taken to retain the best of the old Tunes, while introducing the best of the new ones. The editors have taken it for granted that Choirs and Congregations are desiring, not revolution, but only improvement, in their Service of Song.

ROSWELL DWIGHT HITCHCOCK.
ZACHARY EDDY.
LEWIS WARD MUDGE.

New York: May 1, 1885.

CONTENTS.

CARMINA SANCTORUM.

Invocation.

NICÆA. 11.12.12.10.

Rev. JOHN BACCHUS DYKES (1823—1876), 1861.

1. Ho - LY, ho - ly, ho - ly! Lord God Al - might - y! Ear - ly in the morn - ing our song shall rise to Thee; Ho - ly, ho - ly, ho - ly! Mer - ci - ful and Might - y! God in Three Per - sons, Bles - ed Trin - i - ty!

1

"Which was, and is, and is to come."
Rev. iv. 8.

2 Holy, holy, holy! all the saints adore Thee,
   Casting down their golden crowns around the glassy sea;
   Cherubim and seraphim falling down before Thee,
   Which wert, and art, and evermore shalt be.

3 Holy, holy, holy! though the darkness hide Thee,
   Though the eye of sinful man Thy glory may not see,
   Only Thou art Holy, there is none beside Thee,
   Perfect in power, in love, and purity.

4 Holy, holy, holy! Lord God Almighty!
   All Thy works shall praise Thy Name in earth, and sky, and sea;
   Holy, holy, holy! Lord God Almighty!
   God in Three Persons, Blessed Trinity!

Bp. Reginald Heber (1783—1826), 1827.

(5)

LYONS. 5.5.5.6.D.   FRANCIS JOSEPH HAYDN (1732—1809), 1770.

1. O worship the King, All glorious a - bove; O grate-ful - ly sing His power and His love;

Our Shield and De-fender, The An - cient of days, Pa - vil-ioned in splendor, And gird - ed with praise.

2

The Might and Mercy of God.
Ps. civ.

2 O tell of His might,
    O sing of His grace,
Whose robe is the light,
    Whose canopy space ;
His chariots of wrath
    The thunder-clouds form,
And dark is His path
    On the wings of the storm.

3 Thy bountiful care
    What tongue can recite?
It breathes in the air,
    It shines in the light,
It streams from the hills,
    It descends to the plain,
And sweetly distils
    In the dew and the rain.

4 Frail children of dust,
    And feeble as frail,
In Thee do we trust,
    Nor find Thee to fail :
Thy mercies how tender,
    How firm to the end,
Our Maker, Defender,
    Redeemer, and Friend.
      Sir Robert Grant (1788—1838), 1839. Ab.

3

"Jesus, our King."

1 YE servants of God,
    Your Master proclaim,
And publish abroad
    His wonderful Name ;
The Name all-victorious
    Of Jesus extol ;
His Kingdom is glorious,
    And rules over all.

2 God ruleth on high,
    Almighty to save ;
And still He is nigh ;
    His presence we have.
The great congregation
    His triumph shall sing,
Ascribing salvation
    To Jesus, our King.

3 "Salvation to God,
    Who sits on the throne,"
Let all cry aloud,
    And honor the Son :
The praises of Jesus
    The angels proclaim,
Fall down on their faces,
    And worship the Lamb.

4 Then let us adore,
     And give Him His right,
  All glory, and power,
     And wisdom and might;

All honor and blessing,
   With angels above,
And thanks never ceasing,
   And infinite love.

Rev. Charles Wesley (1708—1788), 1744. Ab.

LUX LUCIS. 7, 8, 7, 7.   JOSEPH BARNBY (1838—   ), 1872.

1. Light of Light, en-light-en me! Now a-new the day is dawn-ing;

Sun of grace, the shad-ows flee, Bright-en Thou my Sab-bath morn-ing:

With Thy joy-ous sun-shine blest, Hap-py is my day of rest.

4

" Light of Light."

2 Fount of all our joy and peace,
     To Thy living waters lead me;
  Thou from earth my soul release,
     And with grace and mercy feed me;
  Bless Thy Word that it may prove
  Rich in fruits that Thou dost love.

3 Kindle Thou the sacrifice
     That upon my lips is lying;
  Clear the shadows from mine eyes,
     That, from every error flying,
  No strange fire may in me glow
  That Thine altar doth not know.

4 Let me with my heart to-day,
     Holy, holy, holy, singing,
  Rapt awhile from earth away,

All my soul to Thee up-springing,
Have a foretaste inly given,
How they worship Thee in Heaven.

5 Rest in me and I in Thee,
     Build a paradise within me:
  O reveal Thyself to me,
     Blessed Love, who died'st to win me;
  Fed from Thine exhaustless urn,
  Pure and bright my lamp shall burn.

6 Hence all care, all vanity,
     For the day to God is holy:
  Come, thou glorious Majesty,
     Deign to fill this temple lowly;
  Naught to-day my soul shall move,
  Simply resting in Thy love.

Rev. Benjamin Schmolke (1672—1737), 1704.
Tr. by Miss Catherine Winkworth (1829—1878), 1858.

DAYSPRING. 7, 8, 7, 3.   JOHANN ANASTASIUS FREYLINGHAUSEN (1670—1739), 1704.

1. DAYSPRING of E-ter-ni-ty, Brightness of the Fa-ther's glo-ry, Dawn on us, that

we may see Clouds and darkness flee be-fore Thee; Drive a-far, with conquering might, All our night.

5

"Morgenglanz der Ewigkeit."

2 Let Thy grace, like morning dew,
   Fall on hearts in Thee confiding;
Thy sweet comfort, ever new,
   Fill our souls with strength abiding;
And Thy quickening eyes behold
     Thy dear fold.

3 Give the flame of love, to burn
   Till the bands of sin it breaketh,
Till, at each new day's return
   Purer light my soul awaketh;
O, ere twilight come, let me
     Rise to Thee.

4 Thou who hast gone up on high,
   Grant that when Thy trumpet soundeth,
When with glory, in the sky,
   Thee the cloud of saints surroundeth,
We may stand among Thine own,
     Round Thy throne.

5 Lead us to the golden shore,
   O Thou rising Sun of Morning,
Lead where tears shall flow no more,
   Where all sighs to songs are turning,
Where Thy glory sheds alway
     Perfect day.

Knorr von Rosenroth (1636—1688), 1684.
Tr. by Rev. John Henry Hopkins (1820—), 1866. Sl. alt.

BADEN. 8. 8. 8. 8. 7.   JOHANN SEBASTIAN BACH (1685—1750).

HO-SAN-NA to the Liv-ing Lord! Ho-san-na to th'In-car-nate Word! To Christ, Cre-a-tor,

Sav-iour, King, Let earth, let Heav'n, ho-san-na sing: Ho-san-na in the high-est!

6

"Hosanna, Lord."

2 "Hosanna," Lord, Thine angels cry;
"Hosanna," Lord, Thy saints reply;
Above, beneath us, and around,
The dead and living swell the sound :
Hosanna in the highest!

3 O Saviour, with protecting care
Return to this Thy house of prayer,
Assembled in Thy sacred Name,
Where we Thy parting promise claim :
Hosanna in the highest!

4 But, chiefest, in our cleansed breast,
Eternal, bid Thy Spirit rest ;
And make our secret soul to be
A temple pure, and worthy Thee :
Hosanna in the highest!

5 So, in the last and dreadful day,
When earth and heaven shall melt away,
Thy flock, redeemed from sinful stain,
Shall swell the sound of praise again :
Hosanna in the highest!

Bp. Reginald Heber (1783–1826), 1811. Ref. alt.

GILEAD. L. M.

ETIENNE HENRI MEHUL (1763–1817), 1807

1. THEE we a - dore, E - ter - nal Lord, We praise Thy Name with one ac - cord;

Thy saints, who here Thy good - ness see, Through all the world do wor - ship Thee

7

"Te Deum Laudamus."

2 To Thee aloud all angels cry,
The heavens and all the powers on high :
Thee, Holy, holy, holy King,
Lord God of Hosts, they ever sing.

3 Th' Apostles join the glorious throng ;
The Prophets swell th' immortal song ;
The Martyrs' noble army raise
Eternal anthems to Thy praise.

4 From day to day, O Lord, do we
Highly exalt and honor Thee :
Thy Name we worship and adore,
World without end, for evermore.

5 Vouchsafe, O Lord, we humbly pray,
To keep us safe from sin this day:
Have mercy, Lord, we trust in Thee ;
O let us ne'er confounded be.

Rev. John Gambold (1711–1771), 1754. Ab. and alt.

8

"The Trinity adored."

1 O HOLY, holy, holy Lord,
Bright in Thy deeds and in Thy Name,
For ever be Thy Name adored,
Thy glories let the world proclaim.

2 O Jesus, Lamb once crucified
To take our load of sins away,
Thine be the hymn that rolls its tide
Along the realms of upper day.

3 O Holy Spirit from above,
In streams of light and glory given,
Thou source of ecstasy and love,
Thy praises ring thro' earth and Heav'n

4 O God Triune, to Thee we owe
Our every thought, our every song ;
And ever may Thy praises flow
From saint and seraph's burning tongue

Rev. James Wallis Eastburn (1797–1819), 1819.

OSWALD. 8.7. *Rev.* JOHN BACCHUS DYKES (1823—1876), 1861.

1. ROUND the Lord in glo-ry seat-ed, Cher-u-bim and ser-a-phim

Filled His Tem-ple and re-peat-ed, Each to each, th'al-ter-nate hymn:

9

Thrice Holy.
Is. vi. 1—3. John xii. 41.

2 "Lord, Thy glory fills the Heaven,
  "Earth is with its fulness stored;
"Unto Thee be glory given,
  "Holy, holy, holy Lord!"

3 Heaven is still with glory ringing;
  Earth takes up the angels' cry,
"Holy, holy, holy," singing,
  "Lord of Hosts, the Lord most High."

4 With His seraph train before Him,
  With His holy Church below,
Thus conspire we to adore Him,
  Bid we thus our anthem flow:

5 "Lord, Thy glory fills the Heaven,
  Earth is with its fulness stored;
Unto Thee be glory given,
  Holy, holy, holy Lord!"

6 Thus Thy glorious Name confessing,
  We adopt the angels' cry,
Holy, holy, holy! blessing
  Thee, the Lord of Hosts most high.
      Bp. Richard Mant (1776—1848), 1837. Ab.

DOXOLOGY.

PRAISE the Father, earth, and Heaven,
  Praise the Son, the Spirit praise;
As it was, and is, be given
  Glory, through eternal days.
      Unknown Author, 1827.

10

God my Refuge and Fortress.
Ps. xci.

1 CALL Jehovah thy Salvation,
  Rest beneath th'Almighty's shade,
In His secret habitation
  Dwell, and never be dismayed.

2 There no tumult can alarm thee,
  Thou shalt dread no hidden snare;
Guile nor violence can harm thee,
  In eternal safeguard there.

3 From the sword, at noonday wasting,
  From the noisome pestilence,
In the depth of midnight, blasting,
  God shall be thy sure defence.

4 God shall charge His angel legions
  Watch and ward o'er thee to keep:
Though thou walk thro' hostile regions,
  Though in desert wilds thou sleep.

5 Since, with pure and firm affection,
  Thou on God hast set thy love,
With the wings of His protection
  He will shield thee from above.

6 Thou shalt call on Him in trouble,
  He will hearken, He will save;
Here for grief reward thee double,
  Crown with life beyond the grave.
      James Montgomery (1771—1854), 1822. Ab.

RATHBUN. 8.7.   ITHAMAR CONKEY (1815—1867), 1851.

1. Praise the Lord, ye Heavens, a-dore Him, Praise Him, an-gels, in the height;

Sun and moon, re-joice be-fore Him; Praise Him, all ye stars of light.

11

Praise from the whole Creation.
Ps. cxlviii.

2 Praise the Lord, for He hath spoken;
  Worlds His mighty voice obeyed;
Laws which never shall be broken,
  For their guidance He hath made.

3 Praise the Lord, for He is glorious;
  Never shall His promise fail;
God hath made His saints victorious;
  Sin and death shall not prevail.

4 Praise the God of our salvation;
  Hosts on high, His power proclaim;
Heaven and earth, and all creation,
  Laud and magnify His Name.

Rev. John Kempthorne (1775—1838), 1809.

12

God is Love.
1 John iv. 8.

1 God is Love; His mercy brightens
  All the path in which we rove;
Bliss He wakes, and woe He lightens:
  God is wisdom, God is love.

2 Chance and change are busy ever;
  Man decays, and ages move;
But His mercy waneth never;
  God is wisdom, God is love.

3 E'en the hour that darkest seemeth
  Will His changeless goodness prove;

From the mist His brightness streameth:
  God is wisdom, God is love.

4 He with earthly cares entwineth
  Hope and comfort from above;
Everywhere His glory shineth:
  God is wisdom, God is love.

Sir John Bowring (1792—1872), 1825.

13

Praise on Earth and in Heaven.
Rev. iv. 11.

1 Praise to Thee, Thou great Creator,
  Praise be Thine from every tongue;
Join, my soul, with every creature,
  Join the universal song.

2 Father, Source of all compassion,
  Pure unbounded grace is Thine:
Hail the God of our salvation,
  Praise Him for His love divine.

3 For ten thousand blessings given,
  For the richest gifts bestowed,
Sound His praise thro' earth and Heaven,
  Sound Jehovah's praise aloud.

4 Joyfully on earth adore Him,
  'Till in Heaven our song we raise;
There, enraptured fall before Him,
  Lost in wonder, love, and praise.

Rev. John Fawcett (1739—1817), 1767. Alt.

DIX. 7. 6l.

CONRAD KOCHER (1786–), 1838.
Arr. by WILLIAM HENRY MONK (1793–), 1861.

1. { God of mer - cy, God of grace, Show the bright - ness of Thy face; }
   { Shine up - on us, Sav - iour, shine, Fill Thy Church with light di - vine; }

And Thy sav - ing health ex - tend Un - to earth's re - mot - est end.

14   "God of Mercy, God of Grace."
                Ps. lxvii.

2 Let the people praise Thee, Lord,
  Be by all that live adored :
  Let the nations shout and sing
  Glory to their Saviour-King ;
  At Thy feet their tribute pay,
  And Thy holy will obey.

3 Let the people praise Thee, Lord,
  Earth shall then her fruits afford :
  God to man His blessing give,
  Man to God devoted live ;
  All below, and all above,
  One in joy, and light, and love.
  Rev. Henry Francis Lyte (1793–1847), 1834.

INNOCENTS. 7.

Ascribed to THEOBALD, King of Navarre (1201–1253).

1. As the sun doth dai - ly rise, Bright'ning all the morn - ing skies,

So to Thee with one ac - cord Lift we up our hearts, O Lord.

15   "Matutinus altiora."

2 Be our Guard in sin and strife ;
  Be the Leader of our life ;
  While we daily search Thy Word,
  Wisdom true impart, O Lord.

3 When the sun withdraws his light,
  When we seek our beds at night,

Thou, by sleepless hosts adored,
Hear the prayer of faith, O Lord.

4 Praise we, with the heavenly host,
  Father, Son, and Holy Ghost ;
  Thee would we with one accord
  Praise and magnify, O Lord.
  King Alfred of England (849–901).
  Tr. by Earl Horatio Nelson (1823–), 1864. Ab.

MESSIAH. 7. D.

LOUIS JOSEPH FERDINAND HEROLD (1791—1833), 1830.
Arr. by GEORGE KINGSLEY (1811—1884), 1838.

1. Praise to God who reigns a - bove, Binding earth and Heav'n in love: All the ar - mies of the sky
Wor - ship His dread sove - reign - ty. Ser - a - phim His prais - es sing, Cher - u - bim on
four - fold wing, Thrones, do - min - ions, princ - es, powers, Ranks of might that nev - er cowers.

16

Christ in Glory.

2 Angel hosts His word fulfil,
 Ruling nature by His will;
 Round His throne archangels pour
 Songs of praise for evermore.
 Yet on man they joy to wait,
 All that bright celestial state;
 For true man their Lord they see,
 Christ, th' incarnate Deity.

3 On the throne our Lord, who died,
 Sits in manhood glorified;
 Where His people faint below,
 Angels count it joy to go.
 O the depths of joy divine,
 Thrilling through those orders nine,
 When the lost are found again,
 When the banished come to reign.

Rev. Richard Meux Benson, 1861. Ab.

17

Thrice Holy.
Is. vi, 3.

1 HOLY, holy, holy Lord
 God of Hosts! When Heaven and earth,
 Out of darkness, at Thy word,
 Issued into glorious birth,

All Thy works before Thee stood,
And Thine eye beheld them good,
While they sang with sweet accord,
Holy, holy, holy Lord!

2 Holy, holy, holy! Thee,
 One Jehovah evermore,
 Father, Son, and Spirit, we,
 Dust and ashes, would adore;
 Lightly by the world esteemed,
 From that world by Thee redeemed,
 Sing we here, with glad accord,
 Holy, holy, holy Lord!

3 Holy, holy, holy! All
 Heaven's triumphant choir shall sing,
 When the ransomed nations fall
 At the footstool of their King:
 Then shall saints and seraphim,
 Hearts and voices, swell one hymn,
 Round the throne with full accord,
 Holy, holy, holy Lord!

James Montgomery (1771—1854), 1826, 1853.

ST. RAPHAEL. 8.7.4.   EDWARD JOHN HOPKINS (1818—   ).

1. In Thy Name, O Lord, as-sembling, We, Thy people, now draw near: Teach us to rejoice with trembling;

Speak, and let Thy ser-vants hear, Hear with meek-ness, Hear Thy Word with god-ly fear.

18

"Speak, for Thy servant heareth."
1 Sam. iii. 10

2 While our days on earth are lengthened,
    May we give them, Lord, to Thee;
Cheered by hope, and daily strengthened,
    May we run, nor weary be,
       Till Thy glory
    Without clouds in Heaven we see.

3 There in worship purer, sweeter,
    Thee Thy people shall adore;
Tasting of enjoyment greater
    Far than thought conceived before;
       Full enjoyment,
    Full, unmixed, and evermore.
         Rev. Thomas Kelly (1769—1855), 1815.

19

Dismission.

1 Lord, dismiss us with Thy blessing,
    Fill our hearts with joy and peace;

Let us now, Thy love possessing,
    Triumph in redeeming grace:
       O refresh us,
    Travelling through this wilderness.

2 Thanks we give, and adoration,
    For Thy Gospel's joyful sound:
May the fruits of Thy salvation
    In our hearts and lives abound;
       May Thy presence
    With us evermore be found.

3 So, whene'er the signal's given
    Us from earth to call away,
Borne on angels' wings to Heaven,
    Glad the summons to obey,
       May we ever
    Reign with Christ in endless day.
         Rev. John Fawcett (1739—1817), 1774.

ADVOCATE. L. M. 6l.   Arr. from JOHANN C. W. A. MOZART (1756—1791).

1. When, streaming from the east-ern skies, The morning light sa-lutes mine eyes, O Sun of

Righteous-ness Di-vine, On me with beams of mer-cy shine: Chase the dark clouds of guilt a-

-way, And turn my dark-ness in - to day, And turn my dark-ness in - to day.

20

"Unto the Lord."
Rom. xiv. 8.

2 And when to Heaven's all-glorious King
My morning sacrifice I bring,
And, mourning o'er my guilt and shame,
Ask mercy in my Saviour's Name,
Then, Jesus, cleanse me with Thy blood,
And be my advocate with God.

3 When each day's scenes and labors close,
And wearied nature seeks repose,

With pardoning mercy richly blest,
Guard me, my Saviour, while I rest;
And as each morning sun shall rise,
O lead me onward to the skies.

4 And at my life's last setting sun,
My conflicts o'er, my labors done,
Jesus, Thy Heavenly radiance shed,
To cheer and bless my dying bed;
And from death's gloom my spirit raise,
To see Thy face, and sing Thy praise.

William Shrubsole, Jr. (1759—1829), 1813. Ab. and alt.

ITALIAN HYMN. 6.6.4.6.6.6.4.

FELICE GIARDINI (1716—1796), 1769.

1. Come, Thou Al - might - y King, Help us Thy Name to sing, Help us to praise:

Fa - ther all - glo - ri - ous, O'er all vic - to - ri-ous, Come, and reign o - ver us, An-cient of days.

21

The Trinity invoked.

2 Jesus, our Lord, arise;
Scatter our enemies,
   And make them fall;
Let Thine almighty aid
Our sure defence be made;
Our souls on Thee be stayed:
   Lord, hear our call.

3 Come, Thou Incarnate Word,
Gird on Thy mighty sword,
   Our prayer attend;
Come, and Thy people bless,
And give Thy Word success:
Spirit of Holiness,
   On us descend.

4 Come, Holy Comforter,
Thy sacred witness bear
   In this glad hour:
Thou who Almighty art,
Now rule in every heart,
And ne'er from us depart,
   Spirit of Power.

5 To the great One and Three
Eternal praises be
   Hence, evermore.
His Sovereign Majesty
May we in glory see,
And to eternity
   Love and adore.

Rev. Charles Wesley (1708—1788), 1757.

ALETTA. 7.

WILLIAM BATCHELDER BRADBURY (1816—1868), 1856.

1. Lord, we come be-fore Thee now, At Thy feet we hum-bly bow;

O do not our suit dis-dain, Shall we seek Thee, Lord, in vain?

22

Seeking after God.
Jer. xxix. 13.

2 Lord, on Thee our souls depend
In compassion, now descend;
Fill our hearts with Thy rich grace,
Tune our lips to sing Thy praise.

3 In Thine own appointed way,
Now we seek Thee, here we stay:
Lord, we know not how to go,
Till a blessing Thou bestow.

4 Send some message from Thy Word,
That may joy and peace afford;
Let Thy Spirit now impart
Full salvation to each heart.

5 Comfort those who weep and mourn,
Let the time of joy return;
Heal the sick, the captive free,
Let us all rejoice in Thee.

Rev. William Hammond (—1783), 1745. Ab.

23

Sabbath Evening.

1 For the mercies of the day,
For this rest upon our way,
Thanks to Thee alone be given,
Lord of earth, and King of Heaven.

2 Cold our services have been,
Mingled every prayer with sin;
But Thou canst and wilt forgive:
By Thy grace alone we live.

3 Whilst this thorny path we tread,
May Thy love our footsteps lead;
When our journey here is past,
May we rest with Thee at last.

4 Let these earthly Sabbaths prove
Foretastes of our joys above;
While their steps Thy pilgrims bend
To the rest which knows no end.

O. P., 1826. Ab.

FERRIER. 7.

Rev. JOHN BACCHUS DYKES (1823—1876), 1861.

SEYMOUR. 7.

CARL MARIA von WEBER (1786—1826), 1826.
Arr. by HENRY WELLINGTON GREATOREX (1811—1858), 1849.

1. COME, my soul, thy suit pre-pare, Je-sus loves to an-swer pray'r;

Thou art com-ing to a King. Large pe-ti-tions with thee bring.

24

Asking of God.
1 Kings iii. 5.

2 With my burden I begin,
Lord, remove this load of sin;
Let Thy blood, for sinners spilt,
Set my conscience free from guilt.

3 Lord, I come to Thee for rest,
Take possession of my breast;
There Thy blood-bought right maintain,
And without a rival reign.

4 While I am a pilgrim here,
Let Thy love my spirit cheer;
As my Guide, my Guard, my Friend,
Lead me to my journey's end.

5 Show me what I have to do,
Every hour my strength renew;
Let me live a life of faith,
Let me die Thy people's death.
Rev. John Newton (1725—1807), 1779. Ab.

25

The fading Light.

1 SOFTLY now the light of day
Fades upon my sight away;
Free from care, from labor free,
Lord, I would commune with Thee.

2 Thou, whose all-pervading eye
Naught escapes, without, within,
Pardon each infirmity,
Open fault, and secret sin.

3 Soon, for me, the light of day
Shall forever pass away:
Then, from sin and sorrow free,
Take me, Lord, to dwell with Thee.

4 Thou who, sinless, yet hast known
All of man's infirmity;
Then, from Thine eternal throne,
Jesus, look with pitying eye.
Bp. George Washington Doane (1799—1859), 1824.

26

For the coming week.
Ps. lxxiii. 24.

1 THROUGH the passing of the week,
Father, we Thy presence seek:
'Midst this world's deceitful maze
Keep us, Lord, in all our ways.

2 O, what snares our path beset!
O, what cares our spirits fret!
Let no earthly thing, we pray,
Draw our souls from Thee away.

3 Thou hast set our daily task,
Grace and strength from Thee we ask;
Thou our joys and griefs dost send,
To Thy will our spirits bend.

4 Still in duty's lowly round
Be our patient footsteps found:
With Thy counsel guide us here,
Till in glory we appear.
Bp. William Walsham How (1823—), 1872. Ab.

INTERCESSION. L. M.
Arr. by Rev. JOHN BACCHUS DYKES (1823—1876). 1862.

1. JE - sus, wher - e'er Thy peo - ple meet, There they be - hold Thy Mer - cy - seat;

Wher - e'er they seek Thee, Thou art found, And ev' - ry place is hal - lowed ground.

27 *"Christ always with His people."*

2 For Thou, within no walls confined,
Inhabitest the humble mind;
Such ever bring Thee where they come,
And, going, take Thee to their home.

3 Dear Shepherd of Thy chosen few,
Thy former mercies here renew:
Here to our waiting hearts proclaim
The sweetness of Thy saving Name.

4 Here may we prove the power of prayer
To strengthen faith, and sweeten care,
To teach our faint desires to rise,
And bring all Heaven before our eyes.

5 Lord, we are few, but Thou art near;
Nor short Thine arm, nor deaf Thine ear:
O rend the heavens, come quickly down,
And make a thousand hearts Thine own.
William Cowper (1731—1800), 1760. Ab.

28 *"Jam lucis orto sidere."*

1 WHILE now the daylight fills the sky,
We lift our hearts to God on high,
That He, in all we do or say,
Would keep us free from harm to-day.

2 So when the daylight leaves the sky,
And night's dark hours once more are nigh,
May we, unsoiled by sinful stain,
Sing glory to our God again.
Ambrose of Milan (340—397).
Tr. by Rev. John Mason Neale (1818—1866), Ab. and alt.

ROCKINGHAM. L. M.
LOWELL MASON (1792—1872), 1832.

1. COME, dear - est Lord, de - scend and dwell, By faith and love, in ev' - ry breast;

Then shall we know, and taste, and feel, The joys that can - not be ex - prest.

29 *The Love of God shed abroad in the Heart.*
EPH. iii. 16.

2 Come, fill our hearts with inward strength;
  Make our enlarged souls possess,
  And learn the height and breadth and [length
  Of Thine immeasurable grace.

3 Now to the God, whose power can do
  More than our thoughts or wishes know,
  Be everlasting honors done,
  By all the church, thro' Christ, His Son.
      Rev. Isaac Watts (1674—1748), 1709.

30 *"Gott ist gegenwärtig. O lasset uns anbeten."*
(Abridged form.)

1 LO, God is here : let us adore,
  And own how dreadful is this place ;

Let all within us feel His power,
And silent bow before His face.

2 Lo, God is here : Him day and night
  United choirs of angels sing ;
  To Him, enthroned above all height,
  Let saints their humble worship bring.

3 Lord God of hosts, O may our praise
  Thy courts with grateful incense fill ;
  Still may we stand before Thy face,
  Still hear and do Thy sovereign will.
      Gerhard Tersteegen (1697—1769), 1731.
      Tr. by Rev. John Wesley (1703—1791), 1739. Ab. and alt.

MORNINGTON. S. M.
      Lord GARRET WELLESLEY MORNINGTON (1735—1781), 1760.
      Arr. by LOWELL MASON, 1822.

1. BE - HOLD the throne of grace! The prom - ise calls me near;

There Je - sus shows a smil - ing face, And waits to an - swer prayer.

31 *"Ask what I shall give thee."*
1 KINGS iii. 5.

2 My soul, ask what thou wilt,
  Thou canst not be too bold ;
  Since His own blood for thee He spilt,
  What else can He withhold ?

3 Thine image, Lord, bestow,
  Thy presence and Thy love ;
  I ask to serve Thee here below,
  And reign with Thee above.

4 Teach me to live by faith,
  Conform my will to Thine,
  Let me victorious be in death,
  And then in glory shine.
      Rev. John Newton (1725—1807), 1779. Ab.

32 *Importunity in Prayer.*
LUKE xviii. 1-7.

1 OUR Lord, who knows full well
  The heart of every saint,

Invites us all our griefs to tell,
To pray, and never faint.

2 He bows His gracious ear,
  We never plead in vain ;
  Yet we must wait till He appear,
  And pray, and pray again.

3 Jesus, the Lord, will hear
  His chosen when they cry ;
  And though He may a while forbear,
  He'll help them from on high.

4 Then let us earnest be,
  And never faint in prayer ;
  He loves our importunity,
  And makes our cause His care.
      Rev. John Newton. 1779. Ab. and alt

SHIRLAND. S. M.   SAMUEL STANLEY (1767—1822), 1805.

1. SWEET is the work, O Lord, Thy glo-rious acts to sing, To praise Thy Name, and hear Thy Word, And grate-ful off'-rings bring.

33   *"Sweet is the Work."*

2 Sweet, at the dawning light,
   Thy boundless love to tell ;
And, when approach the shades of night,
   Still on the theme to dwell.

3 Sweet, on this day of rest,
   To join in heart and voice
With those who love and serve Thee best,
   And in Thy Name rejoice.

4 To songs of praise and joy
   Be every Sabbath given,
That such may be our blest employ
   Eternally in Heaven.
         Miss Harriet Auber (1773—1862), 1829. Alt.

34   *Glory begun.*

1 COME, we that love the Lord,
   And let our joys be known :
Join in a song of sweet accord,
   And thus surround the throne.

2 Let those refuse to sing
   That never knew our God ;
But favorites of the heavenly King
   May speak their joys abroad.

3 The men of grace have found
   Glory begun below ;
Celestial fruits on earthly ground
   From faith and hope may grow.

4 The hill of Zion yields
   A thousand sacred sweets

Before we reach the heavenly fields,
   Or walk the golden streets.

5 Then let our songs abound,
   And every tear be dry ;
We're marching thro' Immanuel's ground
   To fairer worlds on high.
         Rev. Isaac Watts (1674—1748), 1707. Ab

35   *The Sabbath given to our Fathers.*
          Ps. lxxxi

1 SING to the Lord, our Might,
   With holy fervor sing ;
Let hearts and instruments unite
   To praise our heavenly King.

2 This is His holy house,
   And this His festal day,
When He accepts the humblest vows
   That we sincerely pay.

3 The Sabbath to our sires
   In mercy first was given ;
The Church her Sabbaths still requires
   To speed her on to Heaven.

4 We still, like them of old,
   Are in the wilderness ;
And God is still as near His fold,
   To pity and to bless.

5 Then let us open wide
   Our hearts for Him to fill ;
And He that Israel then supplied,
   Will help His Israel still.
         Rev. Henry Francis Lyte (1793—1847), 1834.

RENOVATION. S. M.

JOHANN NEPOMUK HUMMEL (1778—1837).

1. THE day, O Lord, is spent, A - bide with us, and rest; Our
hearts' de - sires are ful - ly bent On mak - ing Thee our guest.

36

The Day far spent.
LUKE xxiv. 29.

2 We have not reached that land,
  That happy land, as yet,
Where holy angels round Thee stand,
  Whose sun can never set.

3 Our sun is sinking now,
  Our day is almost o'er;
O Sun of Righteousness, do Thou
  Shine on us evermore.
            Rev. John Mason Neale (1818—1866), 1854.

37   *The Worship that never ceases.*

1 OUR day of praise is done;
  The evening shadows fall;
Yet pass not from us with the sun,
  True Light that lightenest all.

2 Around the throne on high
  Where night can never be,
The white-robed harpers of the sky
  Bring ceaseless hymns to Thee.

3 Too faint our anthems here;
  Too soon of praise we tire;
But, O the strains, how full and clear,
  Of that eternal choir.

4 Yet, Lord, to Thy dear will
  If Thou attune the heart,
We in Thine angels' music still
  May bear our lower part.

5 'Tis Thine each soul to calm,
  Each wayward thought reclaim,
And make our daily life a psalm
  Of glory to Thy Name.

6 A little while, and then
  Shall come the glorious end;
And songs of angels and of men
  In perfect praise shall blend.
            Rev. John Ellerton (1826—), 1867.

38

"Hath not where to lay His Head."
LUKE ix. 58.

1 ALMIGHTY God, to-night
  To Thee for help we pray;
To whom the darkness is as light,
  And midnight like the day.

2 Thy tender love and care
  Prepares our peaceful bed;
But Thou, O Saviour, hadst not where
  To lay Thy blessed head.

3 O keep us now from harm,
  As Thou hast done before;
And let Thine everlasting arm
  Be round us evermore.

4 Let holy angels stand
  About us every night,
Until they bear us to the land
  Of everlasting light.
            Rev. John Mason Neale, 1854.   Ab.

EVENING HYMN. L. M.   THOMAS TALLIS (1529—1585). 1585.

1. A - WAKE, my soul, and with the sun Thy dai - ly stage of du - ty run;

Shake off dull sloth, and joy - ful rise To pay thy morn - ing sac - ri - fice.

39   *Morning Hymn.*

2 Wake, and lift up thyself, my heart,
And with the angels bear thy part,
Who, all night long, unwearied sing
High praise to the eternal King.

3 All praise to Thee who safe hast kept,
And hast refreshed me whilst I slept;
Grant, Lord, when I from death shall wake,
I may of endless life partake.

4 Lord, I my vows to Thee renew;
Disperse my sins as morning dew;
Guide my first springs of thought and will,
And with Thyself my spirit fill.

5 Direct, control, suggest this day,
All I design, or do, or say;
That all my powers, with all their might,
In Thy sole glory may unite.

        Bp. Thomas Ken (1637—1711), 1697, 1709. Ab.

40   *Evening Hymn.*

1 ALL praise to Thee, my God, this night,
For all the blessings of the light:
Keep me, O keep me, King of kings,
Beneath Thine own almighty wings.

2 Forgive me, Lord, for Thy dear Son,
The ill that I this day have done;
That with the world, myself, and Thee,
I, ere I sleep, at peace may be.

3 Teach me to live, that I may dread
The grave as little as my bed;
To die, that this vile body may
Rise glorious at the awful day.

4 O may my soul on Thee repose,
And may sweet sleep my eyelids close;
Sleep, that shall me more vigorous make,
To serve my God when I awake.

5 When in the night I sleepless lie,
My soul with heavenly thoughts supply,
Let no ill dreams disturb my rest,
No powers of darkness me molest.

6 Praise God, from whom all blessings flow;
Praise Him, all creatures here below;
Praise Him above, ye Heavenly host;
Praise Father, Son, and Holy Ghost.

        Bp. Thomas Ken. 1697, 1709. Ab.

41   *"Splendor paternæ gloriæ."*

1 O JESUS, Lord of light and grace,
Thou brightness of the Father's face,
Thou fountain of eternal light,
Whose beams disperse the shades of night.

2 Come, Holy Sun of heavenly love,
Come in Thy radiance from above,
And to our inward hearts convey
The Holy Spirit's cloudless ray.

3 May He our actions deign to bless,
And loose the bonds of wickedness;
From sudden falls our feet defend,
And guide us safely to the end.

4 O hallowed thus be every day;
Let meekness be our morning ray,
Our faith like noontide splendor glow,
Our souls the twilight never know.

Ambrose of Milan (340—397).
Tr. by Rev. John Chandler (1806—1876), 1837. Ab. and alt.

HURSLEY. L. M.

PETER RITTER (1760—1846), 1792.
Arr. by WILLIAM HENRY MONK (1823—), 1861.

1, Sun of my soul, Thou Sav - iour dear, It is not night if Thou be near:

O may no earth - born cloud a - rise To hide Thee from Thy serv - ant's eyes.

42
"Abide with us."
LUKE xxiv. 29.

2 When the soft dews of kindly sleep
My wearied eyelids gently steep,
Be my last thought, how sweet to rest
Forever on my Saviour's breast.

3 Abide with me from morn till eve,
For without Thee I cannot live;
Abide with me when night is nigh,
For without Thee I dare not die.

4 If some poor wandering child of Thine
Have spurned, to-day, the voice divine;
Now, Lord, the gracious work begin;
Let him no more lie down in sin.

5 Watch by the sick; enrich the poor
With blessings from Thy boundless store;
Be every mourner's sleep to-night,
Like infant's slumbers, pure and light.

6 Come near and bless us when we wake,
Ere through the world our way we take;
Till, in the ocean of Thy love,
We lose ourselves in Heaven above.

Rev. John Keble (1792—1866), 1827. Ab.

43
Evening Praise and Prayer.
Ps. iv.

1 Thus far the Lord has led me on,
Thus far His power prolongs my days;
And every evening shall make known
Some fresh memorial of His grace.

2 Much of my time has run to waste,
And I perhaps am near my home;
But He forgives my follies past,
And gives me strength for days to come.

3 I lay my body down to sleep;
Peace is the pillow for my head,
While well-appointed angels keep
Their watchful stations round my bed.

4 Faith in His Name forbids my fear;
O may Thy presence ne'er depart;
And, in the morning, make me hear
The love and kindness of Thy heart.

5 Thus, when the night of death shall come,
My flesh shall rest beneath the ground;
And wait Thy voice to rouse my tomb,
With sweet salvation in the sound.

Rev. Isaac Watts (1674—1748), 1709. Ab.

STOCKWELL. 8.7.

Rev. DARIUS ELIOT JONES (1815—1881), 1847.

1. SAV - IOUR, breathe an eve - ning bless - ing, Ere re - pose our spir - its seal;

Sin and want we come con - fess - ing, Thou canst save, and Thou canst heal.

44 *Evening Blessing.*

2 Though destruction walk around us,
  Though the arrow past us fly,
Angel-guards from Thee surround us,
  We are safe, if Thou art nigh.

3 Though the night be dark and dreary,
  Darkness cannot hide from Thee;
Thou art He who, never weary,
  Watchest where Thy people be.

4 Should swift death this night o'ertake us,
  And our couch become our tomb,
May the morn in Heaven awake us,
  Clad in light and deathless blóom.

James Edmeston (1791—1867), 1820.

45 *Evening Shadows.*

1 TARRY with me, O my Saviour,
  For the day is passing by;
See, the shades of evening gather,
  And the night is drawing nigh.

2 Deeper, deeper grow the shadows,
  Paler now the glowing west;
Swift the night of death advances;
  Shall it be the night of rest?

3 Feeble, trembling, fainting, dying,
  Lord, I cast myself on Thee;
Tarry with me through the darkness;
  While I sleep, still watch by me.

4 Tarry with me, O my Saviour;
  Lay my head upon Thy breast
Till the morning, then awake me:
  Morning of eternal rest.

Mrs. Caroline Sprague Smith (1827—   ), 1855. Ab.

46 *An Evening Prayer.*

1 HEAR my prayer, O Heavenly Father,
  Ere I lay me down to sleep:
Bid Thine angels, pure and holy,
  Round my bed their vigil keep.

2 Great my sins are, but Thy mercy
  Far outweighs them every one;
Down before Thy cross I cast them,
  Trusting in Thy help alone.

3 Keep me, through this night of peril,
  Underneath its boundless shade;
Take me to Thy rest, I pray Thee,
  When my pilgrimage is made.

4 None shall measure out Thy patience
  By the span of human thought;
None shall bound the tender mercies
  Which Thy holy Son has brought.

5 Pardon all my past transgressions;
  Give me strength for days to come;
Guide and guard me with Thy blessing,
  Till Thine angels bid me home.

Miss Harriet Parr, 1856. Sl. alt.

WESTMINSTER. 8.7. JOSEPH PERRY HOLBROOK (1822—).

1. Vain - ly through night's wea - ry hours, Keep we watch, lest foes a - larm;

Vain our bul - warks, and our tow - ers, But for God's pro - tect - ing arm.

47 *Our Need of God.*
Ps. cxxvii.

2 Vain were all our toil and labor,
  Did not God that labor bless;
  Vain, without His grace and favor,
  Every talent we possess.

3 Vainer still the hope of Heaven,
  That on human strength relies;

But to him shall help be given,
  Who in humble faith applies.

4 Seek we, then, the Lord's Anointed;
  He will grant us peace and rest;
  Ne'er was suppliant disappointed,
  Who thro' Christ his prayer addressed.

Miss Harriet Auber (1773—1862), 1829.

LAUS MATUTINA. 11.10. JOHN STAINER (1840—). 1872.

1. Now, when the dusk - y shades of night re - treat - ing Be - fore the sun's red ban - ner swift - ly flee;

Now, when the ter - rors of the dark are fleet - ing, O Lord, we lift our thank-ful hearts to Thee.

48 *Walking in the Light of the Lord.*
Is. ii. 5.

2 Look from the height of Heaven, and send to cheer us
  Thy light and truth, and guide us onward still;
  Still let Thy mercy, as of old, be near us,
  And lead us safely to Thy holy Hill.

3 So, when that Morn of endless light is waking,
  And shades of evil from its splendors flee,
  Safe may we rise, this earth's dark vale forsaking,
  Through all the long bright Day to dwell with Thee.

Rev. Benjamin Hall Kennedy (1804—), 1863.

LAUDAMUS. 7, 8, 7. 7.

PETER RITTER (1760—1846), 1792.
Arr. by JOHN HENRY CORNELL (1828—), 1885.

HARK! the loud ce - les - tial hymn, An - gel - choirs a - bove are rais - ing;
Cher - u - bim and ser - a - phim In un - ceas - ing cho - rus prais - ing,

Fill the heav'ns with sweet ac - cord: Ho - ly! ho - ly! ho - ly Lord!

49   *"Te Deum Laudamus."*

2 Lo! the apostolic train
   Join Thy sacred Name to hallow!
Prophets swell the loud refrain,
   And the white-robed martyrs follow;
And from morn till set of sun,
Through the church the song goes on.

3 Holy Father, Holy Son,
   Holy Spirit, Three we name Thee,
While in essence, only One,

Undivided God, we claim Thee;
And, adoring, bend the knee,
While we own the mystery.

4 Spare Thy people, Lord, we pray,
   By a thousand snares surrounded:
Keep us without sin to-day,
   Never let us be confounded.
Lo! I put my trust in Thee,
Never, Lord, abandon me.
    Rev. Clarence Augustus Walworth (1820—), 1853. Ab.

MERRIAL. 6. 5.

JOSEPH BARNBY (1838—), 1868.

1. Now the day is o - ver, Night is draw - ing nigh,

Shad - ows of the eve - ning Steal a - cross the sky.

Steal a - cross the sky.

50   *The Day is over*

2 Jesus, give the weary
  Calm and sweet repose;
  With Thy tenderest blessing
  May our eyelids close.

3 Grant to little children
  Visions bright of Thee;
  Guard the sailors tossing
  On the deep blue sea.

4 Through the long night-watches,
  May Thine angels spread
  Their white wings above me,
  Watching round my bed.

5 When the morning wakens,
  Then may I arise,
  Pure and fresh and sinless
  In Thy holy eyes.
  Rev. Sabine Baring-Gould (1834—   ), 1865. Ab.

YOAKLEY. L. M. 6 l.   WILLIAM YOAKLEY. 1820.

1. { Sweet Sav - iour, bless us ere we go; Thy word in - to our minds in - still; }
   { And make our luke - warm hearts to glow With low - ly love and fer - vent will. }

Thro' life's long day and death's dark night, O gen - tle Je - sus, be our Light.

51   *"The Lord is my Light."*
         Ps. xxvii. 1.

2 The day is done, its hours have run;
  And Thou hast taken count of all—
  The scanty triumphs grace hath won,
  The broken vow, the frequent fall.
  Through life's long day and death's dark
      night,
  O gentle Jesus, be our Light.

3 Grant us, dear Lord, from evil ways
  True absolution and release;
  And bless us, more than in past days,
  With purity and inward peace.
  Through life's long day and death's dark
      night,
  O gentle Jesus, be our Light.

4 Do more than pardon; give us joy,
  Sweet fear, and sober liberty,
  And loving hearts without alloy,
  That only long to be like Thee.
  Through life's long day and death's dark
      night,
  O gentle Jesus, be our Light.

5 For all we love, the poor, the sad,
  The sinful, unto Thee we call;
  O let Thy mercy make us glad;
  Thou art our Jesus and our All.
  Through life's long day and death's dark
      night,
  O gentle Jesus, be our Light.
  Rev. Frederick William Faber (1814—1863), 1849. Ab.

CAPETOWN. 7.7.7.5.   FRIEDRICH FILITZ (1804—1860).

1. THREE in One, and One in Three, Rul-er of the earth and sea,

Hear us, while we lift to Thee Ho-ly chant and psalm.

52   *"Three in One, and One in Three."*

2 Light of lights, with morning, shine:
    Lift on us Thy light divine;
    And let charity benign
        Breathe on us her balm.

3 Light of lights, when falls the even,
    Let it close on sin forgiven;

Fold us in the peace of Heaven,
    Shed a holy calm.

4 Three in One, and One in Three,
    Dimly here we worship Thee:
    With the saints hereafter we
        Hope to bear the palm.
           Rev. Gilbert Rorison (1821—1869), 1850. Alt.

ANATOLIUS. 7.6,8.8.   ARTHUR HENRY BROWN (1830—   ), 1874.

1. THE day is past and o-ver; All thanks, O Lord, to Thee; I pray Thee that of-fence-less

The hours of dark may be: O Je-sus, keep me in Thy sight, And save me thro' the com-ing night.

53   *"The Day is past."*

2 The toils of day are over:
    We raise our hymn to Thee,
And ask, that free from peril,
    The hours of dark may be:
O Jesus, keep us in Thy sight,
And guard us through the coming night.

3 Be Thou our souls' Preserver,
    O God, for Thou dost know
How many are the perils
    Through which we have to go:
O loving Jesus, hear our call,
And guard and save us from them all.
       Bp. Anatolius of Constantinople (—458).
    Tr. by Rev. John Mason Neale (1818—1866), 1862. Ab.

NIGHTFALL. 11.11.11.5.
JOSEPH BARNBY (1838–), 1872.

1. Now God be with us, for the night is clos-ing: The light and dark-ness are of His dis-pos-ing, And 'neath His shad-ow here to rest we yield us, For He will shield us.

54

"The Darkness and the Light are both alike to Thee."

2 Let evil thoughts and spirits flee before us;
  Till morning cometh, watch, O Master, o'er us;
  In soul and body Thou from harm defend us,
     Thine angels send us.

3 We have no refuge; none on earth to aid us,
  Save Thee, O Father, who Thine own hast made us;
  But Thy dear presence will not leave them lonely
     Who seek Thee only.

4 Father, Thy Name be praised, Thy Kingdom given,
  Thy will be done on earth as 'tis in Heaven,
  Keep us in life, forgive our sins, deliver
     Us now and ever.

"Bohemian Brethren Collection," 1531.
Tr. by Miss Catherine Winkworth (1829–1878), 1863. Ab.

FLEMMING. 11.11.11.5.
FRIEDRICH FERDINAND FLEMMING (1778–1813), 1810.

EVENTIDE. 10.

WILLIAM HENRY MONK (1823—), 1861.

1. A - BIDE with me: fast falls the e - ven - tide; The dark-ness deep - ens; Lord, with me a - bide;

When oth - er help - ers fail, and comforts flee, Help of the helpless, O a - bide with me.

55

"Fast falls the Eventide."

2 Swift to its close ebbs out life's little day;
Earth's joys grow dim, its glories pass away;
Change and decay in all around I see;
O Thou, who changest not, abide with me.

3 I need Thy presence every passing hour:
What but Thy grace can foil the tempter's power?
Who like Thyself my guide and stay can be?
Through cloud and sunshine, O abide with me.

4 I fear no foe, with Thee at hand to bless;
Ills have no weight, and tears no bitterness;
Where is death's sting? where, grave, thy victory?
I triumph still, if Thou abide with me.

5 Hold Thou Thy cross before my closing eyes;
Shine through the gloom and point me to the skies;
Heaven's morning breaks, and earth's vain shadows flee;
In life, in death, O Lord, abide with me.

Rev. Henry Francis Lyte (1793—1847), 1847. Ab.

DOXOLOGY.

All praise and glory to the Father be
And Son and Spirit, undivided Three,
As hath been alway, shall be, and is now,
To Thee, O God, the everlasting Thou.

Bp. Edward Henry Bickersteth (1825—), 1870.

WORDSWORTH. 10. 6l.

HENRY SMART (1812—1879), 1870.

1. The day is gen-tly sink-ing to a close, Faint-er and yet more faint the sun-light glows;

O brightness of Thy Father's glo-ry, Thou, E-ter-nal Light of light, be with us now;

Where Thou art pres-ent dark-ness can-not be; Mid-night is glo-rious noon, O Lord, with Thee.

56 *"Fainter and yet more faint."*

2 Our changeful lives are ebbing to an end,
Onward to darkness and to death we tend;
O Conqueror of the grave, be Thou our Guide,
Be Thou our light in death's dark eventide;
Then in our mortal hour will be no gloom,
No sting in death, no terror in the tomb.

3 Thou, who in darkness walking didst appear
Upon the waves, and Thy disciples cheer,
Come, Lord, in lonesome days, when storms assail,
And earthly hopes and human succors fail:
When all is dark, may we behold Thee nigh,
And hear Thy voice, "Fear not, for it is I."

4 The weary world is mouldering to decay,
Its glories wane, its pageants fade away:
In that last sunset, when the stars shall fall,
May we arise, awakened by Thy call,
With Thee, O Lord, forever to abide
In that blest Day which has no eventide.

Bp. Christopher Wordsworth (1807—1885). 1862.

SUNSET. L. M. D.
WILHELM MEYER LUTZ (1879—).

1. At e - ven, ere the sun was set, The sick, O Lord, a - round Thee lay; O in what di - vers

pains they met, O with what joy they went a - way. Once more 'tis e - ven-tide, and we, Oppressed with various

ills, draw near: What if Thy form we can - not see? We know and feel that Thou art here.

57

Sunset Prayer.
Mark i. 32.

2 O Saviour Christ, our woes dispel,
   For some are sick, and some are sad,
And some have never loved Thee well,
   And some have lost the love they had ;
And none, O Lord, have perfect rest,
   For none are wholly free from sin :
And they who fain would serve Thee best,
   Are conscious most of wrong within.

3 O Saviour Christ, Thou too art Man ;
   Thou hast been troubled, tempted, tried ;
Thy kind but searching glance can scan
   The very wounds that shame would hide ;
Thy touch has still its ancient power,
   No word from Thee can fruitless fall ;
Hear in this solemn evening hour,
   And in Thy mercy heal us all.

Rev. Henry Twells (1823—), 1868. Ab.

58

At Home with God everywhere.

1 My Lord, how full of sweet content,
I pass my years of banishment :
Where'er I dwell, I dwell with Thee,
In heaven, in earth, or on the sea.
To me remains nor place, nor time :
My country is in every clime :
I can be calm and free from care
On any shore, since God is there.

2 While place we seek, or place we shun,
The soul finds happiness in none ;
But with a God to guide our way,
'Tis equal joy, to go or stay.
Could I be cast where Thou art not,
That were indeed a dreadful lot ;
But regions none remote I call,
Secure of finding God in all.

Madame J. B. de la Motte Guyon (1648—1717), 1702.
Tr. by William Cowper (1731—1800), 1782. Ab. and alt.

ANGELUS. L. M.
GEORG JOSEPH, 1657.

LAST BEAM. P. M. Portuguese.

1. FAD-ING, still fad-ing, the last beam is shining, Fa-ther in Heav-en, the day is de-clin-ing,

Safe-ty and in-no-cence fly with the light, Temp-ta-tion and dan-ger walk forth with the night:

From the fall of the shade till the morning bells chime, Shield me from dan-ger, save me from crime.

Fa-ther, have mer-cy, Fa-ther, have mer-cy, Fa-ther, have mer-cy thro' Je-sus Christ our Lord.

59 *"Fading, still fading."*

2 Father in Heaven, O hear when we call,
Hear for Christ's sake, who is Saviour of all:
Feeble and fainting, we trust in Thy might;
In doubting and darkness Thy love be our light;
Let us sleep on Thy breast while the night taper burns,
Wake in Thy arms when morning returns.
    Father, have mercy, etc.

Unknown Author, 1830.

HALLE. 7. 6 l.

PETER RITTER (1760–1846), 1792.

1. { FA - THER, by Thy love and power, Comes a - gain the ev - 'ning hour; }
{ Light has van - ished, la - bors cease, Wea - ry creat - ures rest in peace: }

We to Thee our-selves re - sign, Let our lat - est thoughts be Thine.

60

Evening Hymn.

2 Saviour, to Thy Father bear
This our feeble evening prayer;
Thou hast seen how oft to-day
We, like sheep, have gone astray;
Blessed Saviour, we, through Thee,
Pray that we may pardoned be.

3 Holy Spirit, Breath of balm,
Fall on us in evening's calm;
Yet awhile, before we sleep,
We with Thee will vigil keep.
Melt our spirits, mould our will,
Soften, strengthen, comfort still.

4 Blessèd Trinity, be near
Through the hours of darkness drear;
Father, Son, and Holy Ghost,
Round us set th' angelic host,
Till the flood of morning rays
Wake us to a song of praise.

Prof. Joseph Anstice (1808–1836), 1836. Ab. and alt.

PAX DEI. 10.

Rev. JOHN BACCHUS DYKES (1823–1876).

1. SAVIOUR, a- gain to Thy dear Name we raise. With one ac-cord, our parting hymn of praise;

We rise to bless Thee ere our wor-ship cease, Then, low- ly kneeling, wait Thy word of peace.

61

"Thy Word of Peace."

2 Grant us Thy peace upon our homeward way ;
  With Thee began, with Thee shall end the day ;
  Guard Thou the lips from sin, the hearts from shame,
  That in this house have called upon Thy Name.

3 Grant us Thy peace, Lord, through the coming night ;
  Turn Thou for us its darkness into light ;
  From harm and danger keep Thy children free :
  Darkness and light are both alike to Thee.

4 Grant us Thy peace throughout our earthly life.
  Our balm in sorrow, and our stay in strife ;
  Then, when Thy voice shall bid our conflict cease,
  Call us, O Lord, to Thine eternal peace.

Rev. John Ellerton (1826—), 1868.

ELLERS. 10.   EDWARD JOHN HOPKINS (1818—), 1866.

1. A - GAIN re - turns the day of ho - ly rest, Which, when He made the world, Je-ho-vah blest,

When, like His own, He bade our la-bors cease, And all be pi - e - ty, and all be peace.

62

"The Day of holy Rest."

2 Let us devote this consecrated day
  To learn His will, and all we learn obey ;
  So shall He hear, when fervently we raise
  Our supplications and our songs of praise.

3 Father of Heaven, in whom our hopes confide,
  Whose power defends us, and whose precepts guide,
  In life our Guardian, and in death our Friend,
  Glory supreme be Thine, till time shall end.

Rev. William Mason (1725—1797), 1811.

MENDEBRAS. 7. 6. D. German Melody. Arr. by LOWELL MASON (1792—1872). 1859.

1. { O DAY of rest and glad-ness, O day of joy and light, }
{ O balm of care and sad-ness, Most beau-ti - ful, most bright: } On thee, the high and low - ly,

Through a - ges joined in tune, Sing "Ho-ly, ho - ly, ho - ly," To the Great God Tri - une.

63 *"The Day which the Lord hath made."*
Ps. cxviii. 24.

2 On thee, at the creation,
　The light first had its birth ;
On thee, for our salvation,
　Christ rose from depths of earth ;
On thee our Lord, victorious,
　The Spirit sent from Heaven,
And thus on thee, most glorious,
　A triple light was given.

3 To-day on weary nations
　The heavenly manna falls ;
To holy convocations
　The silver trumpet calls,

Where gospel light is glowing
　With pure and radiant beams,
And living water flowing
　With soul-refreshing streams.

4 New graces ever gaining
　From this our day of rest,
We reach the rest remaining
　To spirits of the blest ;
To Holy Ghost be praises,
　To Father, and to Son ;
The Church her voice upraises
　To Thee, blest Three in One.

Bp. Christopher Wordsworth (1807—1885), 1862. Ab. and alt.

MIRIAM. 7. 6. D. JOSEPH PERRY HOLBROOK (1822—), 1865.

1. THE Day of Res - ur - rec - tion, Earth, tell it out a - broad: The Pass - o - ver of glad - ness,
D. S.—Our Christ hath bro't us o - ver,

Fine. D. S.

The Pass - o - ver of God. From death to life e - ter - nal, From earth un - to the sky,
With hymns of vic - to - ry.

64
Ἀναστάσεως ἡμέρα.

2 Our hearts be pure from evil,
  That we may see aright
The Lord in rays eternal
  Of resurrection-light ;
And, listening to His accents,
  May hear, so calm and plain,
His own "All hail!" and, hearing,
  May raise the victor-strain.

3 Now let the heavens be joyful ;
  Let earth her song begin :
Let the round world keep triumph,
  And all that is therein ;
Invisible and visible,
  Their notes let all things blend,
For Christ the Lord hath risen,
  Our Joy that hath no end.

John of Damascus (—c. 780.)
Tr. by Rev. John Mason Neale (1818—1866), 1862.

LISCHER. H. M.

FRIEDRICH JOHANN CHRISTIAN SCHNEIDER (1786—1853), 1-40.

1. { WELCOME, de-light-ful morn, Thou day of sa-cred rest:
     I hail thy kind re-turn; Lord, make these moments blest; }
From the low train of mor-tal toys,

I soar to reach im-mor-tal joys, I soar to reach im-mor-tal joys.

I soar to reach

65
Sabbath Morning.

2 Now may the King descend,
  And fill His throne of grace :
Thy sceptre, Lord, extend,
  While saints address Thy face ;
Let sinners feel Thy quickening word,
And learn to know and fear the Lord.

3 Descend, celestial Dove,
  With all Thy quickening powers,
Make known a Saviour's love,
  And bless these sacred hours ;
Then shall my soul new life obtain,
Nor sabbaths e'er be spent in vain.

Hayward. In John Dobell's Collection, 1806. Sl. alt.

66
Longing for the House of God.
Ps. lxxxiv.

1 LORD of the worlds above,
  How pleasant and how fair

The dwellings of Thy love,
  Thine earthly temples are !
To Thine abode my heart aspires,
With warm desires, to see my God.

2 O happy souls, that pray
  Where God appoints to hear ;
O happy men, that pay
  Their constant service there !
They praise Thee still; and happy they,
That love the way to Zion's hill.

3 They go from strength to strength,
  Through this dark vale of tears,
Till each arrives at length.
  Till each in Heaven appears :
O glorious seat, when God, our King,
Shall thither bring our willing feet !

Rev. Isaac Watts (1671—1748), 1719. Ab.

SABBATH. 7, 6l.

LOWELL MASON (1792—1872), 1824.

1. SAFE-LY, thro' an-oth-er week, God has brought us on our way; Let us now a bless-ing seek, Wait-ing in His courts to - day: Day of all the week the best, Em-blem of e-ter-nal rest, Day of all the week the best, Em-blem of e-ter-nal rest.

67   *"Safely, through another Week."*

2 While we pray for pardoning grace,
   Through the dear Redeemer's Name,
Show Thy reconciléd face,
   Take away our sin and shame;
From our worldly cares set free,
May we rest this day in Thee.

3 Here we come Thy Name to praise;
   May we feel Thy presence near:
May Thy glory meet our eyes,
   While we in Thy house appear:
Here afford us, Lord, a taste
Of our everlasting feast.

4 May Thy Gospel's joyful sound
   Conquer sinners, comfort saints;
Make the fruits of grace abound,
   Bring relief for all complaints;
Thus may all our Sabbaths prove,
Till we join the Church above.

Rev. John Newton (1725—1807), 1779.

68   *"The Day spring from on high."*
            LUKE i. 78.

1 CHRIST, whose glory fills the skies,
   Christ, the true, the only Light,
Sun of Righteousness, arise,
   Triumph o'er the shades of night:
Day spring from on high, be near,
Day-star, in our hearts appear.

2 Dark and cheerless is the morn,
   Unillumined, Lord, by Thee;
Joyless is the day's return,
   Till Thy mercy's beams we see;
Lord, Thine inward light impart,
Cheering each benighted heart.

3 Visit every soul of Thine,
   Pierce the gloom of sin and grief;
Fill us, Lord, with light divine,
   Scatter all our unbelief;
More and more Thyself display,
Shining to the perfect day.

Rev. Charles Wesley (1708—1788), 1740. Alt.

SWEET HOME. P. M.   Sir HENRY ROWLEY BISHOP (1780–1855), 1829.

1. 'MID scenes of con - fu - sion and creat - ure complaints, How sweet to the soul is com-

mun - ion with saints; To find at the ban - quet of mer - cy there's room, And

*D. S.—*Pre-

Fine.

feel in the pres - ence of Je - sus at home? Home, home, sweet, sweet home;

pare me, dear Sav - iour, for glo - ry, my home.

69

"At Home."

2 Sweet bonds that unite all the children of peace!
  And thrice precious Jesus, whose love cannot cease!
  Though oft from Thy presence in sadness I roam,
  I long to behold Thee in glory, at home.

3 While here in the valley of conflict I stay,
  O give me submission, and strength as my day;
  In all my afflictions to Thee would I come,
  Rejoicing in hope of my glorious home.

4 Whate'er Thou deniest, O give me Thy grace,
  The Spirit's sure witness, and smiles of Thy face;
  Endue me with patience to wait at Thy throne,
  And find, even now, a sweet foretaste of home.

5 I long, dearest Lord, in Thy beauties to shine;
  No more as an exile in sorrow to pine;
  And in Thy dear image arise from the tomb,
  With glorified millions to praise Thee at home.

Rev. David Denham, 1837. Ab.

ARMAGH. C. M.

JAMES TURLE (1802—1882).

1. BLEST Day of God, most calm, most bright, The first and best of days:

The toil-er's rest, the saint's de-light, A day of joy and praise.

70 *"Most calm, most bright."*

2 My Saviour's face did make thee shine,
   His rising did thee raise;
   This made thee heavenly and divine
   Beyond all other days.

3 The first-fruits do a blessing prove
   To all the sheaves behind;
   And they, that do a Sabbath love,
   A happy week shall find.

4 My Lord on thee His Name did fix,
   Which makes thee rich and gay;
   Amid His golden candlesticks
   My Saviour walks this day.

5 This day must I 'fore God appear,
   For, Lord, this day is Thine:
   O let me spend it in Thy fear,
   The day shall then be mine.
                Rev. John Mason (1634—1694), 1683. Alt.

71 *Sweet Rest.*

1 My Lord, my Love, was crucified,
   He all the pains did bear:
   But in the sweetness of His rest
   He makes His servants share.

2 How sweetly rest Thy saints above
   Who in Thy bosom lie;
   The Church below doth rest in hope
   Of that felicity.

3 Thou, Lord, who daily feed'st Thy sheep,
   Mak'st them a weekly feast;
   Thy flocks assemble in their folds
   On this Thy day of rest.

4 Welcome and dear unto my soul
   Are these sweet feasts of love;
   But what a Sabbath shall I keep
   When I shall rest above!
                Rev. John Mason, 1683. Alt.

WARWICK. C. M.

SAMUEL STANLEY (1767—1822), 1800.

HOLY TRINITY. C. M.   JOSEPH BARNBY (1838—   ), 1861.

1. A - GAIN the Lord of life and light A - wakes the kin - dling ray,

Un - seals the eye - lids of the morn, And pours in - creas - ing day.

72   *The Lord's Day Morning.*

2 O what a night was that which wrapt
   A heathen world in gloom ;
   O what a sun which broke this day
   Triumphant from the tomb.

3 The powers of darkness leagued in vain
   To blind our Lord in death ;
   He shook their kingdom, when He fell,
   With His expiring breath.

4 And now His conq'ring chariot wheels
   Ascend the lofty skies ;
   While, broke beneath His powerful cross,
   Death's iron sceptre lies.

5 This day be grateful homage paid,
   And loud hosannas sung ;
   Let gladness dwell in every heart,
   And praise on every tongue.

6 Ten thousand, thousand lips shall join
   To hail this welcome morn,
   Which scatters blessings from its wings
   On nations yet unborn.

Mrs. Anna Lætitia Barbauld (1743—1825), 1773, 1825. Ab and alt.

73   *"Our rising God."*

1 BLEST morning, whose young dawning
      Beheld our rising God ;   [rays
   That saw Him triumph o'er the dust,
      And leave His dark abode.

2 In the cold prison of a tomb
      The dead Redeemer lay,
   Till the revolving skies had brought
      The third, th' appointed day.

3 Hell and the grave unite their force
      To hold our God, in vain ;
   The sleeping Conqueror arose,
      And burst their feeble chain.

4 To Thy great Name, Almighty Lord,
      These sacred hours we pay ;
   And loud hosannas shall proclaim
      The triumph of the day.

5 Salvation, and immortal praise,
      To our victorious King ;
   Let heaven and earth, and rocks and seas,
      With glad hosannas ring.

Rev. Isaac Watts (1674—1748), 1709

DUKE STREET. L. M.

JOHN HATTON, c. 1790.

1. O COME, loud an - thems let us sing, Loud thanks to our Al - might - y King;

For we our voic - es high should raise, When our sal - va - tion's Rock we praise.

74

"Let us worship and bow down."
PS. XCV. 1—6.

2 Into His presence let us haste,
To thank Him for His favors past;
To Him address, in joyful songs,
The praise that to His Name belongs.

3 O let us to His courts repair,
And bow with adoration there;
Down on our knees devoutly all
Before the Lord our Maker fall.

Tate and Brady, 1696. Ab.

75

The Eternal Sabbath.
HEB. iv. 9.

1 THINE earthly Sabbaths, Lord, we love;
But there's a nobler rest above;
To that our laboring souls aspire
With ardent hope and strong desire.

2 No more fatigue, no more distress,
Nor sin, nor hell, shall reach the place;
No groans to mingle with the songs
Which warble from immortal tongues.

3 No rude alarms of raging foes;
No cares to break the long repose;
No midnight shade, no clouded sun,
But sacred, high, eternal noon.

4 O long-expected day, begin;
Dawn on these realms of woe and sin:

Fain would we leave this weary road,
And sleep in death, to rest with God.

Rev. Philip Doddridge (1702—1751), 1755. Ab. and alt.

76

The Christian Farewell.
2 COR. xiii. 11.

1 THY presence, everlasting God,
Wide o'er all nature spreads abroad;
Thy watchful eyes, which cannot sleep,
In every place Thy children keep.

2 While near each other we remain,
Thou dost our lives and souls sustain;
When absent, Thou dost make us share
Thy smiles, Thy counsels, and Thy care.

3 To Thee we all our ways commit,
And seek our comforts at Thy feet;
Still on our souls vouchsafe to shine,
And guard and guide us still as Thine.

4 Give us, O Lord, within Thy house
Again to pay our thankful vows;
Or if that joy no more be known,
O let us meet around Thy throne.

Rev. Philip Doddridge, 1755. Alt.

77

"O luce qui mortalibus."

1 GREAT God, who, hid from mortal sight,
Dost dwell in depths of dazzling light,
Before whose presence angels bow,
With faces veiled, in homage low:

2 Awhile in darkness we remain,
And round us yet are sin and pain;
But soon the everlasting day
Shall chase our shades of night away.

3 Then from its fleshly bonds set free,
The soul shall fly, O God, to Thee:
To see Thee, love Thee, and adore,
Her blissful task for evermore.

Prof. Charles Coffin (1676—1749), 1736.
Tr. by Rev. Sir Henry William Baker (1521—1877), 1861. Ab.
and alt.

EL PARAN. L. M.

JOHANN ABRAHAM PETER SCHULZ (1747—1800).
Arr. by LOWELL MASON (1792—1872), 1839.

1. AN - OTH- ER six days' work is done, An - oth - er Sab - bath is be - gun:

Re - turn, my soul, en - joy thy rest, Im - prove the day thy God hath blest.

78   *"Return, my Soul."*

2 Come, bless the Lord, whose love assigns
So sweet a rest to wearied minds;
Provides an antepast of Heaven,
And gives this day the food of seven.

3 O that our thoughts and thanks may rise,
As grateful incense, to the skies;
And draw from Heaven that sweet repose,
Which none but he that feels it knows.

4 This heavenly calm within the breast
Is the dear pledge of glorious rest,
Which for the Church of God remains,
The end of cares, the end of pains.

5 In holy duties let the day,
In holy pleasures, pass away;
How sweet a Sabbath thus to spend,
In hope of one that ne'er shall end.

Rev. Joseph Stennett (1663—1713), 1732. Ab. and much alt.

79   *"Sacred Rest."*
            Ps. xcii.

1 SWEET is the work, my God, my King,
To praise Thy Name, give thanks, and sing;
To show Thy love by morning light,
And talk of all Thy truth at night.

2 Sweet is the day of sacred rest;
No mortal cares shall seize my breast;
O may my heart in tune be found,
Like David's harp of solemn sound.

3 My heart shall triumph in my Lord,
And bless His works, and bless His Word:
Thy works of grace, how bright they shine,
How deep Thy counsels, how divine!

4 Lord, I shall share a glorious part,
When grace hath well refined my heart,
And fresh supplies of joy are shed,
Like holy oil, to cheer my head.

5 Then shall I see, and hear, and know
All I desired or wished below;
And every power find sweet employ,
In that eternal world of joy.

Rev. Isaac Watts (1674—1748), 1709. Ab. and sl. alt.

LANESBORO. C. M.

WILLIAM DIXON, 1790.

1. How did my heart re - joice to hear My friends de - vout - ly say, "In Zi - on let us

all ap - pear, In Zi - on let us all ap - pear, And keep the sol - emn day!"

80

"I was glad."
Ps. cxxii.

2 I love her gates, I love the road;
    The Church, adorned with grace,
Stands like a palace built for God,
    To show His milder face.

3 Up to her courts, with joys unknown,
    The holy tribes repair;
The Son of David holds His throne,
    And sits in judgment there.

4 Peace be within this sacred place,
    And joy a constant guest;
With holy gifts and heavenly grace,
    Be her attendants blest.

5 My soul shall pray for Zion still,
    While life or breath remains;
There my best friends, my kindred dwell,
    There God, my Saviour, reigns.

Rev. Isaac Watts (1674—1748), 1719. Ab.

81

The Lord's Day Morning.
Ps. v.

1 LORD, in the morning Thou shalt hear
    My voice ascending high;
To Thee will I direct my prayer,
    To Thee lift up mine eye:

2 Up to the hills, where Christ is gone
    To plead for all His saints,
Presenting, at His Father's throne,
    Our songs and our complaints.

3 Thou art a God, before whose sight
    The wicked shall not stand;
Sinners shall ne'er be Thy delight,
    Nor dwell at Thy right hand.

4 But to Thy house will I resort,
    To taste Thy mercies there;
I will frequent Thy holy court,
    And worship in Thy fear.

5 O may Thy Spirit guide my feet
    In ways of righteousness;
Make every path of duty straight,
    And plain before my face.

Rev. Isaac Watts, 1719.

82

"The Day the Lord hath made."
Ps. cxviii.

1 THIS is the day the Lord hath made,
    He calls the hours His own;
Let Heaven rejoice, let earth be glad,
    And praise surround the throne.

2 To-day He rose and left the dead,
    And Satan's empire fell;
To-day the saints His triumphs spread,
    And all His wonders tell.

3 Hosanna to th' anointed King,
    To David's holy Son;
Help us, O Lord, descend and bring
    Salvation from the throne.

4 Blest be the Lord, who comes to men
  With messages of grace;
  Who comes in God His Father's Name,
  To save our sinful race.

5 Hosanna, in the highest strains
  The Church on earth can raise;
  The highest heavens, in which He reigns,
  Shall give Him nobler praise.

Rev. Isaac Watts, 1719.

LEONI. 6. 6. 8. 4. D.

Hebrew Melody.

1. With glad-some feet we press To Zi-on's ho-ly mount,

Where gush-es from its deep re-cess The cool-ing fount!

O hap-py, hap-py hill, The joy of ev-'ry saint!

With sweet Si-lo-am's crys-tal rill, That cheers the faint.

83 *God's House.*

2 Great City, blest of God,
    Jerusalem the free!
  With ceaseless step the path be trod,
    That leads to Thee!
  The martyrs' bleeding feet,
    The saints with woundless breast,
  Alike have sought Thy golden seat,
    To win their rest.

3 We come, with fervent zeal,
    Beneath Thy hallowed dome,
  The pledge of our eternal weal,
    Our happy home!
  Thy house our Zion stands,
    Though reared of earthly stone,
  The type of that, not made with hands,
    Yet still Thine own.

Rev. Robert Corbet Singleton, 1867. Ab

LISBON. S. M.

DANIEL READ (1757—1836), 1785.

1. WEL - COME, sweet day of rest, That saw the Lord a - rise;

Wel - come to this re - vi - ving breast, And these re - joic - ing eyes.

84

The Lord's Day welcomed.

2 The King Himself comes near,
    And feasts His saints to-day;
  Here we may sit, and see Him here,
    And love, and praise, and pray.

3 One day amidst the place
    Where my dear God hath been,
  Is sweeter than ten thousand days
    Of pleasure and of sin.

4 My willing soul would stay
    In such a frame as this,
  And sit, and sing herself away
    To everlasting bliss.
          Rev. Isaac Watts (1674—1748), 1709. Sl. alt.

85

Our Redeemer worshipped.

1 How charming is the place,
    Where my Redeemer God
  Unveils the beauties of His face,
    And sheds His love abroad.

2 Here, on the Mercy-seat,
    With radiant glory crowned,
  Our joyful eyes behold Him sit,
    And smile on all around.

3 To Him their prayers and cries
    Each humble soul presents:
  He listens to their broken sighs,
    And grants them all their wants.

4 To them His sovereign will
    He graciously imparts;
  And in return accepts, with smiles,
    The tribute of their hearts.

5 Give me, O Lord, a place
    Within Thy blest abode,
  Among the children of Thy grace,
    The servants of my God.
          Rev. Samuel Stennett (1727—1795), 1773. Ab.

86

"Stand up, and bless the Lord."
Neh. ix. 5.

1 STAND up, and bless the Lord,
    Ye people of His choice;
  Stand up and bless the Lord, your God,
    With heart, and soul, and voice.

2 O for the living flame,
    From His own altar brought,
  To touch our lips, our minds inspire,
    And wing to Heaven our thought.

3 God is our strength and song,
    And His salvation ours;
  Then be His love in Christ proclaimed
    With all our ransomed powers.

4 Stand up, and bless the Lord,
    The Lord your God adore;
  Stand up, and bless His glorious Name,
    Henceforth for evermore.
          James Montgomery (1771—1854), 1825. Ab

LEIGHTON. S. M.

HENRY WELLINGTON GREATOREX (1813—1858), 1849.

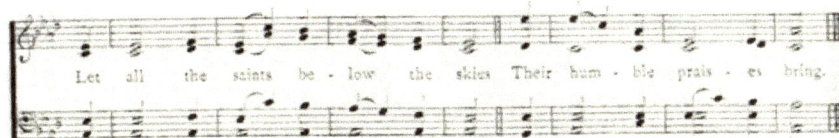

1. To God the On-ly Wise, Our Sav-iour and our King,

Let all the saints be-low the skies Their hum-ble prais-es bring.

87 *"The Only Wise."* JUDE xxiv. 25.

2 'Tis His almighty love,
His counsel and His care,
Preserves us safe from sin and death,
And every hurtful snare.

3 He will present our souls,
Unblemished and complete,
Before the glory of His face,
With joys divinely great.

4 Then all the chosen seed
Shall meet around the throne,
Shall bless the conduct of His grace,
And make His wonders known.

5 To our Redeemer God
Wisdom and power belongs,
Immortal crowns of majesty,
And everlasting songs.
Rev. Isaac Watts, 1709.

88 *God's Sabbath.*

1 LORD, in this sacred hour
Within Thy courts we bend,
And bless Thy love, and own Thy power,
Our Father and our Friend.

2 But Thou art not alone
In courts by mortals trod;
Nor only is the day Thine own
When man draws near to God.

3 Thy temple is the arch
Of yon unmeasured sky;
Thy Sabbath, the stupendous march
Of grand eternity.

4 Lord, may that holier day
Dawn on Thy servants' sight;
And purer worship may we pay
In Heaven's unclouded light.
Rev. Stephen Greenleaf Bulfinch (1809—1870), 1832. Ab.

89 *"The Lord reigneth."* Ps. xcix.

1 EXALT the Lord our God,
And worship at His feet;
His nature is all holiness,
And mercy is His seat.

2 When Israel was His church,
When Aaron was His priest,
When Moses cried, when Samuel prayed,
He gave His people rest.

3 Oft He forgave their sins,
Nor would destroy their race;
And oft He made His vengeance known
When they abused His grace.

4 Exalt the Lord our God,
Whose grace is still the same;
Still He's a God of holiness,
And jealous for His Name.
Rev. Isaac Watts, 1719.

BEMERTON. C. M.

HENRY WELLINGTON GREATOREX (1811—1858), 1849.

1. A - GAIN our earth - ly cares we leave, And in Thy courts ap - pear;

A - gain, with joy - ful feet, we come To meet our Sav - iour here.

90

"To meet our Saviour."

2 Within these walls let holy peace,
  And love, and concord dwell;
  Here give the troubled conscience ease,
  The wounded spirit heal.

3 The feeling heart, the melting eye,
  The humble mind bestow;
  And shine upon us from on high,
  To make our graces grow.

4 May we in faith receive Thy Word,
  In faith present our prayers;
  And, in the presence of our Lord,
  Unbosom all our cares.

5 Show us some token of Thy love,
  Our fainting hope to raise;
  And pour Thy blessing from above,
  That we may render praise.

  Rev. John Newton (1725—1807), 1779. Alt.

91

"We hail the Sacred Day."
Ps. cxxii.

1 WITH joy we hail the sacred day,
  Which God has called His own;
  With joy the summons we obey
  To worship at His throne.

2 Thy chosen temple, Lord, how fair,
  Where willing votaries throng,
  To breathe the humble, fervent prayer,
  And pour the choral song.

3 Spirit of grace, O deign to dwell
  Within Thy Church below;
  Make her in holiness excel,
  With pure devotion glow.

4 Let peace within her walls be found,
  Let all her sons unite,
  To spread with grateful zeal around
  Her clear and shining light.

  Miss Harriet Auber (1773—1862), 1829.

92

Sincerity.

1 LORD, when we bend before Thy throne,
  And our confessions pour,
  Teach us to feel the sins we own,
  And hate what we deplore.

2 Our broken spirits, pitying, see,
  And penitence impart;
  Then let a kindling glance from Thee
  Beam hope upon the heart.

3 When we disclose our wants in prayer,
  May we our wills resign;
  And not a thought our bosom share
  Which is not wholly Thine.

4 Let faith each meek petition fill,
  And waft it to the skies;
  And teach our hearts, 'tis goodness still
  That grants it, or denies.

  Rev. Joseph Dacre Carlyle (1759—1804), 1805. Ab.

VIENNA. 7. Rev. WILLIAM HENRY HAVERGAL (1793–1870).

1. To Thy tem-ple I re-pair, Lord, I love to wor-ship there,

When with-in the veil I meet Christ be-fore the Mer-cy-seat.

93 *"In Thy Courts."*

2 Thou through Him art reconciled,
I through Him become Thy child;
Abba, Father, give me grace
In Thy courts to seek Thy face.

3 While Thy glorious praise is sung,
Touch my lips, unloose my tongue,
That my joyful soul may bless
Thee, the Lord, my Righteousness.

4 While the prayers of saints ascend,
God of love, to mine attend;
Hear me, for Thy Spirit pleads,
Hear, for Jesus intercedes.

5 While I hearken to Thy law,
Fill my soul with humble awe,
Till Thy gospel bring to me
Life and immortality.

6 While Thy ministers proclaim
Peace and pardon in Thy Name,
Through their voice, by faith, may I
Hear Thee speaking from the sky.

7 From Thy house when I return,
May my heart within me burn;
And at evening let me say,
"I have walked with God to-day."
James Montgomery (1771–1854), 1825.

94 *"Still praising Thee."*
Ps. lxxxiv.

1 PLEASANT are Thy courts above,
In the land of light and love;
Pleasant are Thy courts below,
In this land of sin and woe.

2 O, my spirit longs and faints
For the converse of Thy saints,
For the brightness of Thy face,
King of glory, God of grace.

3 Happy souls, their praises flow
Even in this vale of woe;
Waters in the desert rise,
Manna feeds them from the skies.

4 On they go from strength to strength,
Till they reach Thy throne at length;
At Thy feet adoring fall,
Who hast led them safe through all.

5 Lord, be mine this prize to win;
Guide me through a world of sin;
Keep me by Thy saving grace;
Give me at Thy side a place.

6 Sun and Shield alike Thou art;
Guide and guard my erring heart;
Grace and glory flow from Thee,
Shower, O shower them, Lord, on me.
Rev. Henry Francis Lyte (1793–1847), 1834. Ab.

DALSTON. S. P. M.   AARON WILLIAMS (1731–1776), 1763.

1. How pleased and blest was I, To hear the peo-ple cry, "Come,let us seek our God to-day!"

Yes, with a cheer-ful zeal, We haste to Zi-on's hill, And there our vows and hon-ors pay.

95 *"The House of the Lord."*
Ps. cxxii.

2 Zion, thrice happy place,
   Adorned with wondrous grace,
And walls of strength embrace thee round:
   In thee our tribes appear,
   To pray, and praise, and hear
The sacred gospel's joyful sound.

3 There David's greater Son
   Has fixed His royal throne;
He sits for grace and judgment there;
   He bids the saints be glad;
   He makes the sinner sad;
And humble souls rejoice with fear.

4 May peace attend thy gate,
   And joy within thee wait,
To bless the soul of every guest:
   The man that seeks thy peace,
   And wishes thine increase,
A thousand blessings on him rest!

5 My tongue repeats her vows,
   "Peace to this sacred house!"
For there my friends and kindred dwell;
   And since my glorious God
   Makes thee His blest abode,
My soul shall ever love thee well.

Rev. Isaac Watts (1674–1748), 1719.

WAREHAM. L. M.   WILLIAM KNAPP (1698–1768), 1738.

1. How pleas-ant, how di-vine-ly fair, O Lord of hosts, Thy dwell-ings are:

With long de-sire my spir-it faints, To meet th'as-sem-blies of Thy saints.

96 *"From Strength to Strength."*
Ps. lxxxiv.

2 Blest are the saints who sit on high,
Around Thy throne of majesty;
Thy brightest glories shine above,
And all their work is praise and love.

3 Blest are the souls who find a place
Within the temple of Thy grace;
There they behold Thy gentler rays,
And seek Thy face, and learn Thy praise.

4 Blest are the men whose hearts are set
To find the way to Zion's gate;
God is their strength, and, thro' the road,
They lean upon their Helper, God.

5 Cheerful they walk with growing strength,
Till all shall meet in Heaven at length;
Till all before Thy face appear,
And join in nobler worship there.
Rev. Isaac Watts, 1719. Ab.

WARE. L. M.
GEORGE KINGSLEY (1811–1884), 1853.

1. God in His earth - ly tem-ple lays Foun-da-tions for His heav'n-ly praise;
He likes the tents of Ja-cob well, but still in Zi-on loves to dwell.

97 *The Church the Birth-place of Souls.*
Ps. lxxxvii.

2 His mercy visits every house
That pays its night and morning vows;
But makes a more delightful stay
Where churches meet to praise and pray.

3 What glories were described of old,
What wonders are of Zion told!
Thou City of our God below,
Thy fame shall Tyre and Egypt know.

4 Egypt and Tyre, and Greek and Jew,
Shall then begin their lives anew;
Angels, and men shall join to sing
The hill where living waters spring.

5 When God makes up His last account
Of natives in His holy mount,
'Twill be an honor to appear
As one new-born or nourished there.
Rev. Isaac Watts, 1719.

98 *Millions of Worshippers.*

1 MILLIONS within Thy courts have met,
Millions this day before Thee bowed;
Their faces Zion-ward were set,
Vows with their lips to Thee they vowed.

2 Soon as the light of morning broke
O'er island, continent, or deep,
Thy far-spread family awoke,
Sabbath all round the world to keep.

3 And not a prayer, a tear, a sigh,
Hath failed this day some suit to gain;
To those in trouble Thou wert nigh:
Not one hath sought Thy face in vain.

4 Yet one prayer more, and be it one,
In which both Heaven and earth accord:
Fulfil Thy promise to Thy Son;
Let all that breathe call Jesus Lord.
James Montgomery (1771–1854), 1853. Ab. and sl. alt.

BROWNELL. L. M. 6 l.

Arr. from FRANCIS JOSEPH HAYDN (1732—1809), 1787.

1. THE Lord my pasture shall prepare, And feed me with a shepherd's care;

His presence shall my wants supply, And guard me with a watchful eye;

My noonday walks He shall attend, And all my midnight hours defend.

99

The Lord our Shepherd.
Ps. xxiii.

2 When in the sultry glebe I faint,
Or on the thirsty mountain pant,
To fertile vales, and dewy meads,
My weary, wandering steps He leads,
Where peaceful rivers, soft and slow,
Amid the verdant landscape flow.

3 Though in the paths of death I tread,
With gloomy horrors overspread,
My steadfast heart shall fear no ill,
For Thou. O Lord, art with me still:
Thy friendly crook shall give me aid,
And guide me through the dreadful shade.

4 Though in a bare and rugged way,
Through devious, lonely wilds I stray,
Thy bounty shall my pains beguile:
The barren wilderness shall smile,

With sudden greens and herbage crowned,
And streams shall murmur all around.

Joseph Addison (1672—1719), 1712.

100

The Shadow of the Altar.

1 FORTH from the dark and stormy sky,
Lord, to Thine altar's shade we fly;
Forth from the world, its hope and fear,
Saviour, we seek Thy shelter here:
Weary and weak, Thy grace we pray;
Turn not, O Lord, Thy guests away.

2 Long have we roamed in want and pain,
Long have we sought Thy rest in vain;
Wildered in doubt, in darkness lost,
Long have our souls been tempest-tost:
Low at Thy feet our sins we lay;
Turn not, O Lord, Thy guests away.

Bp. Reginald Heber (1783—1826), 1825.

OLD HUNDREDTH. L. M.

LOUIS BOURGEOIS, 1551.

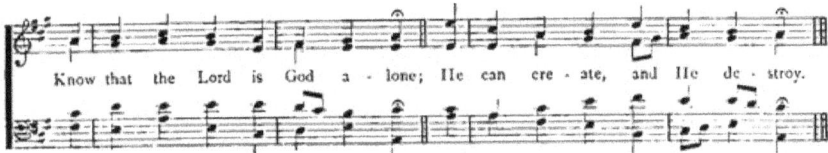

1. BE - FORE Je - ho - vah's aw - ful throne, Ye na - tions, bow with sa - cred joy;

Know that the Lord is God a - lone; He can cre - ate, and He de - stroy.

101

Grateful Adoration.
Ps. c.

2 His sovereign power, without our aid,
  Made us of clay, and formed us men;
And when, like wand'ring sheep, we
    strayed,
  He brought us to His fold again.

3 We are His people, we His care,
  Our souls and all our mortal frame:
What lasting honors shall we rear,
  Almighty Maker, to Thy Name?

4 We'll crowd Thy gates with thankful
    songs,
  High as the heavens our voices raise;
And earth, with her ten thousand tongues,
  Shall fill Thy courts with sounding
    praise.

5 Wide as the world is Thy command,
  Vast as eternity Thy love;
Firm as a rock Thy truth must stand,
  When rolling years shall cease to move.
Rev. Isaac Watts (1674—1748), 1719. Ab. and alt.
Rev. John Wesley (1703—1791), 1741.

102

"Sing to the Lord."
Ps. c.

1 ALL people that on earth do dwell,
  Sing to the Lord with cheerful voice:

Him serve with fear, His praise forth tell,
  Come ye before Him, and rejoice.

2 The Lord, ye know, is God indeed,
  Without our aid He did us make:
We are His flock, He doth us feed,
  And for His sheep He doth us take.

3 O enter then His gates with praise,
  Approach with joy His courts unto:
Praise, laud, and bless His Name always,
  For it is seemly so to do.

4 For why? the Lord our God is good,
  His mercy is forever sure:
His truth at all times firmly stood,
  And shall from age to age endure.
Rev. William Kethe, 1561.

103

"Praise Him, all ye People."
Ps. cxvii.

1 FROM all that dwell below the skies,
  Let the Creator's praise arise:
Let the Redeemer's Name be sung,
  Through every land, by every tongue.

2 Eternal are Thy mercies, Lord;
  Eternal truth attends Thy Word;
Thy praise shall sound from shore to shore
  Till suns shall rise and set no more.
Rev. Isaac Watts, 1719.

CREATION. L. M. D.

FRANCIS JOSEPH HAYDN (1732—1809), 1798.

1. THE spa-cious firm-a-ment on high, With all the blue e-the-real sky,

And span-gled heav'ns, a shin-ing frame, Their Great O-rig-i-nal pro-claim.

Th' un-wea-ried sun, from day to day, Does his Cre-a-tor's pow'r dis-play,

And pub-lish-es to ev-'ry land The work of an Al-might-y Hand.

104   *"The Heavens declare the Glory of God."*
         Ps. xix.

2 Soon as the evening shades prevail,
   The moon takes up the wondrous tale,
   And nightly to the listening earth
   Repeats the story of her birth ;
   Whilst all the stars that round her burn,
   And all the planets in their turn,
   Confirm the tidings as they roll,
   And spread the truth from pole to pole.

3 What though in solemn silence all
   Move round the dark terrestrial ball?
   What though no real voice nor sound
   Amid their radiant orbs be found?
   In reason's ear they all rejoice,
   And utter forth a glorious voice ;
   For ever singing, as they shine,
   "The Hand that made us is Divine."

Joseph Addison (1672—1719), 1712.

TRURO. L. M.

CHARLES BURNEY (1726—1814), 1769.

1. HIGH in the heav'ns, e - ter - nal God, Thy good - ness in full glo - ry shines;

Thy truth shall break thro' ev - 'ry cloud That veils and dark - ens Thy de - signs.

105

Providence and Grace.
Ps. xxxvi. 5—9.

2 Forever firm Thy justice stands,
As mountains their foundations keep;
Wise are the wonders of Thy hands;
Thy judgments are a mighty deep.

3 My God, how excellent Thy grace,
Whence all our hope and comfort springs;
The sons of Adam in distress
Fly to the shadow of Thy wings.

4 Life, like a fountain rich and free,
Springs from the presence of my Lord;
And in Thy light our souls shall see
The glories promised in Thy Word.

Rev. Isaac Watts (1674—1748), 1719. Ab.

106

God's Glory and Nearness to us.
Acts xvii. 24—28.

1 LORD of all being; throned afar,
Thy glory flames from sun and star;
Centre and soul of every sphere,
Yet to each loving heart how near.

2 Sun of our life, Thy quickening ray
Sheds on our path the glow of day;
Star of our hope, Thy softened light
Cheers the long watches of the night.

3 Our midnight is Thy smile withdrawn;
Our noontide is Thy gracious dawn;
Our rainbow arch Thy mercy's sign;
All, save the clouds of sin, are Thine.

4 Lord of all life, below, above,
Whose light is truth, whose warmth is love,
Before Thy ever-blazing throne
We ask no lustre of our own.

5 Grant us Thy truth to make us free,
And kindling hearts that burn for Thee,
Till all Thy living altars claim
One holy light, one heavenly flame.

Oliver Wendell Holmes (1809—   ), 1848.

107

"Bless the Lord."
Ps. ciii.

1 BLESS, O my soul, the Living God,
Call home thy thoughts that rove abroad;
Let all the powers within me join
In work and worship so divine.

2 Bless, O my soul, the God of grace;
His favors claim thy highest praise;
Why should the wonders He hath wrought
Be lost in silence and forgot?

3 'Tis He, my soul, that sent His Son
To die for crimes which thou hast done;
He owns the ransom, and forgives
The hourly follies of our lives.

4 Let the whole earth His power confess;
Let the whole earth adore His grace:
The Gentile with the Jew shall join
In work and worship so divine.

Rev. Isaac Watts, 1719. Ab.

MISSIONARY CHANT. L. M.

HENRICH CHRISTOPHER ZEUNER (1795—1857), 1832.

1. PRAIS-ES to Him, whose love has given, In Christ, His Son, the Life of Heaven;

Who for our dark-ness gives us light, And turns to day our deep-est night.

108 *God Triune praised.*

2 Praises to Him, in grace who came,
To bear our woe, and sin, and shame;
Who lived to die, who died to rise,
The God-accepted sacrifice.

3 Praises to Him, the chain who broke,
Opened the prison, burst the yoke,
Sent forth its captives glad and free,
Heirs of an endless liberty.

4 Praises to Him, who sheds abroad
Within our hearts the love of God;
The Spirit of all truth and peace,
Fountain of joy and holiness!

5 To Father, Son, and Spirit now
The hands we lift, the knees we bow;
To Thee, Jehovah, thus we raise
The sinner's endless song of praise.

Rev. Horatius Bonar (1808—), 1861. Ab. and alt.

109 *"Whose Love profound."*

1 FATHER of Heaven, whose love profound
A ransom for our souls hath found,
Before Thy throne we sinners bend:
To us Thy pardoning love extend.

2 Almighty Son, Incarnate Word,
Our Prophet, Priest, Redeemer, Lord,

Before Thy throne we sinners bend:
To us Thy saving grace extend.

3 Eternal Spirit, by whose breath
The soul is raised from sin and death,
Before Thy throne we sinners bend:
To us Thy quickening power extend.

4 Jehovah, Father, Spirit, Son,
Mysterious Godhead, Three in One,
Before Thy throne we sinners bend:
Grace, pardon, life, to us extend.

Edward Cooper, 1805.

110 *"Mightier than the mighty Sea."*
Ps. xciii 3—5.

1 THE floods, O Lord, lift up their voice,
The mighty floods lift up their roar;
The floods in tumult loud rejoice,
And climb in foam the sounding shore.

2 But mightier than the mighty sea,
The Lord of glory reigns on high:
Far o'er its waves we look to Thee,
And see their fury break and die.

3 Thy word is true, Thy promise sure,
That ancient promise, sealed in love;
Here be Thy temple ever pure,
As Thy pure mansions shine above.

Bp. George Burgess (1809—1866), 1840

RUSSIAN HYMN L. M. ALEXIS THEODORE LWOFF (1799–1870), 1833.

1. KINGDOMS and thrones to God be - long; Crown Him, ye na - tions, in your song;

His wondrous names and powers re - hearse; His hon - ors shall en - rich your verse.

---

111 *The Majesty and Mercy of God.*
Ps. lxviii.

2 He shakes the heavens with loud alarms;
How terrible is God in arms!
In Israel are His mercies known,
Israel is His peculiar throne.

3 Proclaim Him King, pronounce Him blest;
He's your defence, your joy, your rest;
When terrors rise, and nations faint,
God is the strength of every saint.
Rev. Isaac Watts (1674–1748), 1719

112 *Wonders of Creation and Grace.*
Ps. cxxxvi.

1 GIVE to our God immortal praise;
Mercy and truth are all His ways:
Wonders of grace to God belong;
Repeat His mercies in your song.

2 He built the earth, He spread the sky,
And fixed the starry lights on high:
Wonders of grace to God belong;
Repeat His mercies in your song.

3 He sent His Son with power to save,
From guilt, and darkness, and the grave:
Wonders of grace to God belong;
Repeat His mercies in your song.

4 Thro' this vain world He guides our feet,
And leads us to His heavenly seat:
His mercies ever shall endure,
When this vain world shall be no more.
Rev. Isaac Watts, 1719. Ab.

113 *Guiding and Guarding.*
Ps. cvii.

1 GIVE thanks to God; He reigns above;
Kind are His thoughts, His Name is Love:
His mercy ages past have known,
And ages long to come shall own.

2 Let the redeeméd of the Lord
The wonders of His grace record;
Israel, the nation whom He chose,
And rescued from their mighty foes.

3 He feeds and clothes us all the way,
He guides our footsteps lest we stray;
He guards us with a powerful hand,
And brings us to the heavenly land.

4 O let the saints with joy record
The truth and goodness of the Lord:
How great His works! how kind His ways!
Let every tongue pronounce His praise.
Rev. Isaac Watts, 1719. Ab.

FULTON. 7.

WILLIAM BATCHELDER BRADBURY (1816—1868).

1. Let us, with a glad - some mind, Praise the Lord, for He is kind:

For His mer - cies shall en - dure, Ev - er faith - ful, ev - er sure.

114   *Enduring Mercies.*
        Ps. cxxxvi.

2 He, with all-commanding might,
Filled the new-made world with light;
All things living He doth feed,
His full hand supplies their need.

3 He His chosen race did bless
In the wasteful wilderness;
He hath, with a piteous eye,
Looked upon our misery.

4 Let us therefore warble forth
His high majesty and worth:
For His mercies shall endure,
Ever faithful, ever sure.
      John Milton (1608—1674), 1624. **Ab. and alt.**

115   *Thanks and Praise.*
        Ps. cvii; cxvii.

1 THANK and praise Jehovah's Name,
For His mercies, firm and sure,
From eternity, the same,
   To eternity endure.

2 Let the ransomed thus rejoice,
Gathered out of every land;
As the people of His choice,
   Plucked from the destroyer's hand.

3 Praise Him, ye who know His love,
Praise Him from the depths beneath,

Praise Him in the heights above;
Praise your Maker, all that breathe.

4 For His truth and mercy stand,
Past, and present, and to be,
Like the years of His right hand,
Like His own eternity.
      James Montgomery (1771—1854), 1822. **Ab.**

116   *"Praise Him"*
        Ps. cl.

1 PRAISE the Lord; His glories show,
Saints within His courts below,
Angels round His throne above,
Praise Him, all that share His love.

2 Earth, to Heaven exalt the strain,
Send it, Heaven, to earth again;
Age to age, and shore to shore,
Praise Him, praise Him, evermore.

3 Praise the Lord; His goodness trace,
All the wonders of His grace,
All that He hath borne and done,
All He sends us through His Son.

4 Strings and voices, hands and hearts,
In the concert bear your parts;
All that breathe, your Lord adore,
Praise Him, praise Him evermore.
      Rev. Henry Francis Lyte (1793—1847), 1834, 1841.

MONKLAND. 7.   JOHN P. WILKES, 1861.

1. HAL - LE - LU - JAH, raise, O raise To our God the song of praise:

All His ser - vants, join to sing God our Sav - iour and our King.

117 *The Condescension of God.*
Ps. cxiii.

2 Blessèd be for evermore
That dread Name which we adore:
O'er all nations God alone,
Higher than the heavens His throne.

3 Yet to view the heavens He bends;
Yea, to earth He condescends;
Passing by the rich and great,
For the low and desolate.

4 He can raise the poor to stand
With the princes of the land;
Wealth upon the needy shower;
Set the meanest high in power.

5 He the broken spirit cheers,
Turns to joy the mourner's tears;
Such the wonders of His ways:
Praise His Name, forever praise.

Josiah Conder (1789—1855), 1837. Ab.

118 *Redeeming Love.*

1 SWEET the time, exceeding sweet,
When the saints together meet;
When the Saviour is the theme,
When they join to sing of Him.

2 Sing we then eternal love,
Such as did the Father move:
He beheld the world undone,
Loved the world, and gave His Son.

3 Sing the Son's amazing love:
How He left the realms above,
Took our nature and our place,
Lived and died to save our race.

4 Sing we, too, the Spirit's love:
With our wretchèd hearts He strove,
Took the things of Christ, and showed
How to reach His blest abode.

Rev. George Burder (1752—1832), 1779. Ab. and alt.

SOLITUDE. 7.   LEWIS THOMAS DOWNES (1827—), 1850.

CULBACH. 7.

German. Arr. by Rev. WILLIAM HENRY HAVERGAL (1793—1870), 1861.

1. Songs of praise the an - gels sang, Heav'n with hal - le - lu - jahs rang,

When Je - ho - vah's work be - gun, When He spake, and it was done.

119

"Songs of Praise."
Job xxxviii. 7.

2 Songs of praise awoke the morn,
When the Prince of Peace was born;
Songs of praise arose, when He
Captive led captivity.

3 Heaven and earth must pass away,
Songs of praise shall crown that day;
God will make new heavens, new earth,
Songs of praise shall hail their birth.

4 Saints below, with heart and voice,
Still in songs of praise rejoice;
Learning here, by faith and love,
Songs of praise to sing above.

5 Borne upon their latest breath,
Songs of praise shall conquer death;
Then, amidst eternal joy,
Songs of praise their powers employ.

James Montgomery (1771—1854), 1819, 1853. Ab.

120

Mercies that never fail.

1 Holy, holy, holy Lord,
Be Thy glorious Name adored:
Lord, Thy mercies never fail;
Hail, celestial Goodness, hail!

2 Though unworthy, Lord, Thine ear
Deign our humble songs to hear;
Purer praise we hope to bring,
When around Thy throne we sing.

3 While on earth ordained to stay,
Guide our footsteps in Thy way,
Till we come to dwell with Thee,
Till we all Thy glory see.

4 Then, with angel-harps, again
We will wake a nobler strain;
There, in joyful songs of praise,
Our triumphant voices raise.

5 Lord, Thy mercies never fail:
Hail, celestial Goodness, hail!
Holy, holy, holy, Lord,
Be Thy glorious Name adored.

Rev. Benjamin Williams, 1778. Ab.

121

"Te Deum laudamus."

1 God eternal, Lord of all,
Lowly at Thy feet we fall:
All the earth doth worship Thee,
We amidst the throng would be.

2 All the holy angels cry,
Hail, thrice holy, God most High:
Lord of all the heavenly powers,
Be the same loud anthem ours.

3 God eternal, mighty King,
Unto Thee our praise we bring:
Seated on Thy judgment-throne,
Number us among Thine own.

Rev James Elwin Millard, 1848. Ab. and alt.

LAUS SEMPITERNA. L. P. M.

Arr. from LUDWIG SPOHR (1784—1859).

1. I'LL praise my Mak - er with my breath, And, when my voice is lost in death,

Praise shall em - ploy my no - bler powers: My days of praise shall ne'er be past,

While life, and thought, and be - - ing last, Or im - mor - tal - i - ty en-dures.

122

Endless Praise.
Ps. cxlvi.

2 Happy the man, whose hopes rely
On Israel's God: He made the sky,
And earth, and seas, with all their train;
His truth forever stands secure;
He saves th' opprest, He feeds the poor,
And none shall find His promise vain.

3 The Lord hath eyes to give the blind;
The Lord supports the sinking mind;
He sends the laboring conscience peace;

He helps the stranger in distress,
The widow and the fatherless,
And grants the prisoner sweet release

4 I'll praise Him while He lends me breath,
And, when my voice is lost in death,
Praise shall employ my nobler powers:
My days of praise shall ne'er be past,
While life, and thought, and being last,
Or immortality endures.

Rev. Isaac Watts (1674—1748), 1719. Ab

NASHVILLE. L. P. M.

From a Gregorian Chant. Arr. by LOWELL MASON (1792—1872), 1832.

ST. GEORGE'S CHAPEL. 7. D.

Sir GEORGE JOB ELVEY (1816—   ). 1860.

1. From the vast and veil-ed throng, Round the Fath-er's heav'n-ly throne, Swells the ev-er-

last-ing song: Glo-ry be to God a-lone! Round Im-man-uel's cross of pain

Mor-tal men, in tribes un-known, Sing to Him who once was slain: Glo-ry be to God a-lone!

123 *"Glory be to God alone."*

2 Blend, ye raptured songs, in one,
Men redeemed, your Father own;
Angels, worship ye the Son:
Glory be to God alone!

Spirit, 'tis within Thy light,
Streaming far from cross and throne,
Earth and Heaven their songs unite:
Glory be to God alone!

Rev. Hervey Doddridge Ganse (1822—   ), 1872.

DARWALL. H. M.

Rev. JOHN DARWALL (1731—1789), 1770.

1. The Lord Je-ho-vah reigns, His throne is built on high; The gar-ments He as-sumes Are light and

maj-es-ty: His glo-ries shine with beams so bright, No mor-tal eye can bear the sight.

124 *" The Lord reigneth."*
Ps. xciii ; xcvii.

2 The thunders of His hand
  Keep the wide world in awe ;
His wrath and justice stand
  To guard His holy law ;
And where His love resolves to bless,
His truth confirms and seals the grace.

3 Through all His ancient works,
  Surprising wisdom shines ;
Confounds the powers of hell,
  And breaks their cursed designs ;
Strong is His arm, and shall fulfil
His great decrees, His sovereign will.

4 And can this mighty King
  Of Glory condescend?
And will He write His Name,
  My Father and my Friend?
I love His Name, I love His Word :
Join, all my powers, and praise the Lord.
  Rev. Isaac Watts (1674—1748), 1709.

125 *Praise from all Creatures.*
Ps. cxlviii.

1 Ye tribes of Adam, join
  With Heaven, and earth, and seas,
And offer notes divine
  To your Creator's praise.
Ye holy throng of angels bright,
In words of light, begin the song.

2 The shining worlds above
  In glorious order stand,
Or in swift courses move,

By His supreme command :
He spake the word, and all their frame
From nothing came, to praise the Lord.

3 He moved their mighty wheels
  In unknown ages past,
And each His word fulfils,
  While time and nature last :
In different ways His works proclaim
His wondrous Name, and speak His praise.
  Rev. Isaac Watts, 1719. Ab.

126 *"Take up the Strain."*

1 Shall hymns of grateful love
  Through Heaven's high arches ring,
And all the hosts above
  Their songs of triumph sing ;
And shall not we take up the strain,
And send the echo back again?

2 Shall they adore the Lord,
  Who bought them with His blood,
And all the love record
  That led them home to God ;
And shall not we take up the strain,
And send the echo back again?

3 O spread the joyful sound,
  The Saviour's love proclaim,
And publish all around
  Salvation through His Name ;
Till all the world take up the strain,
And send the echo back again.
  Rev. James J. Cummins (—1867), 1839. Ab.

HADDAM. H. M.   Arr. by LOWELL MASON (1792—1872), 1822.

MELCOMBE. L. M.
SAMUEL WEBBE (1740—1816).

1. My God, in whom are all the springs Of bound - less love, and grace un - known,

Hide me be - neath Thy spread - ing wings, Till the dark cloud is o - ver - blown.

127 *Exalted above the Heavens.*
Ps. lvii.

2 Up to the heavens I send my cry;
  The Lord will my desires perform:
  He sends His angels from the sky,
  And saves me from the threat'ning storm.

3 High o'er the earth Thy mercy reigns,
  And reaches to the utmost sky;
  His truth to endless years remains,
  When lower worlds dissolve and die.

4 Be Thou exalted, O my God,
  Above the heavens where angels dwell;
  Thy power on earth be known abroad,
  And land to land Thy wonders tell.
  Rev. Isaac Watts (1674—1748), 1719. Ab.

128 *The All-seeing God.*
Ps. cxxxix.

1 LORD, Thou hast searched and seen me
    through;
  Thine eye commands with piercing view,

My rising and my resting hours,
My heart and flesh with all their powers.

2 My thoughts, before they are my own,
  Are to my God distinctly known;
  He knows the words I mean to speak,
  Ere from my opening lips they break.

3 Within Thy circling power I stand;
  On every side I find Thy hand;
  Awake, asleep, at home, abroad,
  I am surrounded still with God.

4 Amazing knowledge, vast and great,
  What large extent, what lofty height:
  My soul, with all the powers I boast,
  Is in the boundless prospect lost.

5 O may these thoughts possess my breast,
  Where'er I rove, where'er I rest,
  Nor let my weaker passions dare
  Consent to sin, for God is there.
  Rev. Isaac Watts, 1719.

BLENDON. L. M.
FELICE GIARDINI (1716—1796).

129 *The Pillars of Cloud and Fire.*
Ex. xiii. 21. **L. M.**

1 WHEN Israel, of the Lord beloved,
　Out from the land of bondage came,
　Her fathers' God before her moved,
　An awful guide, in smoke and flame.

2 By day, along th' astonished lands,
　The cloudy pillar glided slow;
　By night, Arabia's crimsoned sands
　Returned the fiery column's glow.

3 Thus present still, though now unseen
　O Lord, when shines the prosperous day,
　Be thoughts of Thee a cloudy screen,
　To temper the deceitful ray.

4 And O, when gathers on our path,
　In shade and storm, the frequent night,
　Be Thou long-suffering, slow to wrath,
　A burning and a shining light.

Sir Walter Scott (1771—1832), 1820. Ab. and alt.

DALSTON. S. P. M.

AARON WILLIAMS (1731—1776), 1760.

1. THE Lord Je - ho - vah reigns, And roy - al state main - tains,

His head with aw - ful glo - ries crowned: Ar - rayed in robes of light,

Be - girt with sov - 'reign might, And rays of maj - es - ty a - round.

130 *The Majesty and Might of God.*
Ps. xciii.

2 Upheld by Thy commands,
　The world securely stands,
And skies and stars obey Thy word:
　Thy throne was fixed on high
　Before the starry sky:
Eternal is Thy kingdom, Lord.

3 Let floods and nations rage,
　And all their powers engage;
Let swelling tides assault the sky:

　The terrors of Thy frown
　Shall beat their madness down;
Thy throne for ever stands on high.

4 Thy promises are true,
　Thy grace is ever new;
There fixed, Thy church shall he'er remove:
　Thy saints with holy fear
　Shall in Thy courts appear,
And sing Thine everlasting love.

Rev. Isaac Watts, 1719.

BRADFORD. C. M.

GEORGE FREDERICK HANDEL (1685—1759), 1741.

1. Great God, how in - fi - nite art Thou, What worth - less worms are we:

Let the whole race of creat - ures bow, And pay their praise to Thee.

131   *God infinite and eternal.*

2 Thy throne eternal ages stood,
   Ere seas or stars were made ;
 Thou art the ever-living God,
   Were all the nations dead.

3 Eternity, with all its years,
   Stands present in Thy view ;
 To Thee there's nothing old appears,
   Great God, there's nothing new.

4 Our lives thro' various scenes are drawn,
   And vexed with trifling cares ;
 While Thine eternal thought moves on
   Thine undisturbed affairs.

5 Great God, how infinite art Thou,
   What worthless worms are we ;
 Let the whole race of creatures bow,
   And pay their praise to Thee.
         Rev. Isaac Watts (1674—1748), 1709. Ab.

132   *Feared and loved.*

1 My God, how wonderful Thou art,
   Thy majesty how bright,
 How beautiful Thy Mercy-seat
   In depths of burning light.

2 How dread are Thine eternal years,
   O Everlasting Lord ;
 By prostrate spirits day and night
   Incessantly adored.

3 O how I fear Thee, living God,
   With deepest, tenderest fears,
 And worship Thee with trembling hope,
   And penitential tears.

4 Yet I may love Thee too, O Lord,
   Almighty as Thou art ;
 For Thou hast stooped to ask of me
   The love of my poor heart.

5 No earthly father loves like Thee,
   No mother half so mild
 Bears and forbears, as Thou hast done
   With me, Thy sinful child.

6 Father of Jesus, love's reward,
   What rapture will it be,
 Prostrate before Thy throne to lie,
   And gaze, and gaze on Thee,
     Rev. Frederick William Faber (1814—1863), 1849. Ab.

133   *God our Help, and Security.*
        Ps. xc.

1 O God, our help in ages past,
   Our hope for years to come ;
 Our shelter from the stormy blast,
   And our eternal home :

2 Under the shadow of Thy throne
   Thy saints have dwelt secure ;
 Sufficient is Thine arm alone,
   And our defence is sure.

3 Before the hills in order stood,
  Or earth received her frame,
  From everlasting Thou art God,
  To endless years the same.

4 A thousand ages, in Thy sight,
  Are like an evening gone;
  Short as the watch that ends the night,
  Before the rising sun.

5 Time, like an ever-rolling stream,
  Bears all its sons away;
  They fly, forgotten, as a dream
  Dies at the opening day.

6 O God, our help in ages past,
  Our hope for years to come,
  Be Thou our guard while troubles last,
  And our eternal home.

Rev. Isaac Watts, 1719. Ab. and sl. alt.

CHURCH. C. M.

JOSEPH PERRY HOLBROOK (1822—).

1. JE - HO - VAH, God, Thy gra - cious pow'r On ev - 'ry hand we see;

O may the bless - ings of each hour Lead all our thoughts to Thee.

134 *The constant Goodness of God.*
Ps. cxxxix.

2 If on the wings of morn we speed
  To earth's remotest bound,
  Thy hand will there our footsteps lead,
  Thy love our path surround.

3 Thy power is in the ocean deeps,
  And reaches to the skies;
  Thine eye of mercy never sleeps,
  Thy goodness never dies.

4 From morn till noon, till latest eve,
  Thy hand, O God, we see;
  And all the blessings we receive,
  Proceed alone from Thee.

5 In all the changing scenes of time,
  On Thee our hopes depend;
  Through every age, in every clime,
  Our Father, and our Friend.

Rev. John Thomson (1782—1818), 1810. Sl. alt.

DUNDEE. C. M.

GUILLAUME FRANCK, 1545.

ST. ANN. C. M.
                 WILLIAM CROFT (1677—1727). 1712.

1. The Lord our God is clothed with might; The winds o - bey His will;

He speaks, and in His heav'n - ly height The roll - ing sun stands still.

135   *The Majesty of God.*

2 Rebel, ye waves, and o'er the land
   With threatening aspect roar:
   The Lord uplifts His awful hand,
   And chains you to the shore.

3 Howl, winds of night, your force combine;
   Without His high behest,
   Ye shall not in the mountain pine
   Disturb the sparrow's nest.

4 His voice sublime is heard afar,
   In distant peals it dies;
   He yokes the whirlwind to His car,
   And sweeps the howling skies.

5 Ye nations, bend, in reverence bend;
   Ye monarchs, wait His nod;
   And bid the choral song ascend,
   To celebrate our God.
                Henry Kirke White (1785—1806), 1806.

136   *The Sovereignty of God.*

1 Keep silence, all created things,
   And wait your Master's nod;
   My soul stands trembling while she sings
   The honors of her God.

2 Life, death, and hell, and worlds unknown,
   Hang on His firm decree;
   He sits on no precarious throne,
   Nor borrows leave to be.

3 His providence unfolds the book,
   And makes His counsels shine;
   Each opening leaf, and every stroke,
   Fulfils some deep design.

4 In Thy fair book of life and grace
   O may I find my name,
   Recorded in some humble place,
   Beneath my Lord, the Lamb.
            Rev. Isaac Watts (1674—1748), 1706. Ab. and alt.

137   *Resignation to God's Will.*

1 Since all the varying scenes of time
   God's watchful eye surveys,
   O who so wise to choose our lot,
   Or to appoint our ways?

2 Good, when He gives, supremely good;
   Nor less when He denies;
   E'en crosses, from His sovereign hand,
   Are blessings in disguise.

3 Why should we doubt a Father's love,
   So constant and so kind?
   To His unerring gracious will
   Be every wish resigned.

4 In Thy fair book of life divine,
   My God, inscribe my name;
   There let it fill some humble place
   Beneath my Lord, the Lamb.
           Rev. James Hervey (1714—1758), 1746. Alt.

GENEVA. C. M.

JOHN COLE (1774?—1855), 1800.

1. WHEN all Thy mer - cies, O my God,)
When all Thy mercies, O my God, } My ris - ing soul sur - veys,

When all Thy mercies, O my God,

Trans-port - ed with the view, I'm lost In won - der, love, and praise.

Trans-port-ed with the view, I'm lost

138 *Mercies of God recounted.*

2 Unnumbered comforts to my soul
   Thy tender care bestowed,
 Before my infant heart conceived
   From whom those comforts flowed.

3 When worn with sickness, oft hast Thou
   With health renewed my face ;
 And, when in sins and sorrows sunk,
   Revived my soul with grace.

4 Ten thousand thousand precious gifts
   My daily thanks employ :
 Nor is the least a cheerful heart
   That tastes those gifts with joy.

5 Through every period of my life
   Thy goodness I'll pursue ;
 And after death, in distant worlds,
   The glorious theme renew.

6 Through all eternity to Thee
   A joyful song I'll raise ;
 For O, eternity's too short
   To utter all Thy praise.
                Joseph Addison (1672—1719), 1712. Ab.

139 *God's Omniscience.*
Ps. cxxxix.

1 IN all my vast concerns with Thee,
   In vain my soul would try
 To shun Thy presence, Lord, or flee
   The notice of Thine eye.

2 Thine all-surrounding sight surveys
   My rising and my rest,
 My public walks, my private ways,
   And secrets of my breast.

3 My thoughts lie open to the Lord,
   Before they're formed within ;
 And ere my lips pronounce the word,
   He knows the sense I mean.

4 If o'er my sins I seek to draw
   The curtains of the night,
 Those flaming eyes that guard Thy law
   Would turn the shades to light.

5 The beams of noon, the midnight hour,
   Are both alike to Thee :
 O may I ne'er provoke that power
   From which I cannot flee.
                Rev. Isaac Watts, 1719. Ab.

SPOHR. C. M. 6l.

Arr. from LUDWIG SPOHR (1784—1859), 1835.

1. BE - YOND, be - yond that bound - less sea, A - bove that dome of sky,

Far - ther than thought it - self can flee, Thy dwell - ing is on high;

Yet dear the aw - ful thought to me That Thou, my God, art nigh

140　*Far off, yet near.*
ACTS xvii. 24, 27.

2 We hear Thy voice when thunders roll
　Through the wide fields of air;
The waves obey Thy dread control;
　Yet still Thou art not there:
Where shall I find Him, O my soul,
　Who yet is everywhere?

3 O not in circling depth or height,
　But in the conscious breast,
Present to faith, though vailed from sight,
　There doth His Spirit rest:
O come, Thou Presence Infinite,
　And make Thy creature blest.

Josiah Conder (1789—1855), 1822. Ab.

ST. MARTIN'S. C. M.

WILLIAM TANSUR (1699—1774), 1735.

1. THE Lord de - scend - ed from a - bove, And bowed the heavens most high;

And un - der - neath His feet He cast The dark - ness of the sky,

141 *"He bowed the Heavens."*
Ps. xviii.

2 On cherub and on cherubim
  Full royally He rode ;
  And on the wings of all the winds
  Came flying all abroad.

3 He sat serene upon the floods,
  Their fury to restrain ;

And He, as Sovereign Lord and King,
For evermore shall reign.

4 The Lord will give His people strength
  Whereby they shall increase ;
  And He will bless His chosen flock
  With everlasting peace.

Thomas Sternhold (　—1549),　. Ab. and alt.

THATCHER. S. M.

GEORGE FREDERICK HANDEL (1685—1759), 1732.

1. My soul, re-peat His praise, Whose mer-cies are so great; Whose an-ger is so slow to rise, So read-y to a-bate.

142 *Abounding Compassion of God.*
Ps. ciii. 8—12.

2 God will not always chide ;
  And when His strokes are felt,
  His strokes are fewer than our crimes,
  And lighter than our guilt.

3 High as the heavens are raised
  Above the ground we tread,
  So far the riches of His grace
  Our highest thoughts exceed.

4 His power subdues our sins,
  And His forgiving love,
  Far as the east is from the west,
  Doth all our guilt remove.

Rev. Isaac Watts (1674—1748), 1719.

143 *"He knoweth our Frame."*
Ps. ciii. 13—18.

1 THE pity of the Lord
  To those that fear His Name,

Is such as tender parents feel :
He knows our feeble frame.

2 He knows we are but dust,
  Scattered with every breath ;
  His anger, like a rising wind,
  Can send us swift to death.

3 Our days are as the grass,
  Or like the morning flower ;
  If one sharp blast sweep o'er the field,
  It withers in an hour.

4 But Thy compassions, Lord,
  To endless years endure,
  And children's children ever find
  Thy words of promise sure.

Rev. Isaac Watts, 1719.

ARMSTRONG. 8.7.D.

Arr. from HENRY BRINLEY RICHARDS (1819—).

1. FATHER, Thine E - lect who lov - est With an ev - er - last-ing love; Saviour, who the bar re - mov - est

D. S.—List to Thy glad peo - ple sing - ing,

From the ho - ly home a - bove; Spir - it, dai - ly meetness bring-ing For the glo - ry there up - stored:

"Ho - ly, ho - ly, ho - ly, Lord!"

144   *"Holy, holy, holy, Lord."*

2 Lord, with sin-bound souls Thou bearest,
  Struggling towards this strain divine;
Glad on mortal lips Thou hearest
  That thrice awful Name of Thine.
But Thou listenest, O how sweetly!
  When from holy lips outpoured,
Rings through Heaven this strain full
  "Holy, holy, holy, Lord!" [meetly,

3 Shall we, Lord, meet voices never
  Bring to that eternal hymn?
Hallow us to help th' endeavor
  Of Thy pure-lipped seraphim:
Hark! their own high strain we bring
  Listen to the full accord! [Thee;
Sweet the song we ever sing Thee,
  "Holy, holy, holy, Lord!"
            Thomas Hornblower Gill (1819—), 1860. Ab.

145   *Perpetual Pentecost.*

1 DAY divine, when sudden streaming
  To the Lord's first lovers came
Glory new and treasures teeming,
  Mighty gifts and tongues of flame!
Day to happy souls commended,
  When the Holy Ghost was given,
When the Comforter descended,
  And brought down the joy of Heaven!

2 Hath the Holy Ghost been holden
  By those ancient saints alone?
Only may the ages olden
  Call the Comforter their own?
Wonders we may not inherit,
  Signs and tongues we may not crave;
Yet we still receive the Spirit,
  Still the Comforter we have.

3 Sure the Holy Ghost is dwelling
  With the souls that holier grow;
Signs most glorious, all excelling,
  Witness brightest we may show:
Hope that makes ashaméd never,
  Perfect peace that passeth thought,
Mighty joy that stayeth ever,
  Love Divine that changeth not.
            Thomas Hornblower Gill, 1860. Ab.

146   *Dismission.*

LORD, dismiss us with Thy blessing,
  Bid us now depart in peace;
Still on heavenly manna feeding,
  Let our faith and love increase:
Fill each breast with consolation:
  Up to Thee our hearts we raise;
When we reach our blissful station,
  Then we'll give Thee nobler praise.
            Rev. Robert Hawker (1753—1827), 1794.

STANLEY. 7. D.

FRANZ ABT (1819—1885), 1812.
Arr. by JOSEPH PERRY HOLBROOK (1822—).

1. WATCHMAN, tell us of the night, What its signs of promise are: Traveller,
o'er yon mountain's height, See that glo - ry - beam-ing star!
Watchman, does its beauteous ray Aught of joy or hope fore - tell? Trav - eller, yes; it brings the day— Prom - ised day of Is - ra - el, Prom - ised day of Is - ra - el.

CHORUS.

147   *"What of the Night?"*
Is. xxi. 11.

2 Watchman, tell us of the night;
   Higher yet that star ascends:
Traveller, blessedness and light,
   Peace and truth, its course portends.
Watchman, will its beams alone
   Gild the spot that gave them birth?
Traveller, ages are its own,
   See, it bursts o'er all the earth.

3 Watchman, tell us of the night,
   For the morning seems to dawn:
Traveller, darkness takes its flight,
   Doubt and terror are withdrawn,
Watchman, let thy wanderings cease;
   Hie thee to thy quiet home:
Traveller, lo, the Prince of Peace,
   Lo, the Son of God is come!
                Sir John Bowring (1792—1872), 1825. Sl. alt.

ANGLIA. C. M. D.   English Carol.

1. WHILE shep-herds watched their flocks by night, All seat-ed on the ground,
The an-gel of the Lord came down, And glo-ry shone a-round.

"Fear not," said he, for might-y dread Had seized their trou-bled mind;

"Glad tid-ings of great joy I bring To you, and all man-kind.

148

Song of the Angels.
Luke ii. 7–15.

2 "To you, in David's town, this day,
   Is born of David's line,
The Saviour, who is Christ, the Lord;
   And this shall be the sign:
The Heavenly Babe you there shall find
   To human view displayed,
All meanly wrapped in swathing bands,
   And in a manger laid."

3 Thus spake the seraph, and forthwith
   Appeared a shining throng
Of angels, praising God, and thus
   Addressed their joyful song:
"All glory be to God on high,
   And to the earth be peace;
Good-will henceforth from Heaven to men
   Begin, and never cease."

Nahum Tate (1652–1715), 1703.

ZERAH. C. M. 6l.   LOWELL MASON (1792–1872), 1837.

NEWBOLD. C. M. 51.   GEORGE KINGSLEY (1811—1884).

1. HARK, the glad sound, the Sav-iour comes, The Sav-iour prom - ised long; Let ev-'ry heart prepare a throne, And ev-'ry voice a song, And ev-'ry voice a song.

149   *"Hark, the glad Sound."*
Is. lxi.

2 He comes, the prisoners to release
  In Satan's bondage held;
The gates of brass before Him burst,
  The iron fetters yield.

3 He comes, from thickest films of vice
  To clear the mental ray,
And on the eyeballs of the blind
  To pour celestial day.

4 He comes, the broken heart to bind,
  The bleeding soul to cure,
And with the treasures of His grace
  T' enrich the humble poor.

5 Our glad hosannas, Prince of Peace,
  Thy welcome shall proclaim,
And Heaven's eternal arches ring
  With Thy belovéd Name.
        Rev. Philip Doddridge (1702—1751), 1735.

150   *The Messiah's Coming and Kingdom.*
Is. ix. 1—7.

1 THE race that long in darkness pined
  Have seen a glorious Light;
The people dwell in day, who dwelt
  In death's surrounding night.

2 To hail Thy rise, Thou better Sun,
  The gathering nations come,
Joyous as when the reapers bear
  The harvest-treasures home.

3 To us a Child of Hope is born,
  To us a Son is given;
Him shall the tribes of earth obey,
  Him all the hosts of Heaven.

4 His Name shall be the Prince of Peace
  Forevermore adored,
The Wonderful, the Counsellor,
  The great and mighty Lord.

5 His power increasing still shall spread;
  His reign no end shall know;
Justice shall guard His throne above,
  And peace abound below.
        Rev. John Morrison (1749—1798), 1770. Ab.

ANNUNCIATION. C. M.   GEORGE MURSELL GARRETT (1834—). 1872.

HERALD ANGELS. 7. D.

FELIX MENDELSSOHN-BARTHOLDY (1809—1847), 1846.

1. HARK, the her- ald an-gels sing, "Glo - ry to the new-born King! Peace on earth, and mer - cy mild,

God and sin- ners reconciled!" { Joy - ful, all ye na- tions, rise, / Join the tri-umph of the skies; } U - ni - ver - sal nat - ure say,

"Christ the Lord is born to-day," U - ni - ver - sal nat - ure say, "Christ the Lord is born to - day."

151
"The Herald Angels."

2 Christ, by highest Heaven adored!
Christ, the everlasting Lord!
Late in time behold Him come,
Offspring of a Virgin's womb!
Veiled in flesh the Godhead see,
Hail, th' incarnate Deity!
Pleased as man with men to dwell,
Jesus, our Immanuel.

3 Hail, the heavenly Prince of Peace!
Hail, the Sun of Righteousness!
Light and life to all He brings,
Risen with healing in His wings.
Mild He lays His glory by,
Born that man no more may die,
Born to raise the sons of earth,
Born to give them second birth.

Rev. Charles Wesley (1708—1788), 1739. Ab. and alt

152
"He has come."

1 HE has come, the Christ of God;
Left for us His glad abode;
Stooping from His throne of bliss,

To this darksome wilderness!
He has come, the Prince of Peace;
Come to bid our sorrows cease;
Come to scatter, with His light,
All the shadows of our night.

2 He, the mighty King, has come,
Making this poor earth His home;
Come to bear our sin's sad load,
Son of David, Son of God.
He has come, whose Name of grace
Speaks deliverance to our race;
Left for us His glad abode,
Son of Mary, Son of God.

3 Unto us a Child is born;
Ne'er has earth beheld a morn
Out of all the morns of time
Half so glorious in its prime.
Unto us a Son is given;
He has come from God's own Heaven,
Bringing with Him from above
Holy peace, and holy love.

Rev. Horatius Bonar (1808—), 1857. Sl. alt.

ADESTE FIDELES. P. M.   MARC ANTOINE PORTOGALLO (1765—1830).

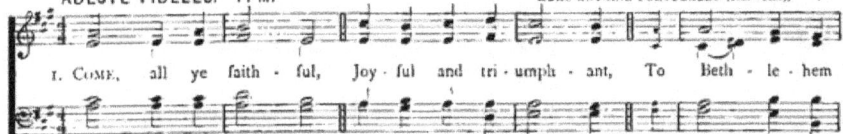

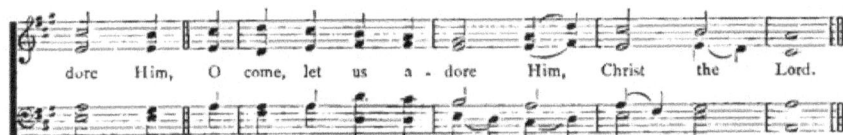

1. COME, all ye faith - ful, Joy - ful and tri - umph - ant, To Beth - le - hem has - ten now with glad ac - cord; Come, and be - hold Him Born, the King of an - gels, O come, let us a - dore Him, O come, let us a - dore Him, O come, let us a - dore Him, Christ the Lord.

153   *"Adeste Fideles."*

2 Sing, choirs of angels,
    Sing in exultation,
Through Heaven's high arches be your praises poured
    Now to our God be
    Glory in the highest:
O come, let us adore Him, Christ the Lord.

3 Yea, Lord, we bless Thee,
    Born for our salvation;
Jesus, forever be Thy Name adored;
    Word of the Father,
    Now in flesh appearing:
O come, let us adore Him, Christ the Lord.

Unknown Author, of uncertain date.
Tr. by Rev. Frederick Oakeley (1802—1880), 1841. Ab. and alt.

CAROL. C. M. D.   RICHARD STORRS WILLIS (1819—   d. 1860.

1. IT came up-on the midnight clear, That glo-rious song of old, From an-gels bend-ing near the earth, To touch their harps of gold: "Peace on earth, good-will to men From Heav'n's all-gracious King." The world in solemn still-ness lay To hear the an-gels sing.

154   *Christmas Carol.*

2 Still through the cloven skies they come,
    With peaceful wings unfurled;
And still their heavenly music floats
    O'er all the weary world:
Above its sad and lowly plains
    They bend on hovering wing,
And ever o'er its Babel sounds
    The blessèd angels sing.

3 But with the woes of sin and strife
    The world has suffered long;
Beneath the angel-strain have rolled
    Two thousand years of wrong;
And man, at war with man, hears not
    The love-song which they bring:
O hush the noise, ye men of strife,
    And hear the angels sing.

4 And ye, beneath life's crushing load
    Whose forms are bending low,
Who toil along the climbing way,
    With painful steps and slow.—

Look now; for glad and golden hours
    Come swiftly on the wing:
O rest beside the weary road,
    And hear the angels sing.

5 For lo, the days are hastening on,
    By prophet-bards foretold,
When with the ever-circling years
    Comes round the age of gold:
When peace shall over all the earth
    Its ancient splendors fling,
And the whole world give back the song
    Which now the angels sing.
          Rev. Edmund Hamilton Sears (1810—1876), 1850.

155   *Christmas Song.*

1 CALM on the listening ear of night
    Come Heaven's melodious strains,
Where wild Judea stretches far
    Her silver-mantled plains;
Celestial choirs, from courts above,
    Shed sacred glories there;
And angels, with their sparkling lyres,
    Make music on the air.

2 The answering hills of Palestine
  Send back the glad reply,
And greet from all their holy heights
  The Day-spring from on high :
O'er the blue depths of Galilee
  There comes a holier calm ;
And Sharon waves in solemn praise
  Her silent groves of palm.

3 Glory to God ! the lofty strain
  The realm of ether fills ;
How sweeps the song of solemn joy
  O'er Judah's sacred hills !
"Glory to God !" the sounding skies
  Loud with their anthems ring:
"Peace on the earth ; good-will to men,
  From Heaven's eternal King."

Rev. Edmund Hamilton Sears, 1835. **Ab.**

HUMMEL. C. M.

HIENRICH CHRISTOPHER ZEUNER (1795—1857), 1832.

1. O Lord, how good, how great art Thou, In Heav'n and earth the same;

There an - gels at Thy foot - stool bow, Here babes Thy grace pro - claim.

156

God's great Love for Man.
Ps. viii.

2 When glorious in the nightly sky
  Thy moon and stars I see,
O, what is man, I wondering cry,
  To be so loved by Thee.

3 To him Thou hourly deign'st to give
  New mercies from on high ;
Didst quit Thy throne with him to live,
  For him in pain to die.

4 Close to Thine own bright seraphim
  His favored path is trod ;
And all beside are serving him,
  That he may serve his God.

5 O Lord, how good, how great art Thou,
  In Heaven and earth the same ;
There angels at Thy footstool bow,
  Here babes Thy grace proclaim.

Rev. Henry Francis Lyte (1793—1847), 1834.

157

The glad Approach.

1 Messiah, at Thy glad approach
  The howling winds are still ;

Thy praises fill the lonely waste,
  And breathe from every hill.

2 The hidden fountains, at Thy call,
  Their sacred stores unlock ;
Loud in the desert sudden streams
  Burst living from the rock.

3 The incense of the Spring ascends
  Upon the morning gale ;
Red o'er the hill the roses bloom,
  The lilies in the vale.

4 Renewed, the earth a robe of light,
  A robe of beauty wears ;
And in new heavens a brighter sun
  Leads on the promised years.

5 Let Israel to the Prince of Peace
  The loud hosanna sing ;
With hallelujahs and with hymns,
  O Zion, hail thy King.

Michael Bruce (1746—1767), 1781. **Ab.**

LAUD. C. M.

Rev. JOHN BACCHUS DYKES (1825—1876), 1861.

1. Joy to the world, the Lord is come: Let earth re-ceive her King;

Let ev - 'ry heart pre - pare Him room, And Heav'n and nat - ure sing.

158 *"Joy to the World."*
Ps. xcviii.

2 Joy to the earth, the Saviour reigns:
  Let men their songs employ;
  While fields and floods, rocks, hills, and
  Repeat the sounding joy.   [plains,

3 No more let sins and sorrows grow,
  Nor thorns infest the ground:
  He comes to make His blessings flow
  Far as the curse is found.

4 He rules the world with truth and grace,
  And makes the nations prove
  The glories of His righteousness,
  And wonders of His love.
            Rev. Isaac Watts (1674—1748), 1709.

159 *"The Lord reigneth."*
Ps. xcvi.

1 Sing to the Lord, ye distant lands,
  Ye tribes of every tongue:
  His new discovered grace demands
  A new and nobler song.

2 Say to the nations, Jesus reigns,
  God's own almighty Son;
  His power the sinking world sustains,
  And grace surrounds His throne.

3 Behold He comes, He comes to bless
  The nations as their God;
  To show the world His righteousness,
  And send His truth abroad.
            Rev. Isaac Watts, 1719. Ab.

ANTIOCH. C. M.

From GEORGE FREDERICK HANDEL.   Arr. by LOWELL MASON (1792—1872), 1836.

1. Joy to the world, the Lord is come: Let earth re-ceive her King; Let ev-'ry heart prepare Him room,

And Heav'n and nat-ure sing,   And Heav'n and nature sing,   And Heav'n, And Heav'n and nature sing.

sing............

And Heav'n and nature sing,   And Heav'n and nature sing,

AVISON. P. M.

CHARLES AVISON (1710—1770).

1. Shout the glad tid-ings, ex-ult-ing-ly sing,......... Je-ru-sa-lem tri-umphs, Mes-

1st & 2d verses. | *Ending for 3d verse.* Fine.

si-ah is King! -si-ah is King, Mes-si-ah is King, Mes-si-ah is King!

1. Zi-on the mar-vel-ous sto-ry be tell-ing, The Son of the

high-est, how low-ly His birth, The bright-est arch-an-gel in

D.C.

glo-ry ex-cel-ling, He stoops to re-deem thee, He reigns up-on earth.

160

"Shout the glad Tidings."

2 Tell how He cometh; from nation to nation,
   The heart-cheering news, let the earth echo round;
How free to the faithful He offers salvation,
   How His people with joy everlasting are crowned.
      Shout the glad tidings, &c.

3 Mortals, your homage be gratefully bringing,
   And sweet let the gladsome hosanna arise;
Ye angels, the full hallelujah be singing;
   One chorus resound through the earth and the skies.
      Shout the glad tidings, &c.

Rev. William Augustus Muhlenberg (1796—1877), 1823.

LEILA. 11.10.   Arr. from MICHAEL COSTA (1810—   ).

1. BRIGHT - EST and best of the sons of the morn - ing,

Dawn on our dark - ness, and lend us Thine aid: Star of the East, the ho-

- ri - zon a - dorn - ing, Guide where our in - fant Re - deem - er is laid.

161   *"Brightest and Best."*

2 Cold on His cradle the dew-drops are shining,
   Low lies His head with the beasts of the stall;
Angels adore Him in slumber reclining,
   Maker, and Monarch, and Saviour of all.

3 Say, shall we yield Him, in costly devotion,
   Odors of Edom, and offerings divine,
Gems of the mountain, and pearls of the ocean,
   Myrrh from the forest, or gold from the mine?

4 Vainly we offer each ample oblation;
   Vainly with gifts would His favor secure:
Richer by far is the heart's adoration;
   Dearer to God are the prayers of the poor.

5 Brightest and best of the sons of the morning,
   Dawn on our darkness, and lend us Thine aid
Star of the East, the horizon adorning,
   Guide where our infant Redeemer is laid.

                              Bp. Reginald Heber (1783—1826), 1811.

ORIENT. 11.10.   JOHANN C. W. A. MOZART (1756—1791).

1. BRIGHTEST and best of the sons of the morning, Dawn on our darkness, and lend us thine aid:

Star of the East, the ho - ri - zon a - dorn - ing, Guide where our in - fant Re - deem - er is laid.

LOWLINESS. 7.7.8.8.7.7.

H. R. HANDY (—).

Faster.

1. Who is He in yon - der stall, At whose feet the shepherds fall? 'Tis the Lord! O wondrous sto - ry!

rall.

'Tis the Lord, the King of glo - ry! At His feet we humbly fall; Crown Him, crown Him, Lord of all!

162

"Crowned with Glory."
Heb. ii. 19.

2 Who is He in deep distress,
Fasting in the wilderness?
'Tis the Lord! O wondrous story!
'Tis the Lord, the King of glory!
At His feet we humbly fall;
Crown Him, crown Him, Lord of all!

3 Who is He that stands and weeps
At the grave where Lazarus sleeps?
'Tis the Lord! O wondrous story!
'Tis the Lord, the King of glory!
At His feet we humbly fall;
Crown Him, crown Him, Lord of all!

4 Lo, at midnight, who is He
Prays in dark Gethsemane?
'Tis the Lord! O wondrous story!
'Tis the Lord, the King of glory!
At His feet we humbly fall;
Crown Him, crown Him, Lord of all!

5 On the cross, lo! who is He
Sheds His precious blood for me?
'Tis the Lord! O wondrous story!
'Tis the Lord, the King of glory!
At His feet we humbly fall;
Crown Him, crown Him, Lord of all!

6 Who is He that from the grave
Comes to heal and help and save?
'Tis the Lord! O wondrous story!
'Tis the Lord, the King of glory!
At His feet we humbly fall;
Crown Him, crown Him, Lord of all!

7 Who is He that on yon throne
Reigns as King of kings alone?
'Tis the Lord! O wondrous story!
'Tis the Lord, the King of glory!
At His feet we humbly fall;
Crown Him, crown Him, Lord of all!

B. R. Handy (—). . Ab.

WIMBORNE. L. M.

JOHN WHITAKER, 1849.

1. All praise to Thee, e-ter-nal Lord, Clothed in the garb of flesh and blood;
Choos-ing a man-ger for Thy throne, While worlds on worlds are Thine a-lone.

163

"Gelobet seist Du, Jesu Christ."

2 Once did the skies before Thee bow;
A virgin's arms contain Thee now:
Angels who did in Thee rejoice
Now listen for Thine infant voice.

3 A little child Thou art our guest,
That weary ones in Thee may rest;
Forlorn and lowly is Thy birth,
That we may rise to Heaven from earth.

4 Thou comest in the darksome night
To make us children of the light,
To make us, in the realms divine,
Like Thine own angels round Thee shine.

Rev. Martin Luther (1483—1546), 1524. Ab.

164

"The Prince of Salem."

1 WHEN Jordan hushed his waters still,
And silence slept on Zion's hill; [night
When Bethlehem's shepherds thro' the
Watched o'er their flocks by starry light:

2 Hark, from the midnight hills around,
A voice of more than mortal sound
In distant hallelujahs stole,
Wild murmuring o'er the raptured soul.

3 On wheels of light, on wings of flame,
The glorious hosts of Zion came;
High Heaven with songs of triumph rung,
While thus they struck their harps, and
sung:

4 "O Zion, lift thy raptured eye,
The long-expected hour is nigh;
Renewed, creation smiles again,
The Prince of Salem comes to reign.

5 "He comes to cheer the trembling heart,
Bid Satan and his host depart;
Again the Day-star gilds the gloom,
Again the bowers of Eden bloom."

Thomas Campbell (1777—1844), 1820. Ab.

165

"Von Himmel hoch da komm ich her."

1 GOOD news from Heaven the angels
bring,
Glad tidings to the earth they sing:
To us this day a Child is given,
To crown us with the joy of Heaven.

2 To us that blessedness He brings,
Which from the Father's bounty springs:
That in the heavenly realm we may
With Him enjoy eternal day.

3 Were earth a thousand times as fair,
Beset with gold and jewels rare,
She yet were far too poor to be
A narrow cradle, Lord, for Thee.

4 Ah, dearest Jesus, Holy Child,
Make Thee a bed, soft, undefiled,
Within my heart, that it may be
A quiet chamber kept for Thee.

Rev. Martin Luther, 1535
Tr. by Rev. Arthur Tozer Russell (1806—1874), 1848. Ab

DROSTANE. L. M. Rev. JOHN BACCHUS DYKES (1823—1876), 1859.

1. When marshalled on the night-ly plain, The glit-t'ring host be-stud the sky; One star a-lone of all the train Can fix the sin-ner's wan-d'ring eye.

166 *"The Star of Bethlehem."*

2 Hark! hark! to God the chorus breaks,
 From every host, from every gem;
 But one alone the Saviour speaks,
 It is the Star of Bethlehem.

3 Once on the raging seas I rode,
 The storm was loud, the night was dark,
 The ocean yawned, and rudely blowed
 The wind that tossed my foundering
 bark.

4 Deep horror then my vitals froze;
 Death-struck, I ceased the tide to stem;
 When suddenly a star arose,
 It was the Star of Bethlehem.

5 It was my guide, my light, my all,
 It bade my dark forebodings cease;
 And, thro' the storm and danger's thrall,
 It led me to the port of peace.

6 Now safely moored, my perils o'er,
 I'll sing, first in night's diadem,
 Forever and for evermore,
 The Star, the Star of Bethlehem.
 Henry Kirke White (1785—1806), 1806.

167 *"Quæ stella sole pulchrior."*

1 What star is this, with beams so bright,
 Which shame the sun's less radiant light?
 It shines t' announce a new-born King,
 Glad tidings of our God to bring.

2 'Tis now fulfilled what God decreed,
 "From Jacob shall a star proceed:"
 And lo, the Eastern sages stand,
 To read in Heaven the Lord's command.

3 O Jesus, while the star of grace
 Invites us now to seek Thy face,
 May we no more that grace repel,
 Or quench that light which shines so well.
 Prof. Charles Coffin (1676—1749), 1736. Alt.
 Tr. by Rev. John Chandler (1806—1876), 1837. Ab.

168 *"Macht hoch die Thür"*
 Ps. xxiv.

1 Lift up your heads, ye mighty gates,
 Behold the King of glory waits;
 The King of kings is drawing near,
 The Saviour of the world is here.

2 O blest the land, the city blest
 Where Christ, the Ruler, is confest:
 O happy hearts and happy homes,
 To whom this King of triumph comes.

3 Redeemer, come, I open wide
 My heart to Thee; here, Lord, abide:
 Let me Thy mighty presence feel,
 Thy grace and love in me reveal.

4 So come, my Sovereign, enter in;
 Let new and nobler life begin:
 Thy Holy Spirit guide us on,
 Until our shining goal is won.
 Rev. George Weissel (1590—1635), Bet. 1623—1635.
 Tr. by Miss Catherine Winkworth (1829—1878), 1855. Ab. and alt.

REGENT SQUARE. 8.7.4.   HENRY SMART (1812—1879), 1867.

1. An-gels, from the realms of glo-ry, Wing your flight o'er all the earth,

Ye who sang cre-a-tion's sto-ry, Now pro-claim Mes-si-ah's birth:

Come and wor-ship, Come and wor-ship, Wor-ship Christ, the new-born King.

169   *"Good Tidings of great Joy."*
LUKE ii. 10.

2 Shepherds, in the field abiding,
    Watching o'er your flocks by night,
God with man is now residing;
    Yonder shines the infant-light;
      Come and worship,
Worship Christ, the new-born King.

3 Sages, leave your contemplations,
    Brighter visions beam afar;
Seek the great Desire of nations;
    Ye have seen His natal star:
      Come and worship,
Worship Christ, the new-born King.

4 Saints before the altar bending,
    Watching long in hope and fear,
Suddenly the Lord, descending,
    In His temple shall appear:
      Come and worship,
Worship Christ, the new-born King.
    James Montgomery (1771—1854), 1819, 1825. Ab. and alt.

170   *Christ's Coming.*

1 JESUS came, the Heavens adoring,
    Came with peace from realms on high;
Jesus came for man's redemption,
    Lowly came on earth to die:
      Hallelujah! Hallelujah!
Came in deep humility.

2 Jesus comes to hearts rejoicing,
    Bringing news of sins forgiven;
Jesus comes in sounds of gladness,
    Leading souls redeemed to Heaven:
      Hallelujah! Hallelujah!
Now the gate of death is riven.

3 Jesus comes in joy and sorrow,
    Shares alike our hopes and fears;
Jesus comes whate'er befalls us,
    Glads our hearts, and dries our tears:
      Hallelujal! Hallelujah!
Cheering e'en our failing years.

4 Jesus comes on clouds triumphant,
  When the heavens shall pass away;
Jesus comes again in glory:
  Let us then our homage pay,
  Hallelujah! ever singing,
  Till the dawn of endless day.

Rev. Godfrey Thring (1823—), 1866. Ab.

DIX. 7. 6 l.

German. Arr. by WILLIAM HENRY MONK (1823—), 1864.

1. As with glad - ness men of old Did the guid - ing star be - hold;

As with joy they hailed its light, Lead - ing on - ward, beam - ing bright;

So, most gra - cious Lord, may we Ev - er - more be led to Thee.

171

"Leading onward."
MATT. ii. 10

2 As with joyful steps they sped
To that lowly manger-bed,
There to bend the knee before
Him whom Heaven and earth adore;
So may we with willing feet
Ever seek the Mercy-seat.

3 As they offered gifts most rare
At that manger rude and bare;
So may we with holy joy,
Pure, and free from sin's alloy,
All our costliest treasures bring,
Christ, to Thee, our heavenly King.

4 Holy Jesus, every day
Keep us in the narrow way;
And, when earthly things are past,
Bring our ransomed souls at last
Where they need no star to guide,
Where no clouds Thy glory hide.

5 In the heavenly country bright,
Need they no created light;
Thou its Light, its Joy, its Crown,
Thou its Sun, which goes not down:
There forever may we sing
Alleluias to our King.

William Chatterton Dix (1837—), 1860.

WILMOT. 8.7.

CARL MARIA VON WEBER (1786–1826).

1. HARK! what mean those ho - ly voi - ces, Sweet - ly sound - ing through the skies?

Lo, th'an - gel - ic host re - joic - es; Heav'n - ly hal - le - lu - jahs rise.

172
"Those holy Voices."

2 Listen to the wondrous story,
   Which they chant in hymns of joy:
"Glory in the highest, glory,
   Glory be to God most high.

3 "Peace on earth, good-will from Heaven,
   Reaching far as man is found;
Souls redeemed, and sins forgiven,
   Loud our golden harps shall sound.

4 "Christ is born, the great Anointed;
   Heaven and earth His glory sing:
Glad receive whom God appointed
   For your Prophet, Priest, and King.

5 "Hasten, mortals, to adore Him;
   Learn His Name and taste His joy:
Till in Heaven you sing before Him,
   "Glory be to God most high."
                    Rev. John Cawood (1775–1852), 1819. Ab.

173
Desired of all Nations.

1 COME, Thou long-expected Jesus,
   Born to set Thy people free:
From our fears and sins release us,
   Let us find our rest in Thee.

2 Israel's Strength and Consolation,
   Hope of all the earth Thou art;
Dear Desire of every nation,
   Joy of every longing heart.

3 Born Thy people to deliver,
   Born a Child, and yet a King,
Born to reign in us for ever.
   Now Thy gracious Kingdom bring.

4 By Thine own eternal Spirit,
   Rule in all our hearts alone;
By Thine all-sufficient merit,
   Raise us to Thy glorious throne.
                    Rev. Charles Wesley, (1708–1788), 1744.

174
"The Brightness of His Glory."
Heb. i. 3.

1 BRIGHTNESS of the Father's glory,
   Shall Thy praise unuttered lie?
Fly, my tongue, such guilty silence,
   Sing the Lord who came to die.

2 Did archangels sing Thy coming?
   Did the shepherds learn their lays?
Shame would cover me ungrateful,
   Should my tongue refuse to praise.

3 From the highest throne of glory,
   To the cross of deepest woe—
All to ransom guilty captives;
   Flow, my praise, forever flow.

4 Go, return, immortal Saviour,
   Leave Thy footstool, take Thy throne;
Thence return, and reign forever;
   Be the Kingdom all Thine own.
                    Rev. Robert Robinson (1735–1790), 1774. Sl. alt.

ST. ANN. C. M.

WILLIAM CROFT (1677—1727), 1712.

1. Bright was the guid-ing star that led, With mild be-nig-nant ray,

The Gen-tiles to the low-ly shed, Where the Re-deem-er lay.

175

The brighter Light.

2 But lo, a brighter, clearer light
　Now points to His abode;
　It shines through sin and sorrow's night,
　To guide us to our God.

3 O haste to follow where it leads,
　The gracious call obey;
　Be rugged wilds, or flowery meads,
　The Christian's destined way.

4 O gladly tread the narrow path
　While light and grace are given;
　Who meekly follow Christ on earth,
　Shall reign with Him in Heaven.

Miss Harriet Auber (1773—1862), 1829.

176

"Face to Face."

1 O Thou, who by a star didst guide
　The wise men on their way,
　Until it came and stood beside
　The place where Jesus lay:

2 Although by stars Thou dost not lead
　Thy servants now below,
　Thy Holy Spirit, when they need,
　Will show them how to go.

3 As yet we know Thee but in part;
　But still we trust Thy word,

That blessèd are the pure in heart,
　For they shall see the Lord.

4 O Saviour, give us then Thy grace,
　To make us pure in heart,
　That we may see Thee face to face
　Hereafter, as Thou art.

Rev. John Mason Neale (1818—1866), 1850.

177

"Divine crescebas puer."

1 In stature grows the Heavenly Child,
　With death before His eyes;
　A Lamb unblemished, meek, and mild,
　Prepared for sacrifice.

2 The Son of God His glory hides
　With parents mean and poor;
　And He who made the Heaven abides
　In dwelling-place obscure.

3 Those mighty hands, that stay the sky,
　No earthly toil refuse;
　And He, who set the stars on high,
　A humble trade pursues.

4 He whom the choirs of angels praise,
　At whose command they fly,
　His earthly parents now obeys,
　And lays His glory by.

Santolius Victorinus (1630—1697), Ab
Tr. by Rev. John Chandler (1806—1876), 1837. Alt.

MANOAH. C. M.

FRANCIS JOSEPH HAYDN (1732—1809), 1801.
Arr. from GIOACCHIMO ROSSINI (1792—1868).

1. BE - HOLD, where, in a mor - tal form, Ap - pears each grace di - vine:

The vir - tues, all in Je - sus met, With mild - est ra - diance shine.

178 "Who went about doing Good."
ACTS x. 38.

2 To spread the rays of heavenly light,
   To give the mourner joy,
To preach glad tidings to the poor,
   Was His divine employ.

3 Lowly in heart, to all His friends
   A Friend and Servant found,
He washed their feet, He wiped their tears,
   And healed each bleeding wound.

4 'Midst keen reproach, and cruel scorn,
   Patient and meek He stood ;
His foes, ungrateful, sought His life,
   Who labored for their good.

5 To God He left His righteous cause,
   And still His task pursued ;
With humble prayer, and holy faith,
   His fainting strength renewed.

6 In the last hour of deep distress,
   Before His Father's throne,
With soul resigned, He bowed, and said,
   "Thy will, not mine, be done."

7 Be Christ our pattern and our guide,
   His image may we bear ;

O may we tread His holy steps,
   His joy and glory share.
        Prof. William Enfield (1741—1797), 1771. Alt.

179 "Grace is poured into Thy Lips."
Ps. xlv. 2.

1 WHAT grace, O Lord, and beauty shone
   Around Thy steps below :
What patient love was seen in all
   Thy life and death of woe.

2 Forever on Thy burdened heart
   A weight of sorrow hung ;
Yet no ungentle, murmuring word
   Escaped Thy silent tongue.

3 Thy foes might hate, despise, revile,
   Thy friends unfaithful prove ;
Unwearied in forgiveness still,
   Thy heart could only love.

4 O give us hearts to love like Thee,
   Like Thee, O Lord, to grieve
Far more for others' sins, than all
   The wrongs that we receive.

5 One with Thyself, may every eye
   In us, Thy brethren, see
The gentleness and grace that springs
   From union, Lord, with Thee.
        Sir Edward Denny (1796—), 1839.

HAMBURG. L. M.   Arr. by LOWELL MASON (1792—1872). 1825.

1. My dear Re - deem - er, and my Lord, I read my du - ty in Thy Word;

But in Thy life the law ap - pears, Drawn out in liv - ing char - ac - ters.

180
Christ our Pattern.
1 PET. ii. 21.

2 Such was Thy truth, and such Thy zeal,
Such deference to Thy Father's will,
Such love, and meekness so divine,
I would transcribe and make them mine.

3 Cold mountains and the midnight air
Witnessed the fervor of Thy prayer;
The desert Thy temptations knew,
Thy conflict and Thy victory, too.

4 Be Thou my pattern; make me bear
More of Thy gracious image here;
Then God, the Judge, shall own my name
Amongst the followers of the Lamb.
Rev. Isaac Watts (1674—1748), 1709.

181
Christ's Works of Mercy.

1 WHEN, like a stranger on our sphere,
The lowly Jesus sojourned here;
Where'er He went, affliction fled,
And sickness reared her drooping head.

2 The eye that rolled in irksome night
Beheld His face, for He was light;
The opening ear, the loosened tongue,
His precepts heard, His praises sung.

3 Demoniac madness, dark and wild,
With melancholy transport smiled;
The storm of horror ceased to roll,
And reason lightened through the soul.

4 His touch the outcast leper healed,
His lips the sinner's pardon sealed;
Warm tears o'er Lazarus He shed,
Then spake the word that raised the dead.
James Montgomery (1771—1854.) 1797. Ab.

182
The Meekness of Christ.

1 How beauteous were the marks divine,
That in Thy meekness used to shine,
That lit Thy lonely pathway, trod
In wondrous love, O Son of God.

2 O who like Thee, so calm, so bright,
So pure, so made to live in light?
O who like Thee did ever go
So patient, through a world of woe?

3 O who like Thee, so humbly bore
The scorn, the scoffs of men, before?
So meek, forgiving, godlike, high,
So glorious in humility?

4 And death, that sets the prisoner free,
Was pang, and scoff, and scorn to Thee;
Yet love through all Thy torture glowed,
And mercy with Thy life-blood flowed.

5 O in Thy light be mine to go,
Illuming all my way of woe;
And give me ever, on the road,
To trace Thy footsteps, O my God.
Bp. Arthur Cleveland Coxe (1818—), 1840. Ab.

VARINA. C. M. D.

JOHANN C. H. RINK (1770—1846).
Arr. by GEORGE FREDERICK ROOT (1820—1895), 1848.

1. O, WHERE is He that trod the sea, O, where is He that spake,
And de-mons from their vic-tims flee, The dead their slum-bers break;

The pal-sied rise in free-dom strong, The dumb men talk and sing.

And from blind eyes, be-night-ed long, Bright beams of morn-ing spring.

183 *"O, where is He that trod the Sea?"*

2 O, where is He that trod the sea,
   'Tis only He can save;
To thousands hungering wearily,
   A wondrous meal He gave:
Full soon, with food celestial fed,
   Their mystic fare they take;
'Twas springtide when He blest the bread,
   And harvest when He brake.

3 O, where is He that trod the sea,
   My soul, the Lord is here:
Let all Thy fears be hushed in thee;
   To leap, to look, to hear,
Be thine: thy needs He'll satisfy:
   Art thou diseased, or dumb?
Or dost thou in thy hunger cry?
   "I come," said Christ, "I come."
Rev. Thomas Toke Lynch (1818—1871), 1855. Ab. and sl. alt.

184 *The Demoniac of Gadara.*
MARK v. 1—21.

1 THE winds were howling o'er the deep,
   Each wave a watery hill;
The Saviour wakened from His sleep:

He spake, and all was still.
The madman in a tomb had made
   His mansion of despair:
Woe to the traveller who strayed
   With heedless footsteps there.

2 The chains hung broken from his arm,
   Such strength can hell supply;
And fiendish hate, and fierce alarm,
   Flashed from his hollow eye.
He met that glance so thrilling sweet,
   He heard those accents mild;
And, melting at Messiah's feet,
   Wept like a weanéd child.

3 O, madder than the raving man,
   O, deafer than the sea:
How long the time since Christ began
   To call in vain to me.
Yet could I hear Him once again,
   As I have heard of old,
Methinks He should not call in vain
   His wanderer to the fold.
Bp. Reginald Heber (1783—1826), 1827. Ab.

ST. LUKE. C. M. D.   JOSEPH BARNBY (1838—). 1-76.

1. Thine arm, O Lord, in days of old Was strong to heal and save; It tri-umphed o'er dis-ease and death, O'er dark-ness and the grave; To Thee they went, the blind, the dumb, The pal-sied and the lame, The lep-er with his taint-ed life, The sick with fev-ered frame.

185 *"And He healed them."*

2 And lo, Thy touch brought life and health,
  Gave speech, and strength, and sight;
And youth renewed and frenzy calmed
  Owned Thee, the Lord of light:
And now, O Lord, be near to bless,
  Almighty as of yore,
In crowded street, by restless couch,
  As by Gennesaret's shore.

3 Though Love and Might no longer heal
  By touch, or word or look;
Though they that do Thy work must read
  Thy laws in nature's book:
Yet come to heal the sick man's soul,
  Come, cleanse the lep'rous taint;
Give joy and peace where all is strife,
  And strength where all is faint.

4 Be Thou our great Deliverer still,
  Thou Lord of life and death;
Restore and quicken, soothe and bless
  With Thine almighty breath.

To hands that work and eyes that see
  Give wisdom's heavenly lore.
That whole and sick, and weak and strong,
  May praise Thee evermore.
                Rev. Edward Hayes Plumptre (1821—   ), 1865.

186   *The Fellowship of Suffering.*

1 O Lord, when we the path retrace
  Which Thou on earth hast trod,
To man Thy wondrous love and grace,
  Thy faithfulness to God:
Thy love, by man so sorely tried,
  Proved stronger than the grave;
The very spear that pierced Thy side
  Drew forth the blood to save.

2 Unmoved by Satan's subtle wiles,
  Or suffering, shame, and loss,
Thy path, uncheered by earthly smiles,
  Led only to the cross.
Give us Thy meek, Thy lowly mind:
  We would obedient be;
And all our rest and pleasure find
  In fellowship with Thee.
        James George Deck (1802—   ), 1838. Ab

MOUNT HERMON. L. M. D.

Sir JOHN GOSS (1800—1880), 1872.

1. O Mas - ter, it is good to be High on the mount - ain here with Thee;

Where stand re - vealed to mor - tal gaze Those glo - rious saints of oth - er days;

Who once re - ceived on Ho - reb's height Th'e - ter - nal laws of truth and right;

Or caught the still small whis - per, higher Than storm, than earthquake, or than fire.

187   *"It is good for us to be here."*   MATT. xvii. 4.

2 O Master, it is good to be
  With Thee, and with Thy faithful Three:
  Here, where the apostle's heart of rock
  Is nerved against temptation's shock;
  Here, where the son of thunder learns
  The thought that breathes, and word that
    burns;
  Here, where on eagle's wings we move
  With Him whose last best creed is love.

3 O Master, it is good to be
  Entranced, enrapt, alone with Thee:
  And watch Thy glistering raiment glow

Whiter than Hermon's whitest snow,
The human lineaments that shine
Irradiant with a light divine:
Till we too change from grace to grace,
Gazing on that transfigured face.

4 O Master, it is good to be
  Here on the holy mount with Thee:
  When darkling in the depths of night,
  When dazzled with excess of light,
  We bow before the heavenly voice
  That bids bewildered souls rejoice,
  Though love wax cold, and faith be dim,
  "This is My Son, O hear ye Him."

Rev. Arthur Penrhyn Stanley (1815—1881), 1872.

DROSTANE. L. M. Rev. JOHN BACCHUS DYKES (1823–1876), 1859.

1. Ride on, ride on in maj-es-ty! Hark, all the tribes Ho-san-na cry;

O Sav-iour meek, pur-sue Thy road With palms and scat-ter'd gar-ments strow'd.

188 *The Triumphal Entry into Jerusalem.*
MATT. xxi. 1—11

2 Ride on, ride on in majesty!
In lowly pomp, ride on to die:
O Christ, Thy triumphs now begin
O'er captive death and conquered sin.

3 Ride on, ride on in majesty!
The wingéd squadrons of the sky
Look down with sad and wondering eyes
To see th' approaching sacrifice.

4 Ride on, ride on in majesty!
Thy last and fiercest strife is nigh:
The Father on His sapphire throne
Expects His own anointed Son.

5 Ride on, ride on in majesty!
In lowly pomp, ride on to die:
Bow Thy meek head to mortal pain,
Then take, O God, Thy power, and reign.
Rev. Henry Hart Milman (1791–1868), 1827. Alt.

PARK STREET. L. M. FREDERICK MARC ANTOINE VENUA (1788–), 1810.

1. Ride on, ride on in maj-es-ty! Hark, all the tribes Ho-san-na cry; O Sav-iour

meek, pur-sue Thy road With palms and scatter'd garments strow'd, With palms and scatter'd garments strow'd.

OLIVE'S BROW. L. M.　　　　　　　　WILLIAM BATCHELDER BRADBURY (1816—1868), 1853.

1. 'Tis mid-night; and on Ol-ive's brow The star is dimmed that late-ly shone:

'Tis mid-night; in the gar-den, now, The suff'ring Sav-iour prays a-lone.

189　　　*Christ in Gethsemane.*

2 'Tis midnight; and from all removed,
　The Saviour wrestles lone with fears;
　E'en that disciple whom He loved
　Heeds not his Master's grief and tears.

3 'Tis midnight; and for others' guilt
　The Man of Sorrows weeps in blood;

Yet He that hath in anguish knelt
　Is not forsaken by His God.

4 'Tis midnight; and from ether-plains
　Is borne the song that angels know;
　Unheard by mortals are the strains
　That sweetly soothe the Saviour's woe.
　　　Rev. William Bingham Tappan (1794—1849), 1819.

THEODORA. 7.　　　　　　　From GEORGE FREDERICK HANDEL (1685—1759), 1749.

1. When on Si-nai's top I see God de-scend in maj-es-ty,

To pro-claim His ho-ly law, All my spir-it sinks with awe.

190　　　*The three Mountains.*

2 When, in ecstasy sublime,
　Hermon's glorious steep I climb,
　At the too transporting light,
　Darkness rushes o'er my sight.

3 When on Calvary I rest,
　God, in flesh made manifest,
　Shines in my Redeemer's face,
　Full of beauty, truth, and grace.

4 Here I would forever stay,
Weep and gaze my soul away:
Thou art Heaven on earth to me,
Lovely, mournful Calvary.

James Montgomery (1771—1854), 1812. Sl. alt.

GETHSEMANE. 7. 6l.
RICHARD REDHEAD (1820—). 1853.

1. Go to dark Geth-sem-a-ne, Ye that feel the tempt-er's power;

Your Re-deem-er's con-flict see; Watch with Him one bit-ter hour:

Turn not from His griefs a-way; Learn of Je-sus Christ to pray.

191
Gethsemane.

2 Follow to the judgment-hall,
View the Lord of life arraigned:
O the wormwood and the gall!
O the pangs His soul sustained!
Shun not suffering, shame, or loss;
Learn of Him to bear the cross.

3 Calvary's mournful mountain climb;
There, adoring at His feet,
Mark that Miracle of time,
God's own sacrifice complete:
"It is finished," hear the cry;
Learn of Jesus Christ to die.

4 Early hasten to the tomb,
Where they laid His breathless clay:
All is solitude and gloom;
Who hath taken Him away?
Christ is risen; He meets our eyes;
Saviour, teach us so to rise.

James Montgomery 1822, 1853.

192
"Venit a cælo Mediator alto."

1 Zion's daughter, weep no more,
Though thy troubled heart be sore:
He of whom the psalmist sung,
He who woke the prophet's tongue,
Christ, the Mediator blest,
Brings thee everlasting rest.

2 In a garden man became
Heir of sin, and death, and shame:
Jesus in a garden wins
Life, and pardon for our sins;
Through His hour of agony,
Praying in Gethsemane.

3 There for us He intercedes:
There with God the Father pleads;
Willing there for us to drain
To the dregs the cup of pain,
That in everlasting day
He may wipe our tears away.

Roman Breviary.
Tr. by Rev. Sir Henry Williams Baker (1821—1877), 1861. Ab.

TRURO. L. M.

CHARLES BURNEY (1726—1814). 1760.

1. The roy - al ban - ners for - ward go, The cross shines forth in mys - tic glow;

Where He in flesh, our flesh who made, Our sen - tence bore, our ran - som paid;

193   *"Vexilla Regis prodeunt."*

2 Where deep for us the spear was dyed,
Life's torrent rushing from His side,
To cleanse us in the precious flood
Of water mingled with His blood.

3 O tree of glory, tree most fair,
Ordained those holy limbs to bear,
How bright in purple robe it stood,
The purple of a Saviour's blood!

4 Upon its arms, so widely flung,
The weight of this world's ransom hung :
The price which none but He could pay,
And spoiled the spoiler of his prey.

5 To Thee, Eternal Three in One,
Let homage meet by all be done :
As by the cross Thou dost restore,
So rule and guide us evermore.

Venantius Fortunatus (530—609), c. 575.
Tr. by Rev. John Mason Neale (1818—1866), 1851. Ab. and alt.

PASSION CHORALE. 7. 6. D.

HANS LEO HASSLER (1564—1612), 1601.
Har. by JOHANN SEBASTIAN BACH (1685—1750).

1. O sa - cred Head, now wound - ed, With grief and shame weighed down,
Now scorn - ful - ly sur - round - ed With thorns, Thine on - ly crown;

O sa - cred Head, what glo - ry, What bliss, till now was Thine!

Yet, though de - spised and gor - y, I joy to call Thee mine.

194 *"Salve, caput cruentatum."*

2 What Thou, my Lord, hast suffered
　Was all for sinners' gain ;
Mine, mine was the transgression,
　But Thine the deadly pain ;
Lo, here I fall, my Saviour !
　'Tis I deserve Thy place ;
Look on me with Thy favor,
　Vouchsafe to me Thy grace.

3 The joy can ne'er be spoken,
　Above all joys beside,
When in Thy body broken
　I thus with safety hide :
My Lord of life, desiring
　Thy glory now to see,
Beside the cross expiring,
　I'd breathe my soul to Thee.

4 What language shall I borrow
　To thank Thee, dearest Friend,
For this Thy dying sorrow,
　Thy pity without end ?

O make me Thine forever ;
　And should I fainting be,
Lord, let me never, never,
　Outlive my love to Thee.

5 And when I am departing,
　O part not Thou from me ;
When mortal pangs are darting,
　Come, Lord, and set me free ;
And when my heart must languish
　Amidst the final throe,
Release me from mine anguish,
　By Thine own pain and woe.

6 Be near me when I'm dying,
　O show Thy cross to me ;
And for my succor flying,
　Come, Lord, and set me free :
These eyes, new faith receiving,
　From Jesus shall not move ;
For he who dies believing,
　Dies safely, through Thy love.

Bernard of Clairvaux (1091—1153),
Rev. Paul Gerhardt (1606—1676), 1659.
Rev. James Waddell Alexander (1804—1859), 1830.　A6.

CRUCIFIX. 7. 6. D.　　　　Greek Melody. Arr. by Bp. REGINALD HEBER (1783—1826).

STABAT MATER. 8.8.7. D. Rev. JOHN BACCHUS DYKES (1823—1876), 1874.

1. NEAR the cross was Ma - ry weep - ing, There her mourn - ful sta - tion keep - ing,

Gaz - ing on her dy - ing Son: There in speech - less an - guish groan - ing,

Yearn - ing, trem - bling, sigh - ing, moan - ing, Thro' her soul the sword had gone.

195 *"Stabat Mater dolorosa."*

2 But we have no need to borrow
  Motives from the mother's sorrow,
    At our Saviour's cross to mourn.
  'Twas our sins brought Him from Heaven,
  These the cruel nails had driven:
    All His griefs for us were borne.

3 When no eye its pity gave us,
  When there was no arm to save us,
    He His love and power displayed:

By His stripes He wrought our healing,
By His death, our life revealing,
  He for us the ransom paid.

4 Jesus, may Thy love constrain us,
  That from sin we may refrain us,
    In Thy griefs may deeply grieve:
  Thee our best affections giving,
  To Thy glory ever living,
    May we in Thy glory live.

Jacoponi da Todi (—1306).
Tr. by Rev. James Waddell Alexander (1804—1859), 1842. Vs. 1.
Rev. Henry Mills (1786—1867), 1845. Vs. 2, 3, 4. Ab.

GENOA. 8.8.7. D. JOSEPH BARNBY (1838—   ).

1. FROM the cross the blood is fall - ing, And to us a voice is call - ing,

Like a tram - pet sil - ver - clear, 'Tis the voice an - nounc - ing par - don,

"It is fin-ished," is its bur-den, Par-don to the far and near.

196 *God is Love.*

2 God is love:—we read the writing
Traced so deeply in the smiting
Of the glorious surety there.
God is light:—we see it beaming,
Like a heavenly dayspring gleaming,
So divinely sweet and fair.

3 Cross of shame, yet tree of glory,
Round thee winds the one great story
Of this ever-changing earth;
Centre of the true and holy,
Grave of human sin and folly,
Womb of nature's second birth.

Rev. Horatius Bonar (1808—), 1866. Ab.

DONCASTER. L. M.   EDWARD MILLER (1731—1807), 1790.

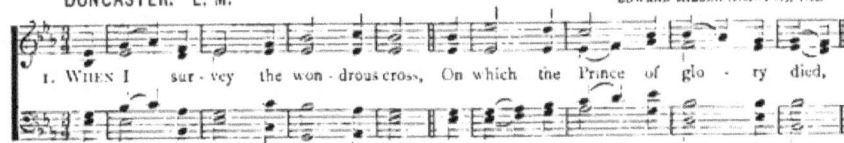

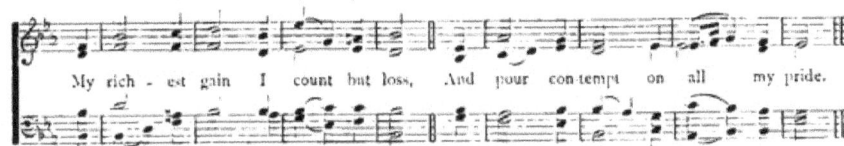

1. WHEN I sur-vey the won-drous cross, On which the Prince of glo-ry died,

My rich-est gain I count but loss, And pour con-tempt on all my pride.

197 *"The wondrous Cross."*

2 Forbid it, Lord, that I should boast,
Save in the death of Christ, my God:
All the vain things that charm me most,
I sacrifice them to His blood.

3 See, from His head, His hands, His feet,
Sorrow and love flow mingled down:
Did e'er such love and sorrow meet,
Or thorns compose so rich a crown?

4 His dying crimson, like a robe,
Spreads o'er His body on the tree;
Then I am dead to all the globe,
And all the globe is dead to me.

5 Were the whole realm of nature mine,
That were a present far too small;
Love so amazing, so divine,
Demands my soul, my life, my all.

Rev. Isaac Watts, (1674—1748), 1709.

FEDERAL STREET. L. M.   HENRY KEMBLE OLIVER (1800—1885), 1832.

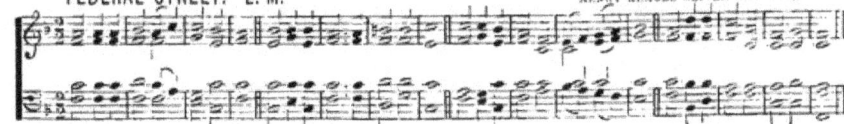

AVON. C. M.   HUGH WILSON, 1768.

1. A - las! and did my Sav - iour bleed? And did my Sov - 'reign die?

Would He de - vote that sa - cred head For such a worm as I?

198   *Before the Cross.*

2 Was it for crimes that I had done
   He groaned upon the tree?
   Amazing pity! grace unknown!
   And love beyond degree!

3 Well might the sun in darkness hide,
   And shut his glories in,
   When God, the mighty Maker, died
   For man the creature's sin.

4 Thus might I hide my blushing face,
   While His dear cross appears:
   Dissolve, my heart, in thankfulness,
   And melt, mine eyes, to tears.

5 But drops of grief can ne'er repay
   The debt of love I owe:
   Here, Lord, I give myself away;
   'Tis all that I can do.
            Rev. Isaac Watts (1674—1748), 1709. Ab.

199   *Kneeling at the Cross.*

1 O JESUS, sweet the tears I shed,
   While at Thy cross I kneel,
   Gaze on Thy wounded, fainting head,
   And all Thy sorrows feel.

2 My heart dissolves to see Thee bleed,
   This heart so hard before:
   I hear Thee for the guilty plead,
   And grief o'erflows the more.

3 'Twas for the sinful Thou didst die,
   And I a sinner stand:
   What love speaks from Thy dying eye,
   And from each pierced hand.

4 I know this cleansing blood of Thine
   Was shed, dear Lord, for me:
   For me, for all, O Grace divine,
   Who look by faith on Thee.

5 O Christ of God, O spotless Lamb,
   By love my soul is drawn;
   Henceforth, for ever, Thine I am;
   Here life and peace are born.

6 In patient hope, the cross I'll bear,
   Thine arm shall be my stay;
   And Thou, enthroned, my soul shalt spare,
   On Thy great judgment-day.
            Rev. Ray Palmer (1808—   ), 1867.

200   *"He dies."*

1 BEHOLD the Saviour of mankind
   Nailed to the shameful tree:
   How vast the love that Him inclined
   To bleed and die for thee!

2 Hark, how He groans, while nature shakes,
   And earth's strong pillars bend;
   The temple's veil in sunder breaks,
   The solid marbles rend.

3 'Tis done, the precious ransom's paid,
 "Receive my soul," He cries:
See where He bows His sacred head
He bows His head and dies.

4 But soon He'll break death's envious
 And in full glory shine: [chain,
O Lamb of God, was ever pain,
Was ever love like Thine?

Rev. Samuel Wesley (1662—1735), 1709.

ST. CROSS. L. M.   Rev. JOHN BACCHUS DYKES (1823—1876), 1861.

1. O COME, and mourn with me a - while; O come ye to the Sav - iour's side;

O come, to - geth - er let us mourn: Je - sus, our Lord, is cru - ci - fied.

201   *"Our Lord is crucified."*

2 Have we no tears to shed for Him,
 While soldiers scoff and Jews deride?
Ah, look how patiently He hangs:
Jesus, our Lord, is crucified.

3 How fast His hands and feet are nailed;
 His throat with parching thirst is dried;
His failing eyes are dimmed with blood:
Jesus, our Lord, is crucified.

4 Seven times He spake, seven words of love;
 And all three hours His silence cried

For mercy on the souls of men:
Jesus, our Lord, is crucified.

5 Come, let us stand beneath the cross;
 So may the blood from out His side
Fall gently on us drop by drop:
Jesus, our Lord, is crucified.

6 A broken heart, a fount of tears
 Ask, and they will not be denied;
Lord Jesus, may we love and weep,
Since Thou for us art crucified.

Rev. Frederick William Faber (1814—1863), 1849. Ab. and alt.

ASHWELL. L. M.   LOWELL MASON (1792—1872), 1842.

DEWITT. C. M.

UZZIAH CHRISTOPHER BURNAP (1834—), 1870.

1. I SEE the crowd in Pi - late's hall, I mark their wrath - ful mien;

Their shouts of "cru - ci - fy" ap - pall, With blas - phe - my be - tween.

202   *In Pilate's Hall.*

2 And of that shouting multitude
    I feel that I am one;
And in that din of voices rude,
    I recognize my own.

3 I see the scourges tear His back,
    I see the piercing crown,
And of that crowd who smite and mock
    I feel that I am one.

4 Around yon cross the throng I see,
    Mocking the Sufferer's groan;
Yet still my voice it seems to be,
    As if I mocked alone.

5 'Twas I that shed the sacred blood,
    I nailed Him to the tree,
I crucified the Christ of God,
    I joined the mockery.

6 Yet not the less that blood avails
    To cleanse away my sin;
And not the less that cross prevails
    To give me peace within.
             Rev. Horatius Bonar (1808—), 1857.

203   *At the Cross.*

1 I SAW One hanging on a tree,
    In agonies and blood;
Who fixed His languid eyes on me,
    As near His cross I stood.

2 Sure, never till my latest breath,
    Can I forget that look;
It seemed to charge me with His death,
    Though not a word He spoke.

3 My conscience felt and owned the guilt,
    And plunged me in despair,
I saw my sins His blood had spilt,
    And helped to nail Him there.

4 Alas, I knew not what I did,
    But all my tears were vain;
Where could my trembling soul be hid,
    For I the Lord had slain.

5 A second look He gave, that said,
    "I freely all forgive;
This blood is for thy ransom paid,
    I die that thou mayest live."
        Rev. John Newton (1725—1807), 1779. Ab.

NAOMI. C. M.

HANS GEORG NAEGELI (1773—1836), 1872.
Arr. by LOWELL MASON (1792—1872), 1836.

SHAWMUT. S. M.

Arr. by LOWELL MASON (1792–1872), 1832.

1. O'ER-WHELMED in depths of woe, Up - on the tree of scorn

Hangs the Re - deem - er of man - kind, With rack - ing an - guish torn.

204   *"Servo dolorum turbine."*

2 See how the nails those hands
   And feet so tender rend;
See down His face, and neck, and breast,
   His sacred blood descend.

3 Hark, with what awful cry
   His spirit takes its flight,
That cry, it pierced His Mother's heart,
   And whelmed her soul in night.

4 Earth hears, and to its base
   Rocks wildly to and fro;
Tombs burst; seas, rivers, mountains quake;
   The veil is rent in two.

5 The sun withdraws his light;
   The midday heavens grow pale;
The moon, the stars, the universe
   Their Maker's death bewail.

6 Shall man alone be mute!
   Come, youth and hoary hairs,
Come, rich and poor, come, all mankind,
   And bathe those feet in tears.

7 Come, fall before His cross
   Who shed for us His blood;
Who died the Victim of pure love,
   To make us sons of God.

8 Jesus, all praise to Thee,
   Our joy and endless rest;
Be Thou our guide while pilgrims here,
   Our crown amid the blest.

                    Roman Breviary.
Tr. by Rev. Edward Caswall (1814–1878), 1849.

205   *"The Heavenly Lamb."*

1 Not all the blood of beasts
   On Jewish altars slain,
Could give the guilty conscience peace,
   Or wash away the stain.

2 But Christ, the heavenly Lamb,
   Takes all our sins away;
A sacrifice of nobler name,
   And richer blood, than they.

3 My faith would lay her hand
   On that dear head of Thine,
While like a penitent I stand,
   And there confess my sin.

4 My soul looks back to see
   The burdens Thou didst bear,
When hanging on the cursèd tree,
   And hopes her guilt was there.

5 Believing, we rejoice
   To see the curse remove;
We bless the Lamb with cheerful voice,
   And sing His bleeding love.

                    Rev. Isaac Watts, (1674–1748), 1709.

GOUDA. C. M.

BERTHOLD TOURS (1838—). 1872.

1. THERE is a green hill far a - way, With - out a cit - y wall,
Where the dear Lord was cru - ci - fied, Who died to save us all.

206 *"The dear Lord."*

2 We may not know, we cannot tell
What pains He had to bear;
But we believe it was for us
He hung and suffered there.

3 He died that we might be forgiven,
He died to make us good,
That we might go at last to Heaven,
Saved by His precious blood.

4 There was no other good enough
To pay the price of sin;
He only could unlock the gate
Of Heaven, and let us in.

5 O, dearly, dearly has He loved,
And we must love Him, too,
And trust in His redeeming blood,
And try His works to do.

Mrs. Cecil Frances Alexander (1823—), 1848.

GERONTIUS. C. M.

WILLIAM HENRY MONK (1823—). 1868.

1. PRAISE to the Ho - liest in the height, And in the depth be praise:
In all His words most won - der - ful, Most sure in all His ways.

207 *"The Lord from Heaven."*
1 COR. XV. 47.

2 O loving wisdom of my God!
When all was sin and shame,
A second Adam to the fight,
And to the rescue, came.

3 O generous love! that He, who smote
In Man for man the foe,
The double agony in Man
For man should undergo;

4 And in the garden secretly,
  And on the cross on high,
  Should teach His brethren, and inspire
  To suffer and to die.

5 Praise to the Holiest in the height,
  And in the depth be praise:
  In all His words most wonderful,
  Most sure in all His ways.

     Rev. John Henry Newman (1801—), 1867. Ab.

208   *"There laid they Jesus."*
         John xix. 42.

1 COME, see the place where Jesus lies:
  The last sad rite is done;
  With aching hearts, and weeping eyes,
  The faithful few are gone.

2 They washed with tears each bloody trace
  On those dear limbs that lay;
  Then spread the napkin o'er His face,
  And turned and went their way.

3 By the sealed stones with grounded spears
  The guards their vigils keep:
  They wist not other eyes than theirs
  Watch o'er the Saviour's sleep.

                          C. M.

4 'Tis done! O Death, thy Victor-guest
  Hath smoothed thy visage grim;
  O Grave, thou place of blessèd rest
  To all who sleep in Him!

     Rev. Thomas Edwards Hankinson (1805—1843), 1843. Ab.

GETHSEMANE. 7.6l.   RICHARD REDHEAD (1820—), 1853.

1. Rest - ing from His work to - day, In the tomb the Sav - iour lay;
Still He slept, from head to feet Shroud - ed in the wind - ing sheet,
Ly - ing in the rock a - lone, Hid - den by the seal - ed stone.

209   *Christ in the Tomb.*

2 Late at even there was seen,
  Watching long, the Magdalene;
  Early, ere the break of day,
  Sorrowful she took her way
  To the holy garden glade,
  Where her buried Lord was laid.

3 So with Thee, till life shall end,
  I would solemn vigil spend;
  Let me hew Thee, Lord, a shrine

In this rocky heart of mine,
  Where in pure embalmèd cell
  None but Thee may ever dwell.

4 Myrrh and spices will I bring,
  True affection's offering;
  Close the door from sight and sound
  Of the busy world around;
  And in patient watch remain
  Till my Lord appear again.

     Rev. Thomas Whytehead (1815—1843), 1842. Ab. and alt.

FESTA DIES. 11.

JOHN BAPTISTE CALKIN (1827—).

1. "WELCOME, hap-py morn - ing," age to age shall say; Hell to - day is vanquished, Heav'n is

won to - day! Lo! the Dead is Liv-ing, God for ev - er-more; Him, their true Cre-

ff In unison.

"Wel-come, hap-py morn-ing," age to age shall say;

- a - tor, all His works a - dore! Inst.

Hell to-day is vanquished, Heav'n is won to - day! Lo! the Dead is

rall.

Liv - ing, God for ev-er-more; Him, their true Cre - a - tor, all His works a - dore!

rall.

210　　"*Salve festa dies.*"

2 Earth her joy confesses, clothing her for spring,
All good gifts returned with her returning King:
Bloom in every meadow, leaves on every bough,
Speak His sorrows ended, hail His triumph now.
　"Welcome, happy morning," &c.

3 Thou, of life the Author, death didst undergo,
Tread the path of darkness, saving strength to show:
Come then, True and Faithful, now fulfil Thy word;
'Tis Thine own third morning, rise, my buried Lord!
　"Welcome, happy morning," &c.

4 Loose the souls long prisoned, bound with Satan's chain;
All that now is fallen raise to life again;
Show Thy face in brightness, bid the nations see,
Bring again our daylight: day returns with Thee!
　"Welcome, happy morning," &c.

Venantius Fortunatus (530—609),
Tr. by Rev. John Ellerton (1826—　), 1871? Ab.

CHIMES. C. M.　　LOWELL MASON (1792—1872).

1. I say to all men, far and near, That He is risen a-gain;
That He is with us now and here, And ev-er shall re-main.

211　　"*Ich sage jedem, dass Er lebt.*"

2 And what I say, let each this morn
　Go tell it to his friend,
That soon in every place shall dawn
　His Kingdom without end.

3 The fears of death and of the grave
　Are whelmed beneath the sea,

And every heart, now light and brave,
　May face the things to be.

4 The way of darkness that He trod
　To Heaven at last shall come,
And he who hearkens to His Word
　Shall reach His Father's home.

Friedrich von Hardenberg (1772—1801), 1799.
Tr. by Miss Catherine Winkworth (1829—1878), 1858. Ab.

MARCELLUS. 8.8.8.4.   GIOVANNI PIERLUIGI DA PALESTRINA (1524?—1594).

1. THE strife is o'er, the bat - tle done; The vic - to - ry of life is won;

The song of tri - umph has be - gun; Hal - le - lu - jah!

212   *"Finita jam sunt proelia."*

2 The three sad days are quickly sped,
  He rises glorious from the dead ;
  All glory to our risen Head ;
    Hallelujah !

3 He closed the yawning gates of hell ;
  The bars from Heaven's high portals fell ;

Le hymns of praise His triumphs tell.
  Hallelujah !

4 Lord, by the stripes which wounded Thee,
  From death's dread sting Thy servants
  That we may live and sing to Thee. [free,
    Hallelujah !

Unknown Author of the 12th century.
Tr. by Rev. Robert Corbet Singleton (   ), 1861. Ab.

REDCLIFF. 8.8.8.4.   EDWARD JOHN HOPKINS (1818—), 1863.

1. MORN'S rose - ate hues have decked the sky; The Lord has risen with vic - to - ry:

Let earth be glad, and raise the cry, Al - le - lu - ia!

213   *Risen with victory.*

2 The Prince of life with death has striven,
  To cleanse the earth His blood has given ;
  Has rent the veil, and opened Heaven :
    Alleluia !

3 Our bodies mouldering to decay,
  Are sure to rise to heavenly day ;

For He by rising burst the way :
  Alleluia !

4 O praise the Father and the Son,
  Who has for us the triumph won,
  And Holy Ghost, the Three in One ;
    Alleluia !

Nicolas le Tourneaux (1640—1686),
Tr. by William Cooke (1821—), 1872. Ab.

214   *"Mundi renovatio."*   8.8.8.4.

1 EARTH blooms afresh in joyous dyes;
In Christ's arising all things rise;
A solemn joy o'er nature lies;
   Alleluia!

2 Now peace the sea, the sky doth fill, [hill;
Heaven's breath wakes fair each vale and

Spring pours thro' barren hearts and chill;
   Alleluia!

3 Life wins from death the glorious prey;
The Cherub's sword is turned away,
And Eden's paths are free to-day;
   Alleluia!

Adam of St. Victor (—1192),
Tr. by A. M. E., 1884.

HASTINGS. C. L. M.   THOMAS HASTINGS (1784—1872), 1831.

1. How calm and beau-ti-ful the morn, That gilds the sa-cred tomb,
Where Christ the cru-ci-fied was borne, And veiled in mid-night gloom!
O weep no more the Sav-iour slain, The Lord is risen, He lives a-gain.

215   *He lives again.*

2 Ye mourning saints, dry every tear
For your departed Lord;
"Behold the place, He is not here,"
The tomb is all unbarred:
The gates of death were closed in vain,
The Lord is risen, He lives again.

3 Now cheerful to the house of prayer
Your early footsteps bend;
The Saviour will Himself be there,
Your Advocate and Friend:
Once by the law your hopes were slain,
But now in Christ ye live again.

4 How tranquil now the rising day!
'Tis Jesus still appears,
A risen Lord, to chase away
Your unbelieving fears:
O weep no more your comforts slain,
The Lord is risen, He lives again.

5 And when the shades of evening fall,
When life's last hour draws nigh,
If Jesus shines upon the soul,
How blissful then to die!
Since He has risen that once was slain,
Ye die in Christ to live again.

Thomas Hastings (1784 1872 , 1832.

MOZART. 7.

JOHANN C. W. A. MOZART (1756—1791). 1779.

1. "Christ, the Lord, is risen to-day," Sons of men and an - gels say. Raise your joys and triumphs high; Sing, ye heavens; and earth, re - ply; Sing, ye heavens; and earth re - ply.

216

"He is not here."
MARK xvi. 6.

2 Love's redeeming work is done,
Fought the fight, the battle won.
Lo, our Sun's eclipse is o'er;
Lo, He sets in blood no more.

3 Vain the stone, the watch, the seal;
Christ has burst the gates of hell;
Death in vain forbids His rise:
Christ has opened Paradise.

4 Lives again our glorious King:
Where, O death, is now thy sting?

Once He died our souls to save:
Where thy victory, O grave?

5 Soar we now where Christ has led,
Following our exalted Head:
Made like Him, like Him we rise;
Ours the cross, the grave, the skies.

6 Hail, the Lord of earth and Heaven!
Praise to Thee by both be given:
Thee we greet triumphant now;
Hail, the Resurrection Thou!

Rev. Charles Wesley (1708—1788), 1739. Ab.

EASTER HYMN. 7.4.D.

HENRY CAREY (1692—1743).

1. "Christ, the Lord, is risen to - day," Al - le - lu - ia. Sons of men and an - gels say, Al - le - lu - ia, Raise your joys and triumphs high; Al - le - lu - ia.

Sing, ye heav'ns; and earth, re - ply. Al - - le - - lu - - ia.

MIGDOL. L. M.

LOWELL MASON (1792—1872), 1841.

1. Our Lord is ris - en from the dead, Our Je - sus is gone up on high;

The pow'rs of hell are cap - tive led, Dragg'd to the port - als of the sky.

217 *"Our Lord is risen."* Ps. xxiv.

2 There His triumphal chariot waits,
  And angels chant the solemn lay :—
"Lift up your heads, ye heavenly gates,
  Ye everlasting doors, give way."

3 "Loose all your bars of massy light,
  And wide unfold the ethereal scene ;
He claims these mansions as His right ;
  Receive the King of glory in."

4 "Who is this King of glory, who?"
  "The Lord that all His foes o'ercame ;
The world, sin, death, and hell o'erthrew ;
  And Jesus is the conqueror's name."

5 Lo, His triumphal chariot waits,
  And angels chant the solemn lay :—
"Lift up your heads, ye heavenly gates,
  Ye everlasting doors, give way."

6 "Who is this King of glory, who?"
  "The Lord of glorious power possessed,

The King of saints and angels, too ;
  God over all, forever blest."
  Rev. Charles Wesley, 1743. Ab.

218 *"He lives."*

1 "I know that my Redeemer lives :"
  What comfort this sweet sentence gives,
  He lives, He lives, who once was dead,
  He lives, my ever-living Head.

2 He lives to bless me with His love,
  He lives to plead for me above,
  He lives my hungry soul to feed,
  He lives to help in time of need.

3 He lives, my kind, my faithful Friend,
  He lives and loves me to the end,
  He lives, and while He lives I'll sing,
  He lives, my Prophet, Priest, and King.

4 He lives, and grants me daily breath,
  He lives, and I shall conquer death,
  He lives my mansion to prepare,
  He lives to bring me safely there.
  Rev. Samuel Medley (1738—1799), 1789. Ab.

BETHABARA. 8.7.D.

HENRY SMART (1812—1879).

1. AL - LE - LU - IA! Al - le - lu - ia! Hearts to Heav'n and voi - ces raise; Sing to God a hymn of glad - ness, Sing to God a hymn of praise: He who on the cross a vic - tim For the world's sal - va - tion bled, Je - sus Christ, the King of glo - ry, Now is ris - en from the dead.

219   *"He is risen, as He said."*
                 MATT. xxviii. 6.

2 Now the iron bars are broken,
  Christ from death to life is born,
Glorious life, and life immortal,
  On this holy Easter morn:
Christ has triumphed, and we conquer
  By His mighty enterprise,
We with Him to life eternal
  By His resurrection rise.

3 Christ is risen, Christ the first-fruits
  Of the holy harvest-field,
Which will all its full abundance
  At His second coming yield;
Then the golden ears of harvest
  Will their heads before Him wave,
Ripened by His glorious sunshine,
  From the furrows of the grave.

4 Christ is risen, we are risen!
  Shed upon us heavenly grace,
Rain, and dew, and gleams of glory
  From the brightness of Thy face,
So that we, with hearts in Heaven,
  Here on earth may fruitful be,
And by angel-hands be gathered,
  And be ever, Lord, with Thee.

5 Alleluia! Alleluia!
  Glory be to God on high,
To the Father, and the Saviour,
  Who has gained the victory;
Glory to the Holy Spirit,
  Fount of love and sanctity:
Alleluia! Alleluia!
  To the Triune Majesty.

               Bp. Christopher Wordsworth (1807—1885), 1865

AUSTRIAN HYMN. 8.7.D.

FRANCIS JOSEPH HAYDN (1732—1809), 1797.

1. { SEE the Con-quer'r mounts in tri-umph, See the King in roy-al state, }
{ Rid-ing on the clouds His char-iot To His heav'n-ly pal-ace-gate, }

Hark, the choirs of an-gel voi-ces Joy-ful Hal-le-lu-jahs sing,

And the port-als high are lift-ed, To re-ceive their heav'n-ly King.

220 *Mounting in Triumph.*

2 Who is this that comes in glory,
  With the trump of jubilee?
Lord of battles, God of armies,
  He has gained the victory;
He who on the cross did suffer,
  He who from the grave arose,
He has vanquished sin and Satan,
  He by death has spoiled His foes.

3 Thou hast raised our human nature
  On the clouds to God's right hand,
There we sit in heavenly places,
  There with Thee in glory stand;
Jesus reigns adored by angels,
  Man with God is on the throne,
Mighty Lord, in Thine ascension
  We by faith behold our own.

4 Lift us up from earth to Heaven,
  Give us wings of faith and love,
Gales of holy aspiration
  Wafting us to realms above;
That, with hearts and minds uplifted,
  We with Christ our Lord may dwell,
Where He sits enthroned in glory
  In the heavenly citadel.

5 So at last, when He appeareth,
  We from out our graves may spring,
With our youth renewed like eagles',
  Flocking round our heavenly King,
Caught up on the clouds of Heaven,
  And may meet Him in the air,
Rise to realms where He is reigning,
  And may reign forever there.

Bp. Christopher Wordsworth, 1862. Ab.

LUTON. L. M.   Rev. GEORGE BURDER (1752–1832), 1784.

1. HE dies, the Friend of sin - ners dies; Lo, Sa - lem's daugh - ters weep a - round;

A sol - emn dark - ness veils the skies; A sud - den trem - bling shakes the ground.

221   *Christ dying, rising, and reigning.*

2 Here's love and grief beyond degree;
   The Lord of glory dies for men;
   But lo, what sudden joys I see,
   Jesus, the dead, revives again.

3 The rising God forsakes the tomb,
   Up to His Father's court He flies;
   Cherubic legions guard Him home,
   And shout Him welcome to the skies.

4 Break off your tears, ye saints, and tell
   How high our great Deliverer reigns;
   Sing how He spoiled the hosts of hell,
   And led the monster, Death, in chains.

5 Say, "Live forever, wondrous King,
   Born to redeem, and strong to save!"
   Then ask the monster, "Where's thy
      sting?"   [Grave?"
   "And where's thy victory, boasting

Rev. Isaac Watts (1674–1748), 1706. Ab.
Alt. by Rev. John Wesley (1703–1791).

GLASTONBURY. 7. 6 l.   Rev. JOHN BACCHUS DYKES (1823–1876).

1. LAMB of God, to Thee we cry; By Thy bit - ter ag - o - ny,

By Thy pangs to us un - known, By Thy spir - it's part - ing groan,

Lord, Thy pres - ence let us see; Thou our Light and Sav - iour be.

222   *"To Thee we cry."*

2 Prince of life, to Thee we cry:
  By Thy glorious majesty,
  By Thy triumph o'er the grave,
  By Thy power to help and save,
  Lord, Thy presence let us see;
  Thou our Light and Saviour be.

3 Lord of glory, God most high,
  Man exalted to the sky.
  With Thy love our bosoms fill;
  Help us now to do Thy will,
  Then Thy glory we shall see,
  Thou wilt bring us home to Thee.

  Bp. Richard Mant (1776—1848), 1828. Ab. and alt.

DIADEMATA. S. M. D.

Sir GEORGE JOB ELVEY (1816—   ), 1868.

1. Crown Him with many crowns, The Lamb up-on His throne: Hark, how the heav'nly anthem drowns
All mu-sic but its own! With His most precious blood From sin He set us free:
We hail Him as our match-less King Through all e-ter-ni-ty.

223   *The Song of the Seraphs.*

2 Crown Him the Lord of love:
  Behold His hands and side,
  Rich wounds, yet visible above
    In beauty glorified:
  No angel in the sky
    Can fully bear that sight,
  But downward bends his burning eye
    At mysteries so bright.

3 Crown Him the Lord of peace,
    Whose power a sceptre sways,
  From pole to pole, that wars may cease,
    And all be prayer and praise:

His reign shall know no end,
    And round His pierced feet
  Fair flowers of Paradise extend
    Their fragrance ever sweet.

4 Crown Him the Lord of Heaven,
    One with the Father known,
  One with the Spirit through Him given
    From yonder radiant throne!
  To Thee be endless praise,
    For Thou for us hast died:
  Be Thou, O Lord, through endless days
    Adored and magnified.

  Matthew Bridges (1800—   ), 1848. Ab. and alt.

HERALD ANGELS. 7. D.   FELIX MENDELSSOHN-BARTHOLDY (1809–1847), 1846.

1. Hail. the day that sees Him rise, Ravish'd from our wish-ful eyes; Christ, a-while to mor-tals giv'n,

Re - as-cends His native Heav'n. { There the glo-rious tri-umph waits; } Wide un-fold the ra-diant scene,
{ Lift your heads, e-ter-nal gates; }

Take the King of glo-ry in, Wide un-fold the ra-diant scene, Take the King of glo-ry in.

224   *Christ re-ascending.*

2 Him though highest Heaven receives,
Still He loves the earth He leaves:
Though returning to His throne,
Still He calls mankind His own.
See, He lifts His hands above;
See, He shows the prints of love;
Hark, His gracious lips bestow
Blessings on His Church below.

3 Still for us His death He pleads;
Prevalent, He intercedes;
Near Himself prepares our place,
Harbinger of human race.
Lord, though parted from our sight,
High above yon azure height,
Grant our hearts may thither rise,
Following Thee beyond the skies.

Rev. Charles Wesley (1708—1788), 1739. Ab.

225   *"Our Brother glorified."*
1 Tim. iii. 16.

1 CHRIST to Heaven is gone before
In the body here He wore;
He that as our Brother died,
Is our Brother glorified.
Fear not, ye of little faith,
For He hath abolished death;
Death, no longer now we die,
We but follow Christ on high.

2 And before each fainting one,
Dreading the dark way alone,
Now appear His footsteps bright,
Far diffusing holiest light.
As our Shepherd He is there,
With the comfort of His care;
Fear no evil, doubt no more,
Christ to Heaven is gone before.

George Rawson (1807—), 1857. Ab.

ST. PATRICK. 7. D.

Sir ARTHUR SULLIVAN (1842—). 1874.

1. HE is gone! and we re - main In this world of sin and pain; In the void which
He has left, On this earth of Him be - reft, We have still His work to do,
We can still His path pur - sue; Seek Him both in friend and foe, In ourselves His im - age show.

226 *"He is gone, and we remain."*

2 He is gone! unto their goal
World and church must onward roll;
For behind we leave the past;
Forward all our glances cast:
Still His words before us range
Through the ages as they change;
Whereso'er the truth shall lead,
He will give whate'er we need.

3 He is gone! but we once more
Shall behold Him as before,
In the Heaven of heavens the same
As on earth He went and came:
In the many mansions there,
Place for us He will prepare:
In that world, unseen, unknown,
He and we shall yet be one.

Rev. Arthur Penrhyn Stanley (1815—1881), 1859. Ab. and sl. alt.

227 *"Gazing up."*

1 MASTER, Lord, to Thee we cry,
On Thy throne exalted high;
See Thy faithful servants, see,
Ever gazing up to Thee.
Grant, though parted from our sight,
High above yon azure height,
Grant our hearts may thither rise,
Following Thee beyond the skies.

2 Ever may we upward move,
Wafted on the wings of love;
Looking when our Lord shall come,
Looking for our heavenly home:
Then may we with Thee remain,
Partners of Thine endless reign;
There Thy face unclouded see,
Find our Heaven of heavens in Thee.

Rev. Charles Wesley, 1739. Ab. and alt.

WORSHIPPED.

DORT. 6.6.4.6.6.6.4.

LOWELL MASON (1792—1872), 1831.

1. RISE, glo-rious Conquer'r, rise In - to Thy na - tive skies; As-sume Thy right; And where, in many a fold, The clouds are backward roll'd, Pass thro' those gates of gold, And reign in light.

228

Reigning in Light.

2 Victor o'er death and hell,
Cherubic legions swell
    The radiant train :
Praises all Heaven inspire ;
Each angel sweeps his lyre,
And claps his wings of fire,
    Thou Lamb once slain.

3 Enter, incarnate God !
No feet but Thine have trod
    The serpent down :
Blow the full trumpets, blow,
Wider yon portals throw,
Saviour, triumphant, go,
    And take Thy crown.

4 Lion of Judah, Hail !
And let Thy Name prevail
    From age to age :
Lord of the rolling years,
Claim for Thine own the spheres,
For Thou hast bought with tears
    Thy heritage.

Matthew Bridges (1800—   ), 1848. Ab.

229

"Worthy the Lamb !"

1 GLORY to God on high,
Let praises fill the sky !
    Praise ye His Name.

Angels His Name adore,
Who all our sorrows bore,
And saints cry evermore,
    "Worthy the Lamb !"

2 All they around the throne
Cheerfully join in one,
    Praising His Name.
We who have felt His blood
Sealing our peace with God,
Spread His dear fame abroad :
    "Worthy the Lamb !"

3 Join all the human race,
Our Lord and God to bless ;
    Praise ye His Name !
In Him we will rejoice,
Making a cheerful noise,
And say with heart and voice,
    "Worthy the Lamb !"

4 Though we must change our place,
Our souls shall never cease
    Praising His Name ;
To Him we'll tribute bring,
Laud Him our gracious King,
And without ceasing sing,
    "Worthy the Lamb !"

Rev. James Allen (1734—1804), 1761. Ab.

ST. LAWRENCE. 8.7,61.

CHARLES STEGGALL (1826—).

1. JE - sus comes, His con - flict o - ver, Comes to claim His great re - ward;

An - gels round the Vic - tor hov - er, Crowd - ing to be - hold their Lord;

Haste, ye saints, your trib - ute bring, Crown Him, ev - er - last - ing King.

230

The Victor crowned.

2 Yonder throne, for Him erected,
  Now becomes the Victor's seat;
  Lo, the Man on earth rejected!
  Angels worship at His feet:
  Haste, ye saints, your tribute bring,
  Crown Him, everlasting King.

3 Day and night they cry before Him,
  "Holy, holy, holy Lord!"
  All the powers of Heaven adore Him,
  All obey His sovereign word;
  Haste, ye saints, your tribute bring,
  Crown Him, everlasting King.

Rev. Thomas Kelly (1769—1855), 1809.

231

"Pange lingua gloriosi."

1 SING, my tongue, the Saviour's triumph,
  Tell His story far and wide;
  Tell aloud the famous story

Of His body crucified;
How upon the cross a Victim,
Languishing in death He died.

2 Thrice ten years among us dwelling,
  All the time to flesh assigned;
  Born for this, He meets His passion,
  To His agony resigned;
  On the cross the Lamb is lifted,
  There the sacrifice they bind.

3 Equal praises to the Father,
  Equal praises to the Son,
  Equal praises to the Spirit,
  While unending ages run;
  Praise for all in earth and Heaven,
  To th' Eternal Three in One.

Claudianus Mamertus (—474).
Tr. by Rev. John Mason Neale (1818—1866), 1851. Ab. and much alt.

122

ALEXANDER. S. M.

HEINRICH CHRISTOPHER ZEUNER (1795—1857), 1832.

1. The Lord on high as·cends, Once more to take His seat: Ce-
·les·tial pow'rs re·joic·ing fly, His glad re·turn to greet.

232   *"Ascendens in altum Dominus."*

2 The mighty battle gained,
    The world's great prince undone,
Before His Father He presents
    The mortal palm He won.

3 Upborne above the clouds,
    Sweet hope He sheds on all:
He flings the gates of Eden back,
    Shut fast by Adam's fall.

4 To our Redeemer's Name
    All thanks and praise be given,
That He hath borne our mortal shape,
    To tread the courts of Heaven.

5 May we, while waiting Christ,
    To heavenly works arise,
And ever live such saintly lives,
    That we may reach the skies.

Ambrose of Milan (340—397),
Tr. by Rev. Robert Corbet Singleton, 1870. Ab.

ALMSGIVING. 8. 8. 8. 4.

Rev. JOHN BACCHUS DYKES (1823—1876).

1 Sov'reign of Heav'n, who didst pre·vail O'er death and with Thy life·blood dye
The path by which we hope to scale Yon star·ry sky:

233 *"Hear us, O Christ."*

2 Look down in mercy from Thy throne
  At God's right hand, O Lord, and see
Us who are lingering here alone,
  Orphaned of Thee.

3 Hear us, O Christ, for we were born
  Out of the travail of Thy soul;

When by the spear Thy side was torn
  To make us whole.

4 Thy toils and anguish at an end,
  Thou wearest now a glorious crown:
The hour is come; send, Saviour, send
  The Spirit down.

C. Stuart Calverley (—1884), 1872. Ab.

VICTORY. 8.7.4.

HARRY HOBART BRADLE (1828—), 1858.

1. Look, ye saints, the sight is glo - rious, See "the Man of Sor - rows" now;

From the fight re - turned vic - to - rious, Ev - 'ry knee to Him shall bow;

Crown Him, crown Him; Crowns be - come the Vic - tor's brow.

234 *"He shall reign forever and ever."*
    Rev. xi. 15.

2 Crown the Saviour, angels, crown Him:
  Rich the trophies Jesus brings:
In the seat of power enthrone Him,
  While the vault of Heaven rings:
Crown Him, crown Him;
  Crown the Saviour "King of kings."

3 Sinners in derison crowned Him,
  Mocking thus the Saviour's claim;
Saints and angels crowd around Him,

Own His title, praise His Name:
Crown Him, crown Him;
  Spread abroad the Victor's fame.

4 Hark, those bursts of acclamation!
  Hark, those loud triumphant chords!
Jesus takes the highest station:
  O what joy the sight affords!
Crown Him, crown Him;
  "King of kings, and Lord of lords."

Rev. Thomas Kelly (1769—1855), 1809.

BROWN. C. M.
WILLIAM BATCHELDER BRADBURY (1816—1868). 1844.

1. The head that once was crown'd with thorns Is crown'd with glo - ry now;
A roy - al di - a - dem a - dorns The might - y Vic - tor's brow.

235 *"Perfect through Sufferings."*
Heb. ii. 10.

2 The joy of all who dwell above,
   The joy of all below
To whom He manifests His love,
   And grants His Name to know:

3 They suffer with their Lord below,
   They reign with Him above;
Their profit and their joy to know
   The mystery of His love.

4 The cross He bore is life and health,
   Though shame and death to Him;
His people's hope, His people's wealth,
   Their everlasting theme.
                    Rev. Thomas Kelly (1769—1855), 1820. Ab.

236 *The universal Anthem.*
Rev. v. 11—13.

1 COME, let us join our cheerful songs
   With angels round the throne;
Ten thousand thousand are their tongues,
   But all their joys are one.

2 "Worthy the Lamb that died," they cry,
   "To be exalted thus;"
"Worthy the Lamb," our lips reply,
   "For He was slain for us."

3 Jesus is worthy to receive
   Honor and power divine;
And blessings, more than we can give,
   Be, Lord, forever Thine.

4 Let all that dwell above the sky,
   And air, and earth, and seas,
Conspire to lift Thy glories high,
   And speak Thine endless praise.

5 The whole creation join in one,
   To bless the sacred Name
Of Him that sits upon the throne,
   And to adore the Lamb.
                    Rev. Isaac Watts (1674—1748), 1709.

237 *"The Desire of all Nations."*
Hag. ii. 7.

1 INFINITE excellence is Thine,
   Thou glorious Prince of grace!
Thy uncreated beauties shine
   With never-fading rays.

2 Sinners, from earth's remotest end,
   Come bending at Thy feet;
To Thee their prayers and songs ascend,
   In Thee their wishes meet.

3 Millions of happy spirits live
   On Thy exhaustless store;
From Thee they all their bliss receive,
   And still Thou givest more.

4 Thou art their triumph, and their joy;
   They find their all in Thee;
Thy glories will their tongues employ
   Through all eternity.
                    Rev. John Fawcett (1739—1817), 1782. Ab.

NATIVITY. C. M.

HENRY LAHEE (1826—).

1. Be-hold the glo-ries of the Lamb, A-midst His Fa-ther's throne;
Pre-pare new hon-ors for His Name, And songs be-fore un-known.

238

To the Lamb that was slain.
Rev. v. 6—12.

2 Let elders worship at His feet,
    The church adore around,
With vials full of odors sweet,
    And harps of sweeter sound.

3 Those are the prayers of all the saints,
    And these the hymns they raise:
Jesus is kind to our complaints,
    He loves to hear our praise.

4 Now to the Lamb that once was slain,
    Be endless blessings paid;
Salvation, glory, joy remain
    Forever on Thy head.

5 Thou hast redeemed our souls with blood,
    Hast set the prisoners free,
Hast made us kings and priests to God,
    And we shall reign with Thee.
        Rev. Isaac Watts, 1709. Ab.

239   *The Gates opened.*

1 Come, let us lift our joyful eyes
    Up to the courts above,
And smile to see our Father there,
    Upon a throne of love.

2 Now we may bow before His feet,
    And venture near the Lord:
No fiery cherub guards His seat,
    Nor double flaming sword.

3 The peaceful gates of heavenly bliss
    Are opened by the Son;
High let us raise our notes of praise,
    And reach th' almighty throne.

4 To Thee ten thousand thanks we bring
    Great Advocate on high;
And glory to th' eternal King,
    Who lays His anger by.
        Rev. Isaac Watts, 1709. Ab. and sl. alt.

240   *"Our ascended Priest."*

1 Come, let us join in songs of praise
    To our ascended Priest;
He entered Heaven, with all our names
    Deep graven on His breast.

2 Below He washed our guilt away,
    By His atoning blood;
Now He appears before the throne,
    And pleads our cause with God.

3 Clothed with our nature still, He knows
    The weakness of our frame,
And how to shield us from the foes
    Which He Himself o'ercame.

4 O may we ne'er forget His grace,
    Nor blush to wear His Name;
Still may our hearts hold fast His faith,
    Our mouths His praise proclaim.
        Rev. Alexander Pirie (—1804), 1786. Ab. and sl. alt.

CORONATION. C. M.

OLIVER HOLDEN (1756—1831), 1793.

1. All hail the pow'r of Je - sus' Name! Let an - gels prostrate fall, Bring forth the roy - al di - a - dem,

And crown Him Lord of all, Bring forth the roy - al di - a - dem, And crown Him Lord of all.

241

"And crown Him Lord of all."
ACTS x. 36.

2 Crown Him, ye morning stars of light,
  Who fixed this floating ball;
  Now hail the strength of Israel's might,
  And crown Him Lord of all.

3 Crown Him, ye martyrs of your God,
  Who from His altar call;
  Extol the stem of Jesse's rod,
  And crown Him Lord of all.

4 Ye seed of Israel's chosen race,
  Ye ransomed of the fall,

Hail Him, who saves you by His grace,
  And crown Him Lord of all.

5 Sinners, whose love can ne'er forget
  The wormwood and the gall,
  Go, spread your trophies at His feet,
  And crown Him Lord of all.

6 Let every kindred, every tribe,
  On this terrestrial ball,
  To Him all majesty ascribe,
  And crown Him Lord of all.

Rev. Edward Perronet (—1792), 1780. Ab. and alt.

MILES LANE. C. M.

Rev. WILLIAM SHRUBSOLE (1729—1797), 1793.
Har. by Rev. JOHN BACCHUS DYKES (1823—1876), 1861.

1. All hail the pow'r of Je - sus' Name! Let an - gels pros-trate fall, Bring forth the roy - al

di - a - dem, And crown Him, crown Him, crown Him, crown Him Lord of all.

SILOAM. C. M.

ISAAC BEVERLY WOODBURY (1819—1858), 1842.

1. O MEAN may seem this house of clay, Yet 'twas the Lord's a - bode;
Our feet may mourn this thorn - y way, Yet here Em - man - uel trod.

242
Our double Kindred to Emmanuel.
1 COR. XV. 47, 49.

2 This fleshly robe the Lord did wear;
This watch the Lord did keep;
These burdens sore the Lord did bear;
These tears the Lord did weep.

3 O vale of tears no longer sad,
Wherein the Lord did dwell!
O happy robe of flesh that clad
Our own Emmanuel!

4 But not this fleshly robe alone
Shall link us, Lord, to Thee;
Not only in the tear and groan
Shall the dear kindred be.

5 We shall be reckoned for Thine own,
Because Thy Heaven we share,
Because we sing around Thy throne,
And Thy bright raiment wear.

6 O mighty grace, our life to live,
To make our earth divine!
O mighty grace, Thy Heaven to give,
And lift our life to Thine!

Thomas Hornblower Gill (1819—), 1860. Ab.

243
"The Incarnate Mystery."
1 COR. I. 22—29.

1 DEAREST of all the names above,
My Jesus and my God,
Who can resist Thy heavenly love,
Or trifle with Thy blood?

2 'Tis by the merits of Thy death
The Father smiles again.
'Tis by Thine interceding breath
The Spirit dwells with men.

3 Till God in human flesh I see,
My thoughts no comfort find:
The holy, just, and sacred Three
Are terrors to my mind.

4 But if Immanuel's face appear,
My hope, my joy, begins:
His Name forbids my slavish fear;
His grace removes my sins.

5 While Jews on their own law rely,
And Greeks of wisdom boast,
I love th' incarnate Mystery,
And there I fix my trust.

Rev. Isaac Watts, (1674—1748), 1709.

128

WARSAW. H. M.

THOMAS CLARK ( ), 1806.

1. REJOICE, the Lord is King, Your Lord and King a - dore; Mortals, give thanks and sing, And tri-umph ev - er - more: Lift up your heart, lift up your voice, Re-joice, a - gain I say, re - joice.

244

"The Lord is King."

2 Jesus the Saviour reigns,
　　The God of truth and love ;
　When He had purged our stains,
　　He took His seat above :
　Lift up your heart, lift up your voice,
　Rejoice, again I say, rejoice.

3 His kingdom cannot fail,
　　He rules o'er earth and Heaven ;
　The keys of death and hell
　　Are to our Jesus given :
　Lift up your heart, lift up your voice,
　Rejoice, again I say, rejoice.

4 Rejoice in glorious hope ;
　　Jesus, the Judge, shall come,
　And take His servants up
　　To their eternal home ;
　We soon shall hear th' archangel's voice,
　The trump of God shall sound, Rejoice.

Rev. Charles Wesley (1708—1788), 1748. Ab.

ST. ALBINUS. 7. 8. 4.

HENRY JOHN GAUNTLETT (1806—1876), 1872.

1. JE - sus lives! no lon - ger now Can thy ter - rors, Death, ap - pal us; Je - sus lives! by this we know Thou, O Grave, canst not en - thral us. Al - le - lu - ia!

245   *"Jesus lebt!"*

2 Jesus lives! henceforth is death
But the gate of life immortal;
This shall calm our trembling breath,
When we pass its gloomy portal.
Alleluia!

3 Jesus lives for us He died;
Then, alone to Jesus living,
Pure in heart may we abide,
Glory to our Saviour giving.
Alleluia!

4 Jesus lives! our hearts know well
Naught from us His love shall sever;
Life, nor death, nor powers of hell
Tear us from His keeping ever.
Alleluia!

5 Jesus lives! to Him the throne
Over all the world is given:
May we go where He is gone,
Rest and reign with Him in Heaven.
Alleluia!

Christian Fürchtegott Gellert (1715—1769), 1757
Tr. by Miss Frances Elizabeth Cox (   ), 1841

BONAR. 8.8.7.D.   JOHN BAPTISTE CALKIN (1827—   ), 1872

1. Up-ward, where the stars are burn-ing, Si-lent, si-lent in their turn-ing, Round the nev-er-chang-ing pole; Up-ward, where the sky is bright-est, Up-ward, where the blue is light-est, Lift I now my long-ing soul

246   *Dwelling in the Heavens*
Ps. cxxiii. 1

2 Where the Lamb on high is seated,
By ten thousand voices greeted:
Lord of lords, and King of kings.
Son of man, they crown, they crown Him,
Son of God, they own, they own Him:
With His Name the palace rings.

3 Blessing, honor, without measure,
Heavenly riches, earthly treasure,
Lay we at His blesséd feet.
Poor the praise that now we render,
Loud shall be our voices yonder,
When before His throne we meet.

Rev. Horatius Bonar (1808—   ), 1866   Ab.

MORNING HYMN. L. M.   FRANCOIS DIPPOLITE BARTHELEMON (1741—1808).

1. O Sav - iour, who for man hast trod The wine - press of the wrath of God,

As - cend, and claim a - gain on high, The glo - ry left for us to die.

247   *"Opus peregisti tuum."*

2 A radiant cloud is now Thy seat,
And earth lies stretched beneath Thy feet ;
Ten thousand thousands round Thee sing,
And share the triumph of their King.

3 Our great High Priest and Shepherd Thou
Within the veil art entered now,
To offer there Thy precious blood
Once poured on earth a cleansing flood.

4 O Christ, our Lord, of Thy dear care
Thy lowly members heaven-ward bear ;
Be ours with Thee to suffer pain,
With Thee for evermore to reign.
Prof. Charles Coffin (1676—1749), 1736.
Tr. by Rev. John Chandler (1806—1876), 1837. Ab. and much alt.

248   *"Nobis Olympo Redditus."*

1 O Christ, uplifted to the sky,
Preparing us a place on high,
Sad exiles from the land above,
O draw us home with words of love.

2 Of every good the fountain, Lord,
Thou soon shalt be our rich reward :
What lasting joys shall then remain,
To match Thy people's briefest pain.

3 Our eyes unveiled, in blissful state,
Shall view Thee, O how good ! how great !

On Thee our ceaseless love shall pour,
And Thee our ceaseless song adore.

4 Thou ne'er dost quit a favored race :
In pledge of Thy redeeming grace,
O send Thy Spirit from Thy throne,
To take and seal us for Thine own.
Santolius Victorinus (1630—1697).
Tr. by Rev. Robert Corbet Singleton, 1867. Ab. and alt.

249   *Our Priest and King.*

1 Now to the Lord, who makes us know
The wonders of His dying love,
Be humble honors paid below,
And strains of noble praise above.

2 'Twas He who cleansed our foulest sins,
And washed us in His precious blood ;
'Tis He who makes us priests and kings,
And brings us rebels near to God.

3 To Jesus, our atoning Priest,
To Jesus, our eternal King,
Be everlasting power confest,
And every tongue His glory sing.

4 Behold, on flying clouds He comes,
And every eye shall see Him move ;
Tho' with our sins we pierced Him once,
He now displays His pard'ning love.
Rev. Isaac Watts (1674—1748), 1707. Ab. and alt.

GROSTETE. L. M. HENRY WELLINGTON GREATOREX (1811—1858). 1849.

1. O Christ, our King, Cre - a - tor, Lord, Sav - iour of all who trust Thy word,

To them who seek Thee ev - er near, Now to our prais - es bend Thine ear.

250 *"Rex Christe, factor omnium."*

2 In Thy dear cross a grace is found,
It flows from every streaming wound,
Whose power our inbred sin controls,
Breaks the firm bond, and frees our souls.

3 Thou didst create the stars of night,
Yet Thou hast veiled in flesh Thy light;
Hast deigned a mortal form to wear,
A mortal's painful lot to bear.

4 When Thou didst hang upon the tree,
The quaking earth acknowledged Thee;
When Thou didst there yield up Thy
breath,
The world grew dark as shades of death.

5 Now in the Father's glory high,
Great Conqueror, never more to die,
Us by Thy mighty power defend,
And reign through ages without end.

Gregory the Great (540—604).
Tr. by Rev. Ray Palmer (1808—   ), 1858.

251 *The enthroned High Priest.*

1 WHERE high the heavenly temple stands,
The house of God not made with hands,
A great High Priest our nature wears,
The Guardian of mankind appears.

2 He who for men their surety stood,
And poured on earth His precious blood,
Pursues in Heaven His mighty plan,
The Saviour and the Friend of man.

3 Though now ascended up on high,
He bends on earth a brother's eye;
Partaker of the human name,
He knows the weakness of our frame.

4 Our fellow-sufferer yet retains
A fellow-feeling of our pains;
And still remembers in the skies
His tears, and agonies, and cries.

5 In every pang, that rends the heart,
The Man of Sorrows had a part;
Touched with the feeling of our grief,
He to the sufferer sends relief.

6 With boldness, therefore, at the throne,
Let us make all our sorrows known,
And ask the aid of heavenly power,
To help us in the evil hour.

Michael Bruce (1746—1767), 1781. Alt.

AUTUMN. 8.7. D.

Spanish Melody.

1. HAIL, Thou once de - spis - ed Je - sus, Hail, Thou Gal - i - le - an King!

Thou didst suf - fer to re - lease us, Thou didst free sal - va - tion bring:

D. S. By Thy mer - its we find fa - vor; Life is giv - en through Thy Name.

Hail, Thou ag - o - niz - ing Sav - iour, Bear - er of our sin and shame;

252   "*Enthroned in Glory.*"

2 Paschal Lamb, by God appointed,
   All our sins on Thee were laid ;
By almighty love anointed,
   Thou hast full atonement made :
All Thy people are forgiven
   Through the virtue of Thy blood ;
Opened is the gate of Heaven ;
   Peace is made 'twixt man and God.

3 Jesus, hail, enthroned in glory,
   There forever to abide ;
All the heavenly hosts adore Thee,
   Seated at Thy Father's side.
There for sinners Thou art pleading ;
   There Thou dost our place prepare ;
Ever for us interceding
   Till in glory we appear.
            Rev. John Bakewell (1721—1819), 1760. Alt.
     Rev. Augustus Montague Toplady (1740—1778), 1776.

253   "*Thou art worthy.*"
     (Second part of preceding Hymn.)

1 WORSHIP, honor, power, and blessing,
   Thou art worthy to receive ;
Loudest praises, without ceasing,
   Meet it is for us to give.

Help, ye bright angelic spirits,
   Bring your sweetest, noblest lays ;
Help to sing our Saviour's merits,
   Help to chant Immanuel's praise.

2 Soon we shall, with those in glory,
   His transcendent grace relate ;
Gladly sing th' amazing story
   Of His dying love so great :
In that blessed contemplation
   We for evermore shall dwell,
Crowned with bliss and consolation,
   Such as none below can tell.
            Rev. John Bakewell, 1760. Alt.
     Rev. Augustus Montague Toplady, 1776

254   "*On the right Hand of God.*"
     1 Pet. iii. 22.

1 CHRIST, above all glory seated,
   King eternal, strong to save,
Dying, Thou hast death defeated,
   Buried, Thou hast spoiled the grave.
Thou art gone, where now is given,
   What no mortal might could gain :
On th' eternal throne of Heaven,
   In Thy Father's power to reign.

2 We, O Lord, with hearts adoring,
  Follow Thee above the sky :
Hear our prayers Thy grace imploring,
  Lift our souls to Thee on high.

So when Thou again in glory
  On the clouds of Heaven shalt shine,
We Thy flock shall stand before Thee,
  Owned forevermore as Thine.

Bp. James Russell Woodford (1820—), 1863. Ab.

GUIDANCE. 8.7. D.

Arr. from FRIEDRICH von FLOTOW (1812—1883), 1868.

1. { Al - le - lu - ia, sing to Je - sus, His the scep-tre, His the throne; }
   { Al - le - lu - ia, His the tri - umph, His the (Omit)................ } vic - to - ry a -

- lone; Hark, the songs of peace-ful Zi - on Thun-der like a might - y flood, Je - sus

out of ev - 'ry na - tion, Hath redeemed us by His blood, Hath redeemed us by His blood.

255 *"A Priest forever."* Ps. cx. 4.

2 Alleluia, not as orphans,
    We are left in sorrow now ;
  Alleluia, He is near us,
    Faith believes, nor questions how :
  Tho' the cloud from sight received Him,
    When the forty days were o'er,
  Shall our hearts forget His promise,
    "I am with you evermore?"

3 Alleluia, Bread of angels,
    Thou on earth our Food, our Stay,
  Alleluia, here the sinful
    Flee to Thee from day to day ;
  Intercessor, Friend of sinners,
    Earth's Redeemer, plead for me,
  Where the songs of all the sinless
    Sweep across the crystal sea.

William Chatterton Dix (1837—), 1867. Ab.

256 *"I am with you alway."* MATT. xxviii. 20.

1 ALWAYS with us, always with us,
    Words of cheer, and words of love :
  Thus the risen Saviour whispers,
    From His dwelling-place above.
  With us when the storm is sweeping
    O'er our pathway dark and drear,
  Waking hope within our bosoms,
    Stilling every anxious fear.

2 With us in the lonely valley,
    When we cross the chilling stream ;
  Lighting up the steps to glory
    Like the ancient prophet's dream.
  Always with us, always with us,
    Pilot in the surging main,
  Guiding to the distant Heaven,
    Where we shall be home again.

Rev. Edwin Henry Nevin (1814—), 1858. Ab

GONE BACK TO HEAVEN.

HARWELL. 8.7.6 l.

LOWELL MASON (1792—1872), 1840.

1. Come, ye faithful, raise the anthem, Cleave the skies with shouts of praise: Sing to Him who found the ransom,
Sing to Him who found the ransom,

Ancient of e - ter - nal days: God e - ter - nal, Word Incarnate, Whom the Heav'n of heav'ns obeys,
Ancient of e - ter - nal days:

---

257 *"Raise the Anthem."*

2 Ere He raised the lofty mountains,
  Formed the sea, or built the sky,
Love eternal, free, and boundless,
  Forced the Lord of Life to die;
Lifted up the Prince of princes
  On the throne of Calvary.

3 Now on those eternal mountains
  Stands the sapphire throne, all bright,
Where unceasing hallelujahs
  They upraise, the sons of light:
Zion's people tell His praises,
  Victor after hard-won fight.

4 Bring your harps and bring your incense,
  Sweep the string and pour the lay;
Let the earth proclaim His wonders,
  King of that celestial day:
He, the Lamb once slain, is worthy,
  Who was dead and lives for aye.

Rev. Job Hupton (1762—1849), 1808. Ab.
Alt. by Rev. John Mason Neale (1818—1866), 1851.

258 Ἰησοῦς ὁ Ζωοδότης.

1 JESUS, Lord of Life eternal,
  Taking those He loved the best,
Stood upon the Mount of Olives,
  And His own the last time blest:
Then, though He had never left it,
  Sought again His Father's breast.

2 Knit is now our flesh to Godhead,
  Knit in everlasting bands:
Call the world to highest festal:
  Floods and oceans, clap your hands:
Angels, raise the song of triumph:
  Make response, ye distant lands.

3 Loosing death with all its terrors
  Thou ascendedst up on high;
And to mortals, now immortal,
  Gavest immortality,
As Thine own disciples saw Thee
  Mounting Victor to the sky.

Joseph of the Studium (—883),
Tr. by Rev. John Mason Neale, 1862. Ab. and alt.

NEANDER. 8.7.6 l.

German. JOACHIM NEANDER (1610—1680), 1679.

SAMSON. L. M.

GEORGE FREDERICK HANDEL (1685—1759), 1742.

1. Come, let us sing the song of songs, The saints in Heav'n be - gan the strain,

The hom - age which to Christ be - longs: "Wor - thy the Lamb, for He was slain!"

259
"The Song of Songs."

2 Slain to redeem us by His blood,
To cleanse from every sinful stain,
And make us kings and priests to God :
"Worthy the Lamb, for He was slain !"

3 To Him, enthroned by filial right,
All power in Heaven and earth proclaim,

Honor, and majesty, and might :
"Worthy the Lamb, for He was slain !"

4 Long as we live, and when we die, [reign,
And while in Heaven with Him we
This song our song of songs shall be :
"Worthy the Lamb, for He was slain !"

James Montgomery (1771—1854,) 1853. Ab. and alt.

HEBER. C. M.

GEORGE KINGSLEY (1811—1884), 1838.

1. Thou art the Way : To Thee a - lone From sin and death we flee ;

And he who would the Fa - ther seek, Must seek Him, Lord, by Thee.

260
"The Way, the Truth, the Life."
John xiv. 6.

2 Thou art the Truth : Thy word alone
True wisdom can impart ;
Thou only canst inform the mind,
And purify the heart.

3 Thou art the Life : the rending tomb
Proclaims Thy conquering arm,

And those who put their trust in Thee
Nor death, nor hell shall harm.

4 Thou art the Way, the Truth, the Life :
Grant us that Way to know,
That Truth to keep, that Life to win,
Whose joys eternal flow.

Bp. George Washington Doane (1799—1859), 1824.

ST. CUTHBERT.   8. 6. 8. 4.   Rev. JOHN BACCHUS DYKES (1823—1876), 1861.

1. Our blest Re-deem - er, ere He breath'd His ten - der last fare - well,

A Guide, a Com - fort - er, be - queath'd With us to dwell.

261   *The Comforter comes.*
           JOHN xvi. 7.

2 He came in semblance of a dove
   With sheltering wings outspread,
The holy balm of peace and love
   On earth to shed.

3 He came sweet influence to impart,
   A gracious, willing guest,
While He can find one humble heart
   Wherein to rest.

4 And His that gentle voice we hear,
   Soft as the breath of even,

That checks each thought, that calms each
      fear,
   And speaks of Heaven.

5 And every virtue we possess,
   And every victory won,
And every thought of holiness
   Are His alone.

6 Spirit of purity and grace,
   Our weakness, pitying, see :
O make our hearts Thy dwelling-place,
   And meet for Thee.

         Miss Harriet Auber (1773—1862), 1829. Ab.

ST. AGNES.   C. M.   Rev. JOHN BACCHUS DYKES, 1858.

1. No track is on the sun - ny sky, No foot-prints on the air :

Je - sus hath gone; the face of earth Is des - o - late and bare.

262 *Pentecost.*
ACTS ii. 1—4.

2 That Upper Room is Heaven on earth:
  Within its precincts lie
  All that earth has of faith, or hope,
  Or Heaven-born charity.

3 He comes! He comes! that mighty Breath
  From Heaven's eternal shores;
  His uncreated freshness fills
  His Bride, as she adores.

4 Earth quakes before that rushing blast,
  Heaven echoes back the sound,
  And mightily the tempest wheels
  That Upper Room around.

5 One moment—and the Spirit hung
  O'er all with dread desire;
  Then broke upon the heads of all
  In cloven tongues of fire.

6 The Spirit came into the Church
  With His unfailing power;
  He is the living Heart that beats
  Within her at this hour.

7 Most tender Spirit, mighty God,
  Sweet must Thy presence be,
  If loss of Jesus can be gain,
  So long as we have Thee!

Rev. Frederick William Faber (1814—1863), 1849. Ab. and sl. alt.

263   *Pentecost.*

1 WHEN God of old came down from
    In power and wrath He came; [Heaven,

Before His feet the clouds were riven,
  Half darkness, and half flame.

2 But when He came the second time,
  He came in power and love;
  Softer than gale at morning prime
  Hovered His holy Dove.

3 The fires, that rushed on Sinai down
  In sudden torrents dread,
  Now gently light, a glorious crown,
  On every sainted head.

4 And, as on Israel's awe-struck ear
  The voice exceeding loud,
  The trump that angels quake to hear,
  Thrilled from the deep dark cloud;

5 So, when the Spirit of our God
  Came down His flock to find,
  A voice from Heaven was heard abroad,
  A rushing mighty wind.

6 It fills the Church of God, it fills
  The sinful world around;
  Only in stubborn hearts and wills
  No place for it is found.

7 Come, Lord, come Wisdom, Love, and
            Power,
  Open our ears to hear;
  Let us not miss th' accepted hour;
  Save, Lord, by love or fear.

Rev. John Keble (1792—1866), 1827.   Ab.

OAKSVILLE. C. M.   HEINRICH CHRISTOPHER ZEUNER (1795—1857). 1839.

ERNAN. L. M.

LOWELL MASON (1792—1872), 1850.

1. COME, O Cre - a - tor Spir - it blest, And in our souls take up Thy rest;

Come, with Thy grace and heav'n-ly aid, To fill the hearts which Thou hast made.

264
"Veni, Creator Spiritus."

2 Great Comforter, to Thee we cry;
O highest gift of God most high,
O Fount of life, O Fire of love,
And sweet anointing from above!

3 Kindle our senses from above,
And make our hearts o'erflow with love;
With patience firm, and virtue high,
The weakness of our flesh supply.

4 Far from us drive the foe we dread,
And grant us Thy true peace instead;
So shall we not, with Thee for Guide,
Turn from the path of life aside.

Rabanus Maurus (776—856),
Tr. by Rev. Edward Caswall (1814—1878), 1849. Ab. and alt.

265
Prayer for Light and Guidance.

1 COME, Holy Spirit, heavenly Dove,
With peace and healing from above;
Be Thou my Light, be Thou my Guide,
O'er every thought and step preside.

2 The light of truth to me display,
That I may know and choose my way;
Plant holy fear within my heart,
That I from God may ne'er depart.

3 Conduct me safe, conduct me far,
From every sin and hurtful snare;

Lead me to God, my final Rest,
In His enjoyment to be blest.

4 Lead me to holiness, the road
That I must take to dwell with God;
Lead me to Christ, the living Way,
Nor let me from His pastures stray.

Rev. Simon Browne (1680—1732), 1720. Ab. and alt.

266
The Operations of the Spirit.

1 ETERNAL Spirit, we confess
And sing the wonders of Thy grace;
Thy power conveys our blessings down
From God the Father and the Son.

2 Enlightened by Thy heavenly ray,
Our shades and darkness turn to day;
Thine inward teachings make us know
Our danger and our refuge, too.

3 Thy power and glory work within,
And break the chains of reigning sin;
Do our imperious lusts subdue,
And form our wretched hearts anew.

4 The troubled conscience knows Thy voice;
Thy cheering words awake our joys;
Thy words allay the stormy wind,
And calm the surges of the mind.

Rev. Isaac Watts (1674—1748), 1709.

PENTECOST. 7.7.7.5.　　　　　Sir ARTHUR SULLIVAN (1842—).

1. Ho - LY Ghost, the In - fi - nite, Shine up - on our nat - ure's night

With Thy bless - ed in - ward light, Com - fort - er Di - vine!

267　　*"Holy Ghost, the Infinite."*

2 We are sinful, cleanse us, Lord ;
  We are faint, Thy strength afford ;
  Lost, until by Thee restored,
  Comforter Divine !

3 Like the dew, Thy peace distil :
  Guide, subdue our wayward will,
  Things of Christ unfolding still,
  Comforter Divine !

4 In us, for us, intercede,
  And with voiceless groaning plead
  Our unutterable need,
  Comforter Divine !

5 In us "Abba, Father," cry,
  Earnest of our bliss on high,
  Seal of immortality,
  Comforter Divine !

6 Search for us the depths of God ;
  Bear us up the starry road,
  To the height of Thine abode,
  Comforter Divine !

George Rawson (1807—1885), 1853. **Ab.**

268　　*"Heavenly Love."*

1 GRACIOUS Spirit, Holy Ghost,
  Taught by Thee, we covet most,
  Of Thy gifts at Pentecost,
  Holy, heavenly Love.

2 Love is kind, and suffers long,
  Love is meek, and thinks no wrong,
  Love than death itself more strong
  Give us heavenly Love.

3 Prophecy will fade away,
  Melting in the light of day ;
  Love will ever with us stay :
  Give us heavenly Love.

4 Faith will vanish into sight,
  Hope be emptied in delight ;
  Love in Heaven will shine more bright :
  Give us heavenly Love.

5 Faith and Hope and Love we see
  Joining hand in hand agree ;
  But the greatest of the three,
  And the best, is Love.

Bp. Christopher Wordsworth (1807—), 1862. **Ab. and alt.**

NELLINE. 7.7.7.5.　　　　　WILLIAM FISK SHERWIN (1826—), 1880.

WESLEY. 8.7.D.   JOHN ZUNDEL (1815—1882), 1870.

1. Love Di - vine, all love ex - cel - ling, Joy of Heav'n, to earth come down;

Fix in us Thy hum - ble dwell - ing, All Thy faith - ful mer - cies crown;

Je - sus, Thou art all com - pas - sion, Pure un - bound - ed love Thou art;

Vis - it us with Thy sal - va - tion, En - ter ev - 'ry trem - bling heart.

269   *"Love Divine."*

2 Breathe, O breathe, Thy loving Spirit
  Into every troubled breast;
Let us all in Thee inherit,
  Let us find that second rest;
Take away our power of sinning,
  Alpha and Omega be,
End of faith, as its beginning,
  Set our hearts at liberty.

3 Come, almighty to deliver,
  Let us all Thy life receive;
Suddenly return, and never,
  Never more Thy temples leave.

Thee we would be always blessing,
  Serve Thee as Thy hosts above,
Pray, and praise Thee without ceasing,
  Glory in Thy perfect love.

4 Finish then Thy new creation,
  Pure, and spotless let us be;
Let us see Thy great salvation
  Perfectly restored in Thee:
Changed from glory into glory,
  Till in Heaven we take our place,
Till we cast our crowns before Thee,
  Lost in wonder, love, and praise.

Rev. Charles Wesley (1708—1788), 1747. Sn. alt.

270 *Prayer for Light.* 8.7. D.

1 LIGHT of those whose dreary dwelling
Borders on the shades of death,
Come, and by Thy love's revealing
Dissipate the clouds beneath:
The new heaven and earth's Creator,
In our deepest darkness rise,
Scattering all the night of nature,
Pouring eye-sight on our eyes.

2 Still we wait for Thine appearing;
Life and joy Thy beams impart,
Chasing all our fears, and cheering
Every poor, benighted heart:

Come, and manifest the favor
God hath for our ransomed race;
Come, Thou glorious God and Saviour,
Come, and bring the gospel-grace.

3 Save us in Thy great compassion,
O thou mild, pacific Prince,
Give the knowledge of salvation,
Give the pardon of our sins;
By Thine all-restoring merit,
Every burdened soul release,
Every weary, wandering spirit
Guide into Thy perfect peace.

Rev. Charles Wesley, 1745.

EIN' FESTE BURG. L. M. 6 l.

Arr. from Rev. MARTIN LUTHER (1483—1546), 1529.

1. COME, Ho - ly Ghost, our souls in - spire, And light - en with ce - les - tial fire;

Thou the an - oint - ing Spir - it art, Who dost Thy sev'n - fold gifts im - part;

Thy bless - ed unc - tion from a - bove, Is com - fort, life, and fire of love.

271 *The Anointing Spirit.*

2 Enable with perpetual light
The dullness of our blinded sight;
Anoint and cheer our soiléd face
With the abundance of Thy grace:
Keep far our foes, give peace at home:
Where Thou art Guide, no ill can come.

3 Teach us to know the Father, Son,
And Thee of both, to be but One;
That through the ages all along,
This still may be our endless song:
All praise, with all the heavenly host,
To Father, Son, and Holy Ghost!

Rabanus Maurus (776—856),
Tr. by Bp. John Cosin (1594—1672), 1627 Alt.

MERCY. 7.

Arr. from LOUIS MOREAU GOTTSCHALK (1829—1869). 1854.

1. GRA - CIOUS Spir - it, Dove di - vine, Let Thy light with - in me shine;

All my guilt - y fears re - move, Fill me full of Heav'n and love.

272   *Prayer for Peace and Rest.*

2 Speak Thy pardoning grace to me,
Set the burdened sinner free,
Lead me to the Lamb of God,
Wash me in His precious blood.

3 Life and peace to me impart,
Seal salvation on my heart,
Breathe Thyself into my breast,
Earnest of immortal rest.

4 Let me never from Thee stray,
Keep me in the narrow way,
Fill my soul with joy divine,
Keep me, Lord, forever Thine.
           John Stocker, 1776. Ab.

273   *Light, Power, Joy.*

1 HOLY GHOST, with light divine,
Shine upon this heart of mine;
Chase the shades of night away,
Turn the darkness into day.

2 Holy Ghost, with power divine,
Cleanse this guilty heart of mine;
Long has sin, without control,
Held dominion o'er my soul.

3 Holy Ghost, with joy divine,
Cheer this saddened heart of mine;

Bid my many woes depart,
Heal my wounded, bleeding heart.

4 Holy Spirit, all divine,
Dwell within this heart of mine,
Cast down every idol-throne;
Reign supreme, and reign alone.
       Rev. Andrew Reed (1787—1862), 1843. Ab.

274   *"Granted is the Saviour's Prayer."*

1 GRANTED is the Saviour's prayer,
Sent the gracious Comforter,
Promise of our parting Lord,
Jesus, to His Heaven restored.

2 God, the everlasting God,
Makes with mortals His abode,
Whom the heavens cannot contain,
He stoops down to dwell in man.

3 Never will He thence depart,
Inmate of a humble heart;
Carrying on His work within,
Striving till He cast out sin.

4 Come, divine and peaceful Guest,
Enter our devoted breast:
Life divine in us renew,
Thou the Gift and Giver, too!
       Rev. Charles Wesley (1708—1788), 1739. Ab. and alt.

HAYDN. S. M.

From FRANCIS JOSEPH HAYDN (1732—1809). 1800.

1. Come, Ho - ly Spir - it, come, Let Thy bright beams a - rise,

Dis - pel the dark - ness from our minds, And o - pen all our eyes.

275   *Prayer for Light and Love.*

2 Revive our drooping faith,
Our doubts and fears remove,
And kindle in our breasts the flame
Of never-dying love.

3 Convince us of our sin,
Then lead to Jesus' blood,
And to our wondering view reveal
The secret love of God.

4 'Tis Thine to cleanse the heart,
To sanctify the soul,
To pour fresh life in every part,
And new-create the whole.

5 Dwell, Spirit, in our hearts,
Our minds from bondage free;
Then we shall know, and praise, and love
The Father, Son, and Thee.

Rev. Joseph Hart (1712—1768), 1759. Ab. and sl. alt.

276   *The Descent of the Spirit.*

1 Lord God, the Holy Ghost,
In this accepted hour,
As on the day of Pentecost,
Descend in all Thy power.

2 Like mighty rushing wind
Upon the waves beneath,
Move with one impulse every mind,
One soul, one feeling breathe.

3 The young, the old, inspire
With wisdom from above;
And give us hearts and tongues of fire
To pray, and praise, and love.

4 Spirit of light, explore,
And chase our gloom away,
With lustre shining more and more
Unto the perfect day.

James Montgomery (1771—1854), 1819, 1825. Ab.

OLMUTZ. S. M.

Gregorian. Arr. by LOWELL MASON (1792—1872). 1832.

ELVET. C. M.   Rev. JOHN BACCHUS DYKES (1823—1876).

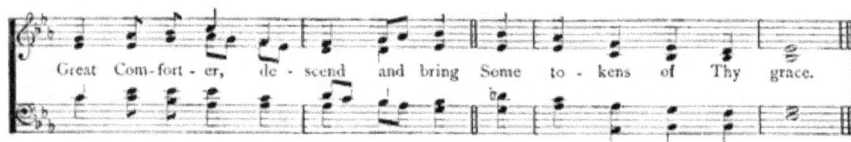

1. Why should the chil - dren   of   a   King   Go   mourn - ing   all   their   days?

Great Com - fort - er,   de - scend   and bring Some   to - kens   of   Thy   grace.

277 *The witnessing and sealing Spirit.*
Rom. viii. 14, 16   Eph. i. 13, 14.

2 Dost Thou not dwell in all the saints,
   And seal the heirs of Heaven?
   When wilt Thou banish my complaints
   And show my sins forgiven?

3 Assure my conscience of her part
   In the Redeemer's blood;
   And bear Thy witness with my heart,
   That I am born of God.

4 Thou art the earnest of His love,
   The pledge of joys to come;
   And Thy soft wings, celestial Dove,
   Will safe convey me home.
                    Rev. Isaac Watts (1674—1748), 1709.

278   *Prayer to the Spirit.*

1 Spirit Divine, attend our prayers,
   And make this house Thy home;
   Descend with all Thy gracious powers,
   O come, Great Spirit, come!

2 Come as the light; to us reveal
   Our sinfulness and woe;
   And lead us in those paths of life
   Where all the righteous go.

3 Come as the fire, and purge our hearts,
   Like sacrificial flame;
   Let our whole soul an offering be
   To our Redeemer's Name.

4 Come as the wind, with rushing sound,
   With Pentecostal grace;
   And make the great salvation known,
   Wide as the human race.

5 Spirit Divine, attend our prayers,
   Make a lost world Thy home;
   Descend with all Thy gracious powers,
   O come, Great Spirit, come!
          Rev. Andrew Reed (1787—1862), 1843. Ab. and sl. alt.

279   *The Spirit's Influences desired.*
ACTS x. 44.

1 Great Father of each perfect gift,
   Behold Thy servants wait;
   With longing eyes and lifted hands,
   We flock around Thy gate.

2 O shed abroad that royal gift,
   Thy Spirit from above,
   To bless our eyes with sacred light,
   And fire our hearts with love.

3 Blest Earnest of eternal joy,
   Declare our sins forgiven;
   And bear, with energy divine,
   Our raptured thoughts to Heaven.

4 Pour down, O God, those copious showers,
   That earth its fruit may yield,
   And change the barren wilderness
   To Carmel's flowery field.
    Rev. Philip Doddridge (1702—1751), 1755. Ab. and sl. alt.

BOARDMAN. C. M.

DEVEREUX. Arr. by GEORGE KINGSLEY (1811—1884). 1853.

1. My soul doth mag - ni - fy the Lord, My spir - it doth re - joice

In God my Sav - iour, and my God; I hear His joy - ful voice.

280

"The Comforter is come."

2 Down from above the blessed Dove
Is come into my breast,
To witness God's eternal love:
This is my heavenly feast.

3 My God, my reconcilèd God,
Creator of my peace:
Thee will I love, and praise, and sing,
Till life and breath shall cease.

Rev. John Mason (—1694), 1683. Ab.

NEW HAVEN. 6. 6. 4. 6. 6. 6. 4.

THOMAS HASTINGS (1784—1872), 1833.

1. Come, Ho - ly Ghost, in love Shed on us from a - bove Thine own bright ray! Di - vine-ly

good Thou art; Thy sa - cred gifts im - part To glad-den each sad heart: O come to - day!

281

"Veni, Sancte Spiritus."

2 Come, tenderest Friend, and best,
Our most delightful Guest,
With soothing power:
Rest, which the weary know,
Shade, 'mid the noontide glow,
Peace, when deep griefs o'erflow,
Cheer us, this hour!

3 Come, Light serene, and still
Our inmost bosoms fill;
Dwell in each breast;
We know no dawn but Thine;

Send forth Thy beams divine,
On our dark souls to shine,
And make us blest!

4 Come, all the faithful bless;
Let all who Christ confess,
His praise employ:
Give virtue's rich reward;
Victorious death accord,
And, with our glorious Lord,
Eternal joy!

Hermannus Contractus? (1013—1054),
Tr. by Rev. Ray Palmer (1808—), 1858.

KELSO. 7.6 l.   EDWARD JOHN HOPKINS (1818—   ), 1872.

1. GRA - CIOUS Spir - it, dwell with me; I my - self would gra - cious be,

And with words that help and heal Would Thy life in mine re - veal,

And with ac - tions bold and meek Would for Christ my Sav - iour speak.

282   *"Dwell with me."*

2 Truthful Spirit, dwell with me ;
   I myself would truthful be,
   And with wisdom kind and clear
   Let Thy life in mine appear,
   And with actions brotherly
   Speak my Lord's sincerity.

3 Tender Spirit, dwell with me ;
   I myself would tender be,
   Shut my heart up like a flower
   At temptation's darksome hour,
   Open it when shines the sun,
   And His love by fragrance own.

4 Silent Spirit, dwell with me ;
   I myself would quiet be,
   Quiet as the growing blade

Which through earth its way has made ;
Silently, like morning light,
Putting mists and chills to flight.

5 Mighty Spirit, dwell with me ;
   I myself would mighty be,
   Mighty so as to prevail
   Where unaided man must fail,
   Ever by a mighty hope
   Pressing on, and bearing up.

6 Holy Spirit, dwell with me ;
   I myself would holy be ;
   Separate from sin, I would
   Choose and cherish all things good,
   And what ever I can be
   Give to Him, who gave me Thee !

   Rev. Thomas Toke Lynch (1818—1871), 187.

EMMANUEL. C. M.   Arr. from LUDWIG von BEETHOVEN (1770—1827).

1. ENTHRONED on high, Al - might - y Lord, Thy Ho - ly Ghost send down ;

Ful - fil in us Thy faith - ful word, And all Thy mer - cies crown.

283 *"Thy Spirit in our Heart."*

2 Though on our heads no tongues of fire
Their wondrous powers impart,
Grant, Saviour, what we more desire,
Thy Spirit in our heart.

3 Spirit of life, and light, and love,
Thy heavenly influence give;
Quicken our souls, born from above,
In Christ that we may live.

4 To our benighted minds reveal
The glories of His grace,
And bring us where no clouds conceal
The brightness of His face.

5 His love within us shed abroad,
Life's ever-springing well:
Till God in us, and we in God,
In love eternal dwell.

Rev. Thomas Haweis (1732—1820), 1792

INVOCATION. 8.7,7.7.8.8.

UZZIAH CHRISTOPHER BURNAP (1834—).

Ho - ly Ghost, dis - pel our sad - ness, Pierce the clouds of sin - ful night;
Come, Thou Source of sweet - est glad - ness, Breathe Thy life and spread Thy light;

Lov - ing Spir - it, God of peace, Great Dis - trib - u - ter of grace,

Rest up - on this con - gre - ga - tion; Hear, O hear, our sup - pli - ca - tion.

284 *"O du allersüss'te Freude."*

2 From that height which knows no measure,
As a gracious shower, descend,
Bringing down the richest treasure
Man can wish, or God can send.
O Thou Glory shining down
From the Father and the Son,
Grant us Thy illumination;
Rest on all this congregation.

3 Come, Thou best of all donations
God can give, or we implore:
Having Thy sweet consolations,
We need wish for nothing more:
Holy Spirit, heavenly Dove.
Now, descending from above,
Rest on all this congregation;
Make our hearts Thy habitation.

Rev. Paul Gerhardt (1606—1676), 1653. Ab.
Tr. by Rev. Augustus Montague Toplady (1740—1778), 1776. Ab.

PRIERE. 7. 3l.   Arr. by WILLIAM HENRY MONK (1823—   ), 1861.

1. Ho - LY Spir - it, Lord of Light, From Thy clear ce-

- les - - tial height, Thy pure beam - ing ra - diance give.

285 *"Veni, Sancte Spiritus."*

2 Come, Thou Father of the poor,
  Come, with treasures which endure,
    Come, Thou Light of all that live.

3 Thou, of all consolers best,
  Visiting the troubled breast,
    Dost refreshing peace bestow.

4 Thou in toil art comfort sweet,
  Pleasant coolness in the heat,
    Solace in the midst of woe.

5 If Thou take Thy grace away,
  Nothing pure in man will stay;
    All his good is turned to ill.

6 Heal our wounds, our strength renew
  On our dryness pour Thy dew;
    Wash the stains of guilt away.

7 Bend the stubborn heart and will,
  Melt the frozen, warm the chill;
    Guide the steps that go astray.

8 Thou, on those who evermore
  Thee confess and Thee adore,
    In Thy sevenfold gifts descend.

9 Give them comfort when they die,
  Give them life with Thee on high;
    Give them joys that never end.

Hermannus Contractus? (1013—1054).
Tr. by Rev. Edward Caswall (1814—1878), 1849. Ab.

286 *Pleading for Mercy.*

1 LORD, in this Thy mercy's day,
  Ere from us it pass away,
    On our knees we fall and pray.

2 Holy Jesus, grant us tears,
  Fill us with heart-searching fears,
    Ere that day of doom appears.

3 Lord, on us Thy Spirit pour,
  Kneeling lowly at the door,
    Ere it close for evermore.

4 By Thy night of agony,
  By Thy supplicating cry,
    By Thy willingness to die,

5 By Thy tears of bitter woe
  For Jerusalem below,
    Let us not Thy love forego.

6 Judge and Saviour of our race,
  Grant us, when we see Thy face,
    With Thy ransomed ones a place.

Rev. Isaac Williams, (1802—1865), 1844. Ab

BARNBY. C. M.

JOSEPH BARNBY (1838—). 1896.

1. A GLO - RY gilds the sa - cred page, Ma - jes - tic, like the sun;

It gives a light to ev - 'ry age, It gives, but bor - rows none.

287 *"The Light and Glory of the Word."*
Ps. cxix. 130. 2 Cor. iv. 4.

2 The hand, that gave it, still supplies
The gracious light and heat;
Its truths upon the nations rise,
They rise, but never set.

3 Let everlasting thanks be Thine,
For such a bright display,
As makes a world of darkness shine
With beams of heavenly day.

4 My soul rejoices to pursue
The steps of Him I love,
Till glory breaks upon my view,
In brighter worlds above.
William Cowper (1731—1800), 1779. Ab.

288 *A Lamp, and a Light.*
Ps. cxix. 105. 2 Tim. iii. 16.

1 How precious is the Book divine,
By inspiration given: ·

Bright as a lamp its doctrines shine,
To guide our souls to Heaven.

2 Its light, descending from above,
Our gloomy world to cheer,
Displays a Saviour's boundless love,
And brings His glories near.

3 It shows to man his wandering ways,
And where his feet have trod;
And brings to view the matchless grace
Of a forgiving God.

4 It sweetly cheers our drooping hearts,
In this dark vale of tears;
Life, light, and joy it still imparts,
And quells our rising fears.

5 This lamp, thro' all the tedious night
Of life, shall guide our way,
Till we behold the clearer light
Of an eternal day.
Rev. John Fawcett (1739—1817), 1782. Ab.

CHESTERFIELD. C. M.

Rev. THOMAS HAWEIS (1732—1820), 1792.

MARLOW. C. M.

English Melody. Arr. by LOWELL MASON (1792—1872), 1832.

1. LA - DEN with guilt, and full of fears, I fly to Thee, my Lord;

And not a glimpse of hope ap - pears, But in Thy writ - ten word.

289 *The Scriptures our only Help and Guide.*

2 This is the field where hidden lies
The pearl of price unknown:
That merchant is divinely wise,
Who makes the pearl his own.

3 This is the judge that ends the strife,
Where wit and reason fail;

My guide to everlasting life,
Through all this gloomy vale.

4 O may Thy counsels, mighty God,
My roving feet command;
Nor I forsake the happy road,
That leads to Thy right hand.

Rev. Isaac Watts (1674—1748), 1709. Ab.

DALLAS. 7.

From MARIA LUIGI CHERUBINI (1760—1842).

1. HO - LY Bi - ble, book di - vine, Pre - cious treas - ure, thou art mine;

Mine to tell me whence I came, Mine to teach me what I am.

290 *"Holy Bible, Book Divine."*

2 Mine to chide me when I rove,
Mine to show a Saviour's love;
Mine art thou to guide my feet,
Mine to judge, condemn, acquit.

3 Mine to comfort in distress,
If the Holy Spirit bless;

Mine to show by living faith
Man can triumph over death.

4 Mine to tell of joys to come,
Light and life beyond the tomb:
Holy Bible, book divine,
Precious treasure, thou art mine.

John Burton (1773—1822), 1805. Alt.

291

"Walte, walte nah und fern."   7.

1 SPREAD, O spread, thou mighty Word,
Spread the kingdom of the Lord,
Wheresoe'er His breath has given
Life to beings meant for Heaven.

2 Tell them how the Father's will
Made the world, and keeps it still;
How He sent His Son to save
All who help and comfort crave.

3 Word of life, most pure and strong,
Lo, for Thee the nations long:
Spread, till from its dreary night
All the world awakes to light.

4 Lord of harvest, let there be
Joy and strength to work for Thee:
Let the nations, far and near,
See Thy light, and learn Thy fear.

Rev. Jonathan Frederic Bahnmaier (1774—1841), 1827.
Tr. by Miss Catherine Winkworth (1827,—1878), 1855. Ab.

KÖNIGSBERG. 7.6.D.

Har. by FELIX MENDELSSOHN-BARTHOLDY (1809—1847).

1. O WORD of God in-car-nate, O Wis-dom from on high, O Truth unchang-ed, un-

-chang-ing, O Light of our dark sky; We praise Thee for the ra-diance That

from the hal-lowed page, A lan-tern to our foot-steps, Shines on from age to age.

292

"O Word of God incarnate."

2 The Church from Thee, her Master,
Received the gift divine;
And still that light she lifteth
O'er all the earth to shine.
It is the golden casket
Where gems of truth are stored;
It is the Heaven-drawn picture
Of Thee, the living Word.

3 It floateth like a banner
Before God's host unfurled;
It shineth like a beacon
Above the darkling world;

It is the chart and compass,
That o'er life's surging sea,
Mid mists, and rocks, and quicksands,
Still guide, O Christ, to Thee.

4 O make Thy Church, dear Saviour,
A lamp of burnished gold,
To bear before the nations
Thy true light, as of old.
O teach Thy wandering pilgrims
By this their path to trace,
Till, clouds and darkness ended,
They see Thee face to face.

Bp. William Walsham How (1823—   ), 1867.

UXBRIDGE. L. M.

LOWELL MASON (1792—1872), 1830.

1. THE heav'ns de-clare Thy glo-ry, Lord, In ev-'ry star Thy wis-dom shines;

But when our eyes be-hold Thy Word, We read Thy Name in fair-er lines.

293 *The two Revelations.*
Ps. xix.

2 The rolling sun, the changing light,
  And nights and days, Thy power confess,
But the blest volume Thou hast writ,
  Reveals Thy justice and Thy grace.

3 Sun, moon, and stars, convey Thy praise
  Round the whole earth, and never stand:
So when Thy truth began its race,
  It touched and glanced on every land.

4 Nor shall Thy spreading gospel rest,
  Till thro' the world Thy truth has run;
Till Christ has all the nations blessed
  That see the light, and feel the sun.

5 Great Sun of Righteousness, arise,
  Bless the dark world with heavenly
    light;
Thy gospel makes the simple wise,
  Thy laws are pure, Thy judgments right.
Rev. Isaac Watts (1674—1748), 1719. Ab.

294 *"God's Word our Guide."*

1 GOD, in the gospel of His Son,
  Makes His eternal counsels known:
Where love in all its glory shines,
  And truth is drawn in fairest lines.

2 Here sinners, of a humble frame,
  May taste His grace, and learn His Name;
May read, in characters of blood,
  The wisdom, power, and grace of God.

3 Here faith reveals to mortal eyes
  A brighter world beyond the skies;
Here shines the light which guides our
    way
From earth to realms of endless day.

4 O grant us grace, Almighty Lord,
  To read and mark Thy holy Word;
Its truth with meekness to receive,
  And by its holy precepts live.
Rev. Benjamin Beddome (1717—1795), 1787. Ab. and alt.
Rev. Thomas Cotterill (1779—1823), 1819. Ab.

295 *Thanks for the Gospel.*

1 LET everlasting glories crown
  Thy head, my Saviour, and my Lord:
Thy hands have brought salvation down,
  And writ the blessings in Thy Word.

2 In vain the trembling conscience seeks
  Some solid ground to rest upon;
With long despair the spirit breaks,
  Till we apply to Christ alone.

3 How well Thy blessed truths agree,
  How wise and holy Thy commands;
Thy promises, how firm they be,
  How firm our hope and comfort stands!

4 Should all the forms that men devise
  Assault my faith with treacherous art,
I'd call them vanity and lies,
  And bind the Gospel to my heart.
Rev. Isaac Watts, 1709. Ab.

SCOTLAND. 12.

JOHN CLARKE (1770–1849), 1800.

1. The voice of free grace cries, Es-cape to the mountain; For A-dam's lost race, Christ has o-pen'd a fount-ain;

{ For sin, and un-cleanness, and ev-'ry trans-gres-sion, His blood flows most free-ly, in streams of sal-va-tion, His blood flows most free-ly, in streams of sal-va-tion. }

{ Hal-le-lu-jah to the Lamb, who hath pur-chased our par-don, We'll praise Him a-gain, when we pass o-ver Jor-dan, We'll praise Him a-gain, when we pass o-ver Jor-dan. }

296

"The Voice of Free Grace."

2 Ye souls that are wounded, O flee to the Saviour;
   He calls you in mercy, 'tis infinite favor;
   Your sins are increaséd as high as a mountain,
   His blood can remove them, it flows from the fountain.
       Hallelujah, &c.

3 With joy shall we stand, when escaped to the shore;
   With harps in our hands, we will praise Him the more;
   We'll range the sweet plains on the banks of the river,
   And sing of salvation for ever and ever.
       Hallelujah, &c.

Rev. Richard Burdsall (1735–1824), 1796. Ab. and alt.

297

"The merciful Saviour."

1 O COME to the merciful Saviour that calls you,
   O come to the Lord who forgives and forgets;
   Though dark be the fortune on earth that befalls you,
   There's a bright home above, where the sun never sets.—REF.

2 O come then to Jesus, whose arms are extended
   To fold His dear children in closest embrace.
   O come, for your exile will shortly be ended,
   And Jesus will show you His beautiful face.—REF.

3 Then come to the Saviour, whose mercy grows brighter
   The longer you look at the depths of His love;
   And fear not, 'tis Jesus, and life's cares grow lighter
   As you think of the home and the glory above.—REF.

Rev. Frederick William Faber (1814–1863), 1849. Ab.

LENOX. H. M.

LEWIS EDSON (1748—1820), 1782.

1. Blow ye the trumpet, blow The glad-ly solemn sound; Let all the nations know, To earth's remotest bound,

The year of ju - bi - lee is come, The year of ju - bi - lee is come; Return, ye ransom'd sinners, home.

The year of ju - bi - lee is come, The year of ju - bi - lee is come; Return, ye ran - som'd sinners, home.

298   "The Year of Jubilee is come."

2 Jesus, our great High-Priest,
    Hath full atonement made;
  Ye weary spirits, rest,
    Ye mournful souls, be glad:
  The year of jubilee is come;
  Return, ye ransomed sinners, home.

3 Extol the Lamb of God,
    The all-atoning Lamb;
  Redemption in His blood
    Throughout the world proclaim:
  The year of jubilee is come;
  Return, ye ransomed sinners, home.

4 Ye, who have sold for naught
    Your heritage above,
  Shall have it back unbought,
    The gift of Jesus' love:
  The year of jubilee is come;
  Return, ye ransomed sinners, home.

5 The Gospel trumpet hear,
    The news of heavenly grace;
  And, saved from earth, appear
    Before your Saviour's face:
  The year of jubilee is come;
  Return, ye ransomed sinners, home.
        Rev. Charles Wesley (1708—1788), 1750.   Ab.

ROSEFIELD. 7. 6l.

Rev. CÆSAR HENRI ABRAHAM MALAN (1787—1864), 1830.

1. { From the cross up - lift - ed high, Where the Sav - iour deigns to die, }
   { What me - lo - dious sounds I hear, Burst - ing on my rav - ish'd ear: }

"Love's re - deem - ing work is done, Come and wel - come, sin - ner, come."

299

"Let him come unto Me."
JOHN vii. 37.

2 "Sprinkled now with blood the throne;
Why beneath thy burdens groan?
On My piercéd body laid,
Justice owns the ransom paid:
Bow the knee, and kiss the Son,
Come and welcome, sinner, come.

3 "Spread for thee, the festal board
See with richest dainties stored;
To thy Father's bosom prest

Yet again a child confest,
Never from His house to roam;
Come and welcome, sinner, come.

4 "Soon the days of life shall end;
Lo! I come, your Saviour, Friend,
Safe your spirits to convey
To the realms of endless day,
Up to My eternal home:
Come and welcome, sinner, come."

Rev. Thomas Hawcis (1732—1820), 1792.

ANGEL TOWER. 7.6.D.

WILLIAM HENRY LONGHURST (1819—

1. O Je - sus, Thou art stand - ing Out - side the fast - clos'd door, In low - ly pa - tience

wait - ing To pass the thres - hold o'er: Shame on us, Chris - tian breth - ren,

His Name and sign who bear, O shame, thrice shame up - on us, To keep Him stand-ing there!

300

Standing at the Door.

2 O Jesus, Thou art knocking:
And lo, that hand is scarred,
And thorns Thy brow encircle,
And tears Thy face have marred.
O love that passeth knowledge,
So patiently to wait!
O sin that hath no equal,
So fast to bar the gate!

3 O Jesus, Thou art pleading
In accents meek and low,
"I died for you, My children,
And will ye treat Me so?"
O Lord, with shame and sorrow
We open now the door:
Dear Saviour, enter, enter,
And leave us never more.

Bp. William Walsham How (1823—), 1854.

ERIE. 8.7. D. CHARLES CROZART CONVERSE (1834—).

1. There's a wideness in God's mer - cy, Like the wideness of the sea: There's a kindness in His

jus - tice, Which is more than lib - er - ty. There is wel come for the sin - ner,

And more gra - ces for the good; There is mer-cy with the Sav iour; There is healing in His blood.

301

Come to Jesus.

2 There is plentiful redemption
In the blood that has been shed;
There is joy for all the members
In the sorrows of the Head.
If our love were but more simple,
We should take Him at His word;
And our lives would be all sunshine
In the sweetness of our Lord.

Rev. Frederick William Faber (1814—1863), 1849. Ab.

302

"In Everything by Prayer."
Phil. iv. 6.

1 WHAT a Friend we have in Jesus,
All our sins and griefs to bear!
What a privilege to carry
Everything to God in prayer!
O what peace we often forfeit,
O what needless pain we bear,

All because we do not carry
Everything to God in prayer!

2 Have we trials and temptations?
Is there trouble anywhere?
We should never be discouraged—
Take it to the Lord in prayer.
Can we find a friend so faithful,
Who will all our sorrows share?
Jesus knows our every weakness:
Take it to the Lord in prayer.

3 Are we weak and heavy laden,
Cumbered with a load of care?
Precious Saviour, still our refuge!
Take it to the Lord in prayer.
Do thy friends despise, forsake thee?
Take it to the Lord in prayer;
In His arms He'll take and shield thee;
Thou wilt find a solace there.

Rev. Horatius Bonar (1808—   )

COME, YE DISCONSOLATE. 11.10.

Choir.

SAMUEL WEBBE (1740—1816), 1790.

1. COME, ye dis-con-so-late, wher-e'er ye lan-guish, Come to the mer-cy-seat, fer-vent-ly kneel,

Congregation.

Here bring your wounded hearts,here tell your an-guish, Earth has no sorrows that Heav'n cannot heal.

303

"Come, ye disconsolate."

2 Joy of the desolate. Light of the straying.
Hope of the penitent, fadeless and pure ;
Here speaks the Comforter, tenderly saying,
Earth has no sorrows that Heaven cannot cure.

3 Here see the Bread of Life, see waters flowing
Forth from the throne of God, pure from above ;
Come to the feast prepared, come, ever knowing
Earth has no sorrows but Heaven can remove.

Thomas Moore (1779—1852), 1816. Vs. 1, 2, Alt.
Thomas Hastings (1784—1872), V. 3.

HENLEY. 11.10.

LOWELL MASON (1792—1872), 1854.

1. COME un-to me, when shadows darkly gath-er, When the sad heart is wea-ry and dis-trest,

Seek-ing for com-fort from your heav'nly Fa-ther, Come un-to me, and I will give you rest.

304

Christ giving Rest

2 Large are the mansions in thy Father's
dwelling, [dim.
Glad are the homes that sorrows never
Sweet are the harps in holy music swelling,
Soft are the tones which raise the
heavenly hymn.

3 There, like an Eden blossoming in
gladness, [rudely pressed ;
Bloom the fair flowers the earth too
Come unto me all ye who droop in
sadness,
Come unto me, and I will give you rest.

Unknown Author, 1854. Ab.

SALVATION FREE.

OLIPHANT. 8.7.4.

PIERRE-MARIE-FRANCOIS de SALES BAILLOT (1771—1842), 1830.
Arr. by LOWELL MASON (1792—1872), 1832.

1. COME, ye sin - ners, poor and wretch-ed, Weak and wounded, sick and sore: Je - sus read - y

stands to save you, Full of pit - y, join'd with pow'r: He is a - ble, He is a - ble,

He is will - ing, doubt no more, He is will - ing, doubt no more.

305

"Come, and welcome."

2 Let not conscience make you linger,
　Nor of fitness fondly dream;
All the fitness He requireth
　Is to feel your need of Him:
　　This He gives you;
　'Tis the Spirit's rising beam.

3 Come, ye weary, heavy-laden,
　Bruised and mangled by the fall;
If you tarry till you're better,

You will never come at all:
　Not the righteous,
Sinners, Jesus came to call.

4 Lo, th' incarnate God, ascended,
　Pleads the merit of His blood:
Venture on Him, venture wholly,
　Let no other trust intrude;
　　None but Jesus
Can do helpless sinners good.

Rev. Joseph Hart (1712—1768), 1759. Ab.

STEPHANOS. 8.5.8.3.

WILLIAM HENRY MONK (1823—). 1861.

1. ART thou weary, art thou languid, Art thou sore dis-trest? "Come to me," saith One, "and coming Be at rest!"

306

Κόπον τε καὶ κάματον.

2 Hath He marks to lead me to Him,
　If He be my Guide?
"In His feet and hands are wound-prints,
　And His side."

3 Is there diadem, as Monarch,
　That His brow adorns?
'Yea, a crown in very surety,
　But of thorns."

4 If I still hold closely to Him,
What hath He at last?
"Sorrow vanquished, labor ended,
Jordan past."

5 If I ask Him to receive me,
Will He say me nay?
"Not till earth, and not till Heaven
Pass away."
Stephen of St. Sabas (725—794).
Tr by Rev. John Mason Neale (1818—1866), 1862. Ab.

GORTON. S. M. LUDWIG von BEETHOVEN (1770—1827).

1. THE Spir - it, in our hearts, Is whis-p'ring, "Sin - ner, come;" The
Bride, the Church of Christ, pro - claims To all His chil - dren, "Come."

307 *"And the Spirit and the Bride say, Come."*
Rev. xvii. 17—20.

2 Let him that heareth, say
To all about him, "Come;"
Let him that thirsts for righteousness,
To Christ, the Fountain, come.

3 Yes, whosoever will,
O let him freely come,
And freely drink the stream of life:
'Tis Jesus bids him come.

4 Lo, Jesus, who invites,
Declares, "I quickly come;"
Lord, even so; I wait Thine hour;
Jesus, my Saviour, come.
Bp. Henry Ustick Onderdonk (1789—1858), 1826.

308 *The Gospel Trumpet.*

1 YE trembling captives, hear;
The gospel-trumpet sounds;
No music more can charm the ear,
Or heal your heart-felt wounds.

2 'Tis not the trump of war,
Nor Sinai's awful roar;
Salvation's news is spread afar,
And vengeance is no more.

3 Forgiveness, love, and peace,
Glad Heaven aloud proclaims;
And earth the jubilee's release
With eager rapture claims.

4 Far, far to distant lands
The saving news shall spread;
And Jesus all His willing bands
In glorious triumph lead.
Samuel Boyce ( ), 1801. Sl alt.

309 *"Behold the Ark of God."*

1 O CEASE, my wandering soul,
On restless wing to roam;
All the wide world, to either pole,
Has not for thee a home.

2 Behold the Ark of God,
Behold the open door;
Hasten to gain that dear abode,
And rove, my soul, no more.

3 There, safe thou shalt abide,
There, sweet shall be thy rest,
And every longing satisfied,
With full salvation blest.
Rev. William Augustus Muhlenberg (1796—1877), 1826. Ab.

BERA. L. M.

JOHN EDGAR GOULD (1822—1875), 1849.

1. RE - TURN, O wan - der - er, re - turn, And seek thine in - jured Fa - ther's face;

Those new de - sires that in thee burn, Were kin - dled by re - claim - ing grace.

310   *"Return!"*   JER. xxxi. 18—22.

2 Return, O wanderer, return,
And seek a Father's melting heart;
Whose pitying eyes thy grief discern,
Whose hand can heal thine inward smart.

3 Return, O wanderer, return,
He heard thy deep repentant sigh,
He saw thy softened spirit mourn,
When no intruding ear was nigh.

4 Return, O wanderer, return,
Thy Saviour bids thy spirit live;
Go to His bleeding feet, and learn
How freely Jesus can forgive.

5 Return, O wanderer, return,
And wipe away the falling tear;
'Tis God who says, "No longer mourn,"
'Tis mercy's voice invites thee near.

Rev. William Bengo Collyer (1782—1854), 1812. Ab.

ZEPHYR. L. M.

WILLIAM BATCHELDER BRADBURY (1816—1868), 1844.

1. BE - HOLD, a Stran - ger at the door: He gen - tly knocks, has knock'd be - fore;

Has wait - ed long, is wait - ing still: You treat no oth - er friend so ill.

311 *Christ knocking at the Door.*
Cant. v 2. Rev. iii. 20.

2 O lovely attitude! He stands
With melting heart, and laden hands:
O matchless kindness! and He shows
This matchless kindness to His foes.

3 Rise, touched with gratitude divine;
Turn out His enemy and thine,
That soul-destroying monster, Sin;
And let the heavenly Stranger in.

4 Admit Him, for the human breast
Ne'er entertained so kind a guest:
Admit Him, ere His anger burn:
His feet, departed, ne'er return!
Rev. Joseph Grigg (—1768), 1765. Ab. and alt.

312 *"Jesu auctor clementia."* L. M.

1 OF Him who did salvation bring,
I could forever think and sing;
Arise, ye needy, He'll relieve:
Arise, ye guilty, He'll forgive.

2 Ask but His grace, and lo, 'tis given;
Ask, and He turns your hell to Heaven:
Though sin and sorrow wound my soul,
Jesus, Thy balm will make it whole.

3 To shame our sins, He blushed in blood;
He closed His eyes to show us God:
Let all the world fall down and know,
That none but God such love can show.

4 'Tis Thee I love, for Thee alone
I shed my tears, and make my moan,
Where'er I am, where'er I move,
I meet the object of my love.

5 Insatiate, to this spring I fly;
I drink, and yet am ever dry:
Ah, who against Thy charms is proof?
Ah, who that loves can love enough?
Bernard of Clairvaux (1091—1153), 1140.
Tr. by Rev. Anthony Wilhelm Boehm (1673—1722), 1712. Alt.

HORTON. 7.

XAVIER SCHNYDER von WARTENSEE (1786—1868), 1826.

1. COME, said Je - sus' sa - cred voice, Come, and make My path your choice;

I will guide you to your home, Wea - ry pil - grim, hith - er come.

313 *"The gracious Call."*
MATT. xi 25—30.

2 Thou who, houseless, sole, forlorn,
Long hast borne the proud world's scorn,
Long hast roamed the barren waste,
Weary pilgrim, hither haste.

3 Ye who, tossed on beds of pain,
Seek for ease, but seek in vain;

Ye, by fiercer anguish torn,
In remorse for guilt who mourn;

4 Hither come, for here is found
Balm that flows for every wound,
Peace that ever shall endure,
Rest eternal, sacred, sure.
Mrs. Anna Laetitia Barbauld (1743—1825), 1825. Ab. and alt.

GREENWOOD. S. M.
JOSEPH EMERSON SWEETSER (1825—1873), 1849.

1. O WHERE shall rest be found, Rest for the wea - ry soul?

'Twere vain the o - cean-depths to sound, Or pierce to ei - ther pole.

314   *The Issues of Life and Death.*

2 The world can never give
   The bliss for which we sigh ;
'Tis not the whole of life to live,
   Nor all of death to die.

3 Beyond this vale of tears
   There is a life above,
Unmeasured by the flight of years ;
   And all that life is love.

4 There is a death, whose pang
   Outlasts the fleeting breath :
O what eternal horrors hang
   Around the second death !

5 Lord God of truth and grace,
   Teach us that death to shun,
Lest we be banished from Thy face,
   And evermore undone.
     James Montgomery (1771—1854), 1819, 1853. **Ab.**

315   *"Out of the Depths."*
      Ps. cxxx.

1 Out of the deep I call
   To Thee, O Lord, to Thee ;
Before Thy throne of grace I fall,
   Be merciful to me.

2 Out of the deep I cry,
   The woful deep of sin,

Of evil done in days gone by,
   Of evil now within.

3 Out of the deep of fear,
   And dread of coming shame,
From morning watch till night is near
   I plead the precious Name.
     Rev. Sir Henry Williams Baker (1821—1877), 1868. **Ab.**

316   *Tears of Penitence.*

1 Did Christ o'er sinners weep,
   And shall our cheeks be dry ?
Let floods of penitential grief
   Burst forth from every eye.

2 The Son of God in tears
   Angels with wonder see :
Be thou astonished, O my soul,
   He shed those tears for thee.

3 He wept that we might weep
   Each sin demands a tear ;
In Heaven alone no sin is found,
   And there's no weeping there.

4 Then tender be our hearts,
   Our eyes in sorrow dim,
Till every tear from every eye
   Is wiped away by Him.
     Rev. Benjamin Beddome (1717—1795), 1787. **Vs. 1. 2. 3**

WARNER. L. M.

GIOACCHIMO ROSSINI (1792—1868).
Arr. by GEORGE KINGSLEY (1811—1884), 1833.

1. With bro - ken heart, and con - trite sigh, A trem - bling sin - ner, Lord, I cry:

Thy pard - 'ning grace is rich and free; O God, be mer - ci - ful to me.

317 *The Prayer of the Publican.*
Luke xviii. 13

2 I smite upon my troubled breast,
With deep and conscious guilt opprest,
Christ and His cross my only plea ;
O God, be merciful to me.

3 Far off I stand with tearful eyes,
Nor dare uplift them to the skies ;
But Thou dost all my anguish see ;
O God, be merciful to me.

Nor alms, nor deeds that I have done,
Can for a single sin atone ;
To Calvary alone I flee ;
O God, be merciful to me.

5 And when, redeemed from sin and hell,
With all the ransomed throng I dwell,
My raptured song shall ever be,
God has been merciful to me.
Rev. Cornelius Elven (1797—), 1852.

318 *Pleading for Pardon.*
Ps. li.

1 Show pity, Lord, O Lord, forgive ;
Let a repenting rebel live :
Are not Thy mercies large and free?
May not a sinner trust in Thee?

2 O wash my soul from every sin,
And make my guilty conscience clean ;
Here on my heart the burden lies,
And past offences pain mine eyes.

3 My lips with shame my sins confess,
Against Thy law, against Thy grace :
Lord, should Thy judgments grow severe,
I am condemned, but Thou art clear.

4 Yet save a trembling sinner, Lord,
Whose hope, still hovering round Thy
Word,
Would light on some sweet promise there,
Some sure support against despair.
Rev. Isaac Watts (1674—1748), 1719. Ab.

319 *"Gott rufet noch."*

1 God calling yet ! shall I not hear?
Earth's pleasures shall I still hold dear?
Shall life's swift passing years all fly,
And still my soul in slumber lie?

2 God calling yet ! and shall He knock,
And I my heart the closer lock?
He still is waiting to receive,
And shall I dare His Spirit grieve?

3 God calling yet ! and shall I give
No heed, but still in bondage live?
I wait, but He does not forsake ;
He calls me still ; my heart, awake !

4 God calling yet ! I cannot stay ;
My heart I yield without delay :
Vain world, farewell, from thee I part ;
The voice of God hath reached my heart.
Gerhard Tersteegen (1697—1769), 1729.
Tr. by Miss Jane Borthwick (1825—), 1854. Ab. and alt.

ST. JOHN. C. M.   JAMES TURLE (1802—1882), 1862.

1. AP PROACH, my soul, the mer - cy - seat Where Je - sus an - swers pray'r;

There hum - bly fall be - fore His feet, For none can per - ish there.

320   *Coming to Christ.*

2 Thy promise is my only plea,
   With this I venture nigh ;
Thou callest burdened souls to Thee,
   And such, O Lord, am I.

3 Bowed down beneath a load of sin,
   By Satan sorely prest,
By war without, and fears within,
   I come to Thee for rest.

4 Be Thou my shield and hiding-place,
   That, sheltered near Thy side,
I may my fierce accuser face,
   And tell him, Thou hast died.

5 O wondrous love, to bleed and die,
   To bear the cross and shame,
That guilty sinners, such as I,
   Might plead Thy gracious Name.

Rev. John Newton (1725—1807), 1779. Ab.

321   *Crying for Mercy.*

1 O LORD, turn not Thy face from me,
   Who lie in woful state,
Lamenting all my sinful life,
   Before Thy mercy-gate :

2 A gate that opens wide to those
   That do lament their sin ;
Shut not that gate against me, Lord,
   But let me enter in.

3 And call me not to strict account
   How I have sojourned here ;
For then my guilty conscience knows
   How vile I shall appear.

4 Mercy, good Lord, mercy I ask ;
   This is my humble prayer ;
For mercy, Lord, is all my suit,
   O let Thy mercy spare.

John Mardley (   ), 1562. Ab. and alt.

AVON. C. M.   HUGH WILSON (   ), 1768.

MERCY-SEAT. C. M.

Arr. from FRITZ SPINDLER (1817–   ).

1. Prostrate, dear Je-sus, at Thy feet, A guilt-y reb-el lies: And up-wards to Thy mer-cy-seat Pre-sumes to lift his eyes, Pre-sumes to lift his eyes.

322 *At Christ's Feet.*

2 O let not justice frown me hence;
　Stay, stay the vengeful storm:
Forbid it, that Omnipotence
　Should crush a feeble worm.

3 If tears of sorrow would suffice
　To pay the debt I owe,
Tears should from both my weeping eyes
　In ceaseless torrents flow.

4 But no such sacrifice I plead
　To expiate my guilt;
No tears but those which Thou hast shed,
　No blood but Thou hast spilt.

5 Think of Thy sorrows, dearest Lord,
　And all my sins forgive;
Justice will well approve the word,
　That bids the sinner live.

　　　Rev. Samuel Stennett (1727–1795), 1787.

323 *"One only."*

1 When wounded sore the stricken soul
　Lies bleeding and unbound,
One only hand, a piercéd hand,
　Can heal the sinner's wound.

2 When sorrow swells the laden breast,
　And tears of anguish flow,
One only heart, a broken heart,
　Can feel the sinner's woe.

3 When penitence has wept in vain
　Over some foul dark spot,
One only stream, a stream of blood,
　Can wash away the blot.

4 Lift up Thy bleeding hand, O Lord ·
　Unseal that cleansing tide;
We have no shelter from our sin
　But in Thy wounded side.

Mrs. Cecil Frances Alexander (1823–   ), 1858. Ab. and sl. alt.

AOMI. C. M.

HANS GEORG NAEGELI (1773–1836), 1828.
Arr. by LOWELL MASON (1792–1872), 1836.

DORRNANCE. 8.7.

ISAAC BEVERLY WOODBURY (1819-1858), 1850.

1. TAKE me, O my Fa-ther, take me, Take me, save me, through Thy Son;

That, which Thou wouldst have me, make me, Let Thy will in me be done.

324 *"Take me."*

2 Long from Thee my footsteps straying,
   Thorny proved the way I trod;
   Weary come I now, and praying,
   Take me to Thy love, my God.

3 Fruitless years with grief recalling,
   Humbly I confess my sin;
   At Thy feet, O Father, falling,
   To Thy household take me in.

4 Freely now to Thee I proffer
   This relenting heart of mine:

Freely, life and soul I offer,
   Gift unworthy love like Thine.

5 Once the world's Redeemer dying,
   Bore our sins upon the tree;
   On that sacrifice relying,
   Now I look in hope to Thee;

6 Father, take me; all forgiving,
   Fold me to Thy loving breast;
   In Thy love for ever living,
   I must be for ever blest.

Rev. Ray Palmer (1808-), 1865.

ALETTA. 7.

WILLIAM BATCHELDER BRADBURY (1816-1868), 1858.

1. DEPTH of mer-cy, can there be Mer-cy still re-serv'd for me?

Can my God His wrath for-bear? Me, the chief of sin-ners, spare?

325 *After a Relapse into Sin*
Heb. x. 29.

2 I have long withstood His grace,
  Long provoked Him to His face;
  Would not hearken to His calls;
  Grieved Him by a thousand falls.

3 Kindled His relentings are;
  Me He now delights to spare;
  Cries, "How shall I give thee up?"
  Lets the lifted thunder drop.

4 There for me the Saviour stands,
  Shows His wounds, and spreads His [hands;
  God is Love: I know, I feel;
  Jesus weeps, but loves me still.
        Rev. Charles Wesley (1708—1788), 1740. Ab.

326 *Rest in Christ.* **7.**

1 JESUS, full of truth and love,
  We Thy kindest word obey:

Faithful let Thy mercies prove,
Take our load of guilt away.

2 Weary of this war within,
  Weary of this endless strife,
  Weary of ourselves and sin,
  Weary of a wretched life;

3 Burdened with a world of grief,
  Burdened with our sinful load,
  Burdened with this unbelief,
  Burdened with the wrath of God:

4 Lo, we come to Thee for ease,
  True and gracious as Thou art;
  Now our groaning soul release,
  Write forgiveness on our heart.
        Rev. Charles Wesley, 1747. Ab. and alt.
        Rev. John Wesley (1703—1791), 1779.

EVEN ME. 8.7,3.3.7.
Arr. by WILLIAM BATCHELDER BRADBURY, 1862.

1. { Pass me not, O gra-cious Fa-ther, Sin-ful though my heart may be; }
  { Thou might'st curse me, but the rath-er Let Thy mer-cy light on me, }

E-ven me, E-ven me, Let Thy mer-cy light on me.

327 *"Bless me, even me also."*
Gen. xxvii. 34.

2 Pass me not, O tender Saviour,
  Let me love and cling to Thee;
  I am longing for Thy favor;
  When Thou comest, call for me,
    Even me.

3 Pass me not, O mighty Spirit,
  Thou canst make the blind to see;

Witnesser of Jesus' merit,
  Speak the word of power to me,
    Even me.

4 Love of God, so pure and changeless,
  Blood of God, so rich and free,
  Grace of God, so strong and boundless,
  Magnify them all in me,
    Even me.
        Mrs. Elizabeth Codner, 1861. Ab.

JESUS BEST AND DEAREST.

CASTELLO. 7.6, 8.8.7.7.
UZZIAH CHRISTOPHER BURNAP (1834— d. 1870.

1. Je - sus, Name all names a - bove, Je - sus, best and dear - est,
Je - sus, Fount of per - fect love, Ho - liest, ten - derest, near - est;
Je - sus, Source of grace com-plet - est, Je - sus, pur - est, Je - sus, sweet - est,
Je - sus, Well of pow'r di - vine, Make me, keep me, seal me Thine.

328   Ἰησοῦ γλυκύτατε.

2 Jesus, open me the gate
   Which the sinner entered,
Who, in his last dying state,
   Wholly on Thee ventured;
Thou, whose wounds are ever pleading,
And Thy passion interceding,
   From my misery let me rise
   To a home in Paradise.

3 Jesus, crowned with thorns for me,
   Scourged for my transgression,
Witnessing, through agony,
   That Thy good confession;

Jesus, clad in purple raiment,
For my evil making payment;
   Let not all Thy woe and pain,
   Let not Calvary, be in vain.

4 When I cross death's bitter sea,
   And its waves roll higher,
Help the more forsaking me
   As the storm draws nigher;
Jesus, leave me not to languish,
Helpless, hopeless, full of anguish:
   Tell me, "Verily, I say,
   "Thou shalt be with Me to-day."

Theoctistus of the Studium (—800),
Tr. by Rev. John Mason Neale (1818—1866), 1862 Ab.

PENITENTIA. 10.   K. DEARLE ( ).

1. WEA - RY of earth and la - den with my sin, I look to Heav'n and long to en - ter in,

But there no e - vil thing may find a home; And yet I hear a voice that bids me "come."

329

Sin Forgiven.

2 So vile I am, how dare I hope to stand
In the pure glory of that holy land?
Before the whiteness of that throne appear?
Yet there are hands stretched out to draw me near;

3 It is the voice of Jesus that I hear;
His are the hands stretched out to draw me near,
And His the blood that can for all atone,
And set me faultless there before the throne.

4 'Twas He who found me on the deathly wild,
And made me heir of Heaven, the Father's child,
And day by day, whereby my soul may live,
Gives me His grace of pardon, and will give.

5 Yea, Thou wilt answer for me, Righteous Lord:
Thine all the merits, mine the great reward:
Thine the sharp thorns, and mine the golden crown;
Mine the life won, and Thine the life laid down.

                    Rev. Samuel John Stone (1839—   ), 1865. Ab.

BARTHOLOMEW. 10.   LOUIS BOURGEOIS (   ), 1551.
                                   Arr. by CLAUDE GOUDIMEL (1510—1572), 1565.

ST. CRISPIN. L. M.

Sir GEORGE JOB ELVEY (1816—).

1. Just as I am, with - out one plea But that Thy blood was shed for me,

And that Thou bidd'st me come to Thee, O Lamb of God, I come, I come.

330

"Just as I am."
John vi. 37.

2 Just as I am, and waiting not
To rid my soul of one dark blot, [spot,
To Thee, whose blood can cleanse each
O Lamb of God, I come.

3 Just as I am, though tossed about
With many a conflict, many a doubt,
With fears within, and foes without,
O Lamb of God, I come.

4 Just as I am, poor, wretched, blind;
Sight, riches, healing of the mind,
Yea, all I need, in Thee to find,
O Lamb of God, I come

5 Just as I am, Thou wilt receive,
Wilt welcome, pardon, cleanse, relieve:
Because Thy promise I believe,
O Lamb of God, I come.

6 Just as I am, Thy love unknown
Has broken every barrier down:
Now, to be Thine, yea, Thine alone,
O Lamb of God, I come.

Miss Charlotte Elliot (1789—1871), 1836.

331

"Christi Blut und Gerechtigkeit.

1 JESUS, Thy blood and righteousness
My beauty are, my glorious dress:
Midst flaming worlds, in these arrayed,
With joy shall I lift up my head.

2 Fully through these absolved I am
From sin and fear, from guilt and shame:
Thy blood washed out the crimson stains,
And white as snow my soul remains.

3 When from the dust of death I rise
To claim my mansion in the skies,
E'en then, this shall be all my plea,
"Jesus hath lived, hath died for me."

4 This spotless robe the same appears
When ruined nature sinks in years:
No age can change its constant hue;
Thy blood preserves it ever new.

5 O let the dead now hear Thy voice;
Now bid Thy banished ones rejoice:
Their beauty this, their glorious dress,
Jesus, Thy blood and righteousness.

Nicolaus Ludwig Zinzendorf (1700—1760), 1739.
Tr. by Rev. John Wesley (1703—1791), 1740. Ab. and sl. alt.

WOODWORTH. L. M.

WILLIAM BATCHELDER BRADBURY (1816—1868), 1849.

ROCK OF AGES. 7. 6l.

Rev. JOHN BACCHUS DYKES (1823—1876), 1861.

1. Rock of a - ges, cleft for me, Let me hide my - self in Thee; Let the wa - ter and the blood,
From Thy riv - en side which flowed, Be of sin the doub - le cure, Cleanse me from its guilt and pow'r.

332   *"Rock of Ages."*

2 Not the labors of my hands
  Can fulfil Thy law's demands;
  Could my zeal no respite know,
  Could my tears for ever flow,
  All for sin could not atone :
  Thou must save, and Thou alone.

3 Nothing in my hand I bring;
  Simply to Thy cross I cling;
  Naked, come to Thee for dress;
  Helpless, look to Thee for grace;
  Foul, I to the fountain fly;
  Wash me, Saviour, or I die.

4 While I draw this fleeting breath,
  When my eye-lids close in death,
  When I soar to worlds unknown,
  See Thee on Thy judgment-throne,
  Rock of ages, cleft for me,
  Let me hide myself in Thee.
  Rev. Augustus Montague Toplady (1740—1778), 1776. Sl. alt.

333   *"He hath borne our Griefs."*
         Is. liii. 4, 5, 12.

1 Surely Christ thy griefs hath borne ;
  Weeping soul, no longer mourn :
  View Him bleeding on the tree :
  Pouring out His life for thee ·
  There thy every sin He bore ;
  Weeping soul, lament no more.

2 Weary sinner, keep thine eyes
  On th' atoning sacrifice :
  There th' incarnate Deity
  Numbered with transgressors see :
  There His Father's absence mourns,
  Nailed and bruised, and crowned with
  thorns.

3 Cast Thy guilty soul on Him,
  Find Him mighty to redeem ;
  At His feet thy burden lay,
  Look thy doubts and cares away ;
  Now by faith the Son embrace,
  Plead His promise, trust His grace.
  Rev. Augustus Montague Toplady, 1759, 1772. Ab.

TOPLADY. 7. 6l.

THOMAS HASTINGS (1784—1872), 1830.

FINE.

D. G.

COWPER. C. M.　　　　　LOWELL MASON (1792—1872), 1830.

1. THERE is a fount-ain fill'd with blood Drawn from Em-man-uel's veins; And sinners, plung'd be-neath that flood, Lose all their guilt-y stains, Lose all their guilt-y stains.

334　　"A Fountain opened."
　　　　ZECH. XIII. 1.

2 The dying thief rejoiced to see
　That fountain in his day;
And there have I, as vile as he,
　Washed all my sins away.

3 Dear dying Lamb, Thy precious blood
Shall never lose its power,
Till all the ransomed Church of God
Be saved, to sin no more.

4 E'er since, by faith, I saw the stream
　Thy flowing wounds supply,
Redeeming love has been my theme,
　And shall be till I die.

5 And when this feeble, stammering tongue
　Lies silent in the grave,
Then in a nobler, sweeter song,
　I'll sing Thy power to save.
　　　William Cowper (1731—1800), 1779.　Ab. and alt.

ST. MAURA. H. M.　　　Sir ARTHUR SULLIVAN (1842—　), 1872.

1. I BRING my sins to Thee, The sins I can-not count, That all may cleans-ed be In Thy once o-pen'd fount. I bring them, Sav-iour, all to Thee; The burden is too great for me.

335　　"Lord, to whom shall we go?"
　　　　JOHN vi. 68.

2 My heart to Thee I bring,
　The heart I cannot read—
A faithless, wandering thing,
　An evil heart indeed.
I bring it, Saviour, now to Thee,
That fixed and faithful it may be.

3 My life I bring to Thee,
　I would not be my own;
O Saviour, let me be
　Thine ever, Thine alone.
My heart, my life, my all I bring
To Thee, my Saviour and my King!
　Miss Frances Ridley Havergal (1836—1879).

BURNHAM. H. M.

WILLIAM CROFT (1677—1727), 1700.

1. Join all the glo - rious names Of wis - dom, love, and pow'r

That ev - er mor - tals knew, That an - gels ev - er bore: All

are too mean to speak His worth, Too mean to set my Sav - iour forth.

336   *Prophet, Priest, and King.*

2 Great Prophet of my God,
   My tongue would bless Thy Name;
By Thee the joyful news
   Of our salvation came:
The joyful news of sins forgiven,
Of hell subdued, and peace with Heaven.

3 Jesus, my great High Priest,
   Offered His blood and died;
My guilty conscience seeks
   No sacrifice beside:
His powerful blood did once atone,
And now it pleads before the throne.

4 My dear Almighty Lord,
   My Conqueror and my King,
Thy sceptre and Thy sword,
   Thy reigning grace I sing:
Thine is the power; behold, I sit,
In willing bonds, beneath Thy feet.
                    Rev. Isaac Watts (1674—1748), 1709. Ab.

337   *"Wounded for our Transgressions."*
                    Is. liii. 5.

1 Thy works, not mine, O Christ,
   Speak gladness to this heart;
They tell me all is done;
   They bid my fear depart:
To whom save Thee, who canst alone
For sin atone, Lord, shall I flee?

2 Thy wounds, not mine, O Christ,
   Can heal my bruisèd soul;
Thy stripes, not mine, contain
   The balm that makes me whole:
To whom save Thee, who canst alone
For sin atone, Lord, shall I flee?

3 Thy cross, not mine, O Christ,
   Has borne the awful load
Of sins that none in Heaven
   Or earth could bear but God:
To whom save Thee, who canst alone
For sin atone, Lord, shall I flee?

4 Thy death, not mine, O Christ,
   Has paid the ransom due;
Ten thousand deaths like mine
   Would have been all too few:
To whom save Thee, who canst alone
For sin atone, Lord, shall I flee?
                    Rev. Horatius Bonar (1808—   ), 1857. Ab.

MERIBAH. C. P. M.

LOWELL MASON (1792—1872), 1839.

1. O Thou that hear'st the pray'r of faith, Wilt Thou not save a soul from death, That casts it-self on Thee?

I have no ref-uge of my own, But fly to what my Lord hath done, And suffer'd once for me.

338   *The Prayer of Faith.*

2 Slain in the guilty sinner's stead,
His spotless righteousness I plead,
    And His availing blood :
Thy merit, Lord, my robe shall be,
Thy merit shall atone for me,
    And bring me near to God.

3 Then snatch me from eternal death,
The Spirit of adoption breathe,
    His consolations send :
By Him some word of life impart,
And sweetly whisper to my heart,
    "Thy Maker is thy Friend."

Rev. Augustus Montague Toplady (1740—1778), 1759. Ab.

ATHENS. C. M. D.

FELICE GIARDINI (1716—1796), 1760.

1. I HEARD the voice of Je-sus say, "Come un-to Me and rest;

Fine.

Lay down, thou wea-ry one, lay down Thy head up-on My breast."
D. S.—I found in Him a rest-ing-place, And He has made me glad.

D. S.

I came to Je-sus as I was, Wea-ry, and worn, and sad;

339 *The Voice from Galilee.*
John i. 16

2 I heard the voice of Jesus say,
  "Behold, I freely give
The living water; thirsty one,
  Stoop down, and drink, and live."
I came to Jesus, and I drank
  Of that life-giving stream;
My thirst was quenched, my soul revived,
  And now I live in Him.

3 I heard the voice of Jesus say,
  "I am this dark world's Light;
Look unto Me, thy morn shall rise,
  And all thy day be bright."
I looked to Jesus, and I found
  In Him my Star, my Sun;
And in that Light of Life I'll walk
  Till all my journey's done.

Rev. Horatius Bonar (1808—   ), 1857. Sl. alt.

LENOX. H. M.   Lewis Edson (1748—1820), 1781.

1. A - RISE, my soul, a - rise, Shake off thy guilt-y fears; The bleed-ing Sac - ri - fice

In my be - half ap - pears; Be - fore the throne my Sure - ty stands, Be-

Be - fore the throne my Sure - ty stands, Be - fore the throne my

fore the throne my Sure - ty stands, My name is writ - ten on His hands.

Sure - ty stands, My name is writ - - - ten on His hands.

340 *"Behold the Man."*

2 He ever lives above,
  For me to intercede,
His all-redeeming love,
  His precious blood, to plead;
His blood atoned for all our race,
And sprinkles now the throne of grace.

3 Five bleeding wounds He bears,
  Received on Calvary;
They pour effectual prayers,
  They strongly plead for me:—
Forgive him, O forgive, they cry,
Nor let that ransom'd sinner die.

4 The Father hears Him pray,
  His dear anointed One:
He cannot turn away
  The presence of His Son:
His Spirit answers to the blood,
And tells me I am born of God.

5 My God is reconciled,
  His pardoning voice I hear,
He owns me for His child;
  I can no longer fear,
With confidence I now draw nigh,
And Father, Abba, Father, cry.

Rev. Charles Wesley (1708—1788), 1742.

SUBJECTION. S. M.

GIOVANNI PAISIELLO (1741—1816).

1. DEAR Lord and Mas - ter mine, Thy hap - py serv - ant see:

My Con - qu'ror, with what joy di - vine Thy cap - tive clings to Thee.

341

Sweet Subjection.

2 I would not walk alone,
  But still with Thee, my God;
  At every step my blindness own,
  And ask of Thee the road.

3 The weakness I enjoy
  That casts me on Thy breast;

The conflicts that Thy strength employ
Make me divinely blest.

4 Dear Lord and Master mine,
  Still keep Thy servant true;
  My Guardian and my Guide divine,
  Bring, bring Thy pilgrim through.

Thomas Hornblower Gill (1819—), 1859. Ab.

HALLE. 7. 6 l.

PETER RITTER (1760—1846). 1788.

1. { JE - sus, Sun of right - eous - ness, Bright - est beam of love di - vine, }
   { With the ear - ly morn - ing rays, Do Thou on our dark - ness shine, }

And dis - pel, with pur - est light, All our long and gloom - y night.

342

"Morgenglanz der Ewigkeit."
Ps. v. 3.

2 Like the sun's reviving ray,
  May Thy love, with tender glow,
  All our coldness melt away,
  Warm and cheer us, forth to go;
  Gladly serve Thee and obey,
  All our life's short earthly day.

3 Thou, our only Hope and Guide,
  Never leave us nor forsake;
  Keep us ever at Thy side,
  Till th' eternal morning break;
  Moving on to Zion's hill,
  Onward, upward, homeward still.

Knorr von Rosenroth (1636—1685), 1664.
Tr. by Miss Jane Borthwick (1825—), 1862. Ab. and alt.

ORTONVILLE. C. M.

THOMAS HASTINGS (1784—1872), 1837.

1. MA - JES - TIC sweetness sits enthron'd Up - on the Sav - iour's brow; His head with ra - diant

glo - ries crown'd, His lips with grace o'er - flow, His lips with grace o'er - flow.

343 *"Majestic Sweetness."*

2 No mortal can with Him compare
   Among the sons of men;
Fairer is He than all the fair
   That fill the heavenly train.

3 He saw me plunged in deep distress,
   He flew to my relief:
For me He bore the shameful cross,
   And carried all my grief.

4 To Him I owe my life and breath,
   And all the joys I have;
He makes me triumph over death,
   He saves me from the grave.

5 To Heaven, the place of His abode,
   He brings my weary feet,
Shows me the glories of my God,
   And makes my joy complete.

6 Since from His bounty I receive
   Such proofs of love divine,
Had I a thousand hearts to give,
   Lord, they should all be Thine.

Rev. Samuel Stennett (1727—1795), 1787.

344 *Singing for Joy.*

1 I've found the pearl of greatest price,
   My heart doth sing for joy:
And sing I must; for Christ is mine,
   Christ shall my song employ.

2 Christ is my Prophet, Priest, and King:
   A Prophet full of light,
My great High-Priest before the throne,
   My King of heavenly might.

3 For He indeed is Lord of lords,
   And He the King of kings:
He is the Sun of righteousness,
   With healing in His wings.

4 Christ is my Peace; He died for me,
   For me He gave His blood;
And as my wondrous Sacrifice,
   Offered Himself to God.

5 Christ Jesus is my All in all,
   My Comfort and my Love,
My Life below, and He shall be
   My Joy and Crown above.

Rev. John Mason (—1694), 1683. Ab. and alt.

BRISTOL. C. M.

EDWARD HODGES (1796—1867).

BARTIMEUS 8. 7.   STEPHEN JENKS (—1856), 1808.

1. "MER - CY, O Thou Son of Da - vid," Thus blind Bar - ti - me - us pray'd;

"Oth - ers by Thy word are sav - ed, Now to me af - ford Thine aid."

345   *Prayer for Sight.*
MARK x. 47, 48.

2 Many for his crying chid him,
    But he called the louder still ;
Till the gracious Saviour bid him
    "Come, and ask Me what you will."

3 Money was not what he wanted,
    Though by begging used to live ;
But he asked, and Jesus granted,
    Alms which none but He could give.

4 "Lord, remove this grievous blindness,
    Let mine eyes behold the day ! "
Straight he saw and, won by kindness,
    Followed Jesus in the way.

5 O methinks I hear him praising,
    Publishing to all around,
"Friends, is not my case amazing?
    What a Saviour I have found !

6 "O that all the blind but knew Him,
    And would be advised by me,
Surely they would hasten to Him,
    He would cause them all to see."
        Rev. John Newton (1725—1807), 1779.

346   *"He received his sight"*
MARK x. 51, 52.

1 LORD, I know Thy grace is nigh me,
    Though Thyself I cannot see ;
Jesus, Master, pass not by me ;
    Son of David, pity me.

2 While I sit in weary blindess,
    Longing for the blesséd light,
Many taste Thy loving-kindness ;
    "Lord, I would receive my sight."

3 I would see Thee and adore Thee,
    And Thy word the power can give ;
Hear the sightless soul implore Thee :
    Let me see Thy face and live.

4 Ah, what touch is this that thrills me?
    What this burst of strange delight?
Lo, the rapturous vision fills me !
    This is Jesus ! this is sight !

5 Room, ye saints that throng behind Him !
    Let me follow in the way ;
I will teach the blind to find Him
    Who can turn their night to day.
        Rev. Hervey Doddridge Ganse (1822—   ), 1869

347   *"Open, Lord, and let me in."*

1 AT the door of mercy sighing
    With the burden of my sin,
Day and night my soul is crying,
    "Open, Lord, and let me in."

2 Waiting 'mid the darkness dreary,
    Stretching out my hands to Thee,
In the refuge for the weary
    Is there not a place for me?

3 Hark, what sounds my ear receiveth,
Sweet as songs of seraphim!
He that in the Lord believeth
Life eternal hath in Him.

4 At the outer door why staying?
Nothing, soul, hast thou to pay:
Christ in love to thee is saying,
"Weary child, come in to-day."

Thomas MacKellar (1812—   ), 1872.

BRADEN. S. M.

WILLIAM BATCHELDER BRADBURY (1816—1868), 1844.

1. I bless the Christ of God; I rest on love di-vine; And
with un-fal-t'ring lip and heart, I call this Sav-iour mine.

348   *"I bless the Christ of God."*

2 His cross dispels each doubt;
I bury in His tomb
Each thought of unbelief and fear,
Each lingering shade of gloom.

3 I praise the God of grace;
I trust His truth and might;
He calls me His, I call Him mine,
My God, my Joy, my Light.

4 'Tis He who saveth me,
And freely pardon gives;
I love because He loveth me,
I live because He lives.

5 My life with Him is hid,
My death has passed away,
My clouds have melted into light,
My midnight into day.

Rev. Horatius Bonar (1808—   ), 1863. Ab.

349   *Christ our Righteousness.*
             1 Cor. i. 30.

1 How heavy is the night
That hangs upon our eyes,

Till Christ, with His reviving light,
Over our souls arise!

2 Our guilty spirits dread
To meet the wrath of Heaven;
But, in His righteousness arrayed,
We see our sins forgiven.

3 Unholy and impure
Are all our thoughts and ways:
His hands infected nature cure,
With sanctifying grace.

4 The powers of hell agree
To hold our souls in vain;
He sets the sons of bondage free,
And breaks the cursèd chain.

5 Lord, we adore Thy ways
To bring us near to God,
Thy sovereign power, Thy healing grace,
And Thine atoning blood.

Rev. Isaac Watts (1674—1748), 1709.

GRACE MAGNIFIED.

NETTLETON. 8.7. D.

Rev. ASAHEL NETTLETON (1783–1844), 1824.

1. COME, Thou Fount of ev-'ry bless-ing, Tune my heart to sing Thy grace;
Streams of mer-cy nev-er ceas-ing, Call for songs of loud-est praise:

Teach me some me-lo-dious son-net, Sung by flam-ing tongues a-bove;

Praise the mount, I'm fix'd up-on it, Mount of God's un-chang-ing love.

350

Grateful Recollection.

2 Here I raise my Ebenezer,
  Hither by Thy help I'm come;
And I hope, by Thy good pleasure,
  Safely to arrive at home:
Jesus sought me, when a stranger,
  Wandering from the fold of God;
He, to rescue me from danger,
  Interposed His precious blood.

3 O to grace how great a debtor,
  Daily I'm constrained to be;
Let that grace now, like a fetter,
  Bind my wandering heart to Thee:
Prone to wander, Lord, I feel it,
  Prone to leave the God I love;
Here's my heart, O take and seal it,
  Seal it from Thy courts above.

Selina, Countess of Huntingdon (1707–1791), 1749.

NEANDER. 8.7, 7.7.

JOACHIM NEANDER (1610–1680), 1679.

1. I WILL love Thee, all my Treas-ure; I will love Thee, all my Strength;
I will love Thee with-out meas-ure, And will love Thee right at length:

I will love Thee, Light di-vine, Till I die and find Thee mine.

351

2 I will praise Thee, Sun of glory,
    For Thy beams have gladness brought;
I will praise Thee, will adore Thee,
    For the light I vainly sought;
Praise Thee that Thy words so blest
Spake my sin-sick soul to rest.

3 I will love in joy or sorrow,
    Crowning joy! will love Thee well;
I will love to-day, to-morrow,
    While I in this body dwell:
I will love Thee, Light divine,
Till I die, and find Thee mine.

Johann Angelus Silesius (1624—1677), 1657.
Tr. by Miss Jane Borthwick (1825—), 1854. Ab.

SILVER STREET. S. M.   ISAAC SMITH (—1800), 1770.

1. GRACE, 'tis a charm - ing sound, Har - mo - nious to mine ear; Heav'n with the ech - o shall re - sound, And all...... the earth shall hear.

352

"*Saving Grace.*"
EPH. ii. 5.

2 Grace first contrived a way
    To save rebellious man,
And all the steps that grace display,
    Which drew the wondrous plan.

3 Grace taught my wandering feet
    To tread the heavenly road;
And new supplies each hour I meet,
    While pressing on to God.

4 Grace all the work shall crown,
    Through everlasting days;
It lays in Heaven the topmost stone,
    And well deserves the praise.

Rev. Philip Doddridge (1702—1751), 1755.

353

"*The Song of Moses and the Lamb.*"
REV. XV. 3

1 AWAKE, and sing the song
    Of Moses and the Lamb;
Wake every heart and every tongue,
    To praise the Saviour's Name.

2 Sing of His dying love;
    Sing of His rising power;
Sing how He intercedes above
    For those whose sins He bore.

3 Sing till we feel our hearts
    Ascending with our tongues;
Sing till the love of sin departs,
    And grace inspires our songs.

4 Sing on your heavenly way,
    Ye ransomed sinners, sing;
Sing on, rejoicing every day
    In Christ th' eternal King.

5 Soon shall ye hear Him say,
    "Ye blessèd children, come:"
Soon will He call you hence away,
    And take His wanderers home.

6 There shall our raptured tongue
    His endless praise proclaim,
And sweeter voices swell the song
    Of Moses and the Lamb.

Rev. William Hammond (—1878), 1745. Ab. and alt.
Rev. Martin Madan (1726—1790), 1760. First 5 vs.

LOVING-KINDNESS. L. M.

American Melody.

1. A-WAKE, my soul, in joy-ful lays, And sing thy great Re-deem-er's praise;
He just-ly claims a song from me, His lov-ing-kind-ness, is so free,
Lov-ing-kind-ness, lov-ing-kind-ness, His lov-ing-kind-ness, is so free.

354 *"The Loving-Kindness of the Lord."* Is. lxiii. 7.

2 He saw me ruined in the fall,
Yet loved me notwithstanding all,
And saved me from my lost estate,
His loving-kindness is so great.

3 Through mighty hosts of cruel foes,
Where earth and hell my way oppose,
He safely leads my soul along,
His loving-kindness is so strong.

4 So when I pass death's gloomy vale,
And life and mortal powers shall fail,
O may my last expiring breath
His loving-kindness sing in death.

5 Then shall I mount, and soar away
To the bright world of endless day;
There shall I sing, with sweet surprise,
His loving-kindness in the skies.

Rev. Samuel Medley (1738—1799), 1787. Ab.

TRANSPORT. L. M.

Arr. from FELIX JACOB LUDWIG MENDELSSOHN-BARTHOLDY (1809—1847).

1. TREM-BLING be-fore Thine aw-ful throne, O Lord, in dust my sins I own;
Jus-tice and mer-cy for my life Con-tend; O smile, and heal the strife.

355
The new Joy.

2 The Saviour smiles; upon my soul
New tides of hope tumultuous roll;
His voice proclaims my pardon found,
Seraphic transport wings the sound.

3 Earth has a joy unknown to Heaven,
The new-born peace of sins forgiven;
Tears of such pure and deep delight,
Ye angels, never dimmed your sight.

4 Ye saw of old, on chaos rise
The beauteous pillars of the skies:
Ye know where morn exulting springs,
And evening folds her drooping wings.

5 Bright heralds of the Eternal Will,
Abroad His errands ye fulfil;
Or, throned in floods of beamy day,
Symphonious in His presence play.

6 Loud is the song, the heavenly plain
Is shaken with the choral strain;
And dying echoes, floating far,
Draw music from each chiming star.

7 But I amid your choirs shall shine,
And all your knowledge shall be mine;
Ye on your harps must learn to hear
A secret chord that mine will bear.

Abraham Lucas Hillhouse (1792—1839), 1822.

CUM NUBIBUS. 8.7.4. HENRY SMART (1813—1879), 1867.

1. Praise, my soul, the King of Heaven; To His feet thy trib-ute bring,
Ran-som'd, heal'd, re-stor'd, for-giv-en, Ev-er-more His prais-es sing:
Al-le-lu-ia! Al-le-lu-ia! Praise the ev-er-last-ing King.

356
"Bless the Lord, O my Soul."
Ps. ciii.

2 Praise Him for His grace and favor
To our fathers in distress;
Praise Him still the same as ever,
Slow to chide, and swift to bless:
Alleluia! Alleluia!
Glorious in His faithfulness.

3 Father-like, He tends and spares us,
Well our feeble frame He knows;
In His hands He gently bears us,
Rescues us from all our foes:
Alleluia! Alleluia!
Praise with us the God of grace.

Rev. Henry Francis Lyte (1793—1847), 1834. Ab. and alt.
Rev. Sir Henry Williams Baker (1821—1877), 1861.

MESSIAH. 7. D.

LOUIS JOSEPH FERDINAND HEROLD (1791–1833), 1839.
Arr. by GEORGE KINGSLEY (1811–1884), 1838.

1. Christ, of all my hopes the Ground, Christ, the Spring of all my joy, Still in Thee may I be found,

Still for Thee my pow'rs em-ploy. Fount-ain of o'er-flow-ing grace, Free-ly from Thy

ful-ness give; Till I close my earth-ly race, May I prove it, "Christ to live."

357 *"To live is Christ, and to die is Gain."*
PHIL. i. 21.

2 When I touch the blessèd shore,
   Back the closing waves shall roll:
Death's dark stream shall never more
   Part from Thee my ravished soul.
Thus, O thus, an entrance give
   To the land of cloudless sky;
Having known it, "Christ to live,"
   Let me know it, "Gain to die."

3 Gain, to part from all my grief;
   Gain, to bid my sins farewell;
Gain, of all my gains the chief,
   Ever with the Lord to dwell:
This Thy people's portion, Lord,
   Peace on earth, and bliss on high;
This their ever-sure reward,
   "Christ to live, and gain to die."

Rev. Ralph Wardlaw (1779–1853), 1817.

SPANISH HYMN. 7. 6l.

Spanish Melody.
FINE.

1. Bless-ed Sav-iour, Thee I love, All my oth-er joys a-bove;
D. C.—Ev-er let my glo-ry be, On-ly, on-ly, on-ly Thee.

D. C.

All my hopes in Thee a-bide, Thou my Hope, and naught be-side,

358   *"Only Thee"*

2 Once again beside the cross,
All my gain I count but loss;
Earthly pleasures fade away;
Clouds they are that hide my day:
Hence, vain shadows, let me see
Jesus, crucified for me.

3 From beneath that thorny crown
Trickle drops of cleansing down;
Pardon from Thy piercéd hand
Now I take, while here I stand;
Only then I live to Thee,
When Thy wounded side I see.

4 Blessed Saviour, Thine am I,
Thine to live, and Thine to die;
Height or depth, or earthly power,
Ne'er shall hide my Saviour more:
Ever shall my glory be,
Only, only, only Thee.

Rev. George Duffield (1818—), 1859.

359   *Happy Trust.*   7.6l.

1 SAVIOUR, happy would I be,
If I could but trust in Thee;
Trust Thy wisdom me to guide;
Trust Thy goodness to provide;
Trust Thy saving love and power;
Trust Thee every day and hour:

2 Trust Thee as the only light
In the darkest hour of night;
Trust in sickness, trust in health;
Trust in poverty and wealth;
Trust in joy, and trust in grief;
Trust Thy promise for relief:

3 Trust Thy blood to cleanse my soul;
Trust Thy grace to make me whole;
Trust Thee living, dying, too;
Trust Thee all my journey through;
Trust Thee till my feet shall be
Planted on the crystal sea.

Rev. Edwin Henry Nevin (1814—), 1858.

PENUEL. L. M. 6l.   American Melody.

1. {
Come, O Thou Trav - el - ler un - known, Whom still I hold, but can - not see;
My com - pa - ny be - fore is gone, And I am left a - lone with Thee;
}

With Thee all night I mean to stay, And wres - tle till the break of day.

360   *Wrestling Jacob.*
      GEN. xxxii. 24

2 I need not tell Thee who I am?
My sin and misery declare;
Thyself hast called me by my name;
Look on Thy hands, and read it there:
But who, I ask Thee, who art Thou?
Tell me Thy Name, and tell me now.

3 My prayer hath power with God; the grace
Unspeakable I now receive:
Through faith I see Thee face to face,

I see Thee face to face and live;
In vain I have not wept and strove.
Thy Nature, and Thy Name, is Love.

4 I know Thee, Saviour, who Thou art,
Jesus, the feeble sinner's Friend;
Nor wilt Thou with the night depart,
But stay and love me to the end:
Thy mercies never shall remove,
Thy Nature, and Thy Name, is Love.

Rev. Charles Wesley (1708—1788), 1742. Ab.

ST. AGNES. C. M.   Rev. JOHN BACCHUS DYKES (1823—1876). 1856.

1. JE - SUS, the ver - y thought of Thee With sweet - ness fills my breast;

But sweet - er far Thy face to see, And in Thy pres - ence rest.

361

"Jesu, dulcis memoria."
Rev. xxii. 4.

2 Nor voice can sing, nor heart can frame,
  Nor can the memory find
A sweeter sound than Thy blest Name,
  O Saviour of mankind!

3 O Hope of every contrite heart,
  O Joy of all the meek,
To those who fall, how kind Thou art!
  How good to those who seek!

4 Jesus, our only Joy be Thou,
  As Thou our Prize wilt be;
Jesus, be Thou our Glory now,
  And through eternity.

Bernard of Clairvaux (1091—1153), 1140.
Tr. by Rev. Edward Caswall (1814—1878), 1849.

362   *"O Deus, ego amo Te."*

1 My God, I love Thee : not because
  I hope for Heaven thereby,
Nor yet because who love Thee not
  Must die eternally.

2 Thou, O my Jesus, Thou didst me
  Upon the cross embrace;
For me didst bear the nails, and spear,
  And manifold disgrace;

3 And griefs, and torments numberless,
  And sweat of agony;
Yea, death itself; and all for me
  Who was Thine enemy.

4 Then why, O blessèd Jesus Christ,
  Should I not love Thee well?
Not for the hope of winning Heaven,
  Nor of escaping hell.

5 Not with the hope of gaining aught,
  Nor seeking a reward;
But as Thyself hast lovèd me,
  O ever-loving Lord.

6 So would I love Thee, dearest Lord,
  And in Thy praise will sing;
Solely because Thou art my God,
  And my eternal King.

Francis Xavier (1506—1552), 1552.
Tr. by Rev. Edward Caswall, 1849. Sl. alt.

DEDHAM. C. M.   WILLIAM GARDINER (1770—1853), 1830.

HOLY TRINITY. C. M.   JOSEPH BARNBY (1838—   ),

1. Do not I love Thee, O my Lord? Be - hold my heart and see;

And turn each curs - ed i - dol out, That dares to ri - val Thee.

363   *" Thou knowest that I love Thee."*
           JOHN xxi. 15.

2 Do not I love Thee from my soul?
   Then let me nothing love;
   Dead be my heart to every joy,
   When Jesus cannot move.

3 Is not Thy Name melodious still
   To mine attentive ear?
   Doth not each pulse with pleasure bound
   My Saviour's voice to hear?

4 Hast Thou a lamb in all Thy flock
   I would disdain to feed?
   Hast Thou a foe before whose face
   I fear Thy cause to plead?

5 Would not my heart pour forth its blood
   In honor of Thy Name,
   And challenge the cold hand of death
   To damp th' immortal flame?

6 Thou know'st I love Thee, dearest Lord,
   But O, I long to soar

Far from the sphere of mortal joys,
And learn to love Thee more.
          Rev. Philip Doddridge (1702—1751), 1755.   Ab.

364   *Christ precious.*
             1 PET. ii. 7.

1 JESUS, I love Thy charming Name,
   'Tis music to mine ear;
   Fain would I sound it out so loud
   That earth and Heaven should hear.

2 All my capacious powers can wish
   In Thee doth richly meet;
   Not to mine eyes is light so dear,
   Nor friendship half so sweet.

3 Thy grace still dwells upon my heart,
   And sheds its fragrance there;
   The noblest balm of all its wounds,
   The cordial of its care.

4 I'll speak the honors of Thy Name
   With my last laboring breath;
   Then, speechless, clasp Thee in mine arms,
   The Conqueror of death.
          Rev. Philip Doddridge, 1755.   Ab.

BOARDMAN. C. M.   Devereux. Arr. by GEORGE KINGSLEY (1811—1884), 1839.

LOVE TO CHRIST.

FABEN. 8.7.D.   JOHN HENRY WILLCOX (1827—1835), 1849.

1. HAIL, my ev-er bless-ed Je-sus! On-ly Thee I wish to sing; To my soul Thy Name is
pre-cious, Thou my Proph-et, Priest, and King: O, what mer-cy flows from Heav-en, O, what
joy and hap-pi-ness! Love I much, I've much for-giv-en; I'm a mir-a-cle of grace.

365   *"I'm a Miracle of Grace."*

2 Once with Adam's race in ruin,
   Unconcerned in sin I lay,
Swift destruction still pursuing,
   Till my Saviour passed that way.
Witness, all ye host of Heaven,
   My Redeemer's tenderness.
Love I much, I've much forgiven;
   I'm a miracle of grace!

3 Shout, ye bright, angelic choir,
   Praise the Lamb enthroned above,
While, astonished, I admire
   God's free grace and boundless love.
That blest moment I received Him
   Filled my soul with joy and peace.
Love I much, I've much forgiven;
   I'm a miracle of grace.

                          John Wingrove, 1806.

366   *Praise for pardoning Grace.*

1 LORD, with glowing heart I'd praise Thee
   For the bliss Thy love bestows,
For the pardoning grace that saves me,
   And the peace that from it flows.
Help, O God, my weak endeavor,
   This dull soul to rapture raise;
Thou must light the flame, or never
   Can my love be warmed to praise.

2 Praise, my soul, the God that sought thee,
   Wretched wanderer, far astray;
Found thee lost, and kindly brought thee
   From the paths of death away.
Praise, with love's devoutest feeling,
   Him who saw thy guilt-born fear,
And, the light of hope revealing,
   Bade the blood-stained cross appear.

3 Lord, this bosom's ardent feeling
   Vainly would my lips express;
Low before Thy footstool kneeling,
   Deign Thy suppliant's prayer to bless.
Let Thy grace, my soul's chief treasure,
   Love's pure flame within me raise;
And since words can never measure,
   Let my life show forth Thy praise.
                    Francis Scott Key (1799—1843), 1857.

DAWN. S. M.

Rev. EDWIN POND PARKER (1836—), 1-72.

1. Je - sus, I live to Thee, The love - li - est and best;

My life in Thee, Thy life in me, In Thy blest love I rest.

367

"We are the Lord's."
Rom. xiv. 8.

2 Jesus, I die to Thee,
   Whenever death shall come;
  To die in Thee is life to me,
   In my eternal home.

3 Whether to live or die,
   I know not which is best;

To live in Thee is bliss to me,
  To die is endless rest.

4 Living or dying, Lord,
  I ask but to be Thine;
  My life in Thee, Thy life in me,
  Makes Heaven forever mine.

Rev. Henry Harbaugh (1818—1867), 1850.

CRUSADER'S HYMN. P. M.

Unknown.

1. Fair-est Lord Je - sus, Rul - er of all nat - ure, O Thou of God and man the Son!

Thee will I cher - ish, Thee will I hon - or, Thou, my soul's glo - ry, joy, and crown.

368

"Schönster Herr Jesu."

2 Fair are the meadows,
  Fairer still the woodlands,
Robed in the blooming garb of spring:
  Jesus is fairer,
  Jesus is purer,
Who makes the woful heart to sing.

3 Fair is the sunshine,
  Fairer still the moonlight,
And the twinkling, starry host:
  Jesus shines brighter,
  Jesus shines purer,
Than all the angels Heaven can boast.

Unknown Author of the 12th century.

BEATITUDE. C. M.

Rev. JOHN BACCHUS DYKES (1823—1876).

1. JE - SUS, these eyes have nev - er seen That ra - diant form of Thine;

The veil of sense hangs dark be - tween Thy bless - ed face and mine.

369

Unseen, but loved.
1 Pet. i. 8.

2 I see Thee not, I hear Thee not,
  Yet art Thou oft with me;
And earth hath ne'er so dear a spot,
  As where I meet with Thee.

3 Like some bright dream that comes un-
  When slumbers o'er me roll, [-sought!
Thine image ever fills my thought,
  And charms my ravished soul.

4 Yet though I have not seen, and still
  Must rest in faith alone,
I love Thee, dearest Lord,—and will,
  Unseen, but not unknown.

5 When death these mortal eyes shall seal,
  And still this throbbing heart,
The rending veil shall Thee reveal,
  All-glorious as Thou art.

Rev. Ray Palmer (1808—   ), 1858.

370

"Jesu decus angelicum."

1 O JESUS, Thou the beauty art
  Of angel-worlds above;
Thy Name is music to the heart,
  Enchanting it with love.

2 O Jesus, Saviour, hear the sighs
  Which unto Thee I send;
To Thee my inmost spirit cries,
  My being's hope and end.

3 Stay with us, Lord, and with Thy light
  Illume the soul's abyss;
Scatter the darkness of our night,
  And fill the world with bliss.

4 O Jesus, King of earth and Heaven,
  Our Life and Joy! to Thee
Be honor, thanks, and blessing given
  Through all eternity!

Bernard of Clairvaux (1091—1153), 1140
Tr. by Rev. Edward Caswall (1814—1878), 1849. Ab. and alt.

GEER. C. M.

HENRY WELLINGTON GREATOREX (1811—1858), 1849.

MANCHESTER. C. M.
ROBERT WAINWRIGHT (1747—1782), c. 1774.

1. How sweet the Name of Je - sus sounds In a be - liev - er's ear;

It soothes his sor - rows, heals his wounds, And drives a - way his fear.

371
The sweet Name.

2 It makes the wounded spirit whole,
  And calms the troubled breast;
  'Tis manna to the hungry soul,
  And to the weary rest.

3 By Thee my prayers acceptance gain,
  Although with sin defiled;
  Satan accuses me in vain,
  And I am owned a child.

4 Weak is the effort of my heart,
  And cold my warmest thought;
  But when I see Thee as Thou art,
  I'll praise Thee as I ought.
  Rev. John Newton (1725—1807), 1779.

372
"O Jesus Christus, wachs in mir."

1 O JESUS Christ, grow Thou in me,
  And all things else recede;
  My heart be daily nearer Thee,
  From sin be daily freed.

2 Each day, let Thy supporting might
  My weakness still embrace;
  My darkness vanish in Thy light,
  Thy life my death efface.

3 In Thy bright beams, which on me fall,
  Fade every evil thought;
  That I am nothing, Thou art all,
  I would be daily taught.

4 Make this poor self grow less and less,
  Be Thou my life and aim,
  O, make me daily, through Thy grace,
  More worthy of Thy Name.

5 Let faith in Thee and in Thy might
  My every motive move;
  Be Thou alone my soul's delight,
  My passion and my love.
  Rev. Johann Caspar Lavater (1741—1801), 1780.
  Tr. by Mrs Elizabeth Lee Smith (1817—   ), 1863. Ab.

HEBER. C. M.
GEORGE KINGSLEY (1811—1884), 1838.

LAUDES DOMINI. 6.6l.   JOSEPH BARNBY (1838—). 1868.

1. WHEN morn - ing gilds the skies, My heart a - wak - ing cries,

May Je - sus Christ be prais'd: A - like at work and pray'r

To Je - sus I re - pair; May Je - sus Christ be prais'd.

373   *Christ praised.*

2 When sleep her balm denies,
My silent spirit sighs,
May Jesus Christ be praised :
When evil thoughts molest,
With this I shield my breast,
May Jesus Christ be praised.

3 The night becomes as day,
When from the heart we say,
May Jesus Christ be praised :

The powers of darkness fear,
When this sweet chant they hear,
May Jesus Christ be praised.

4 In Heaven's eternal bliss
The loveliest strain is this,
May Jesus Christ be praised :
Let air, and sea, and sky
From depth to height reply,
May Jesus Christ be praised.

Rev. Edward Caswall (1814—1878), 1849. Ab.

FERGUSON. S. M.   GEORGE KINGSLEY (1811—1884), 1843.

1. HERE I can firm - ly rest, I dare to boast of this,

That God, the high - est and the best, My Friend and Fa - ther is.

374 *"Ist Gott für mich so trete."*

2 From dangerous snares He saves :
　Where'er He bids me go
　He checks the storms and calms the waves,
　That naught can work me woe.

3 He whispers in my breast
　Sweet words of holy cheer,
　How he who seeks in God his rest
　Shall ever find Him near ;

4 How God hath built above
　A city fair and new,

Where eye and heart shall see and prove
　What faith has counted true.

5 My heart for gladness springs,
　It cannot more be sad,
　For very joy it laughs and sings,
　Sees naught but sunshine glad.

6 The Sun that glads mine eyes
　Is Christ the Lord I love :
　I sing for joy of that which lies
　Stored up for us above.

Rev. Paul Gerhardt (1607—1676), 1646.
Tr. by Miss Catherine Winkworth (1829—1878), 1855　Ab.

JESU PASTOR. 8.7.6l.　　　　　　　JOHN HENRY WILLCOX (1827—1875).

1. Je - sus is the Name we treas - ure ; Name be - yond what words can tell ;
Name of glad - ness, Name of pleas - ure, Ear and heart de - light - ing well ;
Name of sweet - ness, pass - ing meas - ure, Sav - ing us from sin and hell.

375　　　*Christ's Name Precious.*

2 'Tis the Name for adoration,
　Name for songs of victory,
　Name for holy meditation
　In this vale of misery.
　Name for joyful veneration
　By the citizens on high.

3 Jesus is the Name exalted
　Over every other name ;
　In this Name, whene'er assaulted,

We can put our foes to shame ;
　Strength to them who else had halted,
　Eyes to blind, and feet to lame.

4 Therefore we in love adoring,
　This most blesséd Name revere ;
　Holy Jesus, Thee imploring
　So to write it in us here,
　That hereafter heavenward soaring,
　We may sing with angels there.

Unknown Author of the 11th and 13th Century.
Tr. by Rev. John Mason Neale (1818—1866), 1851.　Ab. and alt.

VALENTIA. C. M.

TRAUGOTT MAXIMILIAN EBERWEIN (1775—1831),
Arr. by GEORGE KINGSLEY (1811—1884), 1855.

1. O GIFT of gifts! O grace of faith! My God, how can it be

That Thou, who hast dis - cern - ing love, Shouldst give that gift to me?

376
Converting Grace.

2 How many hearts Thou mightst have had
   More innocent than mine,
How many souls more worthy far
   Of that sweet touch of Thine!

3 Ah, grace, into unlikeliest hearts
   It is thy boast to come,
The glory of thy light to find
   In darkest spots a home.

4 The crowd of cares, the weightiest cross,
   Seem trifles less than light;
Earth looks so little and so low
   When faith shines full and bright.

5 O happy, happy that I am!
   If Thou canst be, O faith,
The treasure that thou art in life,
   What wilt thou be in death?

      Rev. Frederick William Faber (1814—1863), 1848. Ab.

377
"Jesu, Rex admirabilis."

1 O Jesus, King most wonderful,
   Thou Conqueror renowned,
Thou sweetness most ineffable,
   In whom all joys are found:

2 When once Thou visitest the heart,
   Then truth begins to shine,
Then earthly vanities depart,
   Then kindles love divine.

3 O Jesus, Light of all below,
   Thou Fount of life and fire,
Surpassing all the joys we know,
   And all we can desire:

4 May every heart confess Thy Name,
   And ever Thee adore;
And, seeking Thee, itself inflame
   To seek Thee more and more.

5 Thee may our tongues forever bless;
   Thee may we love alone;
And ever in our lives express
   The image of Thine own.

      Bernard of Clairvaux (1091—1153), 1140.
      Tr. by Rev Edward Caswall (1814—1878), 1849. St. alt.

378
Converting Grace commemorated.

1 O FOR a thousand tongues to sing
   My dear Redeemer's praise;
The glories of my God and King,
   The triumphs of His grace.

2 My gracious Master and my God,
   Assist me to proclaim,
To spread, through all the earth abroad,
   The honors of Thy Name.

3 Jesus, the Name that charms our fears,
   That bids our sorrows cease ;
'Tis music in the sinner's ears,
   'Tis life, and health, and peace.

4 He breaks the power of cancelled sin,
   He sets the prisoners free ;
His blood can make the foulest clean,
   His blood availed for me.

Rev. Charles Wesley (1708—1788), 1740. Ab.

SONG. 8.8.8.5.   German Melody. Adams' Church Pastorals, 1864.

1. Sing of Je - sus, sing for - ev - er, Of the love that chang - es nev - er,

Who or what from Him can sev - er Those He makes His own ?

379   *"Sing unto the Lord."* Ps. xxvi. 1.

2 With His blood the Lord has bought
    them ;
When they knew Him not, He sought
    them,
And from all their wanderings brought
    them ;
   His the praise alone.

3 Through the desert Jesus leads them,
With the bread of Heaven He feeds
    them,
And through all the way He speeds
    them
   To their home above.

4 There they see the Lord who bought
    them,
Him who came from Heaven, and sought
    them,
Him who by His Spirit taught them,
   Him they serve and love.

Rev. Thomas Kelly (1769—1855), 1815. Ab.

380   *One Song on Earth and in Heaven.*

1 Saints in glory, we together
Know the song that ceases never ;
Song of songs, Thou art, O Saviour,
   All that endless day.

2 Theme of Adam, when forgiven,
Theme of Abr'am, David, Stephen ;
Souls, ye chant it entering Heaven,
   Now, henceforth, alway.

3 Come, ye angels, round us gather,
While to Jesus we draw nearer ;
In His throne He'll seat forever
   Those for whom He died.

4 Underneath His throne a river,
Clear as crystal, flows forever,
Like His fulness, failing never :
   Hail, enthronèd Lamb !

5 O the unsearchable Redeemer !
Shoreless ocean, sounded never !
Yesterday, to-day, forever,
   Jesus Christ, the same.

Rev. Nehemiah Adams (1806—1878), 1864. Ab.

OLIVET. 6.6.4.6.6.6.4.   LOWELL MASON (1792—1872), 1830.

1. My faith looks up to Thee, Thou Lamb of Cal-va-ry, Sav-iour di-vine: Now hear me while I pray, Take all my guilt a-way, O let me from this day Be whol-ly Thine.

381   *"My Faith looks up to Thee."*

2 May Thy rich grace impart
Strength to my fainting heart,
  My zeal inspire;
As Thou hast died for me,
O may my love to Thee,
Pure, warm, and changeless be,
  A living fire.

3 While life's dark maze I tread,
And griefs around me spread,
  Be Thou my Guide;

Bid darkness turn to day,
Wipe sorrow's tears away,
Nor let me ever stray
  From Thee aside.

4 When ends life's transient dream,
When death's cold, sullen stream
  Shall o'er me roll;
Blest Saviour, then, in love,
Fear and distrust remove;
O, bear me safe above,
  A ransomed soul.

Rev. Ray Palmer (1808—), 1830.

LYTE. 6.6.4.6.6.6.4.   JOSEPH PERRY HOLBROOK (1822—).

1. Je-sus, Thy Name I love, All oth-er names a-bove, Je-sus, my Lord! O Thou art all to me; Noth-ing to please I see, Noth-ing a-part from Thee, Je-sus, my Lord!

382 *"Jesus, my Lord!"*

2 When unto Thee I flee,
Thou wilt my Refuge be,
Jesus, my Lord!
What need I now to fear?
What earthly grief or care,
Since Thou art ever near,
Jesus, my Lord!

3 Soon Thou wilt come again:
I shall be happy then,
Jesus, my Lord!
Then Thine own face I'll see,
Then I shall like Thee be,
Then evermore with Thee,
Jesus, my Lord!

James George Deck (1802—), 1837. Ab.

VOX JESU. C. M. D.

LUDWIG SPOHR (1784—1859).
Arr. by JOSEPH BARNBY (1838—).

1. O Lord, how hap-py is the time When in Thy love I rest; When in my wea-ri-
ness I climb E'en to Thy ten-der breast. The night of sor-row end-eth there:
Thou'rt brighter than the sun; And in Thy par-don, and Thy care, The Heav'n of Heav'n is won.

383 *Safety and Rest in Christ.*

2 Let this world call itself my foe,
Or let the world allure:
I care not for the world; I go
To this dear Friend and sure;
And when life's fiercest storms are sent
Upon life's wildest sea,
My little bark is confident,
Because it holds by Thee.

3 When Thy law threatens endless death
Upon the awful hill,
Straightway from its consuming breath
My soul goes higher still;

Goeth to Jesus, wounded, slain,
And maketh Him her home,
Whence she will not go out again,
And where death cannot come.

4 Thou art my Rest: on Thee I lean;
Thou mak'st my heart to sing,
And to Thy heavenly pastures green
All Thy dear flock dost bring.
That is not losing much of life
Which is not losing Thee.
Who art as present in the strife
As in the victory.

Wolfgang Christopher Dessler (1660—1722), 1692.
Tr. by George Mac Donald (1824—), 1874. Ab. and sl. alt.

HENDON. 7. 5l.

Rev. CÆSAR HENRI ABRAHAM MALAN (1787—1864). 1828.

1. Ask ye what great thing I know That de - lights and stirs me so? What the high reward I win? Whose the name I glo - ry in? Je - sus Christ, the Cru - ci - fied.

384
"The Crucified"

2 What is faith's foundation strong?
   What awakes my lips to song?
   He who bore my sinful load,
   Purchased for me peace with God,
       Jesus Christ, the Crucified.

3 Who defeats my fiercest foes?
   Who consoles my saddest woes?
   Who revives my fainting heart,
   Healing all its hidden smart?
       Jesus Christ, the Crucified.

4 Who is Life in life to me?
   Who the Death of death will be?
   Who will place me on His right
   With the countless hosts of light?
       Jesus Christ, the Crucified.

5 This is that great thing I know;
   This delights and stirs me so:
   Faith in Him who died to save,
   Him who triumphed o'er the grave,
       Jesus Christ, the Crucified.
       Rev. John Samuel Bewley Monsell (1811—1875). 1863.

BREMEN. C. P. M.

THOMAS HASTINGS (1784—1872). 1836.

1. O Love di - vine, how sweet Thou art! When shall I find my will - ing heart All tak - en up by
Thee? { I thirst, and faint, and die to prove } The love of Christ to me.
{ The great - ness of re - deem - ing love, }

385
"Love Divine."

2 God only knows the love of God;
   O that it now were shed abroad
   In this poor, stony heart!
   For love I sigh, for love I pine:
   This only portion, Lord, be mine,
   Be mine this better part.

3 O that I could forever sit
   With Mary at the Master's feet!
   Be this my happy choice,
   My only care, delight, and bliss,
   My joy, my heaven on earth, be this,
   To hear the Bridegroom's voice.
       Rev. Charles Wesley (1708—1788). 1740.   Ab

COLEBROOK. C. P. M.
HENRY SMART (1812—1879), 1872.

1. O could I speak the match - less worth, O could I sound the glo - ries forth,
Which in my Sav - iour shine, I'd soar, and touch the heav'n - ly strings,
And vie with Ga - briel while he sings, In notes al - most di - vine.

386

"*The Matchless Worth.*"
Ps. lxvi. 2.

2 I'd sing the precious blood He spilt,
  My ransom from the dreadful guilt
    Of sin, and wrath divine;
  I'd sing His glorious righteousness,
  In which all-perfect, heavenly dress
    My soul shall ever shine.

3 I'd sing the characters He bears,
  And all the forms of love He wears,
    Exalted on His throne;

In loftiest songs of sweetest praise,
I would to everlasting days
  Make all His glories known.

4 Well, the delightful day will come
When my dear Lord will bring me home,
  And I shall see His face;
Then with my Saviour, Brother, Friend,
A blest eternity I'll spend,
  Triumphant in His grace.

Rev. Samuel Medley (1738—1799), 1789. Ab.

ARIEL. C. P. M.
Arr. from MOZART by LOWELL MASON (1792—1872), 1836.

BLUMENTHAL. 7. D.

JACQUES BLUMENTHAL (1829—). 1-6.

1. PILGRIM, burden'd with thy sin, Come the way to Zi-on's gate: There, till mer-cy lets thee in,
Knock, and weep, and watch, and wait. Knock, He knows the sinner's cry; Weep, He loves the mourner's tears;
Watch, for sav-ing grace is nigh; Wait, till heav'n-ly light ap-pears.

387   *The Pilgrim welcomed.*

2 Hark, it is the Bridegroom's voice:
  "Welcome, pilgrim, to thy rest!"
Now within the gate rejoice,
  Safe, and sealed, and bought and blest:
Safe, from all the lures of vice;
  Sealed, by signs the chosen know;
Bought by love, and life the price;
  Blest, the mighty debt to owe.

3 Holy pilgrim, what for thee
  In a world like this remain?
From thy guarded breast shall flee
  Fear, and shame, and doubt, and pain;
Fear, the hope of Heaven shall fly;
  Shame, from glory's view retire;
Doubt, in certain rapture die;
  Pain, in endless bliss expire.

Rev. George Crabbe (1754—1832), 1807. Ab.

388   *Numbered with God's Sons.*

1 BLESSÉD are the sons of God.
  They are bought with Jesus' blood;
They are ransomed from the grave,
  Life eternal they shall have:
With them numbered may we be,
Here, and in eternity.
With them numbered may we be,
Here, and in eternity.

2 God did love them in His Son,
  Long before the world begun;
All their sins are washed away;
  They shall stand in God's great day:
With them numbered may we be,
Here, and in eternity.
With them numbered may we be,
Here, and in eternity.

3 They are lights upon the earth,
  Children of a heavenly birth,
One with God, with Jesus one;
  Glory is in them begun:
With them numbered may we be,
Here, and in eternity.
With them numbered may we be,
Here, and in eternity.

Rev. Joseph Humphreys (1720—), 1743. Ab.

NUREMBURG. 7.

JOHANN RUDOLPH AHLE (1625—1673), 1664.

1. CHIL-DREN of the heav'n-ly King, As ye jour-ney, sweet-ly sing;

Sing your Sav-iour's worth-y praise, Glo-rious in His works and ways.

389 *"Travelling Home."*

2 We are travelling home to God,
In the way the fathers trod :
They are happy now, and we
Soon their happiness shall see.

3 Shout, ye little flock, and blest,
You on Jesus' throne shall rest ;
There your seat is now prepared,
There your kingdom and reward.

4 Fear not, brethren, joyful stand
On the borders of your land :
Jesus Christ, your Father's Son,
Bids you undismayed go on.

5 Lord, obediently we go,
Gladly leaving all below ;
Only Thou our Leader be,
And we still will follow Thee.
Rev. John Cennick (1717—1755), 1742. Ab.

390 *"Onward go."*

1 OFT in sorrow, oft in woe,
Onward, Christians, onward go :
Bear the toil, maintain the strife,
Strengthened with the Bread of Life.

2 Let not sorrow dim your eye,
Soon shall every tear be dry :
Let not fear your course impede,
Great your strength, if great your need.

3 Let your drooping hearts be glad ;
March in heavenly armour clad ;
Fight, nor think the battle long,
Soon shall victory wake your song.

4 Onward then to glory move ;
More than conquerors ye shall prove ;
Though opposed by many a foe,
Christian soldiers, onward go.
Henry Kirke White (1785—1806), 1806. Very much alt.

391 *"Faint not, Christian."*

1 FAINT not, Christian, though the road,
Leading to thy blest abode,
Darksome be, and dangerous, too ;
Christ, thy Guide, will bring thee through.

2 Faint not, Christian, though the world
Has its hostile flag unfurled ;
Hold the cross of Jesus fast,
Thou shalt overcome at last.

3 Faint not, Christian, though within
There's a heart so prone to sin ;
Christ, the Lord, is over all,
He'll not suffer thee to fall.

4 Faint not, Christian, look on high ;
See the harpers in the sky :
Patient, wait, and thou wilt join
Chant with them of love divine.
Rev. James Harrington Evans (1785—1840), 1833. Ab.

MANNHEIM. 8.7.6|.

FRIEDRICH FILITZ (1804—1860).

1. LEAD us, heav'nly Fa-ther, lead us O'er the world's tempestuous sea; Guard us, guide us, keep us, feed us,

For we have no help but Thee; Yet pos-sess-ing ev-'ry bless-ing, If our God our Fa-ther be.

392

Prayer for Guidance.
NUMBERS X. 33.

2 Saviour, breathe forgiveness o'er us;
    All our weakness Thou dost know;
Thou didst tread this earth before us;
    Thou didst feel its keenest woe;
Lone and dreary, faint and weary,
    Through the desert Thou didst go.

3 Spirit of our God, descending,
    Fill our hearts with heavenly joy,
Love with every passion blending,
    Pleasure that can never cloy;
Thus provided, pardoned, guided,
    Nothing can our peace destroy.

James Edmeston (1791—1867), 1820.

SHEPHERD. 8.7.4.

WILLIAM BATCHELDER BRADBURY (1816—1868), 1862.

1. { SAV - IOUR, like a shep - herd lead us,   Much we need Thy ten - der care; }
    { In Thy pleas - ant past - ures feed us,   For our use Thy folds pre - pare. }

Bless - ed Je - sus, Bless - ed Je - sus, Thou hast bought us, Thine we are;

Bless - ed Je - sus, Bless - ed Je - sus, Thou hast bought us, Thine we are.

393   *"Lead us."*

2 We are Thine, do Thou befriend us,
  Be the guardian of our way;
Keep Thy flock, from sin defend us,
  Seek us when we go astray;
    Blessèd Jesus,
Hear the children when they pray.

3 Early let us seek Thy favor,
  Early let us do Thy will;
Holy Lord, our only Saviour,
  With Thy grace our bosoms fill;
    Blessèd Jesus,
Thou hast loved us, love us still.

Miss Dorothy Ann Thrupp (1779-1847), 1838. Ab.

SALEM. 6.5.D.   HENRY SMART (1812-1879).

1. SAFE across the waters, Foes forever gone, Now we march in safety,
God our guide alone. 'Tis the silent desert, Sand and rock and waste;
But the chain is broken, And the peril past. Onward, then, right onward,
This our watch-word still: Till we reach the glory Of the wondrous hill.

394   *The Desert March.*

2 On through waste and blackness,
  O'er our desert road:
On till Sinai greets us,
  Mountain of our God!
On past Edom's valley,
  Moab's mountain wall,

Jordan's sea-board rushings,
  The pillar-cloud o'er all.
Past the palmy city,
  Rock and hill our road:
On till Salem greets us,
  City of our God.

Rev. Horatius Bonar (1808—), 1861. Ab. and sl. alt.

GUIDE. 5.8.5. American Melody.

1. Je-sus, still lead on, Till our rest be won; And al-though the way be cheer-less, We will fol-low, calm and fear-less: Guide us by Thy hand To our Fa-ther-land, To our Fa-ther-land.

395

"Jesu, geh voran."

2 If the way be drear,
  If the foe be near,
Let not faithless fears o'ertake us,
Let not faith and hope forsake us;
  For, through many a foe,
  To our home we go.

3 When we seek relief
  From a long-felt grief.
When temptations come alluring,
Make us patient and enduring;
  Show us that bright shore,
  Where we weep no more.

4 Jesus, still lead on,
  Till our rest be won;
Heavenly Leader, still direct us,
Still support, console, protect us,
  Till we safely stand
  In our Fatherland.

Nicolaus Ludwig Zinzendorf (1700—1760), 1721.
Tr. by Miss Jane Borthwick (1825—), 1853 Sl. alt.

ST. HUBERT. 5.8.5. Rev. LEICESTER DARWALL (1813—).

1. Je-sus, who can be Once com-par'd with Thee! Source of rest and con-so-la-tion, Life and light, and full sal-va-tion; Son of God, with Thee None compar'd can be!

396 *"Wer ist wohl wie Du?"*

2 Thou hast died for me,
 From all misery
And distress me to deliver,
And from death to save forever;
 I am by Thy blood
 Reconciled to God.

3 Grant me steadiness,
 Lord, to run my race,
Following Thee with love most tender,

So that Satan may not hinder
 Me by craft or force;
 Further Thou my course.

4 When I hence depart,
 Strengthen Thou my heart;
Where Thou art, O Lord, convey me,
In Thy righteousness array me,
 That at Thy right hand
 Joyful I may stand.

Rev. Johann Anastasius Freylinghausen (1670—1739), 1713.
Tr. by Rev. John Gambold (1711—1771), 1754. Ab. and alt.

MIRIAM. 7.6.D.

JOSEPH PERRY HOLBROOK (1822—), 1863.

1. O hap-py band of pil-grims, If on-ward ye will tread, With Je-sus as your Fel-low,
D.S.—O hap-py, if ye hun-ger

To Je-sus as your Head. O hap-py, if ye la-bor As Je-sus did for men:
As Je-sus hun-ger'd then.

397 *The Pilgrims of Jesus.*

2 The cross that Jesus carried
 He carried as your due:
The crown that Jesus weareth
 He weareth it for you.
The faith by which ye see Him,
 The hope in which ye yearn,
The love that through all trouble
 To Him alone will turn:

3 What are they but forerunners
 To lead you to His sight?
What are they save th' effluence
 Of uncreated Light?

The trials that beset you,
 The sorrows ye endure,
The manifold temptations
 That death alone can cure:

4 What are they, but His jewels
 Of right celestial worth?
What are they but the ladder,
 Set up to Heaven on earth?
O happy band of pilgrims,
 Look upward to the skies;
Where such a light affliction
 Shall win you such a prize.

Joseph of the Studium (—883).
Rev. John Mason Neale (1818—1866), 1862. Sl. alt.

206

AUTUMN. 8.7.D.   Spanish Melody.

1. GEN - TLY, Lord, O gen - tly lead us, Pil - grims in this vale of tears,

Through the tri - als yet de - creed us, Till our last great change ap - pears.
D. S.—Let Thy good - ness nev - er fail us, Lead us in Thy per - fect way.

When temp - ta tion's darts as - sail us, When in de - vious paths we stray,

398   "Gently, Lord."

2 In the hour of pain and anguish,
    In the hour when death draws near,
Suffer not our hearts to languish,
    Suffer not our souls to fear;

And, when mortal life is ended,
    Bid us in Thine arms to rest,
Till, by angel bands attended,
    We awake among the blest.
        Thomas Hastings (1784—1872), 1830, 1850, 1859.

SEGUR. 8.7.4.   JOSEPH PERRY HOLBROOK (1822-   ), 1862.

1. GUIDE me, O Thou great Je - ho - vah, Pil - grim through this bar - ren land;

I am weak, but Thou art might - y, Hold me with Thy pow'r - ful hand;

Bread of Heav - en, Bread of Heav - en, Feed me till I want no more.

399 *Prayer for Guidance.*

2 Open now the crystal fountain,
 Whence the healing stream doth flow;
Let the fire and cloudy pillar
 Lead me all my journey through:
 Strong Deliverer,
 Be Thou still my strength and shield.

3 When I tread the verge of Jordan,
 Bid my anxious fears subside;
Death of deaths, and hell's destruction,
 Land me safe on Canaan's side:
 Songs of praises,
 I will ever give to Thee.

Rev. Peter Williams (1719—1796), 1771. v. 1.
Rev. William Williams (1717—1791), 1773. Ab.

PILGRIMAGE. 6.6.8.6.8.7. Sir ARTHUR SULLIVAN (1842—).

1. To Ca - naan's sa - cred bound We haste with songs of joy, Where peace and lib - er - ty are found,

And sweets that nev - er cloy. Hal - le - lu - jah! Hal - le - lu - jah! We are on our way to God.

400 *"On our Way to God."* HEB. xi. 14.

2 Our toils and conflicts cease
 On Canaan's happy shore;
We there shall dwell in endless peace,
 And never hunger more.
 Hallelujah! Hallelujah!
 We are on our way to God.

3 There, in celestial strains,
 Enraptured myriads sing;
There love in every bosom reigns,
 For God Himself is King.
 Hallelujah! Hallelujah!
 We are on our way to God.

Rev. Thomas Kelly (1769—1855), 1812, 1753. Ab.

401 *Pressing onward.*

1 THIS is the day of toil
 Beneath earth's sultry noon;

This is the day of service true,
 But the rest cometh soon.
 Hallelujah! Hallelujah!
 There remains a rest for us.

2 Onward we press in haste,
 Upward our journey still;
Ours is the path the Master trod,
 Through good report and ill.
 Hallelujah! Hallelujah!
 There remains a rest for us.

3 The way may rougher grow,
 The weariness increase;
We gird our loins, and hasten on;
 The end, the end is peace.
 Hallelujah! Hallelujah!
 There remains a rest for us.

Rev. Horatius Bonar (1808—), 1866. Ab.

STRACATHRO. C. M.

Rev. CHARLES HUTCHISON, c. 1680.

1. O God of Beth - el, by whose hand Thy peo - ple still are fed;

Who through this wea - ry pil - grim - age Hast all our fa - thers led;

402

Jacob's Vow.
GEN. xxviii. 20—22.

2 Our vows, our prayers, we now present
  Before Thy throne of grace :
  God of our fathers, be the God
  Of their succeeding race.

3 Through each perplexing path of life
  Our wandering footsteps guide ;

Give us each day our daily bread,
  And raiment fit provide.

4 O spread Thy covering wings around,
  Till all our wanderings cease,
  And, at our Father's loved abode,
  Our souls arrive in peace.

Rev. Philip Doddridge (1702—1751), 1737.
Michael Bruce (1746—1767), 1781. Alt.

ST. HUGH. C. M.

EDWARD JOHN HOPKINS (1818—).

1. Forth to the Land of Prom - ise bound, Our des - ert path we tread;

God's fie - ry pil - lar for our guide, His Cap - tain at our head.

403

The March to Canaan.

2 E'en now we faintly trace the hills,
  And catch their distant blue ;
  And the bright city's gleaming spires
  Rise dimly on our view.

3 Soon, when the desert shall be crossed,
  The flood of death past o'er,

Our pilgrim hosts shall safely land
  On Canaan's peaceful shore.

4 There love shall have its perfect work,
  And prayer be lost in praise ;
  And all the servants of our God
  Their endless anthems raise.

Rev. Henry Alford (1810—1871), 1830.

404 *The High-way to Zion.* **C. M.**
Is. xxxv. 8—10.

1 SING, ye redeeméd of the Lord,
Your great Deliverer sing:
Pilgrims for Zion's city bound,
Be joyful in your King.

2 A hand divine shall lead you on
Through all the blissful road,
Till to the sacred mount you rise,
And see your smiling God.

3 There garlands of immortal joy
Shall bloom on every head;
While sorrow, crying, and distress,
Like shadows all are fled.

4 March on in your Redeemer's strength;
Pursue His footsteps still;
And let the prospect cheer your eye,
While laboring up the hill.
Rev. Philip Doddridge, 1755.

CLINTON. C. M.
JOSEPH PERRY HOLBROOK (1822—).

1. WHEN I can read my ti - tle clear To man-sions in the skies,

I bid fare - well to ev - 'ry fear, And wipe my weep - ing eyes.

405 *Heavenly Hope.*

2 Should earth against my soul engage,
And hellish darts be hurled,
Then I can smile at Satan's rage,
And face a frowning world.

3 Let cares like a wild deluge come,
And storms of sorrow fall;
May I but safely reach my home,
My God, my Heaven, my All;

4 There shall I bathe my weary soul
In seas of heavenly rest,
And not a wave of trouble roll
Across my peaceful breast.
Rev. Isaac Watts (1674—1748), 1709.

406 *Watching for the Morning.*

1 LIGHT of the lonely pilgrim's heart,
Star of the coming day,
Arise, and, with Thy morning beams,
Chase all our griefs away.

2 Come, blesséd Lord, bid every shore
And answering island sing
The praises of Thy royal Name,
And own Thee as their King.

3 Lord, Lord, Thy fair creation groans,
The air, the earth, the sea,
In unison with all our hearts,
And calls aloud for Thee.

4 Thine was the cross, with all its fruits
Of grace and peace divine:
Be Thine the crown of glory now,
The palm of victory Thine.
Sir Edward Denny (1796—), 1839. Ab.

LUX BENIGNA. 10, 4, 10. 10.   Rev. JOHN BACCHUS DYKES (1823—1876), 1861.

1. LEAD, kind - ly Light, a - mid th' en - cir - cling gloom, Lead Thou me on; The night is
dark, and I am far from home, Lead Thou me on; Keep Thou my feet; I
do not ask to see The dis - tant scene; one step e - nough for me.

407

"Lead Thou me on."

2 I was not ever thus, nor prayed that Thou
   Shouldst lead me on ;
I loved to choose and see my path ; but now
   Lead Thou me on !
I loved the garish day, and, spite of fears,
Pride ruled my will. Remember not past
   years !

3 So long Thy power has blest me, sure it still
   Will lead me on
O'er moor and fen, o'er crag and torrent, till
   The night is gone,
And with the morn those angel faces smile
Which I have loved long since, and lost
   awhile !

              Rev. John Henry Newman (1801—   ), 1833.

OLMUTZ. S. M.   Gregorian. Arr. by LOWELL MASON (1792—1872), 1832.

1. YOUR harps, ye trem - bling saints, Down from the wil - lows take; Loud
to the praise of love di - vine Bid ev - 'ry string a - wake.

408

Weak Believers encouraged.

2 Though in a foreign land,
   We are not far from home ;
And nearer to our house above
   We every moment come.

3 His grace will to the end
   Stronger and brighter shine ;
Nor present things, nor things to come,
   Shall quench the spark divine.

4 Soon shall our doubts and fears
  Subside at His control;
  His loving-kindness shall break through
  The midnight of the soul.

5 Blest is the man, O God,
  That stays himself on Thee;
  Who wait for Thy salvation, Lord,
  Shall Thy salvation see.

  Rev. Augustus Montague Toplady (1740—1778), 1772. Ab.

AMSTERDAM. 7.6.D.

JAMES NARES (1715—1783), 1778.

1. Rise, my soul, and stretch thy wings, Thy better portion trace;
   Rise from transitory things Towards Heav'n, thy native place:
   Sun and moon and stars decay; Time shall soon this earth remove;
   Rise, my soul, and haste away To seats pre-par'd above.

409 *"Rise, my Soul."*

2 Rivers to the ocean run,
  Nor stay in all their course;
  Fire, ascending, seeks the sun;
  Both speed them to their source:
  So a soul, that's born of God,
  Pants to view His glorious face,
  Upward tends to His abode,
  To rest in His embrace.

3 Cease, ye pilgrims, cease to mourn,
  Press onward to the prize;
  Soon our Saviour will return
  Triumphant in the skies:
  Yet a season, and you know
  Happy entrance will be given,
  All our sorrows left below,
  And earth exchanged for Heaven.

  Rev. Robert Seagrave (1693—), 1742. Ab.

410 *"Time is winging us away."*

1 Time is winging us away
  To our eternal home;
  Life is but a winter's day,
  A journey to the tomb;
  Youth and vigor soon will flee,
  Blooming beauty lose its charms;
  All that's mortal soon shall be
  Enclosed in death's cold arms.

2 Time is winging us away
  To our eternal home;
  Life is but a winter's day,
  A journey to the tomb;
  But the Christian shall enjoy
  Health and beauty soon, above,
  Far beyond the world's annoy,
  Secure in Jesus' love.

  John Burton (1773—1822), 1815.

NEW JERUSALEM. 7. 6. 7. 7. 7.   Old English Melody.

1. WE are on our jour-ney home, Where Christ our Lord is gone; We shall meet a-round His throne,

When He makes His peo-ple one In the new, In the new Je-ru-sa-lem.

In the new Je-ru-sa-lem.

411   *"New Jerusalem."*

2 We can see that distant home,
   Though clouds rise dark between;
  Faith views the radiant dome,
   And a lustre flashes keen
   ||: From the new :|| Jerusalem.

3 O glory shining far
   From the never-setting Sun,
  O trembling morning-star,
   Our journey's almost done
   ||: To the new :|| Jerusalem.

4 O holy, heavenly home,
   O rest eternal there:
  When shall the exiles come,
   Where they cease from earthly care
   ||: In the new :|| Jerusalem.

5 Our hearts are breaking now
   Those mansions fair to see
  O Lord, Thy heavens bow,
   And raise us up with Thee
   ||: To the new :|| Jerusalem.

Rev. Charles Beecher (1819—   ), 1857.

SCHELL. 10. 10. 11. 12.   UZZIAH CHRISTOPHER BURNAP (1834—), 1869.

1. BREAST the wave, Chris-tian, when it is stron-gest; Watch for day, Chris-tian,

when night is lon-gest; On-ward and on-ward still be thine en-

deav-or; The rest that re-main-eth, en-dur-eth for-ev-er.

412

"*Lay Hold on eternal Life.*"
1 TIM. vi. 12.

2 Fight the fight, Christian, Jesus is o'er thee;
Run the race, Christian, Heaven is before thee;
He who hath promised faltereth never;
O trust in the love that endureth forever.

3 Lift the eye, Christian, just as it closeth;
Raise the heart, Christian, ere it reposeth;
Nothing thy soul from the Saviour shall sever;
Soon shalt thou mount upward to praise Him forever.

Joseph Stammers (1801—   ), 1830. Alt.

LANGRAN. 10.

JAMES LANGRAN (1835—   ), 1862.

1. My feet are worn and wea-ry with the march O'er the rough road and up the steep hill-side;

O Cit-y of our God, I fain would see Thy pastures green, where peaceful wa-ters glide.

413

"*Worn and Weary*"

2 My garments, travel-worn and stained with dust,
    Oft rent by briers and thorns that crowd my way,
Would fain be made, O Lord, my Righteousness,
    Spotless and white in Heaven's unclouded ray.

3 My heart is weary of its own deep sin:
    Sinning, repenting, sinning still again;
When shall my soul Thy glorious presence feel,
    And find, dear Saviour, it is free from stain?

4 Patience, poor soul! the Saviour's feet were worn,
    The Saviour's heart and hands were weary, too;
His garments stained and travel-worn, and old,
    His vision blinded with a pitying dew.

5 Love thou the path of sorrow that He trod;
    Toil on, and wait in patience for thy rest;
O City of our God, we soon shall see
    Thy jasper walls, home of the loved and blest.

S. Roberts. From "Songs in the Night." 1853

WINN. S. M.

WILLIAM WINN (1828—), 1872.

1. SWEET is Thy mer - cy, Lord; Be - fore Thy mer - cy - seat My soul, a - dor - ing, pleads Thy word, And owns Thy mer - cy sweet.

414   "Thy Mercy Sweet."   Ps. cix, 26.

2 My need, and Thy desires,
Are all in Christ complete;
Thou hast the justice truth requires,
And I Thy mercy sweet.

3 Where'er Thy Name is blest,
Where'er Thy people meet,
There I delight in Thee to rest,
And find Thy mercy sweet.

4 Light Thou my weary way,
Place Thou my weary feet,
That while I stray on earth I may
Still find Thy mercy sweet.

5 Thus shall the heavenly host
Hear all my songs repeat
To Father, Son, and Holy Ghost,
My joy, Thy mercy sweet.

Rev. John Samuel Bewley Monsell (1811—1875), 1862.

ASAPH. L. M.

FELIX MENDELSSOHN-BARTHOLDY (1809—1847).

1. O Thou, to whose all - search-ing sight The dark - ness shin - eth as the light, Search, prove my heart, it pants for Thee; O burst these bonds, and set it free.

415   "Seelenbräutigam, o Du Gottes-Lamm."

2 Wash out its stains, refine its dross;
Nail my affections to the cross;
Hallow each thought; let all within
Be clean, as Thou, my Lord, art clean.

3 If in this darksome wild I stray,
Be Thou my Light, be Thou my Way;
No foes, no violence I fear,
No fraud, while Thou, my God, art near.

4 When rising floods my soul o'erflow,
  When sinks my heart in waves of woe,
  Jesus, Thy timely aid impart,
  And raise my head, and cheer my heart.

5 Saviour, where'er Thy steps I see,
  Dauntless, untired, I follow Thee:
  O let Thy hand support me still,
  And lead me to Thy holy hill.

Gerhard Tersteegen (1697—1769),
Tr. by Rev. John Wesley (1703—1791), 1738. Ab.

BANNER. 6.5.D.

Arr. from Sir ARTHUR SULLIVAN (1842—). 1872.

1. Brightly gleams our ban-ner, Point-ing to the sky, Wav-ing wand'rers on-ward To their home on high; Journ'ying o'er a des-ert, Glad-ly thus we pray, Still with hearts u-nit-ed, Sing-ing on our way. Bright-ly gleams our ban-ner, Point-ing to the sky, Wav-ing wan-d'rers on-ward To their home on high.

416 *The Guiding Banner.*

2 All our days direct us
    In the way we go,
  Lead us on victorious
    Over every foe;
  Bid Thine angels shield us,
    When the storm-clouds lower,
  Pardon Thou and save us
    In the last dread hour.
      Brightly gleams, &c.

3 Then with saints and angels
    May we join above,
  Offering prayers and praises
    At Thy throne of love;
  When the toil is over
    Then comes rest and peace,
  Jesus in His beauty,
    Songs that never cease.
      Brightly gleams, &c.

Rev. Thomas Joseph Potter (1823—1873), 1862. Ab

216

ALBAN. 6.5.D.

From FRANCIS JOSEPH HAYDN (1732—1809).

1. FORWARD! be our watch-word, Steps and voic-es join'd; Seek the things be-fore us,

Not a look be-hind: Burns the fie-ry pil-lar At our ar-my's head;

Who shall dream of shrink-ing, By our Cap-tain led? Forward through the des-ert,

Through the toil and fight: Jor-dan flows be-fore us, Zi-on beams with light!

417

"Forward into Light!"
Ex. xiv. 15.

2 Forward, flock of Jesus,
  Salt of all the earth;
Till each yearning purpose
  Spring to glorious birth:
Sick, they ask for healing,
  Blind, they grope for day;
Pour upon the nations
  Wisdom's loving ray.
Forward, out of error,
  Leave behind the night;
Forward through the darkness,
  Forward into light!

3 Far o'er yon horizon
  Rise the city towers,
Where our God abideth;
  That fair home is ours:
Flash the walls with jasper,
  Shine the streets with gold;
Flows the gladdening river
  Shedding joys untold;
Thither, onward thither,
  In the Spirit's might:
Pilgrims to your country,
  Forward into light!

Rev. Henry Alford (1810—1871), 1865   Ab. and alt.

GERTRUDE. 6.5.D.

Sir ARTHUR SULLIVAN (1842—), 1872.

1. ON-WARD, Chris-tian sol - diers, March-ing as to war, With the cross of Je - sus

Go - ing on be - fore. Christ, the Roy - al Mas - ter, Leads a - gainst the foe;

For-ward in - to bat - tle, See, His ban-ners go. On - ward, Chris-tian sol - diers,

March-ing as to war, With the cross of Je - sus Go - ing on be - fore.

418 *"Onward, Christian Soldiers."*

2 Like a mighty army
   Moves the Church of God:
Brothers, we are treading
   Where the saints have trod;
We are not divided,
   All one body we,
One in hope and doctrine,
   One in charity.
      Onward, &c.

3 Crowns and thrones may perish,
   Kingdoms rise and wane,
But the Church of Jesus
   Constant will remain:

Gates of hell can never
   'Gainst that Church prevail:
We have Christ's own promise,
   And that cannot fail.
      Onward, &c.

4 Onward, then, ye people,
   Join our happy throng,
Blend with ours your voices
   In the triumph-song:
Glory, laud, and honor
   Unto Christ our King;
This through countless ages,
   Men and angels sing.
      Onward, &c.

Rev. Sabine Baring-Gould (1834—), 1865. Ab. and sl. alt.

218

ST. ANDREW. 6.5.D.

Rev. JOHN BACCHUS DYKES (1823—1876), 1868.

1. CHRISTIAN, dost thou see them On the ho-ly ground, How the troops of Mid-ian Prowl and prowl a-round? Chris-tian, up and smite them, Count-ing gain but loss; Smite them by the mer-it Of the ho-ly cross.

419

Οὐ γὰρ βλέπεις τοὺς ταράττοντας.

2 Christian, dost thou hear them,
    How they speak thee fair?
 "Always fast and vigil?
    Always watch and prayer?"
 Christian, say but boldly,
    "While I breathe I pray."
 Peace shall follow battle,
    Night shall end in day.

3 "Well I know thy trouble,
    O My servant true;
 Thou art very weary,
    I was weary, too;
 But that toil shall make thee
    Some day all Mine own,
 And the end of sorrow
    Shall be near My throne."

St. Andrew of Crete (66o—732).
Tr. by Rev. John Mason Neale (1818—1866), 1862. Ab.

PARK STREET. L. M.

FREDERICK MARC ANTOINE VENUA (1788—   ), 1810.

1. FIGHT the good fight with all thy might, Christ is thy strength, and Christ thy right; Lay hold on life, and it shall be Thy joy and crown e-ter-nal-ly, Thy joy and crown e-ter-nal-ly.

420 *"The good Fight."*
1 Tim. vi. 12.

2 Run the straight race through God's
  good grace,
  Lift up thine eyes, and seek His face ;
  Life with its way before us lies,
  Christ is the path, and Christ the prize.

3 Cast care aside, upon thy guide
  Lean, and His mercy will provide ;

Lean, and the trusting soul shall prove
Christ is its life, and Christ its love.

4 Faint not nor fear, His arms are near,
  He changeth not, and thou art dear ;
  Only believe, and thou shalt see
  That Christ is all in all to thee.

Rev. John Samuel Bewley Monsell (1811—1875), 1863.

MENDON. L. M.   German. Arr. by LOWELL MASON (1792—1872), 1859.

1. STAND up, my soul, shake off thy fears, And gird the gos - pel arm - or on ;

March to the gates of end - less joy, Where Je - sus, thy great Cap - tain's gone.

421 *"March boldly on."*

2 Hell and thy sins resist thy course,
  But hell and sin are vanquished foes ;
  Thy Jesus nailed them to the cross,
  And sung the triumph when He rose.

3 Then let my soul march boldly on,
  Press forward to the heavenly gate :
  There peace and joy eternal reign,
  And glittering robes for conquerors wait.

4 There shall I wear a starry crown,
  And triumph in almighty grace ;
  While all the armies of the skies
  Join in my glorious Leader's praise.

Rev. Isaac Watts (1674—1748), 1709. Ab. and alt.

422 *Walking by Faith.*

1 'Tis by the faith of joys to come,
  We walk through deserts dark as night ;

Till we arrive at Heaven, our home.
  Faith is our guide, and faith our light.

2 The want of sight she well supplies ;
  She makes the pearly gates appear ;
  Far into distant worlds she pries,
  And brings eternal glories near.

3 Cheerful we tread the desert through,
  While faith inspires a heavenly ray ;
  Though lions roar and tempests blow,
  And rocks and dangers fill the way.

4 So Abr'am, by divine command,
  Left his own house to walk with God ;
  His faith beheld the promised land,
  And fired his zeal along the road.

Rev. Isaac Watts, 1709.

FRANCONIA. S. M.

German Melody, circa 1720.

1. SOL - DIERS of Christ, a - rise, And put your arm - or on, Strong

in the strength which God sup - plies Through His e - ter - nal Son.

423

"*The whole Armor.*"
Eph. vi. 11—18.

2 Strong in the Lord of hosts,
  And in His mighty power,
Who in the strength of Jesus trusts,
  Is more than conqueror.

3 Stand, then, in His great might,
  With all His strength endued,
And take, to arm you for the fight,
  The panoply of God.

4 Leave no unguarded place,
  No weakness of the soul;
Take every virtue, every grace,
  And fortify the whole.

5 To keep your armor bright,
  Attend with constant care,
Still walking in your Captain's sight,
  And watching unto prayer,

Rev. Charles Wesley (17..—1788), 1749. Ab.

VICTORIA. L. M. D.

HENRY LAHEE (1826—), 1861.

1. ARM these Thy sol-diers, mighty Lord, With shield of faith and Spir-it's sword; Forth to the bat-tle

may they go, And bold-ly fight a-gainst the foe, With ban-ner of the cross un-furl'd, And by it

o - vercome the world; And so at last re-ceive from Thee The palm and crown of vic - to - ry.

424 *"Arm these Thy Soldiers."*

2 Come, ever-blessèd Spirit, come,
  And make Thy servants' hearts Thy home;
  May each a living temple be,
  Hallowed for ever, Lord, to Thee;

Enrich that temple's holy shrine
With sevenfold gifts of grace divine;
With wisdom, light, and knowledge bless,
Strength, counsel, fear, and godliness.

Bp. Christopher Wordsworth (1807—1885), 1863. Ab.

LABAN. S. M.   LOWELL MASON (1792—1872), 1830.

1. MY soul, be on thy guard; Ten thou-sand foes a-rise, And
hosts of sin are press-ing hard To draw thee from the skies.

425 *"Be on thy Guard."*

2 O watch, and fight, and pray,
   The battle ne'er give o'er;
  Renew it boldly every day,
   And help divine implore.

3 Ne'er think the victory won,
   Nor once at ease sit down;
  Thine arduous work will not be done
   Till thou receive thy crown.

4 Fight on, my soul, till death
   Shall bring thee to thy God;
  He'll take thee, at thy parting breath,
   To His divine abode.

George Heath, 1781.

426 *"Keep the Charge of the Lord."*
Lev. viii. 35.

1 A CHARGE to keep I have,
   A God to glorify,
  A never-dying soul to save,
   And fit it for the sky;

2 To serve the present age,
   My calling to fulfil:
  O may it all my powers engage
   To do my Master's will.

3 Arm me with jealous care,
   As in Thy sight to live,

And O Thy servant, Lord, prepare
 A strict account to give.

Help me to watch and pray,
 And on Thyself rely,
Assured, if I my trust betray,
 I shall for ever die.

Rev. Charles Wesley, 1762.

427 *"Weigh not thy Life."*

1 My soul, weigh not thy life
   Against thy heavenly crown,
  Nor suffer Satan's deadliest strife
   To beat thy courage down.

2 With prayer and crying strong,
   Maintain the fearful fight,
  And let the breaking day prolong
   The wrestling of the night.

3 The battle soon will yield,
   If thou thy part fulfil;
  For strong as is the hostile shield,
   Thy sword is stronger still.

4 Thine armor is divine,
   Thy feet with victory shod;
  And on thy head shall quickly shine
   The diadem of God.

Rev. Leonard Swain (1821—1869), 1858. Sl. alt.

VIGILATE. 7. 7. 7. 3.

WILLIAM HENRY MONK (1823–). 1874.

1. CHRIS - TIAN, seek not yet re - pose, Cast thy dreams of ease a - way;

Thou art in the midst of foes: Watch and pray.

428   *"Watch and pray."* MARK xiv. 38; Col. iv. 2.

2 Gird thy heavenly armor on,
   Wear it ever, night and day;
   Ambushed lies the evil one:
        Watch and pray.

3 Hear the victors who o'ercame;
   Still they mark each warrior's way;

All with warning voice exclaim:
        Watch and pray.

4 Watch, as if on that alone
   Hung the issue of the day;
   Pray that help may be sent down:
        Watch and pray.

Bp. William Walsham How (1823–), 1872. Ab. and alt.
Miss Charlotte Elliott (1789–1871), 1859.

INNOCENTS. 7.

Ascribed to THEOBALD, King of Navarre (1201–1253).

1. SOL - DIERS, who are Christ's be - low, Strong in faith re - sist the foe:

Bound - less is the pledg'd re - ward Un - to them who serve the Lord.

429   *"He that overcometh."* REV. iii. 21.

2 'Tis no palm of fading leaves
   That the conqueror's hand receives;
   Joys are his, serene and pure,
   Light, that ever shall endure.

3 For the souls that overcome,
   Waits the beauteous heavenly home,
   Where the Blessèd evermore
   Tread, on high, the starry floor.

4 Passing soon, and little worth,
Are the things that tempt on earth ;
Heavenward lift thy soul's regard ;
God Himself is thy Reward.

5 Father, Who the crown dost give,
Saviour, by Whose death we live,
Spirit, Who our hearts dost raise,
Three in One, Thy Name we praise.

Paris Breviary, 1736
Tr. by Rev. J. H. Clark (—).

CHRISTMAS. C. M.

GEORGE FREDERICK HANDEL (1685—1759).

1. Am I a sol-dier of the cross, A foll'wer of the Lamb? And shall I fear to own His cause, Or blush to speak His Name? Or blush to speak His Name?

430

"Quit you like Men."
1 Cor. xvi. 13.

2 Must I be carried to the skies
On flowery beds of ease,
While others fought to win the prize,
And sailed through bloody seas?

3 Are there no foes for me to face?
Must I not stem the flood?
Is this vile world a friend to grace,
To help me on to God?

4 Sure I must fight, if I would reign ;
Increase my courage, Lord ;
I'll bear the toil, endure the pain,
Supported by Thy word.

5 Thy saints, in all this glorious war,
Shall conquer, though they die ;
They view the triumph from afar,
And seize it with their eye.

6 When that illustrious day shall rise,
And all Thine armies shine
In robes of victory through the skies,
The glory shall be Thine.

Rev. Isaac Watts (1674—1748), 1720.

431

Pressing on.
Phil. iii. 12—14.

1 Awake, my soul, stretch every nerve,
And press with vigor on :
A heavenly race demands thy zeal,
And an immortal crown.

2 A cloud of witnesses around
Hold thee in full survey ;
Forget the steps already trod,
And onward urge thy way.

3 'Tis God's all-animating voice
That calls thee from on high ;
'Tis His own hand presents the prize
To thine aspiring eye :—

4 That prize with peerless glories bright,
Which shall new lustre boast,
When victors' wreaths and monarchs' gems
Shall blend in common dust. [gems

5 Blest Saviour, introduced by Thee,
Have I my race begun :
And, crowned with victory, at Thy feet
I'll lay my honors down.

Rev. Philip Doddridge (1702—1751), 1755.

WEBB. 7. 6. D.　　　　　　　　　　　GEORGE JAMES WEBB (1803—　　), 1830.

1. Go for-ward, Christian sol - dier, Be - neath His ban - ner true: The Lord Himself, thy Lead - er,
D. S.—He can, with bread of Heav - en,

Shall all thy foes sub - due. His love fore-tells thy tri - als, He knows thine hourly need;
Thy faint-ing spir - it feed.

432　　*"Go forward, Christian Soldier."*

2 Go forward, Christian soldier,
　Fear not the secret foe;
Far more are o'er thee watching
　Than human eyes can know.
Trust only Christ, thy Captain,
　Cease not to watch and pray;
Heed not the treacherous voices,
　That lure thy soul astray.

3 Go forward, Christian soldier,
　Nor dream of peaceful rest,
Till Satan's host is vanquished,
　And Heaven is all possest;

Till Christ Himself shall call thee
　To lay thine armor by,
And wear, in endless glory,
　The crown of victory.

4 Go forward, Christian soldier,
　Fear not the gathering night;
The Lord has been thy shelter,
　The Lord will be thy light;
When morn His face revealeth,
　Thy dangers all are past;
O pray that faith and virtue
　May keep thee to the last.

Rev. Lawrence Tuttiett (1825—　　), 1866.

FERGUSON. S. M.　　　　　　　　　GEORGE KINGSLEY (1811—1884), 1843.

1. RE - JOICE, ye pure in heart, Re - joice, give thanks and sing; Your

fes - tal ban - ner wave on high, The cross of Christ your King.

433   *Marching on.*

2 Your clear hosannas raise,
　　And alleluias loud ;
　While answering echoes upward float,
　　Like wreaths of incense-cloud.

3 Still lift your standard high,
　　Still march in firm array,
　As warriors through the darkness toil,
　　Till dawns the golden day.

4 At last the march shall end,
　　The wearied ones shall rest,
　The pilgrims find the Father's house,
　　Jerusalem the blest.

5 Then on, ye pure in heart ;
　　Rejoice, give thanks, and sing ;
　Your festal banner wave on high,
　　The cross of Christ your King.

　　　　　　　　Rev. Edward Hayes Plumptre (1821—　), Ab.

UNSELD. 7.6.D.   BENJAMIN CARL UNSELD (1843—　), 1893.

1. STAND up, stand up for Je - sus, Ye sol - diers of the cross ; Lift high His roy - al ban - ner, It must not suf - fer loss : From vic - t'ry un - to vic - t'ry His ar - my shall He lead, Till ev - 'ry foe is vanquish'd, And Christ is Lord in - deed.

434   *"Stand up, stand up for Jesus!"*

2 Stand up, stand up for Jesus,
　The trumpet call obey :
Forth to the mighty conflict,
　In this His glorious day :
"Ye that are men, now serve Him"
　Against unnumbered foes ;
Let courage rise with danger,
　And strength to strength oppose.

3 Stand up, stand up for Jesus,
　Stand in His strength alone ;
The arm of flesh will fail you,
　Ye dare not trust your own :

Put on the gospel armor,
　Each piece put on with prayer ;
Where duty calls, or danger,
　Be never wanting there.

4 Stand up, stand up for Jesus,
　The strife will not be long ;
This day, the noise of battle,
　The next, the victor's song :
To him that overcometh,
　A crown of life shall be ;
He with the King of Glory
　Shall reign eternally.

　　　　　　Rev. George Duffield (1818—　), 1858. Ab.

EIN FESTE BURG. P. M.

Arr. from Rev. MARTIN LUTHER (1483—1546), 1529.

1. A MIGHT-Y For - tress is our God, A bul - wark nev - er fail - ing;

Our Help - er He, a - mid the flood Of mor - tal ills pre - vail - ing.

For still our an - cient foe Doth seek to work us woe; His craft and pow'r are great,

And arm'd with cru - el hate, On earth is not his e - qual.

435 *"A Mighty Fortress."*

2 Did we in our own strength confide,
 Our striving would be losing;
Were not the right man on our side,
 The man of God's own choosing.
Dost ask who that may be?
Christ Jesus, it is He;
Lord Sabaoth is His Name,
From age to age the same,
And He must win the battle.

3 And though this world, with devils filled,
 Should threaten to undo us,
We will not fear, for God hath willed
 His truth to triumph through us.
The Prince of darkness grim,

We tremble not for him;
His rage we can endure,
For lo! his doom is sure:
One little word shall fell him.

4 That word above all earthly powers,
 No thanks to them, abideth:
The Spirit and the gifts are ours
 Through Him who with us sideth.
Let goods and kindred go,
This mortal life also:
The body they may kill;
God's truth abideth still,
 His Kingdom is for ever.

Rev. Martin Luther (1483—1546), 1527.
Tr. by Rev. Frederick Henry Hedge (1805—), 1856?

436 *"Praise Him, all ye People."*
Ps. cxvii. 1. Rom xv. 11
P. M.

1 REJOICE to-day with one accord,
  Sing out with exultation ;
Rejoice and praise our mighty Lord,
  Whose arm hath brought salvation ;
His works of love proclaim
The greatness of His Name ;
  For He is God alone,
  Who hath His mercy shown ;
  Let all His saints adore Him !

2 When in distress to Him we cried,
  He heard our sad complaining ;
Oh, trust in Him, whate'er betide,
  His love is all-sustaining ;

Triumphant songs of praise
To Him our hearts shall raise ;
  Now every voice shall say,
  "O praise our God alway :"
  Let all His saints adore Him !

3 Rejoice to-day with one accord,
  Sing out with exultation ;
Rejoice and praise our mighty Lord,
  Whose arm hath brought salvation ;
His works of love proclaim
The greatness of His Name ;
  For He is God alone,
  Who hath His mercy shown ;
  Let all His saints adore Him !

Rev. Sir Henry Williams Baker (1821—1877), 1861.

SALZBURG. 7. D.
JOHANN SEBASTIAN BACH (1685—1750).

1. { MARCH, march on - ward, sol - diers true! Take through cloud and mist your way,)
{ Yon - der flows the fount of life, Yon - der dwells e - ter - nal day. }

March, though myr - iad foes are nigh, For - ward till you reach the shore,

Then, when all the strife is done, Rest in peace for ev - er - more.

437 *The good Soldier.*
2 Tim. ii. 3.

2 Hark, hark, loud the trumpet sounds !
  Wake, ye children of the light ;
Time is past for sloth and sleep ;
  Wake, and arm you for the fight !
Spear and sword each warrior needs ;
  Foes are round you, friends are few ;
Faint not, though the way be long ;
  Fainting, still your way pursue !

3 See, see, yonder shines your home,
  Gates of pearl, and streets of gold,
Joy, that heart hath never known,
  Bliss, that tongue hath never told.
Victors then through Christ your Lord,
  Gathered round His glorious throne,
Be it yours to sing His praise,
  Praise that He, your King, shall own.

His Royal Highness, Prince Albert (1819—1861), Ab. and sl. alt.

MARCHING TO VICTORY.

GREATHEART. P. M.

JOSEPH BARNBY (1838—). 1869.

We march, we march to vic-to-ry, With the cross of the Lord be-fore us,

D. S.—march, we march, &c.

With His lov-ing eye look-ing down from the sky, And His ho-ly arm spread o'er us,

FINE. vv. 1-2. *Last verse only.*

His ho-ly arm spread o'er us, o'er us. 1. We come in the might of the Lord of light,

His arm

A joy-ful host to meet Him; And we put to flight the ar-mies of night,

D.S.

That the sons of the day may greet Him, The sons of the day may greet Him. We

438   *Marching to Victory.*

2 And the choir of angels with song awaits
   Our march to the golden Zion ;
For our Captain has broken the brazen
         gates,
   And burst the bars of iron.
      We march, we march, &c.

3 Then onward we march, our arms to prove,
      With the banner of Christ before us,
   With His eye of love looking down from
         above,
   And His holy arm spread o'er us
      We march, we march, &c.

Rev. Gerard Moultrie (1839—), 1867. Ab.

ANGELUS. L. M. GEORG JOSEPHI, 1657.

1. JE - SUS, and shall it ev - er be, A mor-tal man a-sham'd of Thee?

A-sham'd of Thee, whom an - gels praise, Whose glo - ries shine through end - less days?

439 *Not ashamed of Jesus.* ROM. i. 16. HEB. ii. 11.

2 Ashamed of Jesus! sooner far
Let evening blush to own a star:
He sheds the beams of light divine
O'er this benighted soul of mine.

3 Ashamed of Jesus, that dear Friend,
On whom my hopes of Heaven depend!
No, when I blush, be this my shame,
That I no more revere His Name.

4 Ashamed of Jesus! yes, I may,
When I've no guilt to wash away,
No tear to wipe, no good to crave,
No fear to quell, no soul to save.

5 Till then, nor is my boasting vain,
Till then I boast a Saviour slain;
And O, may this my glory be,
That Christ is not ashamed of me.
Rev. Joseph Grigg (—1768), 1765. Ab. and alt.
Rev. Benjamin Francis (1734—1799), 1787.

440 *"Take up thy Cross"* MATT. xvi. 24.

1 TAKE up thy cross, the Saviour said,
If thou wouldst My disciple be;
Deny thyself, the world forsake,
And humbly follow after Me.

2 Take up thy cross; let not its weight
Fill thy weak spirit with alarm;
His strength shall bear thy spirit up,
And brace thy heart, and nerve thine arm.

3 Take up thy cross, nor heed the shame,
Nor let thy foolish pride rebel:
Thy Lord for thee the cross endured,
To save thy soul from death and hell.

4 Take up thy cross, and follow Christ,
Nor think till death to lay it down;
For only he who bears the cross
May hope to wear the starry crown.
Rev. Charles William Everest (1814—1877), 1833. Ab and alt.

FEDERAL STREET. L. M. HENRY KEMBLE OLIVER (1800—1885), 1832.

RATHBUN. 8.7.   ITHAMAR CONKEY (1815—1867), 1851.

1. In the cross of Christ I glo-ry, Tow-'ring o'er the wrecks of time;

All the light of sa - cred sto - ry Gath-ers round its head sub-lime.

441
"In the Cross of Christ I glory."
GAL. vi, 14

2 When the woes of life o'ertake me,
  Hopes deceive, and fears annoy,
Never shall the cross forsake me ;
  Lo, it glows with peace and joy.

3 When the sun of bliss is beaming
  Light and love upon my way,
From the cross the radiance streaming
  Adds more lustre to the day.

4 Bane and blessing, pain and pleasure,
  By the cross are sanctified ;
Peace is there, that knows no measure,
  Joys that through all time abide.

5 In the cross of Christ I glory,
  Towering o'er the wrecks of time ;
All the light of sacred story
  Gathers round its head sublime.
         Sir John Bowring (1792—1872), 1825.

442
Hasting on.

1 TAKE, my soul, thy full salvation,
  Rise o'er sin, and fear, and care ;
Joy to find in every station
  Something still to do or bear.

2 Think what Spirit dwells within thee ;
  What a Father's smile is thine :
What a Saviour died to win thee :
  Child of Heaven, shouldst thou repine?

3 Haste thee on from grace to glory,
  Armed by faith, and winged by prayer :
Heaven's eternal day's before thee,
  God's own hand shall guide thee there.

4 Soon shall close thy earthly mission,
  Swift shall pass thy pilgrim days,
Hope soon change to glad fruition,
  Faith to sight, and prayer to praise.
         Rev. Henry Francis Lyte (1793—1847), 1824. Ab.

443
"Follow Me."

1 JESUS calls us : o'er the tumult
  Of our life's wild, restless sea,
Day by day His sweet voice soundeth,
  Softly, clearly—" Follow Me."

2 Jesus calls us, from the evil
  In a world we cannot flee,
From each idol that would keep us,
  Softly, clearly—" Follow Me."

3 Still in joy and still in sadness
  We discern our own decree :
Still He calls, in cares and pleasures,
  Softly, clearly—" Follow Me."

4 Thou dost call us! may we ever
  To Thy call attentive be ;
Give our hearts to Thine obedience,
  Rise, leave all, and follow Thee.
    Mrs. Cecil Frances Alexander (1823—), 1858. Ab. and alt

BETHABARA. 8.7.D. HENRY SMART (1812—1879).

1. Je - sus, I my cross have tak - en, All to leave, and fol - low Thee; Des - ti - tute, de-
spis'd, for - sak - en, Thou, henceforth, my all shalt be: Per - ish, ev - 'ry fond am - bi - tion,
All I've sought, and hop'd, and known; Yet how rich is my con - di - tion, God and Heav'n are still my own!

444 *"Leaving all."* MARK x. 28.

2 Let the world despise and leave me,
  They have left my Saviour, too;
Human hearts and looks deceive me;
  Thou art not, like man, untrue;
And while Thou shalt smile upon me,
  God of wisdom, love, and might,
Foes may hate, and friends may shun me,
  Show Thy face, and all is bright.

3 Go, then, earthly fame and treasure;
  Come, disaster, scorn, and pain!
In Thy service, pain is pleasure;
  With Thy favor, loss is gain.

I have called Thee, Abba, Father;
  I have stayed my heart on Thee:
Storms may howl, and clouds may gather,
  All must work for good to me.

4 Man may trouble and distress me,
  'Twill but drive me to Thy breast;
Life with trials hard may press me,
  Heaven will bring me sweeter rest.
O 'tis not in grief to harm me,
  While Thy love is left to me;
O 'twere not in joy to charm me,
  Were that joy unmixed with Thee.

Rev. Henry Francis Lyte, 1824. Sl. alt.

BAYLEY. 8.7.D. Arr. by JOSEPH PERRY HOLBROOK (1822—).

MAITLAND. C. M. AARON CHAPIN, c. 1805.

1. Must Je - sus bear the cross a - lone, And all the world go free?
No, there's a cross for ev - 'ry one, And there's a cross for me.

445

No Cross, no Crown.

2 How happy are the saints above,
　Who once went sorrowing here!
But now they taste unmingled love,
　And joy without a tear.

3 The consecrated cross I'll bear,
　Till death shall set me free;
And then go home my crown to wear,
　For there's a crown for me.

4 O precious cross! O glorious crown!
　O resurrection day!
Ye angels, from the stars come down,
　And bear my soul away.

Thomas Shepherd (1665—1739), 1692. Vs. 1. Alt.
Prof. George Nelson Allen (1812—1877), 1849. Vs. 2, 3.
Plymouth Collection, 1855. Vs. 4.

446

Christ our Example.
John xiii. 15.

1 Lord, as to Thy dear cross we flee,
　And plead to be forgiven,
So let Thy life our pattern be,
　And form our souls for Heaven.

2 Help us, through good report and ill,
　Our daily cross to bear;
Like Thee, to do our Father's will,
　Our brethren's griefs to share.

3 If joy shall at Thy bidding fly,
　And grief's dark day come on,
We in our turn would meekly cry
　Father, Thy will be done.

4 Should friends misjudge, or foes defame,
　Or brethren faithless prove,
Then, like Thine own, be all our aim
　To conquer them by love.

5 Kept peaceful in the midst of strife,
　Forgiving and forgiven,
O may we lead the pilgrim's life,
　And follow Thee to Heaven.

Rev. John Hampden Gurney (1802—1862), 1838. Ab.

447

"I am not ashamed."
2 Tim. i. 12.

1 I'm not ashamed to own my Lord,
　Or to defend His cause,
Maintain the honor of His word,
　The glory of His cross.

2 Jesus, my God! I know His Name,
　His Name is all my trust;
Nor will He put my soul to shame,
　Nor let my hope be lost.

3 Firm as His throne His promise stands,
　And He can well secure
What I've committed to His hands,
　Till the decisive hour.

4 Then will He own my worthless name
　Before His Father's face,
And in the New Jerusalem
　Appoint my soul a place.

Rev. Isaac Watts (1674—1748), 1709

ROSSINI. 6.4.D.

Arr. from GIACCHIMO ROSSINI (1792—1868).

1. FIERCE was the wild bil - low, Dark was the night, Oars la - bor'd heav - i - ly,

Foam glim - mer'd white, Trem - bled the mar - i - ners, Per - il was high;

Rall.

Last ending.

Then said the God of gods, "Peace! it is I!"

448

Ζοφερᾶς τρικυμίας.

2 Ridge of the mountain-wave,
Lower thy crest!
Wail of Euroclydon,
Be thou at rest!
Sorrow can never be,
Darkness must fly,
Where saith the Light of light,
"Peace! it is I!"

3 Jesus, Deliverer,
Come Thou to me:
Soothe Thou my voyaging
Over life's sea;
Thou, when the storm of death
Roars, sweeping by,
Whisper, Thou Truth of truth,
"Peace! it is I!"

Anatolius of Constantinople (—458).
Tr. by Rev. John Mason Neale (1818—1866), 1862. Alt.

449

Clinging to Christ.

1 CLING to the mighty One,
Cling in thy grief;

Cling to the holy One,
He gives relief;
Cling to the gracious One,
Cling in thy pain;
Cling to the faithful One,
He will sustain.

2 Cling to the living One,
Cling in thy woe;
Cling to the loving One,
Through all below;
Cling to the pardoning One,
He speaketh peace;
Cling to the healing One,
Anguish shall cease.

3 Cling to the piercèd One,
Cling to His side;
Cling to the risen One,
In Him abide;
Cling to the coming One,
Hope shall arise;
Cling to the reigning One,
Joy lights thine eyes.

Henry Bennett (1813—1868), 1852.

HOLLINGSIDE. 7. D.   Rev. JOHN BACCHUS DYKES (1823—1876), 1861.

1. Je - sus, Lov - er of my soul, Let me to Thy bo - som fly, While the bil-lows near - er roll, While the tem - pest still is high; Hide me, O my Sav - iour, hide, Till the storm of life is past; Safe in - to the ha - ven guide; O re-ceive my soul at last.

450   *"Jesus, Lover of my Soul."*

2 Other refuge have I none;
    Hangs my helpless soul on Thee;
Leave, ah! leave me not alone,
    Still support and comfort me.
All my trust on Thee is stayed,
    All my help from Thee I bring;
Cover my defenceless head
    With the shadow of Thy wing.

3 Wilt Thou not regard my call?
    Wilt Thou not accept my prayer?
Lo, I sink, I faint, I fall!
    Lo, on Thee I cast my care.
Reach me out Thy gracious hand!
    While I of Thy strength receive,
Hoping against hope I stand,
    Dying, and behold I live!

4 Thou, O Christ, art all I want ·
    More than all in Thee I find:
Raise the fallen, cheer the faint,
    Heal the sick, and lead the blind.
Just and holy is Thy Name;
    I am all unrighteousness;
False and full of sin I am,
    Thou art full of truth and grace.

5 Plenteous grace with Thee is found,
    Grace to cover all my sin:
Let the healing streams abound,
    Make and keep me pure within.
Thou of life the Fountain art;
    Freely let me take of Thee;
Spring Thou up within my heart,
    Rise to all eternity.

        Rev. Charles Wesley (1708—1788), 1740. Sl. alt.

MARTYN. 7. D.   SIMEON BUTLER MARSH (1798—1875), 1834.

COOPER. 7.6 l.

ALEXANDER SAMUEL COOPER (1835 —), 1872.

1. WHEN this pass-ing world is done, When has sunk yon glar-ing sun; When we stand with Christ in light,

All our fin-ish'd life in sight: Then, Lord, shall we ful-ly know, Not till then, how much we owe.

451

The forgiven Debt.
MATT xviii. 32.

2 When we stand before the throne,
Dressed in beauty not our own;
When we see Thee as Thou art,
Love Thee with unsinning heart:
Then, Lord, shall we fully know,
Not till then, how much we owe.

3 When the praise of Heaven we hear,
Loud as thunders to the ear,
Loud as many waters' noise,
Sweet as harp's melodious voice:
Then, Lord, shall we fully know,
Not till then, how much we owe.

Rev. Robert Murray McCheyne (1813—1843), 1837. Ab.

REFUGE. 7. D.

JOSEPH PERRY HOLBROOK (1822—), 1862.

1. JE-SUS, Lov-er of my soul, Let me to Thy bo-som fly, While the bil-lows near-er

roll, While the tem-pest still is high; Hide me, O my Sav-iour, hide, Till the

storm of life is past; Safe in-to the ha-ven guide; O re-ceive my soul at last.

SPANISH HYMN. 7. D.

Spanish Melody.
FINE.

1. { Lord, Thou art my Rock of strength, And my home is in Thine arms; }
{ Thou wilt send me help at length, And I feel no wild a - larms. }
D.C.—Up to Thee my - self I yield, And my sor - rows are Thine own.

Sin nor death can pierce the shield Thy de - fence has o'er me thrown;

D.C.

452   "Was von aussen und von innen."

2 When my trials tarry long,
  Unto Thee I look and wait,
Knowing none, though keen and strong,
  Can my trust in Thee abate.
And this faith I long have nursed,
  Comes alone, O God, from Thee;
Thou my heart didst open first,
  Thou didst set this hope in me.

3 Mercy's wings o'er me outspread,
  Ever keep me close to Thee;
In the peace Thy love doth shed,
  Let me dwell eternally.
Be my All; in all I do,
  Let me only seek Thy will,
Where the heart to Thee is true,
  All is peaceful, calm, and still.

Rev. August Hermann Franke (1663—1727), 1711.
Tr. by Miss Catherine Winkworth (1829—1876), 1855. Ab. and sl. alt.

BENTLEY. 7. 6. D.

JOHN HULLAH (1812—1884), 1865.

1. To Thee, my God and Sav - iour, My heart ex - ult - ing sings, Re - joic - ing in Thy

fav - or, Al - might - y, King of kings: I'll cel - e - brate Thy glo - ry,

With all Thy saints a - bove, And tell the joy - ful sto - ry Of Thy re - deem - ing love.

453   *"Shew forth His Salvation."*
Ps. xcvi. 2.

2 Soon as the morn with roses
   Bedecks the dewy east,
And when the sun reposes
   Upon the ocean's breast,
My voice in supplication,
   Well pleaséd, Thou shalt hear:
O grant me Thy salvation,
   And to my soul draw near.

3 By Thee through life supported,
   I pass the dangerous road,
With heavenly hosts escorted
   Up to their bright abode;
There cast my crown before Thee,
   Now all my conflicts o'er,
And day and night adore Thee:
   What can an angel more?
                    Rev. Thomas Haweis (1732—1820), 1792.

454   *Rejoicing in God our Saviour.*
Luke i. 47.   7. 6. D.

1 To Thee, O dear, dear Saviour,
   My spirit turns for rest,
My peace is in Thy favor,
   My pillow on Thy breast.
Though all the world deceive me,
   I know that I am Thine;
And Thou wilt never leave me,
   O blessed Saviour mine.

2 O Thou, whose mercy found me,
   From bondage set me free;
And then for ever bound me
   With threefold cords to Thee:
O for a heart to love Thee
   More truly as I ought,
And nothing place above Thee
   In deed, or word, or thought.
          Rev. John Samuel Bewley Monsell (1811—1875), 1863. Ab.

STEPHENS, C. M.

Rev. WILLIAM JONES (1726—1800), 1794.

1. Through all the chang - ing scenes of life, In troub - le and in joy,

The prais - es of my God shall still My heart and tongue em - ploy.

455   *Safety in God.*
Ps. xxxiv.

2 Of His deliverance I will boast,
   Till all that are distressed,
From my example comfort take,
   And charm their griefs to rest.

3 The hosts of God encamp around
   The dwellings of the just;

Deliverance He affords to all
   Who on His succor trust.

4 Fear Him, ye saints, and you will then
   Have nothing else to fear;
Make you His service your delight,
   Your wants shall be His care.
                    Tate and Brady, 1696. Ab.

BREMEN. C. P. M.   THOMAS HASTINGS (1784—1872), 1836.

1. FEAR not, O lit - tle flock, the foe Who mad - ly seeks your o - ver-throw, Dread

not his rage and pow'r; { What tho' your courage sometimes faints, }
{ His seeming triumph o'er God's saints } Lasts but a lit - tle hour.

456   *"Verzage nicht, du Häuflein klein."*

2 Be of good cheer; your cause belongs
To Him who can avenge your wrongs;
    Leave it to Him, our Lord.
Though hidden yet from mortal eyes,
Salvation shall for you arise:
    He girdeth on His sword!

3 As true as God's own Word is true,
Not earth nor hell with all their crew
    Against us shall prevail.
A jest and byword are they grown:
God is with us; we are His own;
    Our victory cannot fail.

4 Amen, Lord Jesus, grant our prayer!
Great Captain, now Thine arm make bare;
    Fight for us once again!
So shall Thy saints and martyrs raise
A mighty chorus to Thy praise,
    World without end. Amen.

Gustavus Adolphus (1594—1632), 1631. In prose.
Rev. Jacob Fabricius (1593—1654), 1631. In verse.
Tr. by Miss Catherine Winkworth (1829—1878), 1855. Alt.

457   *Casting our Care on God.*
      1 PET. v. 7.

1 O LORD, how happy should we be
If we could cast our care on Thee,
    If we from self could rest;
And feel at heart that One above,

In perfect wisdom, perfect love,
    Is working for the best.

2 How far from this our daily life,
How oft disturbed by anxious strife,
    By sudden wild alarms;
O could we but relinquish all
Our earthly props, and simply fall
    On Thine almighty arms!

3 Could we but kneel and cast our load,
E'en while we pray, upon our God,
    Then rise with lightened cheer;
Sure that the Father, who is nigh
To still the famished raven's cry,
    Will hear in that we fear.

4 We cannot trust Him as we should;
So chafes weak nature's restless mood
    To cast its peace away;
But birds and flowerets round us preach,
All, all the present evil teach
    Sufficient for the day.

5 Lord, make these faithless hearts of ours
Such lessons learn from birds and flowers;
    Make them from self to cease,
Leave all things to a Father's will,
And taste, before Him lying still,
    E'en in affliction, peace.

Prof. Joseph Anstice (1808—1836), 1836.

HOLLINGSIDE. 7.D.

Rev. JOHN BACCHUS DYKES (1823—1876), 1861.

1. SAV - IOUR, when in dust to Thee, Low we bow th'a - dor - ing knee;
When, re - pent - ant, to the skies Scarce we lift our weep - ing eyes,
O by all Thy pains and woe Suf - fer'd once for man be - low,
Bend - ing from Thy throne on high, Hear our sol - emn Lit - a - ny.

458 *"Hear our solemn Litany."*

2 By Thy helpless infant years;
By Thy life of want and tears;
By Thy days of sore distress
In the savage wilderness;
By the dread, mysterious hour
Of th' insulting tempter's power;
Turn, O turn a pitying eye,
Hear our solemn Litany!

3 By Thine hour of dire despair;
By Thine agony of prayer;
By the cross, the nail, the thorn,
Piercing spear, and torturing scorn;

By the gloom that veiled the skies
O'er the dreadful sacrifice;
Listen to our humble cry,
Hear our solemn Litany!

4 By Thy deep expiring groan;
By the sad sepulchral stone;
By the vault, whose dark abode
Held in vain the rising God;
O, from earth to Heaven restored,
Mighty, reascended Lord,
Listen, listen to the cry
Of our solemn Litany!

Sir Robert Grant (1785—1838), 1815. Ab. and sl. alt.

LOUVAN. L. M.

VIRGIL CORYDON TAYLOR (1811—), 1847.

1. O DEEM not they are blest a - lone, Whose lives a peace - ful ten - or keep;

The Power, who pit - ies man, has shown A bless - ing for the eyes that weep.

459   *"Blessed are they that mourn."*
     MATT. v. 4.

2 The light of smiles shall fill again
    The lids that overflow with tears;
And weary hours of woe and pain
    Are promises of happier years.

3 There is a day of sunny rest
    For every dark and troubled night;
And grief may bide an evening guest,
    But joy shall come with early light.

4 And thou, who o'er thy friend's low bier
    Sheddest the bitter drops like rain,

Hope that a brighter, happier sphere
    Will give him to thy arms again.

5 Nor let the good man's trust depart,
    Though life its common gifts deny;
Though, with a pierced and broken heart,
    And spurned of men, he goes to die.

6 For God has marked each sorrowing day,
    And numbered every secret tear,
And Heaven's long age of bliss shall pay
    For all His children suffer here.

         William Cullen Bryant (1794—1878), 1824.

WARD. L. M.

Old Scotch Melody. Arr. by LOWELL MASON (1792—1872), 1830.

1. GOD is the Ref - uge of His saints, When storms of sharp dis - tress in - vade;

Ere we can of - fer our complaints, Be - hold Him pres - ent with His aid.

460 *God our Refuge.*
Ps. xlvi.

2 Loud may the troubled ocean roar;
  In sacred peace our souls abide,
  While every nation, every shore,
  Trembles, and dreads the swelling tide.

3 There is a stream, whose gentle flow
  Supplies the city of our God;
  Life, love, and joy, still gliding through,
  And watering our divine abode.

4 That sacred stream, Thy holy Word,
  Our grief allays, our fear controls;
  Sweet peace Thy promises afford,
  And give new strength to fainting souls.

5 Zion enjoys her Monarch's love,
  Secure against a threatening hour;
  Nor can her firm foundations move,
  Built on His truth, and armed with power.

Rev. Isaac Watts (1674—1748), 1719. Alt.

GILEAD. L. M.

ETIENNE HENRI MEHUL (1763—1817), 1807.

1. The Lord is King: lift up thy voice, O earth, and all ye Heav'ns, re - joice;

From world to world the joy shall ring, The Lord Om - nip - o - tent is King.

461 *"The Lord reigneth."*
Ps. xcvii.

2 The Lord is King: who then shall dare
  Resist His will, distrust His care,
  Or murmur at His wise decrees,
  Or doubt His royal promises?

3 The Lord is King: child of the dust,
  The Judge of all the earth is just;
  Holy and true are all His ways:
  Let every creature speak His praise.

4 O, when His wisdom can mistake,
  His might decay, His love forsake,
  Then may His children cease to sing,
  The Lord Omnipotent is King.

Josiah Conder (1789—1855), 1824. Ab.

462 *Divine Protection.*
Ps. cxxi.

1 He lives, the everlasting God,
  That built the world, that spread the flood;

The Heavens with all their hosts He
    made,
  And the dark regions of the dead.

2 He guides our feet, He guards our way;
  His morning smiles bless all the day;
  He spreads the evening veil, and keeps
  The silent hours while Israel sleeps.

3 Israel, a name divinely blest,
  May rise secure, securely rest;
  Thy holy Guardian's wakeful eyes
  Admit no slumber, nor surprise.

4 On thee foul spirits have no power;
  And, in thy last departing hour,
  Angels, that trace the airy road,
  Shall bear thee homeward to thy God.

Rev. Isaac Watts, 1719. Ab.

NAOMI. C. M.

HANS GEORG NAEGELI (1768—1836), 1832.
Arr. by LOWELL MASON (1792—1872), 1836.

1. FA - THER, what-e'er of earth - ly bliss Thy sov - 'reign will de - nies,

Ac - cept - ed at Thy throne of grace, Let this pe - ti - tion rise:—

463 *"A calm, a thankful Heart."*

2 Give me a calm, a thankful heart,
  From every murmur free;
  The blessings of Thy grace impart,
  And make me live to Thee.

3 Let the sweet hope that Thou art mine
  My life and death attend;
  Thy presence through my journey shine,
  And crown my journey's end.

  Miss Anne Steele (1717—1778), 1760. Ab.

464 *"Sweet Will of God."*

1 I worship Thee, sweet Will of God,
  And all Thy ways adore;
  And every day I live, I seem
  To love Thee more and more.

2 I love to kiss each print where Thou
  Hast set Thine unseen feet:

I cannot fear Thee, blessed Will,
  Thine empire is so sweet.

3 I have no cares, O blessed Will,
  For all my cares are Thine;
  I live in triumph, Lord, for Thou
  Hast made Thy triumphs mine.

4 He always wins who sides with God,
  To him no chance is lost;
  God's will is sweetest to him when
  It triumphs at his cost.

5 Ill that He blesses is our good,
  And unblest good is ill;
  And all is right that seems most wrong,
  If it be His sweet will.

  Rev. Frederick William Faber (1814—1863), 1849. Ab.

FAITH. C. M.

Rev. JOHN BACCHUS DYKES (1823—1876).

1. CALM me, my God, and keep me calm, Soft rest - ing on Thy breast;

Soothe me with ho - ly hymn and psalm, And bid my spir - it rest.

465
The inner Calm.

2 Calm me, my God, and keep me calm;
Let Thine outstretchéd wing
Be like the shade of Elim's palm,
Beside her desert spring.

3 Yes, keep me calm, though loud and rude
The sounds my ear that greet;
Calm in the closet's solitude,
Calm in the bustling street;

4 Calm in the hour of buoyant health,
Calm in my hour of pain;
Calm in my poverty or wealth,
Calm in my loss or gain;

5 Calm in the sufferance of wrong,
Like Him who bore my shame,
Calm 'mid the threat'ning, taunting
Who hate Thy holy Name. [throng

Rev. Horatius Bonar (1808—), 1857. Ab.

BYEFIELD. C. M.

THOMAS HASTINGS (1784—1872), 1840.

1. God moves in a mys-te-rious way His won-ders to per-form;
He plants His foot-steps in the sea, And rides up-on the storm.

466
The Mysteries of Providence.

2 Deep in unfathomable mines
Of never-failing skill,
He treasures up His bright designs,
And works His sovereign will.

3 Ye fearful saints, fresh courage take;
The clouds ye so much dread
Are big with mercy, and shall break
In blessings on your head.

4 Judge not the Lord by feeble sense,
But trust Him for His grace;
Behind a frowning providence
He hides a smiling face.

5 His purposes will ripen fast,
Unfolding every hour;
The bud may have a bitter taste,
But sweet will be the flower.

6 Blind unbelief is sure to err,
And scan His work in vain:
God is His own intrepreter,
And He will make it plain.

William Cowper (1731—1800), 1779.

467
Happiness only in God.
Ps. lxxiii. 25.

1 My God, my Portion, and my Love,
My everlasting All,
I've none but Thee in Heaven above,
Or on this earthly ball.

2 Were I possessor of the earth,
And called the stars my own,
Without Thy graces and Thyself,
I were a wretch undone.

3 Let others stretch their arms like seas,
And grasp in all the shore,
Grant me the visits of Thy face,
And I desire no more.

Rev. Isaac Watts (1674—1748), 1709. Ab.

DOMINUS REGIT ME. 8.7.

WILLIAM HENRY MONK (1823—), 1868.

1. THE King of love my Shep-herd is, Whose good-ness fail-eth nev-er;

I noth-ing lack if I am His, And He is mine for ev-er.

468

Never-failing Goodness.

2 Where streams of living water flow
  My ransomed soul He leadeth,
And, where the verdant pastures grow,
  With food celestial feedeth.

3 Perverse and foolish oft I strayed,
  But yet in love He sought me,
And on His shoulder gently laid,
  And home, rejoicing, brought me.

4 In death's dark vale I fear no ill
  With Thee, dear Lord, beside me;
Thy rod and staff my comfort still,
  Thy cross before to guide me.

5 And so through all the length of days
  Thy goodness faileth never;
Good Shepherd, may I sing Thy praise
  Within Thy house for ever.

Rev. Sir Henry Williams Baker (1821—1877), 1868. Ab.

ST. BEDE. C. M. 6 l.

Rev. JOHN BACCHUS DYKES (1823—1876), 1868.

1. FA-THER, I know that all my life Is por-tion'd out for me;

The chang-es that are sure to come I do not fear to see:

I ask Thee for a pre-sent mind, In-tent on pleas-ing Thee.

469
"*My Times are in Thy Hand.*"
Ps. xxxi. 15.

2 I would not have the restless will
  That hurries to and fro,
Seeking for some great thing to do,
  Or secret thing to know:
I would be treated as a child,
  And guided where I go.

3 I ask Thee for the daily strength,
  To none that ask denied,
A mind to blend with outward life,

While keeping at Thy side;
  Content to fill a little space,
    If Thou be glorified.

4 In service which Thy will appoints
  There are no bonds for me;
My inmost heart is taught the truth
  That makes Thy children free:
A life of self-renouncing love
  Is one of liberty.

Miss Anna Lætitia Waring (1820—), 1850. Ab. and alt.

BRATTLE STREET. C. M. D.

IGNACE PLEYEL (1757—1831), 1791.
Arr. by NAHUM MITCHELL (1770—1853), 1812.

1. WHILE Thee I seek, pro-tect-ing Pow'r, Be my vain wish-es still'd;

And may this con-se-crat-ed hour With bet-ter hopes be fill'd.

Thy love the pow'rs of thought be-stow'd, To Thee my thoughts would soar;

Thy mer-cy o'er my life has flow'd, That mer-cy I a-dore.

470   *Habitual Devotion.*

2 In each event of life, how clear
  Thy ruling hand I see:
Each blessing to my soul more dear,
  Because conferred by Thee.
In every joy that crowns my days,
  In every pain I bear,
My heart shall find delight in praise,
  Or seek relief in prayer.

3 When gladness wings my favored hour,
  Thy love my thoughts shall fill:
Resigned, when storms of sorrow lower,
  My soul shall meet Thy will.
My lifted eye, without a tear,
  The lowering storm shall see;
My steadfast heart shall know no fear,
  That heart will rest on Thee.

Miss Helen Maria Williams (1762—1827), 1786.

CONFIDENCE. 7.6.D.   Arr. from FELIX JACOB LUDWIG MENDELSSOHN-BARTHOLDY (1809—1847).

1. In heav'nly love a-bid-ing, No change my heart shall fear; And safe is such con-
fid - ing, For noth-ing chang-es here. The storm may roar with-out me,
My heart may low be laid, But God is round a-bout me, And can I be dis-may'd?

471

"I will fear no Evil."
Ps. xxiii. 4.

2 Wherever He may guide me,
   No want shall turn me back;
My Shepherd is beside me,
   And nothing can I lack.
His wisdom ever waketh,
   His sight is never dim,
He knows the way He taketh,
   And I will walk with Him.

3 Green pastures are before me,
   Which yet I have not seen;
Bright skies will soon be o'er me,
   Where darkest clouds have been.
My hope I cannot measure,

My path to life is free,
My Saviour has my treasure,
   And He will walk with me.
Miss Anna Lætitia Waring (1820—   ), 1850. Sl. alt.

472

"O Jesu, meine Sonne."

1 I KNOW no life divided,
   O Lord of life, from Thee;
In Thee is life provided
   For all mankind and me:
I know no death, O Jesus,
   Because I live in Thee;
Thy death it is which frees us
   From death eternally.

2 I fear no tribulation,
　Since, whatsoe'er it be,
It makes no separation
　Between my Lord and me.
If Thou, my God and Teacher,
　Vouchsafe to be my own,
Though poor, I shall be richer
　Than monarch on his throne.

3 If, while on earth I wander,
　My heart is light and blest,
Ah, what shall I be yonder
　In perfect peace and rest?
O blessed thought in dying,
　We go to meet the Lord,
Where there shall be no sighing,
　A kingdom our reward.

Rev. Carl Johann Philipp Spitta (1801—1859), 1833.
Tr. by Richard Massie, 1860. Ab.

APPLETON. L. M.　　WILLIAM BOYCE (1710—1779).

1. To God I cried when troub-les rose; He heard me, and sub-dued my foes;

He did my ris-ing fears con-trol, And strength dif-fus'd through all my soul.

473　*Restoring and preserving Grace.*
　　　Ps. cxxxviii.

2 The God of Heaven maintains His state,
Frowns on the proud, and scorns the great;
But from His throne descends to see
The sons of humble poverty.

3 Amid a thousand snares I stand,
Upheld and guarded by Thy hand;
Thy words my fainting soul revive,
And keep my dying faith alive.

4 Grace will complete what grace begins,
To save from sorrows and from sins;
The work that wisdom undertakes,
Eternal mercy ne'er forsakes.

Rev. Isaac Watts (1674—1748), 1719. Ab.

474　　*Storm and Rescue.*

1 THE billows swell, the winds are high,
Clouds overcast my wintry sky;
Out of the depths to Thee I call,
My fears are great, my strength is small.

2 O Lord, the pilot's part perform,
And guard and guide me through the
　　　storm;
Defend me from each threatening ill,
Control the waves, say, "Peace, be still!"

3 Amidst the roaring of the sea
My soul still hangs her hope on Thee;
Thy constant love, Thy faithful care,
Is all that saves me from despair.

4 Though tempest-tost and half a wreck,
My Saviour through the floods I seek:
Let neither winds nor stormy main
Force back my shattered bark again.

William Cowper (1731—1800), 1779. Ab.

GOSHEN. 11.   German Melody.

1. The Lord is my Shep-herd, no want shall I know; I feed in green past - ures, safe - fold - ed I rest; He lead - eth my soul where the still wa - ters flow, Re - stores me when wan - d'ring, re - deems when op - press'd.

475   *"I will fear no Evil."*
Ps. xxiii. 4.

2 Through the valley and shadow of death though I stray,
   Since Thou art my Guardian, no evil I fear;
Thy rod shall defend me, Thy staff be my stay;
   No harm can befall, with my Comforter near.

3 In the midst of affliction my table is spread;
   With blessings unmeasured my cup runneth o'er;
With perfume and oil Thou anointest my head;
   O what shall I ask of Thy providence more?

4 Let goodness and mercy, my bountiful God,
   Still follow my steps till I meet Thee above;
I seek, by the path which my forefathers trod,
   Through the land of their sojourn, Thy kingdom of love.
                  James Montgomery (1771—1854), 1822.

476   *"Faint, yet pursuing."*

1 Though faint, yet pursuing, we go on our way;
The Lord is our Leader, His Word is our stay;
Though suffering, and sorrow, and trial be near,
The Lord is our Refuge, and whom can we fear?

2 He raiseth the fallen, He cheereth the faint;
The weak and oppressed, He will hear their complaint;
The way may be weary, and thorny the road,
But how can we falter? our help is in God.

3 Though clouds may surround us, our God is our Light;
  Though storms rage around us, our God is our Might;
  So faint, yet pursuing, still onward we come;
  The Lord is our Leader, and Heaven is our home.

Rev. John Nelson Darby (1800—1882), 1858. Ab.

NEWLAND. S. M.

HENRY JOHN GAUNTLETT (1806—1876), 1867.

1. The Lord my Shep - herd is, I shall be well sup - plied;

Since He is mine, and I am His, What can I want be - side?

477   *The Lord our Shepherd.*
   Ps. xxiii.

2 He leads me to the place
  Where heavenly pasture grows;
  Where living waters gently pass,
  And full salvation flows.

3 If e'er I go astray,
  He doth my soul reclaim;
  And guides me, in His own right way,
  For His most holy Name.

4 While He affords His aid,
  I cannot yield to fear;   [dark shade,
  Though I should walk through death's
  My Shepherd's with me there.

Rev. Isaac Watts (1674—1748), 1719. Ab.

478   *Casting Care on God.*
   1 Pet. v. 7.

1 Where wilt thou put thy trust?
  In a frail form of clay,

That to its element of dust
Must soon resolve away?

2 Where wilt thou cast thy care?
  Upon an erring heart,
  Which hath its own sore ills to bear,
  And shrinks from sorrow's dart?

3 No, place thy trust above
  This shadowy realm of night,
  In Him, whose boundless power and love
  Thy confidence invite.

4 His mercies still endure
  When skies and stars grow dim,
  His changeless promise standeth sure;
  Go, cast thy care on Him.

Mrs. Lydia Howard Huntley Sigourney (1791—1865), 1815. Ab.

DENNIS. S. M.

HANS GEORG NÄGELI (1773—1836), 1832.
Arr. by WILLIAM BATCHELDER BRADBURY (1816—1868), 1849.

250

BRADFORD. C. M.

GEORGE FREDERICK HANDEL (1685—1759), 1741.

1. My God, the Spring of all my joys, The Life of my de-lights,

The Glo - ry of my bright - est days, And Com - fort of my nights:

479   *Light in Darkness.*

2 In darkest shades, if He appear,
  My dawning is begun :
He is my soul's sweet Morning Star,
  And He my rising Sun.

3 The opening heavens around me shine
  With beams of sacred bliss,
While Jesus shows His heart is mine,
  And whispers, I am His.

4 My soul would leave this heavy clay
  At that transporting word ;
Run up with joy the shining way,
  T' embrace my dearest Lord.

5 Fearless of hell and ghastly death,
  I'd break through every foe ;
The wings of love and arms of faith
  Should bear me conqueror through.

Rev. Isaac Watts (1674—1748), 1709.

BETHANY. 6. 4. 6. 4. 6. 6. 4.

Arr. by LOWELL MASON (1792—1872), 1859.

1. Near-er, my God, to Thee, Near-er to Thee: E'en though it be a cross That rais-eth me ;

Still all my song shall be, Near-er, my God, to Thee, Near-er, my God, to Thee, Near-er to Thee.

480   *"Nearer, my God, to Thee."*
GEN. xxviii. 10—12.

2 Though like the wanderer,
  The sun gone down,
Darkness be over me,

My rest a stone ;
Yet in my dreams I'd be
Nearer, my God, to Thee,
Nearer to Thee.

3 There let the way appear
 Steps unto Heaven;
All that Thou sendest me,
 In mercy given;
Angels to beckon me
Nearer, my God, to Thee,
 Nearer to Thee.

4 Then, with my waking thoughts
 Bright with Thy praise,
Out of my stony griefs
 Bethel I'll raise;
So by my woes to be
Nearer, my God, to Thee,
 Nearer to Thee.

5 Or if on joyful wing
 Cleaving the sky,
Sun, moon, and stars forgot,
 Upwards I fly,
Still all my song shall be,
Nearer, my God, to Thee,
 Nearer to Thee.

Mrs. Sarah Flower Adams (1805—1848), 1840.

481

"More Love to Thee!"
JOHN xxi. 17.

1 MORE love to Thee, O Christ,
 More love to Thee!
Hear Thou the prayer I make

On bended knee;
This is my earnest plea,
More love, O Christ, to Thee,
 More love to Thee!

2 Once earthly joy I craved,
 Sought peace and rest;
Now Thee alone I seek,
 Give what is best:
This all my prayer shall be,
More love, O Christ, to Thee,
 More love to Thee!

3 Let sorrow do its work,
 Send grief and pain;
Sweet are Thy messengers,
 Sweet their refrain,
When they can sing with me,
More love, O Christ, to Thee,
 More love to Thee!

4 Then shall my latest breath
 Whisper Thy praise;
This be the parting cry
 My heart shall raise,
This still its prayer shall be,
More love, O Christ, to Thee,
 More love to Thee!

Mrs. Elizabeth Payson Prentiss (1819—1878), 1869.

DOANE. 6.4.6.4.6.6.4.

WILLIAM HOWARD DOANE (1832—   ).

1. MORE love to Thee, O Christ, More love to Thee! Hear Thou the pray'r I make On bend-ed knee; This is my earn-est plea, More love, O Christ, to Thee, More love to Thee! More love to Thee!

MANOAH. C. M.

CARL MARIA von WEBER (1786—1826).
Arr. by HENRY WELLINGTON GREATOREX (1811—1858), 1851.

1. Je - sus, Thine all - vic - to - rious love Shed in my heart a - broad:

Then shall my feet no lon - ger rove, Root - ed and fix'd in God.

482 *The refining Fire of the Holy Spirit.*

2 O that in me the sacred fire
Might now begin to glow;
Burn up the dross of base desire,
And make the mountains flow.

3 O that it now from Heaven might fall,
And all my sins consume:
Come, Holy Ghost, for Thee I call;
Spirit of burning, come.

4 Refining Fire, go through my heart;
Illuminate my soul;
Scatter Thy life through every part,
And sanctify the whole.
Rev. Charles Wesley (1708—1788), 1740. Ab. and alt.

483 *Preservation by Day and Night.*
Ps. cxxi.

1 To Heaven I lift my waiting eyes,
There all my hopes are laid;
The Lord, that built the earth and skies,
Is my perpetual aid.

2 Their feet shall never slide nor fall,
Whom He designs to keep;
His ear attends the softest call,
His eyes can never sleep.

3 Israel, rejoice and rest secure,
Thy Keeper is the Lord;
His wakeful eyes employ His power
For thine eternal guard.

4 Nor scorching sun, nor sickly moon,
Shall have His leave to smite;
He shields thy head from burning noon,
From blasting damps at night.

5 He guards thy soul, He keeps thy breath,
Where thickest dangers come;
Go and return, secure from death,
Till God commands thee home.
Rev. Isaac Watts (1674—1748), 1719. Ab.

484 *God our Portion here and hereafter.*
Ps. lxxiii. 23—28.

1 Thy counsels, Lord, shall guide my feet
Through this dark wilderness;
Thy hand conduct me near Thy seat,
To dwell before Thy face.

2 Were I in Heaven without my God,
'Twould be no joy to me;
And while this earth is my abode,
I long for none but Thee.

3 What if the springs of life were broke,
And flesh and heart should faint?
God is my soul's eternal Rock,
The Strength of every saint.

4 But to draw near to Thee, my God,
Shall be my sweet employ;
My tongue shall sound Thy works abroad,
And tell the world my joy.
Rev. Isaac Watts, 1719. Ab.

BEATITUDE. C. M.

Rev. JOHN BACCHUS DYKES (1823—1876).

1. O for a heart to praise my God, A heart from sin set free;

A heart that al - ways feels Thy blood So free - ly shed for me.

485 *"Make me a clean Heart."*
Ps. li. 10.

2 A heart resigned, submissive, meek,
My dear Redeemer's throne;
Where only Christ is heard to speak,
Where Jesus reigns alone.

3 A humble, lowly, contrite heart,
Believing, true, and clean;
Which neither life nor death can part
From Him that dwells within.

4 A heart in every thought renewed,
And full of love divine;
Perfect, and right, and pure, and good,
A copy, Lord, of Thine.

5 Thy nature, dearest Lord, impart;
Come quickly from above;
Write Thy new Name upon my heart,
Thy new, best Name of Love.

Rev. Charles Wesley, 1742. Ab. and sl. alt.

DIJON. 7.

German.

1. To Thy past - ures fair and large, Heav'n - ly Shep - herd, lead Thy charge,

And my couch, with ten - d'rest care, Mid the spring - ing grass pre - pare.

486 *The Heavenly Shepherd.*
Ps. xxiii.

2 When I faint with summer's heat
Thou shalt guide my weary feet
To the streams that, still and slow,
Through the verdant meadows flow.

3 Safe the dreary vale I tread,
By the shades of death o'erspread,

With Thy rod and staff supplied,
This my guard, and that my guide.

4 Constant to my latest end,
Thou my footsteps shalt attend;
And shalt bid Thy hallowed dome
Yield me an eternal home.

Rev. James Merrick (1720—1769), 1765. Ab. and alt.

MEAR. C. M.   Welsh Air. AARON WILLIAMS (1731—1776), 1760.

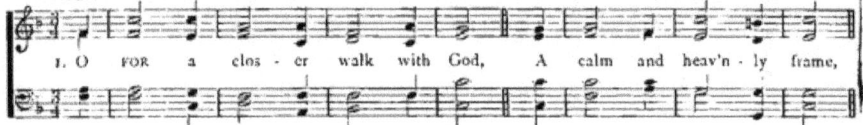

1. O FOR a clos-er walk with God, A calm and heav'n-ly frame,

A light to shine up-on the road That leads me to the Lamb!

487   *"A closer Walk."*   GEN. v. 24. 1 JOHN ii. 6.

2 Return, O holy Dove, return,
   Sweet messenger of rest:
I hate the sins that made Thee mourn,
   And drove Thee from my breast.

3 The dearest idol I have known,
   Whate'er that idol be;
Help me to tear it from Thy throne,
   And worship only Thee.

4 So shall my walk be close with God,
   Calm and serene my frame;
So purer light shall mark the road
   That leads me to the Lamb.

       William Cowper (1731—1800), 1779. Ab.

488   *"Let us return"*   Hos. vi. 1-4.

1 Long hath the night of sorrow reigned;
   The dawn shall bring us light:

God shall appear, and we shall rise
   With gladness in His sight.

2 Our hearts, if God we seek to know,
   Shall know Him and rejoice;
His coming like the morn shall be,
   Like morning songs His voice.

3 As dew upon the tender herb,
   Diffusing fragrance round;
As showers that usher in the spring,
   And cheer the thirsty ground;

4 So shall His presence bless our souls,
   And shed a joyful light;
That hallowed morn shall chase away
   The sorrows of the night.

       Rev. John Morrison (1749—1798), 1781. Ab.

HEATH. C. M.   LOWELL MASON (1792—1872), 1835.

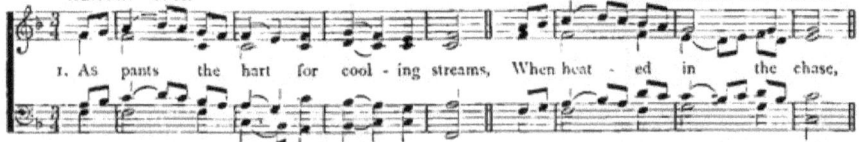

1. As pants the hart for cool-ing streams, When heat-ed in the chase,

So pants my soul, O Lord, for Thee, And Thy re-fresh-ing grace.

489 *Panting for God.*
Ps. xlii.

2 For Thee, the Lord, the living Lord,
My thirsty soul doth pine:
O when shall I behold Thy face,
Thou Majesty Divine?

3 I sigh to think of happier days,
When Thou, O Lord, wast nigh;

When every heart was tuned to praise,
And none so blest as I.

4 Why restless, why cast down, my soul?
Trust God, and thou shalt sing
His praise again, and find Him still
Thy health's eternal Spring.

Tate and Brady, 1696. Alt.
Rev. Henry Francis Lyte (1793—1847), 1834.

AZMON. C. M.

CARL GOTTHILF GLÄSER (1784—1829), 1828.
Arr. by LOWELL MASON, 1839.

1. FA - THER of Love, our Guide and Friend, O lead us gen - tly on,

Un - til life's tri - al - time shall end, And heav'n - ly peace be won.

490 *Constant Trust in God.*

2 We know not what the path may be
As yet by us untrod;
But we can trust our all to Thee,
Our Father, and our God.

3 If called, like Abr'am's child, to climb
The hill of sacrifice,
Some angel may be there in time;
Deliverance shall arise:

4 Or, if some darker lot be good,
O teach us to endure
The sorrow, pain, or solitude,
That makes the spirit pure.

5 Christ by no flowery pathway came;
And we, His followers here,
Must do Thy will and praise Thy Name,
In hope, and love, and fear.

6 And, till in Heaven we sinless bow,
And faultless anthems raise,

O Father, Son, and Spirit, now
Accept our feeble praise.
Rev. William Josiah Irons (1812—1883), 1853.

491 *The gentle Shepherd.*

1 THERE is a little lonely fold,
Whose flock one Shepherd keeps,
Through summer's heat and winter's cold,
With eye that never sleeps.

2 By evil beast, or burning sky,
Or damp of midnight air,
Not one in all that flock shall die
Beneath that Shepherd's care.

3 For if, unheeding or beguiled,
In danger's path they roam,
His pity follows through the wild,
And guards them safely home.

4 O gentle Shepherd, still behold
Thy helpless charge in me;
And take a wanderer to Thy fold,
That, trembling, turns to Thee.
Mrs. Mina Grace Saffery (1773—1858), 1854.

MONSELL. S. M.

JOSEPH BARNBY (1838—), 1868.

1. OUT of the depths of woe, To Thee, O Lord, I cry; Dark-ness sur-rounds me, but I know That Thou art ev-er nigh.

492 *"Out of the Depths."* PS. CXXX.

2 Humbly I wait on Thee,
  Confessing all my sin;
Lord, I am knocking at Thy gate;
  Open, and take me in.

3 Glory to God above!
  The waters soon will cease;
For lo, the swift-returning Dove
  Brings home the sign of peace.

4 Though storms His face obscure,
  And dangers threaten loud,
Jehovah's covenant is sure,
  His bow is in the cloud.
                James Montgomery (1771—1854), 1822. Ab.

493 *"Fear not."*

FEAR not, poor, weary one;
  But struggle bravely yet;
Toil on until thy task is done,
  Until thy sun is set.

2 Though many are thy cares,
  And many are thy fears,
The loving Christ thy burden shares,
  And wipes away thy tears.

3 No distant Christ is He,
  And one that doth not know;

But watches close and constantly
  The path which thou dost go.

4 'Tis when thy heart is tried,
  'Tis in thine hour of grief,
He standeth ever at thy side
  And ever brings relief.
                Rev. Thomas Cogswell Upham (1799—1872), 1872.

494 *All for God.*

TEACH me, my God and King,
  In all things Thee to see,
And what I do in anything,
  To do it as for Thee;

2 To scorn the senses' sway,
  While still to Thee I tend;
In all I do be Thou the Way,
  In all be Thou the End.

3 All may of Thee partake;
  Nothing so small can be
But draws, when acted for Thy sake,
  Greatness and worth from Thee.

4 If done t' obey Thy laws,
  E'en servile labors shine,
Hallowed is toil, if this the cause,
  The meanest work, divine.
                Rev. George Herbert (1593—1632), 1635. Ab

JESUS SALVATOR. S. M. WILLIAM HENRY MONK (1823—).

1. JE - sus, my Strength, my Hope, On Thee I cast my care, With
hum - ble con - fi - dence look up, And know Thou hear'st my pray'r.

495   *Watching and Praying.*
LUKE. XVIII. 1. PHIL. iv. 13.

2 Give me on Thee to wait,
  Till I can all things do ;
On Thee, almighty to create,
  Almighty to renew.

3 I want a godly fear,
  A quick-discerning eye,
That looks to Thee when sin is near,
  And sees the tempter fly ;

4 A spirit still prepared,
  And armed with jealous care,
Forever standing on its guard,
  And watching unto prayer.
    Rev. Charles Wesley (1708—1788), 1742. Ab.

496   *With us on the Sea.*

1 JESUS, one word from Thee
  Fills my sad soul with peace.
My griefs are like a tossing sea:
  They hear Thy voice, and cease.

2 Soon as Thy pitying face
  Shone through my stormy fears,
The storm swept by, nor left a trace,
  Save the sweet dew of tears.

3 And when Thou call'st me, Lord,
  Where thickest dangers be,
Even the waves a path afford :
  I walk the waves with Thee.

4 With Thee within my bark,
  I'll dare death's threatening tide ;
Nor count the passage strange or dark
  With Jesus by my side.

5 Dear Lord, Thy faithful grace
  I know and I adore :
What shall it be to see Thy face
  In Heaven, forevermore !
    Rev. Hervey Doddridge Ganse (1822—), 1872.

STATE STREET. S. M. JONATHAN CALL WOODMAN (1813—), 1844.

PORTUGUESE HYMN. 11.
MARC ANTOINE PORTOGALLO (1763—1830).

1. How firm a foun-da-tion, ye saints of the Lord, Is laid for your faith in His ex-cel-lent Word! What more can He say than to you He hath said, You who un-to Je-sus for ref-uge have fled? You who un-to Je-sus for ref-uge have fled?

497   *"Exceeding great and precious Promises."*
2 Pet. i. 4.

2 "Fear not, I am with thee, O be not dismayed,
For I am thy God, and will still give thee aid;
I'll strengthen thee, help thee, and cause thee to stand,
Upheld by My righteous, omnipotent hand.

3 "When through the deep waters I call thee to go,
The rivers of woe shall not thee overflow;
For I will be with thee thy troubles to bless,
And sanctify to thee thy deepest distress.

4 "When through fiery trials thy pathway shall lie,
My grace all-sufficient shall be thy supply;
The flame shall not hurt thee: I only design
Thy dross to consume, and thy gold to refine.

5 "E'en down to old age, all My people shall prove
My sovereign, eternal, unchangeable love;
And when hoary hairs shall their temples adorn,
Like lambs they shall still in My bosom be borne.

6 "The soul that on Jesus hath leaned for repose
I will not, I will not desert to His foes;
That soul, though all hell should endeavor to shake,
I'll never, no, never, no, never forsake."

George Keith, 1787. Ab

UNIVERSITY COLLEGE. 7.

HENRY JOHN GAUNTLETT (1806—1876).

1. HARK, my soul, it is the Lord; 'Tis thy Sav - iour, hear His word;
Je - sus speaks, and speaks to thee: "Say, poor sin - ner, lov'st thou Me?

498
"Lovest thou Me?"

2 "I delivered thee, when bound,
And, when wounded, healed Thy wound;
Sought thee wandering, set thee right,
Turned thy darkness into light.

3 "Can a woman's tender care
Cease towards the child she bare?
Yes, she may forgetful be,
Yet will I remember thee.

4 "Mine is an unchanging love,
Higher than the heights above,
Deeper than the depths beneath,
Free and faithful, strong as death.

5 "Thou shalt see My glory soon,
When the work of grace is done;
Partner of My throne shalt be;
Say, poor sinner, lovest thou Me?"

6 Lord, it is my chief complaint,
That my love is weak and faint;
Yet I love Thee, and adore;
O for grace to love Thee more!

William Cowper (1731—1800), 1779.

499
"Loving Him who first loved me."

1 SAVIOUR, teach me, day by day,
Love's sweet lesson to obey;
Sweeter lesson cannot be,
Loving Him who first loved me.

2 Teach me all Thy steps to trace,
Strong to follow in Thy grace;
Learning how to love from Thee,
Loving Him who first loved me.

3 Thus may I rejoice to show
That I feel the love I owe;
Singing, till Thy face I see,
Of His love who first loved me.

Miss Jane E. Leeson, 1842. Ab.

HORTON. 7.

XAVIER SCHNYDER von WARTENSEE (1786—1868).

ASWARBY S. M.

SAMUEL WESLEY (1766—1837), 1795.

1. How gen - tle God's com - mands! How kind His pre - cepts are!

"Come, cast your bur - dens on the Lord, And trust His con - stant care."

500 *God's Care a Remedy for ours.*
1 PET. v. 7.

2 While Providence supports,
  Let saints securely dwell;
  That hand, which bears all nature up,
  Shall guide His children well.

3 Why should this anxious load
  Press down your weary mind?
  Haste to your heavenly Father's throne,
  And sweet refreshment find.

4 His goodness stands approved
  Down to the present day;
  I'll drop my burden at His feet,
  And bear a song away.

      Rev. Philip Doddridge (1702—1751), 1755.

501   *Sailing on.*

1 IF, through unruffled seas,
  Toward Heaven we calmly sail,

With grateful hearts, O God, to Thee,
  We'll own the favoring gale.

2 But should the surges rise,
  And rest delay to come,
  Blest be the sorrow, kind the storm,
  Which drives us nearer home.

3 Soon shall our doubts and fears
  All yield to Thy control:
  Thy tender mercies shall illume
  The midnight of the soul.

4 Teach us, in every state,
  To make Thy will our own;
  And when the joys of sense depart,
  To live by faith alone.

    Rev. Augustus Montague Toplady (1740—1778), 1772. Ab. and
much alt.

FRANKLIN SQUARE. S. M.

SYLVANUS BILLINGS POND (1815—1871), before 1850.

1. GIVE to the winds thy fears; Hope, and be un - dis - may'd:

God hears thy sighs, and counts thy tears; God shall lift up thy head.

502 *"Befiehl du deine Wege"*

2 Through waves and clouds and storms,
  He gently clears thy way :
Wait thou His time, so shall this night
  Soon end in joyous day.

3 Far, far above thy thought
  His counsel shall appear,
When fully He the work hath wrought
  That caused thy needless fear.

4 Thou seest our weakness, Lord,
  Our hearts are known to Thee ;
O lift Thou up the sinking hand,
  Confirm the feeble knee.

5 Let us, in life, in death,
  Thy steadfast truth declare,
And publish with our latest breath
  Thy love and guardian care.

Rev. Paul Gerhardt (1606—1676), 1653.
Tr. by Rev. John Wesley (1703—1791), 1739. Ab.

OLNEY. S. M.

LOWELL MASON (1792—1872), 1832.

1. COM - MIT thou all thy griefs And ways in - to His hands, To

His sure truth and ten - der care, Who earth and Heav'n com - mands.

503 *Trust in Providence.*
MATT. vi. 25, 1 PET. v. 7.

2 Who points the clouds their course,
  Whom wind and seas obey,
He shall direct thy wandering feet,
  He shall prepare thy way.

3 Thou on the Lord rely,
  So safe shalt thou go on ;
Fix on His work thy steadfast eye,
  So shall thy work be done.

4 No profit canst thou gain
  By self-consuming care ;
To Him commend thy cause ; His ear
  Attends the softest prayer.

Rev. Paul Gerhardt, 1659.
Tr. by Rev. John Wesley, 1739. Ab.

504 *Safety in God.*
Ps. xxxi.

1 My spirit, on Thy care,
  Blest Saviour, I recline :

Thou wilt not leave me to despair,
  For Thou art Love divine.

2 In Thee I place my trust,
  On Thee I calmly rest ;
I know Thee good, I know Thee just,
  And count Thy choice the best.

3 Whate'er events betide,
  Thy will they all perform ;
Safe in Thy breast my head I hide,
  Nor fear the coming storm.

4 Let good or ill befall,
  It must be good for me ;
Secure of having Thee in all,
  Of having all in Thee.

Rev. Henry Francis Lyte (1793—1847), 1834.

SUBMISSION.

ST. JUDE. 6. D.

CARL MARIA von WEBER (1786—1826), 1820.

1. My Je - sus, as Thou wilt: O may Thy will be mine; In - to Thy

hand of love I would my all re - sign. Through sor - row or through joy,

Con - duct me as Thine own, And help me still to say, My Lord, Thy will be done.

505

"Mein Jesu, wie Du willst."

2 My Jesus, as Thou wilt:
  If needy here and poor,
  Give me Thy people's bread,
  Their portion rich and sure.
The manna of Thy Word
  Let my soul feed upon;
And if all else should fail,
  My Lord, Thy will be done.

3 My Jesus, as Thou wilt:
  Though seen through many a tear,
Let not my star of hope
  Grow dim or disappear.
Since Thou on earth hast wept
  And sorrowed oft alone,
If I must weep with Thee,
  My Lord, Thy will be done

4 My Jesus, as Thou wilt:
  All shall be well for me;
Each changing future scene
  I gladly trust with Thee.
Straight to my home above,
  I travel calmly on,

And sing, in life or death,
  My Lord, Thy will be done.
Rev. Benjamin Schmolke (1672—1737), 1716.
Tr. by Miss Jane Borthwick (1325—   ), 1853. Ab.

506

Longing for Christ.

1 My spirit longs for Thee
  Within my troubled breast,
Unworthy though I be
  Of so divine a Guest.
Of so divine a Guest
  Unworthy though I be,
Yet has my heart no rest
  Unless it come from Thee.

2 Unless it come from Thee,
  In vain I look around;
In all that I can see
  No rest is to be found.
No rest is to be found,
  But in Thy blessed love:
O let my wish be crowned,
  And send it from above.
John Byrom (1691—1763), 1773.

507   *"Thy Way, not mine."*   6. D.

1 Thy way, not mine, O Lord,
    However dark it be!
Lead me by Thine own hand;
    Choose out the path for me.
I dare not choose my lot;
    I would not, if I might;
Choose Thou for me, my God,
    So shall I walk aright.

2 The kingdom that I seek
    Is Thine: so let the way
That leads to it be Thine,
    Else I must surely stray.

Take Thou my cup, and it
    With joy or sorrow fill,
As best to Thee may seem;
    Choose Thou my good and ill.

3 Choose Thou for me my friends,
    My sickness or my health,
Choose Thou my cares for me,
    My poverty or wealth.
Not mine, not mine the choice,
    In things or great or small;
Be Thou my Guide, my Strength,
    My Wisdom, and my All.

Rev. Horatius Bonar (1808–), 1857. Ab.

HANFORD. 8.8.8.4.   Sir ARTHUR SULLIVAN (1842–), 1872.

1. My God and Fa-ther, while I stray Far from my home, on life's rough way,

O teach me from my heart to say, "Thy will be done."

508   *"Thy Will be done."*

2 Though dark my path, and sad my lot,
Let me be still and murmur not,
Or breathe the prayer divinely taught,
    "Thy will be done."

3 Renew my will from day to day;
Blend it with Thine, and take away

All that now makes it hard to say,
    "Thy will be done."

4 Then when on earth I breathe no more,
The prayer oft mixed with tears before
I'll sing upon a happier shore:
    "Thy will be done."

Miss Charlotte Elliott (1789–1871), 1834. Ab.

TROYTE'S CHANT. 8.8.8.4.   ARTHUR HENRY DYKE TROYTE (1811–1857), 1857.

AURELIA. 7, 6. D.

SAMUEL SEBASTIAN WESLEY (1810—1876). 1868.

1. I NEED Thee, pre-cious Je - sus, For I am full of sin; My soul is dark and guilt - y, My heart is dead with - in; I need the cleans-ing fount - ain Where I can al - ways flee, The blood of Christ most pre - cious, The sin - ner's per - fect plea.

509

"He is precious."
1 PET. ii. 7.

2 I need Thee, precious Jesus,
  For I am very poor;
A stranger and a pilgrim,
  I have no earthly store;
I need the love of Jesus
  To cheer me on my way,
To guide my doubting footsteps,
  To be my strength and stay.

3 I need Thee, precious Jesus,
  And hope to see Thee soon,
Encircled with the rainbow,
  And seated on Thy throne:
There, with Thy blood-bought children,
  My joy shall ever be,
To sing Thy praises, Jesus,
  To gaze, my Lord, on Thee.

Rev. Frederick Whitfield (1829—), 1859. Ab. and sl. alt.

510

"Thee, Thee only."

1 LORD Jesus, by Thy passion,
  To Thee I make my prayer;
Thou who in mercy smitest,

Have mercy, Lord, and spare:
O wash me in the fountain
  That floweth from Thy side;
O clothe me in the raiment
  Thy blood hath purified.

2 O bring me, loving Jesus,
  To that most blessed place,
Where angels and archangels
  Look ever on Thy face;
Where gladsome Alleluias
  Unceasingly resound;
Where martyrs, now triumphant,
  Walk robed in white, and crowned.

3 O make my spirit worthy
  To join that ransomed throng;
O teach my lips to utter
  That everlasting song;
O give that last, best blessing
  That even saints can know,
To follow in Thy footsteps
  Wherever Thou dost go.

The Book of Hours, 1865. Ab.

PASTOR BONUS. 7.6.D.

THEODORE EDWARD AYLWARD (1844—   ), 1868.

1. O Jе-sus ev-er pres-ent, O Shepherd ev-er kind, Thy ver-y Name is mu-sic,

To ear, and heart, and mind. It woke my wond'ring child-hood To muse on things a-bove;

It drew my hard-er man-hood With cords of might-y love.

511   *The Good Shepherd.*
        JOHN X. 14.

2 How oft to sure destruction
    My feet had gone astray,
    Wert Thou not, patient Shepherd,
    The Guardian of my way.
    How oft, in darkness fallen,
    And wounded sore by sin,
    Thy hand has gently raised me,
    And healing balms poured in.

3 O Shepherd good, I follow
    Wherever Thou wilt lead;
    No matter where the pasture,
    With Thee at hand to feed.
    Thy voice, in life so mighty,
    In death shall make me bold;
    O bring my ransomed spirit
    To Thine eternal fold.
                Rev. Lawrence Tuttlett (1825—   ), 1866.

512   *God's Way best for us.*

1 OUR yet unfinished story
    Is tending all to this:
    To God the greatest glory,
    To us the greatest bliss.
    Our plans may be disjointed,
    But we may calmly rest:
    What God has once appointed
    Is better than our best.

2 We cannot see before us,
    But our all-seeing Friend
    Is always watching o'er us,
    And knows the very end;
    And when amid our blindness
    His disappointments fall,
    We trust His loving-kindness
    Whose wisdom sends them all.

3 They are the purple fringes
    That hide His glorious feet;
    They are the fire-wrought hinges
    Where truth and mercy meet;
    By them the golden portal
    Of Providence shall ope,
    And lift to praise immortal
    The songs of faith and hope.
    Miss Frances Ridley Havergal (1836—1879), 1872.   **Ab**

IN SORROW.

MILMAN. 7.

RICHARD REDHEAD (1820 —   ).

1. WHEN our heads are bow'd with woe, When our bit - ter tears o'er - flow,

When we mourn the lost, the dear, Je - sus, Son of Ma - ry, hear.

513

"He hath borne our Griefs."
Is. liii. 4.

2 When the solemn death-bell tolls
For our own departing souls,
When our final doom is near,
Jesus, Son of Mary, hear.

3 Thou hast bowed the dying head,
Thou the blood of life hast shed,
Thou hast filled a mortal bier:
Jesus, Son of Mary, hear.

4 When the heart is sad within
With the thought of all its sin,
When the spirit shrinks with fear,
Jesus, Son of Mary, hear.

5 Thou, the shame, the grief hast known;
Though the sins were not Thine own,
Thou hast deigned their load to bear:
Jesus, Son of Mary, hear.

Rev. Henry Hart Milman (1791—1868), 1827. Ab.

ST. BEES. 7.

Rev. JOHN BACCHUS DYKES (1823—1876), 1874.

1. CAST thy bur - den on the Lord, On - ly lean up - on His word;

Thou shalt soon have cause to bless His e - ter - nal faith - ful - ness.

514

"Cast thy Burden upon the Lord."
Ps. lv. 22.

2 Ever in the raging storm
Thou shalt see His cheering form,
Hear His pledge of coming aid:
"It is I, be not afraid."

3 Cast thy burden at His feet;
Linger at His mercy-seat:
He will lead thee by the hand
Gently to the better land.

4 He will gird thee by His power,
In thy weary, fainting hour;
Lean, then, loving, on His word;
Cast thy burden on the Lord.

Rev. Rowland Hill (1744—1833), 1783. V. 1.
George Rawson (1807—   ), 1857. Ab. and much alt.

TREVES. 7.7.7.5.

Arr. by HENRY JOHN GAUNTLETT (1806—1876), 1872.

1. LORD of mer - cy and of might, Of man - kind the Life and Light,
Mak - er, Teach - er in - fi - nite, Je - sus, hear and save.

515   *"Hear and save."*

2 Strong Creator, Saviour mild,
Humbled to a mortal child,
Captive, beaten, bound, reviled,
Jesus, hear and save.

3 Throned above celestial things,
Borne aloft on angels' wings.
Lord of lords, and King of kings,
Jesus, hear and save.

4 Soon to come to earth again.
Judge of angels and of men,
Hear us now, and hear us then,
Jesus, hear and save.

Bp. Reginald Heber (1783—1826), 1811. Ab.

516   *Prayer for Comfort.*

1 In the dark and cloudy day,
When earth's riches flee away,
And the last hope will not stay,
Saviour, comfort me.

2 When the hoard of many years
Like a fleet-cloud disappears,
And the future's full of fears,
Saviour, comfort me.

3 When the secret idol's gone
That my poor heart yearned upon,
Desolate, bereft, alone,
Saviour, comfort me.

4 Thou, who wast so sorely tried,
In the darkness crucified,
Bid me in Thy love confide:
Saviour, comfort me.

5 In these hours of sad distress,
Let me know He loves no less,
Bids me trust His faithfulness:
Saviour, comfort me.

6 Not unduly let me grieve,
Meekly the kind stripes receive,
Let me humbly still believe:
Saviour, comfort me.

Rev. Robert Herrick (1591—1674), 1647. Ab.

BENEDICTION. L. M. 6l.   JOSEPH BARNBY (1838—   ), 1872.

1. WHEN gath'ring clouds a-round I view, And days are dark, and friends are few,

On Him I lean, who not in vain Ex-perienc'd ev-'ry hu-man pain;

He sees my wants, al-lays my fears, And counts and treas-ures up my tears.

517   *Christ able to succor the tempted.*
      Heb. ii. 18.

2 If aught should tempt my soul to stray
From heavenly wisdom's narrow way;
To fly the good I would pursue,
Or do the sin I would not do;
Still He who felt temptation's power,
Shall guard me in that dangerous hour.

3 When sorrowing o'er some stone I bend,
Which covers what was once a friend,
And from his voice, his hand, his smile,
Divides me for a little while;
Thou, Saviour, mark'st the tears I shed,
For Thou didst weep o'er Lazarus dead.

4 And O, when I have safely past
Through every conflict but the last,
Still, still unchanging, watch beside
My painful bed, for Thou hast died;
Then point to realms of cloudless day,
And wipe the latest tear away.

    Sir Robert Grant (1788—1838), 1806, 1812. Ab.

RETREAT. L. M.   THOMAS HASTINGS (1784—1872), 1840.

1. FROM ev-'ry storm-y wind that blows, From ev-'ry swell-ing tide of woes,

There is a calm, a sure re-treat: 'Tis found be-neath the mer-cy-seat.

518 *The Mercy-seat.*

2 There is a place where Jesus sheds
  The oil of gladness on our heads;
  A place than all besides more sweet:
  It is the blood-bought mercy-seat.

3 There is a spot where spirits blend,
  Where friend holds fellowship with friend;
  Though sundered far, by faith they meet
  Around one common mercy-seat.

4 There, there, on eagle wings we soar,
  And time and sense seem all no more;
  And Heaven comes down our souls to greet,
  And glory crowns the mercy-seat.

5 O may my hand forget her skill,
  My tongue be silent, cold, and still,
  This bounding heart forget to beat,
  If I forget the mercy-seat.

          Rev. Hugh Stowell (1799—1865), 1832. Ab.

WELTON. L. M.
       Rev. CÆSAR HENRI ABRAHAM MALAN (1787—1864), 1839.

1. 'Tis thus in sol - i - tude I roam O'er ma - ny a land and toss - ing sea;
And yet, a - far from friends and home, I find, O God, a home in Thee.

519 *Far from Home.*

2 I pass from things of space and time,
  The finite meets or leaves my sight;
  But God expands o'er every clime,
  The clothing of the Infinite.

3 He walks the earth, He rides the air:
  The lightning's speed He leaves behind.
  His Name is Love. And tell me, where
  Is sea or land He cannot find?

4 O, long I've known Him. Could it be
  That if He did not hold me dear,
  He thus would travel land and sea,
  And throw His arms around me here?

5 I could not leave Him, if I would;
  I would not, if the power were given;
  'Twould be to leave the True and Good,
  The soul's Repose, the spirit's Heaven.

      Rev. Thomas Cogswell Upham (1799—1872), 1853. Ab.

520 *Watching and Praying.*

1 They pray the best who pray and watch,
  They watch the best who watch and
    pray,
  They hear Christ's fingers on the latch,
  Whether He comes by night, or day.

2 Whether they guard the gates and watch,
  Or, patient, toil for Him, and wait,
  They hear His fingers on the latch,
  If early He doth come, or late.

3 With trembling joy they hail their Lord,
  And haste His welcome feet to kiss,
  While He, well pleased, doth speak the
    word
  That thrills them with unending bliss:

4 "Well done, My servants, now receive,
  For faithful work, reward and rest,
  And wreaths which busy angels weave,
  To crown the men who serve Me best."

      Rev. Edward Hopper (1818—), 1873.

THE CALM RETREAT.

WELLINGTON. C. M.

HENRY JOHN GAUNTLETT (1806–1876), 1812.

1. FAR from the world, O Lord, I flee, From strife and tu-mult far;

From scenes where Sa-tan wa-ges still His most suc-cess-ful war.

521   *"Far from the world."*

2 The calm retreat, the silent shade,
　　With prayer and praise agree,
　And seem by Thy sweet bounty made
　　For those who follow Thee.

3 There, if Thy Spirit touch the soul,
　　And grace her mean abode,
　O with what peace, and joy, and love
　　She communes with her God!

4 Author and Guardian of my life,
　　Sweet Source of love divine,
　And, all harmonious names in one,
　　My Saviour, Thou art mine!

5 What thanks I owe Thee, and what love,
　　A boundless, endless store,
　Shall echo through the realms above,
　　When time shall be no more!
　　　　　　　William Cowper (1731–1800), 1779. Ab.

522　*Moving the Hand which moves the World.*

1 THERE is an eye that never sleeps
　　Beneath the wing of night;

There is an ear that never shuts,
　　When sink the beams of light.

2 There is an arm that never tires,
　　When human strength gives way;
　There is a love that never fails,
　　When earthly loves decay.

3 That eye is fixed on seraph throngs;
　　That arm upholds the sky;
　That ear is filled with angel songs;
　　That love is throned on high.

4 But there's a power which man can wield,
　　When mortal aid is vain,
　That eye, that arm, that love to reach,
　　That listening ear to gain.

5 That power is prayer, which soars on high.
　　Through Jesus, to the throne,
　And moves the hand which moves the
　　　world,
　　To bring salvation down.
　　　　Rev. John Aikman Wallace (1802–1870), 1839. Ab.

SERENITY. C. M.

WILLIAM VINCENT WALLACE (1815–1865), 1856.

BELMONT. C. M.

SAMUEL WEBBE (1740-1816).

1. Prayer is the soul's sincere desire, Uttered or unexpressed,
The motion of a hidden fire That trembles in the breast.

523 *Prayer.*

2 Prayer is the burden of a sigh,
The falling of a tear,
The upward glancing of an eye,
When none but God is near.

3 Prayer is the simplest form of speech
That infant lips can try;
Prayer the sublimest strains that reach
The Majesty on high.

4 Prayer is the contrite sinner's voice
Returning from his ways,
While angels in their songs rejoice,
And cry, "Behold, he prays!"

5 Prayer is the Christian's vital breath,
The Christian's native air,
His watchword at the gates of death;
He enters Heaven with prayer.

6 O Thou, by whom we come to God,
The Life, the Truth, the Way,
The path of prayer Thyself hast trod:
Lord, teach us how to pray.

James Montgomery (1771-1854), 1819, 1833. Ab.

524 *Evening Twilight.*

1 I love to steal awhile away
From every cumbering care,
And spend the hours of setting day
In humble, grateful prayer.

2 I love, in solitude, to shed
The penitential tear;
And all His promises to plead
Where none but God can hear.

3 I love to think on mercies past,
And future good implore;
And all my cares and sorrows cast
On Him whom I adore.

4 I love, by faith, to take a view
Of brighter scenes in Heaven;
The prospect doth my strength renew,
While here by tempests driven.

5 Thus, when life's toilsome day is o'er,
May its departing ray
Be calm as this impressive hour,
And lead to endless day.

Mrs. Phœbe Hinsdale Brown (1783-1861), 1824.

WOODSTOCK. C. M.

DEODATUS DUTTON, Jr., 1829.

MORNINGTON. S. M.

Lord GARRET WELLESLEY MORNINGTON (1770—1781), 1760.
Arr. by LOWELL MASON (1792—1872), 1822.

1. PRAY, with · out ceas · ing, pray, Your Cap · tain gives the word;

His sum · mons cheer · ful · ly o · bey, And call up · on the Lord.

525

"Pray without ceasing."
1 Thess. v. 17.

2 To God your every want
  In instant prayer display;
Pray always; pray, and never faint;
  Pray, without ceasing, pray.

3 From strength to strength go on;
  Wrestle, and fight, and pray;

Tread all the powers of darkness down,
  And win the well-fought day.

4 Still let the Spirit cry,
  In all His soldiers—"Come,"
Till Christ the Lord descends from high,
  And takes the conquerors home.

Rev. Charles Wesley (1708—1788), 1749. Ab.

ALMSGIVING. 8. 8. 8. 4.

Rev. JOHN BACCHUS DYKES (1823—1876).

1. O LORD of Heaven, and earth, and sea, To Thee all praise and glo · ry be;

How shall we show our love to Thee, Who giv · est all?

526

Christian Giving.

2 Thou didst not spare Thine only Son,
  But gavest Him for a world undone,
And freely with that Blessed One
  Thou givest all.

3 Thou givest the Spirit's blessed dower,
  Spirit of life, and love, and power,

And dost His sevenfold graces shower
  Upon us all.

4 For souls redeemed, for sins forgiven,
  For means of grace, and hopes of Heaven,
What can to Thee, O Lord, be given,
  Who givest all?

Bp. Christopher Wordsworth (1807—1885), 1863. Ab. and alt.

BISHOP. L. M.

JOSEPH PERRY HOLBROOK (1822—), 1862.

1. My gra-cious Lord, I own Thy right To ev-'ry ser-vice I can pay,

And call it my su-preme de-light To hear Thy dic-tates and o-bey.

---

527 *Serving Christ.*
Phil. i. 22.

2 I would not breathe for worldly joy,
   Or to increase my worldly good ;
Nor future days nor powers employ
   To spread a sounding name abroad.

3 'Tis to my Saviour I would live,
   To Him who for my ransom died ;
Nor could the bowers of Eden give
   Such bliss as blossoms at His side.

4 His work my hoary age shall bless,
   When youthful vigor is no more ;
And my last hour of life confess
   His dying love, His saving power.
      Rev. Philip Doddridge (1702—1751), 1755. Ab. and alt.

528 *"Go, labor on."*

1 Go, labor on ; spend and be spent,
   Thy joy to do the Father's will :
It is the way the Master went ;
   Should not the servant tread it still?

2 Go, labor on ; 'tis not for naught ;
   Thine earthly loss is heavenly gain :
Men heed thee, love thee, praise thee not ;
   The Master praises,—what are men?

3 Go, labor on ; enough, while here,
   If He shall praise thee, if He deign

Thy willing heart to mark and cheer :
   No toil for Him shall be in vain.

4 Toil on, and in thy toil rejoice ;
   For toil comes rest, for exile, home ;
Soon shalt thou hear the Bridegroom's voice,
   The midnight peal : "Behold, I come !"
      Rev. Horatius Bonar (1808—), 1857. Ab.

529 *Adorning the Doctrine.*
Titus. ii. 10—13.

1 So let our lips and lives express
   The holy gospel we profess ;
So let our works and virtues shine,
   To prove the doctrine all divine.

2 Thus shall we best proclaim abroad
   The honors of our Saviour God ;
When His salvation reigns within,
   And grace subdues the power of sin.

3 Our flesh and sense must be denied,
   Passion and envy, lust and pride ;
While justice, temperance, truth, and love,
   Our inward piety approve.

4 Religion bears our spirits up,
   While we expect that blessed hope,
The bright appearance of the Lord,
   And faith stands leaning on His word.
      Rev. Isaac Watts (1674—1748), 1709. Sl. alt.

SOUTHPORT. C. M. GEORGE KINGSLEY (1811—1884). 1853.

1. WORK - MAN of God, O lose not heart, But learn what God is like;

And in the dark - est bat - tle - field Thou shalt know where to strike.

530   *The winning Side.*

2 Thrice blest is he to whom is given
   The instinct that can tell
That God is on the field, when He
   Is most invisible.

3 Blest too is he who can divine,
   Where real right doth lie,
And dares to take the side that seems
   Wrong to man's blindfold eye.

4 Then learn to scorn the praise of men,
   And learn to lose with God;
For Jesus won the world through shame,
   And beckons thee His road.

5 For right is right, since God is God,
   And right the day must win;
To doubt would be disloyalty,
   To falter would be sin.
      Rev. Frederick William Faber (1814—1863), 1849. Ab.

531   *Waiting for Light.*

1 O VERY God of very God,
   And very Light of Light,
Whose feet this earth's dark valley trod,
   That so it might be bright;

2 Our hopes are weak, our fears are strong,
   Thick darkness blinds our eyes;
Cold is the night, and O we long
   That Thou, our Sun, wouldst rise.

3 O guide us till our path is done,
   And we have reached the shore
Where Thou, our everlasting Sun,
   Art shining evermore.

4 We wait in faith, and turn our face
   To where the daylight springs,
Till Thou shalt come our gloom to chase,
   With healing on Thy wings.
      Rev. John Mason Neale (1818—1866), 1854. Ab.

532   *"The Poor always with you."*
       MATT. xxvi. 11.

1 LORD, lead the way the Saviour went,
   By lane and cell obscure,
And let our treasure still be spent,
   Like His, upon the poor.

2 Like Him, through scenes of deep distress,
   Who bore the world's sad weight,
We, in their crowded loneliness,
   Would seek the desolate.

3 For Thou hast placed us side by side
   In this wide world of ill;
And that Thy followers may be tried,
   The poor are with us still.

4 Mean are all offerings we can make;
   But Thou hast taught us, Lord,
If given for the Saviour's sake,
   They lose not their reward.
      Rev. William Croswell (1804—1851), 1831.

ST. THOMAS S. M.   WILLIAM TANS'UR (1699—1774), 1743.

1. WE give Thee but Thine own, What - e'er the gift may be;
All that we have is Thine a - lone, A trust, O Lord, from Thee.

533   *"Thine alone."*

2 O, hearts are bruised and dead,
   And homes are bare and cold,
   And lambs, for whom the Shepherd bled,
   Are straying from the fold.

3 To comfort and to bless,
   To find a balm for woe,
   To tend the lone and fatherless,
   Is angels' work below.

4 The captive to release,
   To God the lost to bring,
   To teach the way of life and peace,
   It is a Christ-like thing.

5 And we believe Thy word,
   Though dim our faith may be;
   Whate'er for Thine we do, O Lord,
   We do it unto Thee.
   Bp. William Walsham How (1823—   ), 1854.   Ab.

534   *Waiting Orders from Heaven.*

1 HAPPY the man, who knows
   His Master to obey;
   Whose life of care and labor flows,
   Where God points out the way.

2 He riseth to his task,
   Soon as the word is given;
   Nor waits, nor doth a question ask,
   When orders come from Heaven.

3 Nothing he calls his own;
   Nothing he hath to say;
   His feet are shod for God alone,
   And God alone obey.

4 Give us, O God, this mind,
   Which waits for Thy command,
   And doth its highest pleasure find
   In Thy great work to stand.
   Rev. Thomas Cogswell Upham (1799—1872), 1872.

535   *Bearing One Another's Burdens.*
            GAL. VI. 2.

1 O PRAISE our God to-day,
   His constant mercy bless,
   Whose love hath helped us on our way,
   And granted us success.

2 His arm the strength imparts
   Our daily toil to bear;
   His grace alone inspires our hearts,
   Each other's load to share.

3 O happiest work below,
   Earnest of joy above,
   To sweeten many a cup of woe,
   By deeds of holy love!

4 Lord, may it be our choice
   This blessed rule to keep,
   "Rejoice with them that do rejoice,
   And weep with them that weep."
   Rev. Sir Henry Williams Baker (1821—1877), 1861.   Ab.

ST. MICHAEL. S. M.   From the Psalter (1563) of JOHN DAYE (1522—1584).

1. YE serv-ants of the Lord, Each in his of-fice wait,

Ob-serv-ant of His heav'n-ly word, And watch-ful at His gate.

536   *"The watchful Servant."*
LUKE xii. 35—38.

2 Let all your lamps be bright,
   And trim the golden flame;
Gird up your loins as in His sight,
   For awful is His Name.

3 Watch! 'tis your Lord's command;
   And while we speak, He's near:
Mark the first signal of His hand,
   And ready all appear.

4 O happy servant he,
   In such a posture found!
He shall his Lord with rapture see,
   And be with honor crowned.

5 Christ shall the banquet spread
   With His own royal hand,
And raise that faithful servant's head
   Amid th' angelic band.

Rev. Philip Doddridge (1702—1751), 1755.   Sl. alt.

CHARITAS. 8. 7. D.   Rev. JOHN BACCHUS DYKES (1823—1876), 1874.

1. Lord of Glo-ry, who hast bought us With Thy life-blood as the price, Nev-er grudg-ing

for the lost ones That tre-men-dous sac-ri-fice; And with that hast free-ly giv-en

Blessings, countless as the sand, To th' unthankful and the e-vil, With Thine own un-spar-ing hand.

537 *The Blessedness of Giving.*
Acts xx. 35.

2 Grant us hearts, dear Lord, to yield Thee
   Gladly, freely of Thine own;
  With the sunshine of Thy goodness
   Melt our thankless hearts of stone.
  Wondrous honor hast Thou given
   To our humblest charity,
  In Thine own mysterious sentence,
   "Ye have done it unto Me."

3 Lord of Glory, who hast bought us
   With Thy life-blood as the price,
  Never grudging for the lost ones
   That tremendous sacrifice,
  Give us faith, to trust Thee boldly,
   Hope, to stay our souls on Thee;
  But, O best of all Thy graces,
   Give us Thine own charity.

Mrs. Eliza Sibbald Alderson, 1868. Ab.

538 *The Call to Service.* 8.7.D.

1 We are living, we are dwelling,
   In a grand and awful time,
  In an age on ages telling;
   To be living is sublime.
  Hark, the waking up of nations,
   Gog and Magog, to the fray.
  Hark, what soundeth? is creation
   Groaning for its latter day?

2 Worlds are charging, Heaven beholding,
   Thou hast but an hour to fight;
  Now the blazoned cross unfolding,
   On, right onward, for the right!
  On! let all the soul within you
   For the truth's sake go abroad.
  Strike! let every nerve and sinew
   Tell on ages, tell for God.

Bp. Arthur Cleveland Coxe (1818—), 1840.

HOWARD. C. M.

SAMUEL HOWARD (1710—1782), 1769.

1. Shine on our souls, e-ter-nal God, With rays of beau-ty shine:

O let Thy fa-vor crown our days, And all their round be Thine.

539 *"God's Blessing invoked."*
Ps. xc. 17.

2 Did we not raise our hands to Thee,
   Our hands might toil in vain;
  Small joy success itself could give,
   If Thou Thy love restrain.

3 With Thee let every week begin,
   With Thee each day be spent;

For Thee each fleeting hour improved,
  Since each by Thee is lent.

4 Thus cheer us through this desert road,
   Till all our labors cease;
  And Heaven refresh our weary souls
   With everlasting peace.

Rev. Philip Doddridge, 1755.

STUTTGARD. 8.7.

JOHANN GEORG CHRISTIAN STÖRL (1676—1743).

1. ALL un - seen the Mas - ter walk - eth By the toil - ing serv - ant's side:

Com - fort - a - ble words He speak - eth, While His hands up - hold and guide.

540 *Sufficient Grace.*

2 Grief, nor pain, nor any sorrow
Rends thy heart, to Him unknown;
He to-day, and He to-morrow,
Grace sufficient gives His own.

3 Holy strivings nerve and strengthen,
Long endurance wins the crown:
When the evening shadows lengthen,
Thou shalt lay thy burden down.
Thomas MacKellar (1812—), 1852. Ab. and sl. alt.

KELSO. 7.6 l.

EDWARD JOHN HOPKINS (1818—), 1872.

1. EV - 'RY morn - ing mer - cies new Fall as fresh as morn - ing dew;

Ev - 'ry morn - ing let us pay Trib - ute with the ear - ly day;

For Thy mer - cies, Lord, are sure; Thy com - pas - sion doth en - dure.

541 *"The Lord is Thy Keeper"* Ps. cxxi. 5.

2 Still the greatness of Thy love
Daily doth our sins remove;
Daily, far as east from west,

Lifts the burden from the breast;
Gives unbought, to those who pray,
Strength to stand in evil day.

3 Let our prayers each morn prevail,
That these gifts may never fail;
And, as we confess the sin
And the tempter's power within,
Feed us with the Bread of Life;
Fit us for our daily strife.

4 As the morning light returns,
As the sun with splendor burns,
Teach us still to turn to Thee,
Ever blesséd Trinity,
With our hands our hearts to raise,
In unfailing prayer and praise.

Rev. Horatius Bonar (1808—   ), 1863.

CANONBURY. L. M.

ROBERT SCHUMANN (1810—1856), Op. 23.

1. New ev-'ry morn-ing is the love Our wak-'ning and up-ris-ing prove;

Through sleep and dark-ness safe-ly brought, Re-stor'd to life, and pow'r, and thought.

542 "New every Morning."
LAM. iii. 22, 23.

2 New mercies, each returning day,
Hover round us while we pray;
New perils past, new sins forgiven,
New thoughts of God, new hopes of Heaven

3 If on our daily course our mind
Be set, to hallow all we find,
New treasures still, of countless price,
God will provide for sacrifice.

4 The trivial round, the common task,
Will furnish all we ought to ask,—
Room to deny ourselves, a road
To bring us daily nearer God.

5 Only, O Lord, in Thy dear love
Fit us for perfect rest above;
And help us, this and every day,
To live more nearly as we pray.

Rev. John Keble (1792—1866), 1827. Ab.

543 *Jesus the Best Beloved.*

1 JESUS, my heart within me burns,
To tell Thee all its conscious love;

And from earth's low delights it turns,
To taste a joy like that above.

2 When Thou to me dost condescend,
In love divine, Thou blessed One,
The moments that with Thee I spend,
Seem e'en as Heaven itself begun.

3 Though oft these lips my love have told,
They still the story would repeat;
To me the rapture ne'er grows old
That thrills me, bending at Thy feet.

4 I breathe my words into Thine ear;
I seem to fix mine eyes on Thine;
And sure that Thou dost wait to hear,
I dare in faith to call Thee mine.

5 Reign Thou sole Sovereign of my heart,
My all I yield to Thy control;
O let me never from Thee part,
Thou best Belovéd of my soul.

Rev. Ray Palmer (1808—   ), 1869.

RIVAULX. L. M.   Rev. JOHN BACCHUS DYKES (1823—1876), 1874.

1. My God, how end - less is Thy love: Thy gifts are ev - 'ry even - ing new;

And morn - ing mer - cies from a - bove Gen - tly dis - til like ear - ly dew.

544

For Morning or Evening.
LAM. iii. 23. Is. xlv. 7.

2 Thou spread'st the curtains of the night,
   Great Guardian of my sleeping hours;
Thy sovereign word restores the light,
   And quickens all my drowsy powers.

3 I yield my powers to Thy command;
   To Thee I consecrate my days;
Perpetual blessings from Thy hand
   Demand perpetual songs of praise.
            Rev. Isaac Watts (1674—1748), 1709.

545

Morning Hymn.

1 Lord God of morning and of night,
   We thank Thee for Thy gift of light:
As in the dawn the shadows fly,
   We seem to find Thee now more nigh.

2 Fresh hopes have wakened in the heart,
   Fresh force to do our daily part;
Thy thousand sleeps our strength restore,
   A thousand-fold to serve Thee more.

3 Yet whilst Thy will we would pursue,
   Oft what we would we cannot do;

The sun may stand in zenith skies,
   But on the soul thick midnight lies.

4 O Lord of lights, 'tis Thou alone   [own;
   Canst make our darkened hearts Thine
Though this new day with joy we see,
   O Dawn of God, we cry for Thee.

5 Praise God, our Maker and our Friend;
   Praise Him through time, till time shall
Till psalm and song His Name adore [end;
   Through Heaven's great day of Evermore.
        Francis Turner Palgrave (1824—), 1867.

546

"Aurora jam spargit polum."

1 The dawn is sprinkling in the east
   Its golden shower, as day flows in;
Fast mount the pointed shafts of light:
   Farewell to darkness and to sin.

2 So, Lord, when that last morning breaks,
   Which shrouds in darkness earth and
May it on us, low bending here,   [skies,
   Arrayed in joyful light arise.
        Ambrosian, 4th or 5th century.
Tr. by Rev. Edward Caswall (1814—1878), 1849. Ab. and alt.

GRATITUDE. L. M.   PAUL AMI ISAAC DAVID ROST (1790—1874), 1859.
                                    Arr. by THOMAS HASTINGS (1781—1872), 1837.

POTSDAM. S. M.

JOHANN SEBASTIAN BACH (1685—1750).

1. Our Heav'n-ly Fa-ther calls, And Christ in-vites us near;

With both our friend-ship shall be sweet, And our com-mun-ion dear

547 *Communion with God and Christ.*
1 JOHN i. 3.

2 God pities all my griefs ;
  He pardons every day ;
  Almighty to protect my soul,
  And wise to guide my way.

3 Jesus, my living Head,
  We bless Thy faithful care ;

Mine Advocate before the throne,
  And my Forerunner there.

4 Here fix, my roving heart,
  Here wait, my warmest love,
  Till the communion be complete,
  In nobler scenes above.

Rev. Philip Doddridge (1702—1751), 1755. Ab.

DOWNS. C. M.

LOWELL MASON (1792—1872), 1832.

1. Now that the sun is gleam-ing bright, Im-plore we, bend-ing low,

That He, the un-cre-at-ed Light, May guide us as we go.

548 *"Jam lucis orto sidere."*

2 No sinful word, nor deed of wrong,
  Nor thoughts that idly rove ;
  But simple truth be on our tongue,
  And in our hearts be love.

3 And grant that to Thine honor, Lord,
  Our daily toil may tend ;

That we begin it at Thy word,
  And in Thy favor end.

4 Now to our God, the Father, Son,
  And Holy Spirit, sing :
  With praise to God, the Three in One,
  Let all creation ring.

Paris Breviary, 1736.
Tr. by Rev. John Henry Newman (1801—), 1842. Ab. and alt.

EVENING PRAYER.

TEMPLE. P. M.

EDWARD JOHN HOPKINS (1818—), 1869.

1. God, that mad - est earth and Heav - en, Dark - ness and light; Who the day for toil hast giv - en, For rest the night: May Thine an - gel - guards de - fend us, Slum - ber sweet Thy mer - cy send us, Ho - ly dreams and hopes at - tend us, This live-long night.

549   *Evening Prayer.*

2 And when morn again shall call us
    To run life's way,
May we still, whate'er befall us,
    Thy will obey:
From the power of evil hide us,
In the narrow pathway guide us,
Nor Thy smile be e'er denied us,
    The livelong day.

3 Guard us waking, guard us sleeping,
    And when we die,
May we in Thy mighty keeping
    All peaceful lie:
When the last dread call shall wake us,
Do not Thou, our God, forsake us,
But to reign in glory take us,
    With Thee on high.

Bp. Reginald Heber (1783—1826), 1827. V. 1.
Abp. Richard Whately (1787—1863),   V. 3.

HOLLEY. 7.

GEORGE HEWS (1806—1873), 1835.

1. Ere the wan - ing light de - cay, God of all, to Thee we pray, Thee Thy health - ful grace to send, Thee to guard us and de - fend.

550   *" Te lu.is ante terminum."*

2 Guard from dreams that may affright;
  Guard from terrors of the night;
  Guard from foes, without, within;
  Outward danger, inward sin.

3 Hear the prayer, almighty King;
  Hear Thy praises while we sing,
  Hymning with Thy heavenly host,
  Father, Son, and Holy Ghost.

Ambrose of Milan (340—397),
Tr. by Bp. Richard Mant (1776—1848, 1857. Ab.

NIGHTFALL. 11.11.11.5.   JOSEPH BARNBY (1838—), 1872.

1. BE-HOLD, the shade of night is now re-ced-ing, Kin-dling with splen-dors fair the dawn is
glow-ing, With fer-vent hearts, O let us all im-plore Him, Rul-er Al-might-y:

551   *A Morning Hymn.*

2 That He, our God, will look on us in pity,
  Send strength for weakness, grant us His
    salvation,
  And with a Father's pure affection give us
    Glory eternal.

3 This grace O grant us, Godhead ever-
    blessed,
  Of Father, Son, and Holy Ghost in union,
  Whose praises be through earth's most
    Ever resounding. [distant regions

Gregory (540—604). Tr. by Rev. Ray Palmer (1808—), 1871.

552   *An Evening Hymn.*

1 'MID evening shadows let us all be watch-
    ing,

Ever in psalms our deep devotion waking,
And with one voice hymns to the Lord, the
    Saviour,
    Sweetly be singing.

2 That to the Holy King our songs ascend-
    ing,
We worthily, with all His saints, may enter
The heavenly temple, joyfully partaking
    Life everlasting.

3 This grace O grant us, Godhead ever-
    blessed,
Of Father, Son, and Holy Ghost in union,
Whose praises be through earth's most
    distant regions
    Ever resounding.

Gregory. Tr. by Rev. Ray Palmer, 1871.

FLEMMING. 11.11.11.5.   FRIEDRICH FERDINAND FLEMMING (1778—1813), 1910.

SERENITY C. M.   Arr. from WILLIAM VINCENT WALLACE (1815—1865), 1856.

1. THE twi-light falls, the night is near, I fold my work a-way,

And kneel to One who bends to hear The sto-ry of the day.

553   *"He knoweth the Way that I take."*
              Job xxiii. 10.

2 The old, old story; yet I kneel
  To tell it at Thy call,
  And cares grow lighter as I feel
  That Jesus knows them all.

3 Thou knowest all: I lean my head;
  My weary eyelids close;
  Content and glad awhile to tread
  This path, since Jesus knows.

4 And He has loved me: all my heart
  With answering love is stirred,
  And every anguished pain and smart
  Finds healing in the word.

5 So here I lay me down to rest,
  As nightly shadows fall,
  And lean confiding on His breast
  Who knows and pities all.

                              Unknown Author.

ADRIAN. S. M.   JOHN EDGAR GOULD (1822—1875), 1846.

1. THE day is past and gone, Great God, we bow to Thee;

A-gain, as shades of night steal on, Un-to Thy side we flee.

554   *The final Rest.*

2 O when shall that day come,
  Ne'er sinking in the west,
  That country and that happy home,
  Where none shall break our rest;

3 Where all things shall be peace,
  And pleasure without end,

And golden harps, that never cease,
  With joyous hymns shall blend;

4 Where we, preserved beneath
  The shelter of Thy wing,
  For evermore Thy praise shall breathe,
  And of Thy mercy sing.

                    Rev. William John Blew, 1849. Ab.

NEWTON FERNS 8.7.

SAMUEL SMITH (1804—.913).

1. Ev - er would I fain be read - ing In the an - cient Ho - ly Book,

Of my Sav - iour's gen - tle plead - ing, Truth in ev - 'ry word and look.

555 *"Immer muss ich wieder lesen."*

2 How when children came He blessed them,
Suffered no man to reprove;
Took them in His arms and pressed them
To His heart with words of love.

3 How He healed the sick and dying,
Heard the contrite sinner's moan,
Sought the poor, and stilled their crying,
Called them brothers and His own.

4 Still I read the ancient story,
And my joy is ever new;
How for us He left His glory,
How He still is kind and true.

5 Let me kneel, my Lord, before Thee,
Let my heart in tears o'erflow,
Melted by Thy love adore Thee,
Blest in Thee mid joy or woe.

Miss Luise Hensel (1798—1876), 1820
Tr. by Miss Catherine Winkworth (1829—1878), 1858. Ab. and alt.

THE SWEETEST NAME. 8.7.D.

WILLIAM BATCHELDER BRADBURY (1816—1868), 1861.

1st. 2d. Fine.

1. { There is no Name so sweet on earth, No Name so sweet in Heav - en,
The Name be - fore His wondrous birth To Christ, the Sav - iour, [*Omit . . .*] giv - en.
D.C.—For there's no word ear ev - er heard, So dear, so sweet, as [*Omit . . .*] Je - sus.

REFRAIN.

D.C.

We love to sing a - round our King, And hail Him bless - ed Je - sus;

556 *"No Name so sweet."*

2 And when He hung upon the tree,
They wrote His Name above Him,
That all might see the reason we
For evermore must love Him.—Ref.

3 So now upon His Father's throne,
Almighty to release us
From sin and pains, He gladly reigns,
The Prince and Saviour, Jesus.—Ref.

Rev. George Washington Bethune (1805—1862), 1858. Ab.

ORIOLA. C. M. D.

WILLIAM BATCHELDER BRADBURY (1816—1868).

1. DEAR Je - sus, ev - er at my side, How lov - ing Thou must be,

To leave Thy home in Heav'n to guard A lit - tle child like me!

D.S. The sweet - ness of Thy soft, low voice I am too deaf to hear.

Thy beau - ti - ful and shin - ing face I see not, though so near;

557 *Jesus watching over Children.*

2 I cannot feel Thee touch my hand,
  With pressure light and mild,
To check me as my mother did,
  When I was but a child.
But I have felt Thee in my thoughts,
  Rebuking sin for me;
And, when my heart loves God, I know
  The sweetness is from Thee.

3 And when, dear Saviour, I kneel down,
  Morning and night, to prayer,
Something there is within my heart
  Which tells me, Thou art there.
Yes, when I pray, Thou prayest, too;
  Thy prayer is all for me:
But when I sleep, Thou sleepest not,
  But watchest patiently.

Rev. Frederick William Faber (1814—1863), 1849. Ab. and alt.

ST. SYLVESTER. 8.7.

Rev. JOHN BACCHUS DYKES (1823—1876), 1861.

1. SAV - IOUR, who Thy flock art feed - ing, With the shep - herd's kind - est care,

All the fee - ble gen - tly lead - ing, While the lambs Thy bo - som share;

558 *Committed to the Shepherd's Care.*

2 Now, these little ones receiving,
Fold them in Thy gracious arm ;
There, we know, Thy word believing,
Only there, secure from harm.

3 Never, from Thy pasture roving,
Let them be the lion's prey ;

Let Thy tenderness, so loving,
Keep them all life's dangerous way.

4 Then, within Thy fold eternal,
Let them find a resting-place ;
Feed in pastures ever vernal,
Drink the rivers of Thy grace.

Rev. William Augustus Muhlenberg (1796—1877), 1826.

ITALIAN HYMN. 6, 6, 4, 6, 6, 6, 4.   FELICE GIARDINI (1716—1796), 1760.

1. SHEPHERD of ten - der youth, Guid - ing in love.... and truth Through de - vious ways;

Christ, our tri - umphant King, We come Thy Name to sing; Hith-er our children bring. To shout Thy praise.

559 *Στόμιον πώλων ἀδαῶν.*

2 Thou art our Holy Lord,
The all-subduing Word,
Healer of strife;
Thou didst Thyself abase,
That from sin's deep disgrace
Thou mightest save our race,
And give us life.

3 Thou art the great High Priest,
Thou hast prepared the feast
Of heavenly love;
While in our mortal pain
None calls on Thee in vain ;
Help Thou dost not disdain,
Help from above.

4 Ever be Thou our Guide,
Our Shepherd and our Pride,
Our Staff and Song :
Jesus, Thou Christ of God,
By Thy perennial Word
Lead us where Thou hast trod,
Make our faith strong.

5 So now, and till we die,
Sound we Thy praises high,
And joyful sing :
Infants, and the glad throng
Who to Thy Church belong,
Unite to swell the song
To Christ our King.

From Clement of Alexandria (—217),
Tr. by Rev. Henry Martyn Dexter (1821—), 1846, 1849.

SALVATION. 7. 6. D.

JOHANN C. W. A. MOZART (1756—1791).

1. WHEN, His sal-va-tion bringing, To Zi-on Je-sus came, The chil-dren all stood sing-ing Ho-san-na to His Name. Nor did their zeal of-fend Him, But as He rode a-long, He let them still at-tend Him, And smil'd to hear their song.

560

The Children in the Temple.
MATT. xxi. 15, 16.

2 And since the Lord retaineth
  His love to children still,
Though now as King He reigneth
  On Zion's heavenly hill;
We'll flock around His banner,
  We'll bow before His throne,
And cry aloud, Hosanna
  To David's royal Son.

3 For should we fail proclaiming
  Our great Redeemer's praise,
The stones, our silence shaming,
  Would their hosannas raise.
But shall we only render
  The tribute of our words?
No; while our hearts are tender,
  They too shall be the Lord's.

Rev. John King (1788—1858), 1830.

BADEN. 8. 8. 8. 8. 7.

JOHANN SEBASTIAN BACH (1685—1750).

1. WHEN in the Lord Je-hovah's Name, The Sav-iour low-ly rid-ing came, Loud-est and first an in-fant throng Greet-ed His com-ing with their song, Ho-san-na in the high-est.

561 *For a School Anniversary.*

2 We too are taught to know the Lord,
   To fear His Name, to read His Word;
   And though we simple are and young,
   Can praise Him with our joyful song,
      Hosanna in the highest.

3 Soon shall the Lord again pass by
   To judgment, from His throne on high;

And, from the saints' assembled throng,
Shall burst upon the world the song,
   Hosanna in the highest.

4 Then may our youthful band be found
   With coronals of triumph crowned;
   Raising, the heavenly hosts among,
   Our chorus of eternal song,
      Hosanna in the highest.

                        Rev. Henry Alford (1810—1871), 1845.

LITTLE TRAVELLERS. 7. D.   WILLIAM BATCHELDER BRADBURY (1816—1868).

1. Lit-tle trav'llers Zi - on-ward, Each one ent'ring in - to rest, In the kingdom of your Lord,
In the mansions of the blest: There, to wel-come, Je - sus waits, Gives the crowns His
foll'wers win; Lift your heads, ye gold - en gates! Let the lit - tle trav - 'llers in.

562 *The Little Travellers.*

2 Who are they whose little feet,
   Pacing life's dark journey through,
   Now have reached that heavenly seat,
   They had ever kept in view?
   "I from Greenland's frozen land;"
      "I from India's sultry plain;"
   "I from Afric's barren sand;"
      "I from islands of the main."

3 All our earthly journey past,
   Every tear and pain gone by,
   Here together met at last
   At the portal of the sky:
   Each the welcome, "Come," awaits,
   Conquerors over death and sin;
   Lift your heads, ye golden gates,
   Let the little travellers in.

                        James Edmeston (1791—1867), 1846.

SILOAM. C. M.　　ISAAC BEVERLY WOODBURY (1819—1858), 1850.

1. By cool Si - lo - am's sha - dy rill How sweet the lil - y grows!

How sweet the breath be - neath the hill Of Sha - ron's dew - y rose!

563　*Christ a Pattern for Children.*
LUKE. ii 40.

2 Lo, such the child whose early feet
　The paths of peace have trod;
Whose secret heart, with influence sweet,
　Is upward drawn to God.

3 By cool Siloam's shady rill
　The lily must decay;
The rose that blooms beneath the hill
　Must shortly fade away.

4 And soon, too soon, the wintry hour
　Of man's maturer age
Will shake the soul with sorrow's power,
　And stormy passion's rage.

5 O Thou, whose infant feet were found
　Within Thy Father's shrine,
Whose years, with changeless virtue crowned,
　Were all alike divine,

6 Dependent on Thy bounteous breath,
　We seek Thy grace alone,
In childhood, manhood, age, and death,
　To keep us still Thine own.
　　　Bp. Reginald Heber (1783—1826), 1812.

564　*Christ's Regard for Children.*
MARK x. 13—16.

1 SEE, Israel's gentle Shepherd stands,
　With all-engaging charms;
Hark, how He calls the tender lambs,
　And folds them in His arms!

2 "Permit them to approach," He cries,
　"Nor scorn their humble name;
For 't was to bless such souls as these,
　The Lord of angels came."

3 We bring them, Lord, in thankful hands,
　And yield them up to Thee;
Joyful that we ourselves are Thine,
　Thine let our offspring be.
　　　Rev. Philip Doddridge (1702—1751), 1755.　Ab.

565　*Confession and Covenant.*

1 WITNESS, ye men and angels, now,
　Before the Lord we speak;
To Him we make our solemn vow,
　A vow we dare not break:—

2 That long as life itself shall last,
　Ourselves to Christ we yield;
Nor from His cause will we depart,
　Or ever quit the field.

3 We trust not in our native strength,
　But on His grace rely,
That, with returning wants, the Lord
　Will all our need supply.

4 O guide our doubtful feet aright,
　And keep us in Thy ways;
And, while we turn our vows to prayers,
　Turn Thou our prayers to praise.
　　　Rev. Benjamin Beddome (1717—1795), 1818

CRASSELIUS. L. M.

Hamburger Musikalisches Handbuch, 1690.

1. O HAP-PY day, that fix'd my choice On Thee, my Sav - iour and my God:

Well may this glow-ing heart re - joice, And tell its rap - tures all a - broad.

566 *Rejoicing in our Covenant-Engagements.*
2 CHRON. XV. 15

2 O happy bond, that seals my vows
　To Him who merits all my love :
Let cheerful anthems fill His house,
　While to that sacred shrine I move.

3 'Tis done, the great transaction's done ;
　I am my Lord's, and He is mine :
He drew me, and I followed on,
　Charmed to confess the Voice divine.

4 Now rest, my long divided heart,
　Fixed on this blissful centre, rest ;
With ashes who would grudge to part,
　When called on angels' bread to feast?

5 High heaven, that heard the solemn vow,
　That vow renewed shall daily hear,
Till in life's latest hour I bow,
　And bless in death a bond so dear.
　　　　　　Rev. Philip Doddridge 1755.

567 *"Entirely Thine."*

1 LORD, I am Thine, entirely Thine,
　Purchased and saved by blood divine ;
With full consent Thine I would be,
　And own Thy sovereign right in me.

2 Grant one poor sinner more a place
　Among the children of Thy grace ;
A wretched sinner, lost to God,
　But ransomed by Immanuel's blood.

3 Thine would I live, Thine would I die,
　Be Thine through all eternity ;
The vow is passed beyond repeal ;
　And now I set the solemn seal.

4 Here at that cross where flows the blood
　That bought my guilty soul for God,
Thee, my new Master now I call,
　And consecrate to Thee my all.
　　　　　Rev. Samuel Davies (1724-1761), 1769. Ab.

HEBRON. L. M.

LOWELL MASON (1792-1872), 1830.

CULFORD. 7. D.

EDWARD JOHN HOPKINS (1818—).

1. PEO - PLE of the liv - ing God, I have sought the world a - round, Paths of sin and sor - row trod, Peace and com - fort no - where found. Now to you my spir - it turns, Turns, a fug - i - tive unbless'd; Brethren, where your al - tar burns, O re - ceive me in - to rest.

568   *Choosing the Portion of God's Heritage.*
RUTH i. 16, 17.

2 Lonely I no longer roam,
    Like the cloud, the wind, the wave;
Where you dwell shall be my home,
    Where you die shall be my grave;

Mine the God whom you adore,
    Your Redeemer shall be mine;
Earth can fill my heart no more,
    Every idol I resign.

James Montgomery (1771—1854), 1819, 1853. Ab.

EVERMORE. 7.

HENRY JOHN GAUNTLETT (1806—1876), 1871.

1. THINE for - ev - er!—God of love, Hear us from Thy throne a - bove; Thine for - ev - er may we be, Here and in e - ter - ni - ty.

569   *"Thine for ever!"*

2 Thine forever!—Lord of life,
   Shield us through our earthly strife;
   Thou, the Life, the Truth, the Way,
   Guide us to the realms of day.

3 Thine forever!—Saviour, keep
   These Thy frail and trembling sheep;

Safe alone beneath Thy care,
Let us all Thy goodness share.

4 Thine forever!—Thou our Guide,
   All our wants by Thee supplied,
   All our sins by Thee forgiven,
   Lead us, Lord, from earth to Heaven.

Mrs. Mary Fawler Maude, 1848. Ab.

NEWLAND. S. M.   HENRY JOHN GAUNTLETT, 1851.

1. Dear Sav - iour, I am Thine, By ev - er - last - ing bands;
My name, my heart I would re - sign; My soul is in Thy hands.

570   *One with Christ.*
            1 Cor. vi. 17.

2 To Thee I still would cleave
    With ever growing zeal;
  Let millions tempt me Christ to leave,
    They never shall prevail.

3 His Spirit shall unite
    My soul to Him, my Head;
  Shall form me to His image bright,
    And teach His paths to tread.

4 Death may my soul divide
    From this abode of clay;
  But love shall keep me near His side,
    Through all the gloomy way.

5 Since Christ and we are one,
    What should remain to fear?
  If He in Heaven has fixed His throne,
    He'll fix His members there.
              Rev. Philip Doddridge (1702—1751), 1755. Sl. alt.

571   *Adoption.*
            1 John iii. 1. Gal. iv. 6.

1 Behold what wondrous grace
    The Father hath bestowed

On sinners of a mortal race,
  To call them sons of God.

2 Nor doth it yet appear
    How great we must be made;
  But when we see our Saviour here,
    We shall be like our Head.

3 A hope so much divine
    May trials well endure,
  May purge our souls from sense and sin,
    As Christ the Lord is pure.

4 If in my Father's love
    I share a filial part,
  Send down Thy Spirit, like a dove,
    To rest upon my heart,

5 We would no longer lie
    Like slaves beneath the throne;
  Our faith shall Abba, Father! cry,
    And Thou the kindred own.
              Rev. Isaac Watts (1674—1748), 1709. Ab.

WATCHMAN. S. M.   JAMES LEACH (1762—1798), 1789.

LUDWIG. 7.6.D.   LUDWIG von BEETHOVEN (1770—1827), 1824.

1. Lamb of God, whose bleeding love We now re-call to mind, Send the an-swer

from a-bove, And let us mer-cy find; Think on us who think on Thee;

Ev-'ry struggling soul re-lease; O re-mem-ber Cal-va-ry, And bid us go in peace.

572   *"Bid us go in Peace."*

2 By Thine agonizing pain
    And bloody sweat, we pray,
By Thy dying love to man,
    Take all our sins away;
Burst our bonds and set us free,
    From iniquity release;
O remember Calvary,
    And bid us go in peace.

3 Let Thy blood, by faith applied,
    The sinner's pardon seal;
Speak us freely justified,
    And all our sickness heal;
By Thy passion on the tree,
    Let our griefs and troubles cease;
O remember Calvary,
    And bid us go in peace.

Rev. Charles Wesley (1708—1788), 1745. Ab. and sl. alt.

GRACE. 7.6 l.   Arr. from FRANCIS XAVIER CHWATAL (1808—   ).

1. Till He come, O let the words Lin-ger on the trem-bling chords;

Let the lit-tle while be-tween In their gold-en light be seen;
Let us think how Heav'n and home Lie be-yond that, till He [*Omit.*] come.

573 *"Till He come."*
1 Cor. xi. 26.

2 When the weary ones we love
Enter on their rest above,
Seems the earth so poor and vast,
All our life-joy overcast?
Hush, be every murmur dumb;
It is only, till He come.

3 See, the feast of love is spread,
Drink the wine, and break the bread:
Sweet memorials,—till the Lord
Call us round His heavenly board;
Some from earth, from glory some,
Severed only, till He come.

Bp. Edward Henry Bickersteth (1825—   ), 1861. Ab.

574 *"Bread of Heaven."* 7. 6 l.

1 BREAD of Heaven, on Thee I feed,
For Thy flesh is meat indeed;
Ever may my soul be fed
With this true and living bread;
Day by day with strength supplied,
Through the life of Him who died.

2 Vine of Heaven, Thy blood supplies
This blest cup of sacrifice;
'Tis Thy wounds my healing give;
To Thy cross I look and live.
Thou my Life, O let me be
Rooted, grafted, built on Thee.

Josiah Conder (1789—1855), 1824.

ECCE AGNUS. P. M.   JAMES WILLIAM ELLIOTT (   ),

1. BE-HOLD the Lamb! O Thou for sin-ners slain, Let it not be in vain
That Thou hast died; Thee for my Sav-iour let me take,
Thee, Thee a-lone my ref-uge make, Thy pierc-ed side.

575 *"Behold the Lamb."*

2 Behold the Lamb!
All hail, eternal Word!
Thou everlasting Lord,
Purge out our leaven:
Clothe us with godliness and good,
Feed us with Thy celestial food,
Manna from Heaven.

3 Behold the Lamb!
Worthy is He alone,
Upon the rainbow throne
Of God above:
One with the Ancient of all days,
One with the Paraclete in praise,
All Light, all Love.

Matthew Bridges (1800—   ), 1848. Ab. and alt.

BENEDICTION. L. M. 6l.

JOSEPH BARNBY (1838—). 1872.

1. Je - sus, my Lord, my God, my All, Hear me, blest Sav - iour, when I call;

Hear me, and from Thy dwell-ing - place Pour down the rich - es of Thy grace:

Je - sus, my Lord, I Thee a - dore, O make me love Thee more and more.

576

Adoring Love.

2 Jesus, too late I Thee have sought,
How can I love Thee as I ought;
And how extol Thy matchless fame,
The glorious beauty of Thy Name?
Jesus, my Lord, I Thee adore,
O make me love Thee more and more.

3 Jesus, what didst Thou find in me,
That Thou hast dealt so lovingly?
How great the joy that Thou hast brought,
So far exceeding hope or thought!
Jesus, my Lord, I Thee adore,
O make me love Thee more and more.

4 Jesus, of Thee shall be my song,
To Thee my heart and soul belong;
All that I have or am is Thine,
And Thou, blest Saviour, Thou art mine;
Jesus, my Lord, I Thee adore,
O make me love Thee more and more.

Rev. Henry Collins ( ), 1852.

SEASONS. L. M.

From IGNACE PLEYEL (1757—1831).

1. 'Twas on that dark, that dole - ful night, When pow'rs of earth and hell a - rose

A - gainst the Son of God's de - light, And friends be - tray'd Him to His foes:

577 *The Supper instituted.*
1 Cor. xi. 23.

2 Before the mournful scene began, [brake:
He took the bread, and blessed, and
What love through all His actions ran,
What wondrous words of grace He
spake.

3 "This is My body, broke for sin;
Receive and eat the living food:"
Then took the cup, and blessed the wine,
"'Tis the new covenant in My blood."

4 "Do this," He cried, "'till time shall end,
In memory of your dying Friend;
Meet at My table, and record
The love of your departed Lord."

5 Jesus, Thy feast we celebrate;
We show Thy death, we sing Thy Name,
Till Thou return, and we shall eat
The marriage supper of the Lamb.
Rev. Isaac Watts (1674—1748), 1709. Ab.

578 *"Jesu, Dulcedo cordium."* L. M.

1 Jesus, Thou Joy of loving hearts,
Thou Fount of life, Thou Light of men,
From the best bliss that earth imparts,
We turn unfilled to Thee again.

2 Thy truth unchanged hath ever stood;
Thou savest those that on Thee call;
To them that seek Thee, Thou art good,
To them that find Thee, All in all.

3 We taste Thee, O Thou living Bread,
And long to feast upon Thee still;
We drink of Thee, the Fountain Head,
And thirst, our souls from Thee to fill.

4 O Jesus, ever with us stay;
Make all our moments calm and bright;
Chase the dark night of sin away;
Shed o'er the world Thy holy light.
Bernard of Clairvaux (1091—1153), 1140.
Tr. by Rev. Ray Palmer (1805—   ), 1752. Ab.

579 *At Dismission,* L. M.

1 Dismiss us with Thy blessing, Lord;
Help us to feed upon Thy Word;
All that has been amiss forgive,
And let Thy truth within us live.

2 Though we are guilty, Thou art good;
Wash all our works in Jesus' blood;
Give every fettered soul release,
And bid us all depart in peace.
Rev. Joseph Hart (1712—1768), 1762.

SACRAMENT. 9.8.
EDWARD JOHN HOPKINS (1819—   ).

1. Bread of the world, in mer-cy bro-ken, Wine of the soul, in mer-cy shed,

By whom the words of life were spo-ken, And in whose death our sins are dead:

580 *"Bread of the World."*

2 Look on the heart by sorrow broken,
Look on the tears by sinners shed;

And be Thy feast to us the token
That by Thy grace our souls are fed.
Bp. Reginald Heber (1783—1826), 1827.

ELLESDIE. 8.7.D.

Arr. from JOHANN C. W. A. MOZART (1756—1791).

1. Sweet the mo - ments, rich in bless - ing, Which be - fore the cross I spend;

Life and health and peace pos - sess - ing, From the sin - ner's dy - ing Friend.

D. S.—Pre - cious drops, my soul be - dew - ing, Plead and claim my peace with God.

Here I'll sit, for - ev - er view - ing Mer - cy's streams in streams of blood:

581   *Before the Cross.*

2 Truly blessed is this station,
  Low before His cross to lie,
While I see divine compassion
  Floating in His languid eye.
Here it is I find my Heaven,
  While upon the Lamb I gaze;
Love I much? I've much forgiven;
  I'm a miracle of grace.

3 Love and grief my heart dividing,
  With my tears His feet I'll bathe,
Constant still, in faith abiding,
  Life deriving from His death.
May I still enjoy this feeling,
  In all need to Jesus go;
Prove His blood each day more healing,
  And Himself most deeply know.

Rev. James Allen (1734—1804), 1757. Alt.
Hon. and Rev. Walter Shirley (1725—1786), 1771.

DORRNANCE. 8.7.

ISAAC BEVERLY WOODBURY (1819—1858), 1850.

1. One there is, a - bove all oth - ers, Well de - serves the name of Friend;

His is love be - yond a broth - er's, Cost - ly, free, and knows no end.

582   *"Closer than a Brother."*

2 Which of all our friends, to save us,
  Could or would have shed his blood?
But our Jesus died to have us
  Reconciled in Him to God.

3 When He lived on earth abaséd,
  Friend of sinners was His Name;
Now above all glory raiséd,
  He rejoices in the same.

4 O for grace our hearts to soften:
  Teach us, Lord, at length to love;
We, alas, forget too often
  What a Friend we have above.

Rev. John Newton (1725—1807), 1779. Ab.

583   *Giving the Heart.*   **8.7.**

1 TAKE my heart, O Father, take it!
  Make and keep it all Thine own;

Let Thy Spirit melt and break it,
  This proud heart of sin and stone.

2 Father, make it pure and lowly,
  Fond of peace, and far from strife;
Turning from the paths unholy
  Of this vain and sinful life.

3 Ever let Thy grace surround it;
  Strengthen it with power divine,
Till Thy cords of love have bound it:
  Make it to be wholly Thine.

4 May the blood of Jesus heal it,
  And its sins be all forgiven;
Holy Spirit, take and seal it,
  Guide it in the path to Heaven.

Bartol's Hymns for the Sanctuary, 1849.

PLEYEL'S HYMN. 7.   IGNACE PLEYEL (1757—1831), 1800.

1. At the Lamb's high feast we sing Praise to our vic - to - rious King,
Who hath wash'd us in the tide Flow - ing from His pierc - ed side.

584   *"Ad regias Agni dapes."*

2 Where the paschal blood is poured,
  Death's dark angel sheathes his sword;
Israel's hosts triumphant go
  Through the wave that drowns the foe.

3 Mighty Victim from the sky,
  Hell's fierce powers beneath Thee lie;

Thou hast conquered in the fight,
  Thou has brought us life and light.

4 Hymns of glory and of praise,
  Risen Lord, to Thee we raise;
Holy Father, praise to Thee,
  With the Spirit, ever be!

Roman Breviary.
Tr. by Robert Campbell (1799?—1868), 1850. Ab.

THE FEAST OF LOVE.

ELIZABETHTOWN. C. M.

GEORGE KINGSLEY (1811—1884), 1838.

1. If hu-man kind-ness meets re-turn, And owns the grate-ful tie;

If ten-der thoughts with-in us burn, To feel a friend is nigh;

585 *Grateful and tender Remembrance.*

2 O shall not warmer accents tell
   The gratitude we owe
To Him, who died, our fears to quell,
   Our more than orphan's woe?

3 While yet His anguished soul surveyed
   Those pangs He would not flee,
What love His latest words displayed
   "Meet, and remember Me."

4 Remember Thee, Thy death, Thy shame,
   Our sinful hearts to share!
O memory, leave no other name
   But His recorded there.
   Hon. and Rev. Gerard Thomas Noel (1782—1851), 1813.

586 *At the Table.*

1 How sweet and awful is the place,
   With Christ within the doors,
While everlasting love displays
   The choicest of her stores.

2 While all our hearts, and all our songs,
   Join to admire the feast,
Each of us cry, with thankful tongues,
   ' Lord, why was I a guest?"

3 "Why was I made to hear Thy voice,
   And enter while there's room,
When thousands make a wretched choice,
   And rather starve than come?"

4 'Twas the same love that spread the feast,
   That sweetly forced us in;
Else we had still refused to taste,
   And perished in our sin.

5 Pity the nations, O our God;
   Constrain the earth to come;
Send Thy victorious word abroad,
   And bring the strangers home.
   Rev. Isaac Watts (1674—1748), 1709. Ab.

587 *Remembrance pledged.*

1 ACCORDING to Thy gracious word,
   In meek humility,
This will I do, my dying Lord,
   I will remember Thee.

2 Thy body, broken for my sake,
   My Bread from Heaven shall be;
Thy testamental cup I take,
   And thus remember Thee.

3 When to the cross I turn mine eyes,
   And rest on Calvary,
O Lamb of God, my sacrifice,
   I must remember Thee:

4 And when these failing lips grow dumb,
   And mind and memory flee,
When Thou shalt in Thy kingdom come,
   Jesus, remember me.
   James Montgomery (1771—1854), 1825. Ab.

HODNET. 7.6.D.

SIGISMUND THALBERG (1812—1871), 1868.

1. { O BREAD to pilgrims giv-en, O food that an-gels eat,
   { O Man-na sent from Heaven, [*Omit* . . . .] For heav'n-born natures meet: Give us, for

Thee long pin-ing, To eat till rich-ly fill'd; Till, earth's delights resigning, Our ev-'ry wish is still'd.

588 *"O Esca viatorum."*

2 O Water, life bestowing,
  From out the Saviour's heart,
A fountain purely flowing,
  A fount of love Thou art:
O let us, freely tasting,
  Our burning thirst assuage;
Thy sweetness, never wasting,
  Avails from age to age.

3 Jesus, this feast receiving,
  We Thee unseen adore;
Thy faithful word believing,
  We take, and doubt no more:
Give us, Thou true and loving,
  On earth to live in Thee;
Then, death the veil removing,
  Thy glorious face to see.

Unknown mediæval Author.
Tr. by Rev. Ray Palmer (1808—), 1858.

589 *"Ermuntert euch, ihr Frommen."*

1 REJOICE, rejoice, believers,
  And let your lights appear;
The evening is advancing,
  And darker night is near.
The Bridegroom is arising,
  And soon He will draw nigh;
Up, pray, and watch, and wrestle,
  At midnight comes the cry.

2 See that your lamps are burning,
  Replenish them with oil;
Look now for your salvation,
  The end of sin and toil.
The watchers on the mountain
  Proclaim the Bridegroom near,
Go meet Him as He cometh,
  With hallelujahs clear.

3 Ye saints, who here in patience
  Your cross and sufferings bore,
Shall live and reign forever,
  When sorrow is no more;
Around the Throne of glory
  The Lamb ye shall behold,
In triumph cast before Him
  Your diadems of gold.

4 Our Hope and Expectation,
  O Jesus, now appear;
Arise, thou Sun so longed for,
  O'er this benighted sphere.
With hearts and hands uplifted,
  We plead, O Lord, to see
The day of earth's redemption,
  And ever be with Thee.

Laurentius Laurenti (1660—1722),
Tr. by Miss Jane Borthwick (1825—), 1853. Ab. and sl. alt.

CHRISTMAS. C. M.   GEORGE FREDERICK HANDEL (1685—1759).

1. Give me the wings of faith, to rise With-in the veil, and see The saints a-bove, how great their joys, How bright their glo-ries be, How bright their glo-ries be.

590   *"The Saints above."*

2 Once they were mourning here below,
   And wet their couch with tears;
   They wrestled hard, as we do now,
   With sins, and doubts, and fears.

3 I ask them, whence their victory came?
   They, with united breath,
   Ascribe their conquest to the Lamb,
   Their triumph to His death.

4 They marked the footsteps that He trod;
   His zeal inspired their breast;
   And following their incarnate God,
   Possess the promised rest.

5 Our glorious Leader claims our praise,
   For His own pattern given,
   While the long cloud of witnesses
   Show the same path to Heaven.
          Rev. Isaac Watts (1674—1748), 1709.

591   *One Church, one Army.*

1 Let saints below in concert sing
   With those to glory gone;
   For all the servants of our King
   In earth and Heaven are one.

2 One family, we dwell in Him,
   One Church above, beneath,
   Though now divided by the stream,
   The narrow stream of death.

3 One army of the living God,
   To His command we bow;
   Part of the host have crossed the flood,
   And part are crossing now.

4 Dear Saviour, be our constant Guide;
   Then, when the word is given,
   Bid Jordan's narrow stream divide,
   And land us safe in Heaven.
          Rev. Charles Wesley (1708—1788), 1759. Ab. and alt.

592   *One Song.*

1 Happy the souls to Jesus joined,
   And saved by grace alone;
   Walking in all Thy ways, we find
   Our Heaven on earth begun.

2 The Church triumphant in Thy love,
   Their mighty joys we know;
   They sing the Lamb in hymns above,
   And we in hymns below.

3 Thee, in Thy glorious realm, they praise,
   And bow before Thy throne;
   We, in the kingdom of Thy grace:
   The kingdoms are but one.

4 The holy to the holiest leads;
   From hence our spirits rise;
   And he that in Thy statutes treads
   Shall meet Thee in the skies.
          Rev. Charles Wesley, 1745.

NEEDHAM. C. M.
SAMUEL SEBASTIAN WESLEY (1810—1876), 1872.

1. How sweet, how heav'n-ly is the sight, When those who love the Lord

In one an-oth-er's peace de-light, And so ful-fil His word.

593 *"The golden Chain"*

2 When each can feel his brother's sigh,
   And with him bear a part;
   When sorrow flows from eye to eye,
   And joy from heart to heart;

3 When, free from envy, scorn, and pride,
   Our wishes all above,
   Each can his brother's failings hide,
   And show a brother's love;

4 When love, in one delightful stream,
   Through every bosom flows;
   When union sweet, and dear esteem,
   In every action glows.

5 Love is the golden chain that binds
   The happy souls above;
   And he's an heir of Heaven that finds
   His bosom glow with love.
   Rev. Joseph Swain (1761—1796), 1792.

594 *The ancient Worthies.*

1 RISE, O my soul, pursue the path,
   By ancient worthies trod;
   Aspiring, view those holy men
   Who lived and walked with God.

2 Though dead, they speak in reason's ear,
   And in example live;
   Their faith, and hope, and mighty deeds,
   Still fresh instruction give.

3 'Twas through the Lamb's most precious
   They conquered every foe;   [blood,
   And to His power and matchless grace
   Their crowns and honors owe.

4 Lord, may I ever keep in view
   The patterns Thou hast given;
   And ne'er forsake the blessed path
   Which led them safe to Heaven.
   Rev. John Needham, 1768.

ARMENIA. C. M.
SYLVANUS BILLINGS POND (1815—1871).

304

VOX ANGELICA. P. M.

Rev. JOHN BACCHUS DYKES (1823—1876), 1868.

1. HARK, hark, my soul; An - gel - ic songs are swell - ing O'er earth's green fields, and

o-cean's wave-beat shore: How sweet the truth those bless - ed strains are tell - ing

Of that new life when sin shall be no more. An - gels of Je - sus,

REFRAIN.

An - gels of light, Sing - ing to wel - come the pil - grims of the night,

Sing - ing to wel - come the pil - grims, the pil - grims of the night.

595

"Pilgrims of the Night."

2 Onward we go, for still we hear them singing,
  "Come, weary souls, for Jesus bids you come;"
  And through the dark, its echoes sweetly ringing,
  The music of the Gospel leads us home.—REF.

3 Far, far away, like bells at evening pealing,
  The voice of Jesus sounds o'er land and sea;
  And laden souls, by thousands meekly stealing,
  Kind Shepherd, turn their weary steps to Thee.—REF.

4 Rest comes at length ; though life be long and dreary,
  The day must dawn, and darksome night be past ;
  Life's journey ends in welcome to the weary,
  And Heaven, the heart's true home, will come at last.—REF.

5 Angels, sing on : your faithful watches keeping,
  Sing us sweet fragments of the songs above ;
  Till morning's joy shall end the night of weeping,
  And life's long shadows break in cloudless love.—REF.

Rev. Frederick William Faber (1814—1863), 1849. Ab. and alt

SARUM. 10.10.10.4.

JOSEPH BARNBY (1838—), 1869.

1. For all the saints, who from their la - bors rest, Who Thee by faith be-fore the world con-fest,

Thy Name, O Je - sus, be for - ev - er blest. Al - le - lu - ia, Al - le - lu - ia.

596

" The Fellowship of all the Saints."

2 Thou wast their Rock, their Fortress, and their Light ;
  Thou, Lord, their Captain in the well-fought fight ;
  Thou, in the darkness drear, their Light of light.
  Alleluia.

3 O blest communion, fellowship divine !
  We feebly struggle, they in glory shine ;
  Yet all are one in Thee, for all are Thine.
  Alleluia.

4 The golden evening brightens in the west ;
  Soon, soon to faithful warriors comes the rest ;
  Sweet is the calm of Paradise the blest.
  Alleluia.

5 But lo, there breaks a yet more glorious day ;
  The saints triumphant rise in bright array ;
  The King of Glory passes on His way.
  Alleluia.

6 From earth's wide bounds, from ocean's farthest coast,
  Through gates of pearl streams in the countless host,
  Singing to Father, Son, and Holy Ghost.
  Alleluia.

Bp. William Walsham How (1823—), 1854. Ab.

MONSELL. S. M.

JOSEPH BARNBY (1838—   ), 1868.

1. BLEST be the tie that binds Our hearts in Chris - tian love:

The fel - low - ship of kin - dred minds Is like to that a - bove.

597   *"Blest be the Tie."*

2 Before our Father's throne
　We pour our ardent prayers;
　Our fears, our hopes, our aims are one,
　Our comforts and our cares.

3 We share our mutual woes;
　Our mutual burdens bear;
　And often for each other flows
　The sympathizing tear.

4 When we asunder part,
　It gives us inward pain;
　But we shall still be joined in heart,
　And hope to meet again.

5 This glorious hope revives
　Our courage by the way;
　While each in expectation lives,
　And longs to see the Day.

6 From sorrow, toil, and pain,
　And sin we shall be free;

And perfect love and friendship reign
　Through all eternity.

Rev. John Fawcett (1739—1817), 1772.

598   *Cross and Crown.*

1 O WHAT, if we are Christ's,
　Is earthly shame or loss?
　Bright shall the crown of glory be,
　When we have borne the cross.

2 Keen was the trial once,
　Bitter the cup of woe,
　When martyred saints, baptized in blood,
　Christ's sufferings shared below.

3 Bright is their glory now,
　Boundless their joy above,
　Where, on the bosom of their God,
　They rest in perfect love.

4 Lord, may that grace be ours,
　Like them in faith to bear
　All that of sorrow, grief, or pain
　May be our portion here.

Rev. Sir Henry Williams Baker (1821—1877), 1852. Ab.

BOYLSTON. S. M.

LOWELL MASON (1792—1872), 1832.

ST. THOMAS. S. M.   WILLIAM TANSUR (1699—1774), 1743.

1. I LOVE Thy king - dom, Lord, The house of Thine a - bode,

The church our blest Re - deem - er sav'd With His own pre - cious blood.

599   *Love to the Church.*
            Ps. cxxxvii.

2 I love Thy church, O God:
    Her walls before Thee stand,
  Dear as the apple of Thine eye,
    And graven on Thy hand.

3 For her my tears shall fall,
    For her my prayers ascend;
  To her my cares and toils be given,
    Till toils and cares shall end.

4 Beyond my highest joy
    I prize her heavenly ways,
  Her sweet communion, solemn vows,
    Her hymns of love and praise.

5 Jesus, Thou Friend divine,
    Our Saviour and our King,
  Thy hand from every snare and foe
    Shall great deliverance bring.

6 Sure as Thy truth shall last,
    To Zion shall be given

The brightest glories earth can yield,
  And brighter bliss of Heaven.
            Rev. Timothy Dwight (1752—1817), 1800. Ab.

600   *The Saints of the Lord.*

1 FOR all Thy saints, O Lord,
    Who strove in Thee to live,
  Who followed Thee, obeyed, adored,
    Our grateful hymn receive.

2 For all Thy saints, O Lord,
    Accept our thankful cry,
  Who counted Thee their great reward,
    And strove in Thee to die.

3 They all in life and death,
    With Thee, their Lord in view,
  Learned from Thy Holy Spirit's breath
    To suffer and to do.

4 For this Thy Name we bless,
    And humbly pray that we
  May follow them in holiness,
    And live and die in Thee.
            Bp. Richard Mant (1776—1848), 1837. Ab

BADEA. S. M.   German Melody.

FORMOSA. 8.7.D.   Sir ARTHUR SULLIVAN (1842—), 1872.

1. Through the night of doubt and sorrow, On - ward goes the pil - grim band,

Sing - ing songs of ex - pec - ta - tion, March - ing to the Prom - is'd Land,
D.S. Broth - er clasps the hand of broth - er, And steps fear - less through the night.

And be - fore us through the dark - ness, Gleam - eth clear the guid - ing Light;

601

"Igjennem Nat og Traengsel."

2 One the strain which mouths of thousands
  Lift as from the heart of one ;
One the conflict, one the peril,
  One the march in God begun,
One the gladness of rejoicing
  On the Resurrection shore,
With one Father o'er us shining
  In His love for evermore.

3 Go we onward, pilgrim brothers,
  Visit first the cross and grave,
Where the cross its shadow flingeth,
  Where the boughs of cypress wave.
Then, a shaking as of earthquakes,
  Then, a rending of the tomb,
Then, a scattering of all shadows,
  And an end of toil and gloom.

Bernhardt Severin Ingemann (1789—1862),
Tr. by Rev. Sabine Baring Gould (1834—), 1867. Ab.

602

Prayer for Union.

1 HAIL, Thou God of grace and glory,
  Who Thy Name hast magnified,
By redemption's wondrous story,
  By the Saviour crucified ;
Thanks to Thee for every blessing,
  Flowing from the Fount of love ;
Thanks for present good unceasing,
  And for hopes of bliss above.

2 Hear us, as thus bending lowly,
  Near Thy bright and burning throne,
We invoke Thee, God most holy,
  Through Thy well-belovéd Son ;
Send the baptism of Thy Spirit,
  Shed the pentecostal fire ;
Let us all Thy grace inherit,
  Waken, crown each good desire.

3 Bind Thy people, Lord, in union,
  With the sevenfold cord of love ;
Breathe a spirit of communion
  With the glorious hosts above ;
Let Thy work be seen progressing ;
  Bow each heart, and bend each knee,
Till the world, Thy truth possessing,
  Celebrates its jubilee.

Rev. Thomas William Aveling (1815—), 1844.

AUSTRIAN HYMN. 8.7.D. FRANCIS JOSEPH HAYDN (1732–1809), 1797.

1. { GLO - RIOUS things of thee are spok-en, Zi - on, cit - y of our God! }
{ He whose word can - not be brok-en, Formed thee for His own a - bode: }

On the Rock of a - ges found-ed, What can shake thy sure re - pose?

With sal - va - tion's walls sur - round-ed, Thou may'st smile at all thy foes.

603 *The City of God.* Is. xxxiii. 20, 21.

2 See, the streams of living waters,
Springing from eternal love,
Well supply thy sons and daughters,
And all fear of want remove:
Who can faint, while such a river
Ever flows their thirst t' assuage?
Grace, which, like the Lord, the Giver,
Never fails from age to age.

3 Round each habitation hovering,
See the cloud and fire appear,
For a glory and a covering,
Showing that the Lord is near:
Thus deriving from their banner
Light by night, and shade by day,
Safe they feed upon the manna
Which He gives them when they pray.
Rev. John Newton (1725–1807), 1779.

604 *"The Heavenly City."* Ezek. xxxvii. 27.

1 PRAISE the Rock of our salvation,
Laud His Name from zone to zone;
On that Rock the Church is builded,
Christ Himself the Corner-Stone;
Vain against our rock-built Zion
Winds and waters, fire and hail,
Christ is in her midst; against her
Sin and hell shall not prevail.

2 Stands four-square that heavenly city;
Paved with gold like crystal bright;
Gates of pearl, and walls of jasper,
Emerald and chrysolyte:
Broad and lofty tower its ramparts;
At its gates twelve angels stand;
On its walls twelve names are graven,
Of th' Apostles' chosen band.

3 Where Thou reignest, King of glory,
Throned in everlasting light,
Midst Thy saints, no more is needed
Sun by day, nor moon by night;
Soon may we those portals enter
When this earthly strife is o'er,
There to dwell with saints and angels
In Thy presence evermore.
Rev. Benjamin Webb (1819–   ), 1872. Ab.

FURTH. S. M. D.

FRANCIS JOSEPH HAYDN (1732—1809).

1. How beauteous are their feet, Who stand on Zi-on's hill, Who bring sal-va-tion on their tongues,

And words of peace re-veal, How charming is their voice, How sweet the tid-ings are!

"Zi-on, be-hold thy Sav-iour King; He reigns and triumphs here," He reigns and tri-umphs here.

605

The Blessedness of Gospel-times.
Is. lii. 7—9. Matt. xiii. 16, 17.

2 How happy are our ears,
 That hear this joyful sound,
Which kings and prophets waited for,
 And sought, but never found!
How blessèd are our eyes,
 That see this heavenly light!
Prophets and kings desired it long,
 But died without the sight.

3 The watchmen join their voice,
 And tuneful notes employ;
Jerusalem breaks forth in songs,
 And deserts learn the joy.
The Lord makes bare His arm
 Through all the earth abroad;
Let every nation now behold
 Their Saviour and their God.

Rev. Isaac Watts (1674—1748), 1709.

GLORY. S. M.

Rev. RALPH HARRISON (1748—1810), 1786.

1. Great is the Lord our God, And let His praise be great; He

makes His church-es His a-bode, His most de-light-ful seat.

606 *The Church the Safety of the Nation.*
Ps. xlviii.

2 These temples of His grace,
  How beautiful they stand,
The honors of our native place,
  And bulwarks of our land.

3 Oft have our fathers told,
  Our eyes have often seen,
How well our God secures the fold,
  Where His own sheep have been.

4 In every new distress
  We'll to His house repair;
We'll think upon His wondrous grace,
  And seek deliverance there.
      Rev. Isaac Watts, 1719. Ab.

607 *"Come, Kingdom of our God."* S. M.

1 COME, kingdom of our God,
  Sweet reign of light and love,
Shed peace, and hope, and joy abroad,
  And wisdom from above.

2 Come, kingdom of our God,
  And make the broad earth thine;
Stretch o'er her lands and isles the rod
  That flowers with grace divine.

3 Come, kingdom of our God,
  And raise the glorious throne
In worlds by the undying trod,
  When God shall bless His own.
      Bp. John Johns (1796—1876), 1837. Ab.

608 *The Pilgrim Church.* S. M.

1 FAR down the ages now,
  Much of her journey done,
The pilgrim church pursues her way,
  Until her crown be won.

2 No wider is the gate,
  No broader is the way,
No smoother is the ancient path,
  That leads to light and day.

3 Thus onward still we press
  Through evil and through good,
Through pain and poverty and want,
  Through peril and through blood.

4 Still faithful to our God,
  And to our Captain true,
We follow where He leads the way,
  The kingdom in our view.
      Rev. Horatius Bonar (1808—   ), 1857. Ab.

SICILY. 8.7.4. Sicilian Melody.

Zi - on stands by hills sur - round - ed, Zi - on kept by pow'r di - vine;
All her foes shall be con - found - ed, Though the world in arms com - bine.
Hap - py Zi - on! Hap - py Zi - on! What a fa - vored lot is thine!

609 *Zion secure.*
Ps. cxxv. 2.

2 Every human tie may perish;
  Friend to friend unfaithful prove;
Mothers cease their own to cherish;
  Heaven and earth at last remove;
||: But no changes :||
  Can attend Jehovah's love.

3 In the furnace God may prove thee,
  Thence to bring thee forth more bright,
But can never cease to love thee;
  Thou art precious in His sight:
||: God is with thee, :||
  God thine everlasting light.
      Rev. Thomas Kelly (1769—1855), 1806. Ab.

IRENAEUS. H. M.

Rev. WM. HENRY HAVERGAL (1793—1870), 1849.

1. CHRIST is our Cor-ner-stone, On Him a-lone we build; With His true saints a-lone The courts of Heav'n are fill'd; On His great love our hopes we place Of present grace, and joys a-bove.

610   *Christ the Corner-Stone.*

2 O, then, with hymns of praise
    These hallowed courts shall ring;
Our voices we will raise
    The Three in One to sing;
And thus proclaim in joyful song,
    Both loud and long, that glorious Name.

3 Here, gracious God, do Thou
    Forevermore draw nigh;
Accept each faithful vow,
    And mark each suppliant sigh;
In copious shower, on all who pray,
    Each holy day, Thy blessings pour.

4 Here may we gain from Heaven
    The grace which we implore,
And may that grace, once given,
    Be with us evermore,
Until that day when all the blest
    To endless rest are called away.

Unknown Author of the 8th century.
Tr. by Rev. John Chandler (1806—1876), 1837.

COLUMBA. 7.

JOHN BAPTISTE CALKIN (1827—), 1872.

1. LORD of hosts! to Thee we raise Here a house of pray'r and praise: Thou Thy peo-ple's hearts pre-pare, Here to meet for praise and pray'r.

611   *On opening a Place of Worship.*

2 Let the living here be fed
    With Thy Word, the heavenly Bread;

Here in hope of glory blest,
May the dead be laid to rest.

3 Here to Thee a temple stand,
While the sea shall gird the land ;
Here reveal Thy mercy sure,
While the sun and moon endure.

4 Hallelujah ! earth and sky
To the joyful sound reply ;
Hallelujah ! hence ascend
Prayer and praise till time shall end.

James Montgomery (1771–1854), 1825.

ST. ETHELDREDA. C. M.   Bp. THOMAS TURTON (1780–1864), 1862.

1. O Thou, whose own vast tem - ple stands, Built o - ver earth and sea,

Ac - cept the walls that hu - man hands Have rais'd to wor - ship Thee.

612   *God's Blessing invoked.*

2 Lord, from Thine inmost glory send,
Within these walls t' abide,
The peace that dwelleth without end
Serenely by Thy side.

3 May erring minds, that worship here,
Be taught the better way ;
And they who mourn, and they who fear,
Be strengthened as they pray.

4 May faith grow firm, and love grow warm,
And pure devotion rise,
While round these hallowed walls the
Of earth-born passion dies. [storm

William Cullen Bryant (1794–1878), 1835.

613   *Prayer of Dedication.*
Ps. cxxxii.

1 ARISE, O King of grace, arise,
And enter to Thy rest :

Lo, Thy church waits with longing eyes,
Thus to be owned and blest.

2 Enter with all Thy glorious train,
Thy Spirit and Thy Word ;
All that the ark did once contain
Could no such grace afford.

3 Here, mighty God, accept our vows,
Here let Thy praise be spread ;
Bless the provisions of Thy house,
And fill Thy poor with bread.

4 Here let the Son of David reign,
Let God's Anointed shine.
Justice and truth His court maintain,
With love and power divine.

5 Here let Him hold a lasting throne,
And as His kingdom grows,
Fresh honors shall adorn His crown,
And shame confound His foes.

Rev. Isaac Watts (1674–1748), 1719.

MEAR. C. M.   Welsh Air. AARON WILLIAMS (1731–1776), 1760.

NEALE. 8. 7. 61.

HENRY SMART (1812—1879).

1. CHRIST is made the sure Foun - da - tion, Christ the Head and Cor - ner - Stone,

Chos - en of the Lord, and pre - cious, Bind - ing all the church in one,

Ho - ly Zi - on's help for - ev - er, And her con - fi - dence a - lone.

614

"Angulare Fundamentum."

2 All that dedicated city,
  Dearly loved of God on high,
In exultant jubilation
  Pours perpetual melody;
God the One in Three adoring
  In glad hymns eternally.

3 To this temple, where we call Thee,
  Come, O Lord of hosts, to-day:
With Thy wonted loving-kindness,

Hear Thy servants as they pray;
And Thy fullest benediction
  Shed within its walls alway.

4 Here vouchsafe to all Thy servants
  What they ask of Thee to gain,
What they gain from Thee forever
  With the blessed to retain,
And hereafter in Thy glory
  Evermore with Thee to reign.

Unknown Author of the 8th century.
Tr. by Rev. John Mason Neale (1818—1866), 1851. Ab. and alt.

ROSE HILL. L. M.

JOSEPH EMERSON SWEETZER(1825—1873), 1849.

1. THE per - fect world, by A - dam trod, Was the first tem - ple, built by God;

His fi - at laid the cor - ner - stone, And heav'd its pil - lars one by one.

615

God's Temple.

2 He hung its starry roof on high,
The broad, illimitable sky :
He spread its pavement, green and bright,
And curtained it with morning light.

3 The mountains in their places stood,
The sea, the sky, and all was good ;

And when its first pure praises rang,
The morning stars together sang.

4 Lord, 'tis not ours to make the sea,
And earth, and sky, a house for Thee
But in Thy sight our offering stands,
A humbler temple, made with hands.

Nathaniel Parker Willis (1807—1867), 1826. Ab.

AURELIA. 7. 6. D.

SAMUEL SEBASTIAN WESLEY (1810—1876), 1868.

1. THE Church's one Foun-da-tion, Is Je-sus Christ her Lord; She is His new cre-

a-tion, By wa-ter and the word: From Heav'n He came and sought her To

be His ho-ly Bride; With His own blood He bought her, And for her life He died.

616

The One Foundation.
EPH. ii. 20.

2 Elect from every nation,
Yet one o'er all the earth,
Her charter of salvation
One Lord, one faith, one birth ;
One holy Name she blesses,
Partakes one holy food,
And to one hope she presses,
With every grace endued.

3 'Mid toil and tribulation,
And tumult of her war,
She waits the consummation
Of peace for evermore ;

Till with the vision glorious
Her longing eyes are blest,
And the great Church victorious
Shall be the Church at rest.

4 The saints their watch are keeping,
Their cry goes up, "how long?"
And soon the night of weeping
Shall be the morn of song.
O happy ones and holy !
Lord, give us grace, that we
Like them, the meek and lowly,
On high may dwell with Thee.

Rev. Samuel John Stone (1839—), 1866. Ab. and sl. alt.

ROMBERG. C. M.

THOMAS HASTINGS (1784—1872).

1. Lord, who didst bless Thy cho - sen band, And forth com - mis - sion'd send

To spread Thy Name from land to land, To Thee our hymns as - cend.

617   *Our Lord's Apostles.*

2 The princes of Thy Church were they,
   Chiefs unsubdued in fight,
Soldiers on earth of Heaven's array,
   The world's unerring light.

3 Theirs the firm faith of holy birth,
   The hope that looks above,

And, trampling on the powers of earth,
   Their Saviour's perfect love.

4 In them the heavens exulting own
   The Father's might revealed,
Thy triumph gained, begotten Son,
   Thy Spirit's influence sealed.

Bp. Richard Mant (1776—1848), 1837. Ab.

OUSELEY. L. M.

Rev. Sir FREDERICK ARTHUR GORE OUSELEY (1825—), 1872.

1. "Go, preach My gos - pel," saith the Lord, Bid the whole earth My grace re - ceive;

He shall be sav'd that trusts My word, And he con-demn'd that won't be - lieve.

618   *The great Commission.*
      MARK xvi. 15.

2 I'll make your great commission known;
   And ye shall prove My gospel true,
By all the works that I have done,
   By all the wonders ye shall do.

3 Go, heal the sick; go, raise the dead;
   Go, cast out devils in My Name;
Nor let My prophets be afraid,
   Though Greeks reproach, and Jews
      blaspheme.

4 Teach all the nations My commands,
　I'm with you till the world shall end;
　All power is trusted to My hands,
　I can destroy, and I defend."

5 He spake, and light shone round His head;
　On a bright cloud to Heaven He rode;
　They to the farthest nations spread
　The grace of their ascended God.

Rev. Isaac Watts (1674—1748), 1709. Sl. alt.

MISSIONARY CHANT. L. M.　　　　HEINRICH CHRISTOPHER ZEUNER (1795—1857), 1832.

1. Ye Chris-tian her - alds, go, pro-claim Sal - va-tion thro' Im - man - uel's Name;

To dis-tant climes the tid-ings bear, And plant the Rose of Sha - ron there.

619　"*Go ye into the World.*"
　　　MARK xvi. 15.

2 He'll shield you with a wall of fire,
　With flaming zeal your breast inspire,
　Bid raging winds their fury cease,
　And hush the tempest into peace.

3 And when our labors all are o'er,
　Then we shall meet to part no more,
　Meet, with the blood-bought throng to fall,
　And crown our Jesus Lord of all.

Mrs. Voke, 1816.

620　*Ordination of a Minister.*

1 FATHER of mercies, in Thy house,
　Smile on our homage, and our vows;
　While, with a grateful heart, we share
　These pledges of our Father's care.

2 The Saviour, when to Heaven He rose,
　In splendid triumph o'er His foes,
　Scattered His gifts on men below,
　And wide His royal bounties flow.

3 Hence sprung th' apostles' honored name,
　Sacred beyond heroic fame;
　In lowlier forms, to bless our eyes,
　Pastors from hence, and teachers rise.

4 So shall the bright succession run,
　Through the last courses of the sun;
　While unborn churches, by their care,
　Shall rise and flourish, large and fair.

Rev. Philip Doddridge (1702—1751), 1745. Ab.

621　*The Spirit accompanying the Word.*

1 O SPIRIT of the living God,
　In all Thy plenitude of grace,
　Where'er the foot of man hath trod,
　Descend on our apostate race.

2 Give tongues of fire, and hearts of love,
　To preach the reconciling Word;
　Give power and unction from above,
　Whene'er the joyful sound is heard.

3 Be darkness, at Thy coming, light,
　Confusion, order in Thy path;
　Souls without strength inspire with might;
　Bid mercy triumph over wrath.

4 Baptize the nations; far and nigh
　The triumphs of the cross record;
　The name of Jesus glorify,
　Till every kindred call Him Lord.

James Montgomery (1771—1854), 1825. **Ab.**

DUKE STREET. L. M.

JOHN HATTON, c. 1790.

1. Je - sus shall reign wher-e'er the sun Does his suc - ces - sive jour - neys run;

His king - dom stretch from shore to shore, Till moons shall wax and wane no more.

622

Christ's Dominion.
Ps. lxxii.

2 To Him shall endless prayer be made,
   And praises throng to crown His head;
   His Name, like sweet perfume, shall rise
   With every morning sacrifice.

3 Blessings abound where'er He reigns;
   The prisoner leaps to lose his chains;
   The weary find eternal rest,
   And all the sons of want are blest.

4 Let every creature rise and bring
   Peculiar honors to our King;
   Angels descend with songs again,
   And earth repeat the loud Amen.

Rev. Isaac Watts (1674—1748), 1719.   Ab. and sl. alt.

623

For a Missionary Meeting.

1 ASSEMBLED at Thy great command,
   Before Thy face, dread King, we stand;

The voice that marshaled every star,
Has called Thy people from afar.

2 We meet, through distant lands to spread
   The truth for which the martyrs bled;
   Along the line, to either pole,
   The thunder of Thy praise to roll.

3 Our prayers assist, accept our praise,
   Our hopes revive, our courage raise,
   Our counsels aid; and, O impart
   The single eye, the faithful heart.

4 Forth with Thy chosen heralds come,
   Recall the wandering spirits home;
   From Zion's mount send forth the sound,
   To spread the spacious earth around.

Rev. William Bengo Collyer (1782—1854), 1812.   Ab.

ENSIGN. L. M.

JOHN BAPTISTE CALKIN (1827—   ), 1872.

1. Fling out the ban - ner: let it float Sky - ward and sea - ward, high and wide;

The sun, that lights its shin - ing folds, The cross, on which the Sav - iour died.

624 *"Fling out the Banner."*

2 Fling out the banner: angels bend
    In anxious silence o'er the sign,
And vainly seek to comprehend
    The wonder of the Love divine.

3 Fling out the banner: heathen lands
    Shall see from far the glorious sight;
And nations, crowding to be born,
    Baptize their spirits in its light.

4 Fling out the banner: let it float
    Skyward and seaward, high and wide:
Our glory only in the cross,
    Our only hope, the Crucified.

5 Fling out the banner: wide and high,
    Seaward and skyward let it shine;
Nor skill, nor might, nor merit ours;
    We conquer only in that sign.
              Bp. George Washington Doane (1799—1859), 1824. Ab.

ST. ANN. C. M.   WILLIAM CROFT (1677—1727), 1712.

1. O WHERE are kings and em - pires now Of old that went and came?

But, Lord, Thy Church is pray - ing yet, A thou - sand years the same.

625 *The immovable Kingdom.*
        DAN. ii. 44.

2 We mark her goodly battlements,
    And her foundations strong;
We hear within the solemn voice
    Of her unending song.

3 For not like kingdoms of the world
    Thy holy Church, O God!   [ing her,
Though earthquake shocks are threaten-
    And tempests are abroad;

4 Unshaken as eternal hills,
    Immovable she stands,
A mountain that shall fill the earth,
    A house not made by hands.
              Bp. Arthur Cleveland Coxe (1818—   ), 1839. Alt.

626 *The Spirit creating all Things new.*

1 SPIRIT of power and might, behold
    A world by sin destroyed;
Creator, Spirit, as of old,
    Move on the formless void.

2 Give Thou the word: that healing sound
    Shall quell the deadly strife,
And earth again, like Eden crowned,
    Produce the tree of life.

3 If sang the morning stars for joy
    When nature rose to view,
What strains will angel-harps employ
    When Thou shalt all renew!

4 And if the sons of God rejoice
    To hear a Saviour's Name,
How shall the ransomed raise their voice,
    To whom that Saviour came!

5 So every kindred, tongue, and tribe,
    Assembling round the throne,
The new creation shall ascribe
    To sovereign love alone.
              James Montgomery (1771—1854), 1825, 1853.

MISSIONARY HYMN. 7.6.D.   LOWELL MASON (1792—1872), 1823.

1. From Greenland's i - cy mount - ains, From In - dia's cor - al   strand, Where Af - ric's sun - ny

fount - ains Roll down their gold - en sand; From many an   an - cient riv - er,

From many a palmy plain, They call us to de - liv - er Their land from er - ror's chain.

627   *"From Greenland's Icy Mountains."*

2 What though the spicy breezes
   Blow soft o'er Ceylon's isle,
  Though every prospect pleases,
   And only man is vile:
  In vain with lavish kindness
   The gifts of God are strown,
  The heathen in his blindness
   Bows down to wood and stone.

3 Can we, whose souls are lighted
   With wisdom from on high,
  Can we to men benighted
   The lamp of life deny?
  Salvation, O salvation!
   The joyful sound proclaim,
  Till each remotest nation
   Has learnt Messiah's Name.

4 Waft, waft, ye winds, His story,
   And you, ye waters, roll,
  Till, like a sea of glory,
   It spreads from pole to pole;
  Till o'er our ransomed nature,
   The Lamb for sinners slain,
  Redeemer, King, Creator,
   In bliss returns to reign.

           Bp. Reginald Heber (1783—1826), 1819.

628   *"Hail to the Lord's Anointed!"*

1 Hail to the Lord's Anointed,
   Great David's greater Son;
  Hail, in the time appointed,
   His reign on earth begun!
  He comes to break oppression,
   To set the captive free,
  To take away transgression,
   And rule in equity.

2 He comes with succor speedy
   To those who suffer wrong;
  To help the poor and needy,
   And bid the weak be strong;
  To give them songs for sighing,
   Their darkness turn to light,
  Whose souls, condemned and dying,
   Were precious in His sight.

3 For Him shall prayer unceasing
   And daily vows ascend;
  His kingdom still increasing,
   A kingdom without end.
  O'er every foe victorious,
   He on His throne shall rest,
  From age to age more glorious,
   All-blessing and all-blest.

       James Montgomery (1771—1854), 1822. Ab.

WEBB. 7. 6. D.

GEORGE JAMES WEBB (1803—). 1830.

1. THE morn-ing light is break-ing, The dark-ness dis-ap-pears; The sons of earth are wak-ing
D.S.—Of na-tions in com-mo-tion,

Fine.

D.S.

To pen-i-ten-tial tears: Each breeze that sweeps the o-cean Brings tid-ings from a-far
Pre-par'd for Zi-on's war.

629 *"The Morning Light is breaking."*

2 See heathen nations bending
    Before the God we love,
And thousand hearts ascending,
    In gratitude above;
While sinners, now confessing,
    The gospel call obey,
And seek the Saviour's blessing,
    A nation in a day.

3 Blest river of salvation,
    Pursue thine onward way;
Flow thou to every nation,
    Nor in thy riches stay;
Stay not, till all the lowly
    Triumphant reach their home;
Stay not, till all the holy
    Proclaim, "The Lord is come."
        Rev. Samuel Francis Smith (1808—), 1831. Ab.

630 *The final Triumph.*

1 WHEN shall the voice of singing
    Flow joyfully along,
When hill and valley, ringing
    With one triumphant song,
Proclaim the contest ended,
    And Him, who once was slain,
Again to earth descended,
    In righteousness to reign?

2 Then from the craggy mountains
    The sacred shout shall fly;
And shady vales and fountains
    Shall echo the reply:
High tower and lowly dwelling
    Shall send the chorus round,
All hallelujah swelling
    In one eternal sound.
        James Edmeston (1791—1867), 1822. Alt.

631 *The good Tidings.*

1 How beauteous, on the mountains,
    The feet of him that brings,
Like streams from living fountains,
    Good tidings of good things;
That publisheth salvation,
    And jubilee release,
To every tribe and nation,
    God's reign of joy and peace.

2 Lift up thy voice, O watchman,
    And shout, from Zion's towers,
Thy hallelujah chorus,
    "The victory is ours!"
The Lord shall build up Zion
    In glory and renown,
And Jesus, Judah's Lion,
    Shall wear His rightful crown.
        Benjamin Gough (1805—), 1863. Ab. and sl. alt.

ANVERN. L. M.

German. Arr. by LOWELL MASON (1792—1872), 1840.

1. ARM of the Lord, a - wake, a - wake, Put on Thy strength, the na - tions shake; And let the

ritard.

world, a - dor - ing, see Triumphs of mer - cy wrought by Thee, Triumphs of mer - cy wrought by Thee.

632

"*Awake, awake.*"
Is. li. 9.

2 Say to the heathen from Thy throne,
"I am Jehovah, God alone!"
Thy voice their idols shall confound,
And cast their altars to the ground.

3 No more let human blood be spilt,
Vain sacrifice for human guilt;
But to each conscience be applied
The blood that flowed from Jesus' side.

4 Almighty God, Thy grace proclaim,
In every clime, of every name,
Till adverse power before Thee fall,
And crown the Saviour, Lord of all.

William Shrubsole, Jr. (1759—1829), 1795. Ab.

633

Prayer for speedy Triumph.

1 SOON may the last glad song arise
Through all the millions of the skies,
That song of triumph, which records
That all the earth is now the Lord's.

2 Let thrones, and powers, and kingdoms be
Obedient, mighty God, to Thee;
And over land, and stream, and main,
Wave Thou the sceptre of Thy reign.

3 O that the anthem now might swell,
And host to host the triumph tell,
That not one rebel heart remains,
But over all the Saviour reigns.

Baptist Magazine, 1816.

HARMONY GROVE. L. M.

HENRY KEMBLE OLIVER (1800—1885), 1839.

1. LOOK from Thy sphere of end - less day, O God of mer - cy and of might;

In pit - y look on those who stray, Be - night - ed, in this land of light.

634 *Prayer for Home Missions.*

2 In peopled vale, in lonely glen,
  In crowded mart, by stream or sea,
How many of the sons of men
  Hear not the message sent from Thee.

3 Send forth Thy heralds, Lord, to call
  The thoughtless young, the hardened old,
A scattered, homeless flock, till all
  Be gathered to Thy peaceful fold.

4 Send them Thy mighty word to speak,
  Till faith shall dawn, and doubt depart,
To awe the bold, to stay the weak,
  And bind and heal the broken heart.

5 Then all these wastes, a dreary scene,
  That make us sadden as we gaze,
Shall grow with living waters green,
  And lift to Heaven the voice of praise.

William Cullen Bryant (1794—1878), 1840.

LANCASHIRE. 7. 6. D.   HENRY SMART (1812—1879), 1867

1. Up - lift the blood - red ban - ner, And shout, with trum - pet's sound, De -
liv'rance to the cap - tive, And free - dom to the bound; Earth's ju - bi - lee of glo - ry,
The year of full re - lease: O tell the wondrous sto - ry, Go forth and pub - lish peace.

635 *"Uplift the Blood-red Banner."*

2 Go forth, confessors, martyrs,
  With zeal and love unpriced,
And preach the blood of sprinkling,
  And live, or die, for Christ;
For Christ claim every nation,
  Your banner wide unfurled;
Go forth and preach salvation,
  Salvation for the world.

Benjamin Gough (1805—   ), 1865. Ab.

636 *"The Salvation of Israel."*
Ps. xiv.

1 O THAT the Lord's salvation
  Were out of Zion come,
To heal His ancient nation,
  To lead His outcasts home.
How long the holy city
  Shall heathen feet profane?
Return, O Lord, in pity;
  Rebuild her walls again.

2 Let fall Thy rod of terror,
  Thy saving grace impart;
Roll back the veil of error,
  Release the fettered heart.
Let Israel, home returning,
  Her lost Messiah see;
Give oil of joy for mourning,
  And bind Thy Church to Thee.

Rev. Henry Francis Lyte (1793—1847), 1834

324

ITALIAN HYMN. 6.6.4,6.6.6.4.

FELICE GIARDINI (1716—1796), 1769.

1. LORD of all power and might, Fa - ther of love and light, Speed on Thy Word

O let the gos - pel sound All the wide world around, Wher-ev - er man is found: God speed His Word.

637 *"Speed on Thy Word."*

2 Hail, blessed Jubilee:
   Thine, Lord, the glory be;
      Praise we the Lord:
   Thine was the mighty plan,
   From Thee the work began;
   Away with praise of man,
      Glory to God!

3 Lo, what embattled foes,
   Stern in their hate, oppose
      God's holy Word:
   One for His truth we stand,
   Strong in His own right hand,
   Firm as a martyr-band:
      God shield His Word.

4 Onward shall be our course,
   Despite of fraud or force;
      God is before:
   His word ere long shall run
   Free as the noon-day sun;
   His purpose must be done:
      God bless His Word.

Rev. Hugh Stowell (1799—1865), 1854. Sl. alt.

638 *"Let there be Light!"*
GEN. i. 3. 2 COR. iv. 6.

1 THOU, whose almighty word
   Chaos and darkness heard,

And took their flight;
Hear us, we humbly pray,
And where the gospel's day
Sheds not its glorious ray,
   "Let there be light!"

2 Thou, who didst come to bring
   On Thy redeeming wing
      Healing and sight,
   Health to the sick in mind,
   Sight to the inly blind,
   O, now to all mankind
      "Let there be light!"

3 Spirit of truth and love,
   Life-giving, holy Dove,
      Speed forth Thy flight:
   Move o'er the water's face,
   Bearing the lamp of grace,
   And in earth's darkest place
      "Let there be light!"

4 Blessed and Holy Three,
   Glorious Trinity,
      Wisdom, Love. Might;
   Boundless as ocean's tide,
   Rolling in fullest pride,
   Through the world, far and wide,
      "Let there be light!"

Rev. John Marriott (1780—1825), 1816

REGENT SQUARE. 8.7.4.

HENRY SMART (1813—1879), 1867.

1. On the mountain's top ap-pear-ing, Lo, the sa-cred her-ald stands, Welcome news to Zi - on bearing,

Zi - on long in hos-tile lands: Mourning cap-tive, Mourning cap-tive, God Him-self will loose thy bands.

639   *Good Tidings to Zion.*
Is. lii. 7.

2 Has thy night been long and mournful?
  Have thy friends unfaithful proved?
Have thy foes been proud and scornful,
  By thy sighs and tears unmoved?
    Cease thy mourning:
  Zion still is well-beloved.

3 God, thy God, will now restore thee;
  He Himself appears thy Friend;
All thy foes shall flee before thee;
  Here their boasts and triumphs end:
    Great deliverance
  Zion's King vouchsafes to send.

Rev. Thomas Kelly (1769—1855), 1806. Ab.

640   *Light in the Darkness.*
Matt. iv. 16.

1 O'er the gloomy hills of darkness,
  Look, my soul, be still and gaze;

Sun of Righteousness, arising,
  Bring the bright, the glorious day:
    Send the Gospel
  To the earth's remotest bound.

2 Kingdoms wide that sit in darkness,
  Grant them, Lord, Thy glorious light,
And from eastern coast to western
  May the morning chase the night;
    And redemption,
  Freely purchased, win the day.

3 Fly abroad, thou mighty Gospel,
  Win and conquer, never cease:
May thy lasting wide dominions
  Multiply, and still increase;
    Sway Thy sceptre,
  Saviour, all the world around.

Rev. William Williams (1717—1791), 1772. Ab. and alt.

ZION. 8.7.4.

THOMAS HASTINGS (1784—1872), 1830.

ATHENS. C. M. D.

FELICE GIARDINI (1716—1796), 1760.

1. A - WAKE, a - wake, put on Thy strength, O arm of Christ the Lord;

A - wake, as in the an - cient days, Fresh tri - umphs now re - cord.

D.S.—That joy might spring in sad - den'd hearts, And mourners cease to weep.

Thou dry - est up the might - y sea, The wa - ters of the deep,

641

"Put on Thy Strength."
Is. li. 9.

2 Thy ransomed people passed the wave,
  They trod the Red Sea floor;
The cloudy pillar frowned behind,
  But smiled with light before.
Lift up Thine arm, display Thy light,
  Again to guard and guide:
Beneath Thy banner, mighty Lord,
  We too have crossed the tide.

3 On, on we haste with holy zeal,
  Since Thou the path hast blest;
The distant mountains rise in view,
  Thy seat of peace and rest.
There lies the City of our God,
  The City beaming bright;
Where shines nor sun, nor moon, nor star,
  The Lamb its only light.

T. T. N, 1870. Ab.

OLIVET. 6. 6. 4. 6. 6. 6. 4.

LOWELL MASON (1792—1872), 1830.

1. CHRIST for the world we sing; The world to Christ we bring, With lov - ing zeal; The poor, and

them that mourn, The faint and o - verborne, Sin - sick and sor - row-worn, Whom Christ doth heal.

642   *"Christ for the World."*

2 Christ for the world we sing;
The world to Christ we bring,
With fervent prayer:
The wayward and the lost,
By reckless passion tossed,
Redeemed, at countless cost,
From dark despair.

3 Christ for the world we sing;
The world to Christ we bring,
With one accord;
With us the work to share,
With us reproach to dare,
With us the cross to bear,
For Christ our Lord.

4 Christ for the world we sing;
The world to Christ we bring,
With joyful song;
The new-born souls, whose days,
Reclaimed from error's ways,
Inspired with hope and praise,
To Christ belong.

Rev. Samuel Wolcott (1813—   ), 1869.

ARLINGTON. C. M.   THOMAS AUGUSTINE ARNE (1710—1778), 1744.

1. Great God, the na - tions of the earth Are by cre - a - tion Thine;

And in Thy works, by all be - held, Thy ra - diant glo - ries shine.

643   *The Gospel for all Nations.*
    Mark xiii. 10.

2 But, Lord, Thy greater love has sent
Thy gospel to mankind,
Unveiling what rich stores of grace
Are treasured in Thy mind.

3 Lord, when shall these glad tidings spread
The spacious earth around,
Till every tribe, and every soul,
Shall hear the joyful sound?

4 Smile, Lord, on each divine attempt
To spread the gospel's rays,
And build on sin's demolished throne
The temples of Thy praise.

Rev. Thomas Gibbons (1720—1785), 1769. Ab. and alt.

644   *"The Glory of the latter Day."*

1 O God, our God, Thou shinest here,
Thine own this latter day;
To us Thy radiant steps appear:
We watch Thy glorious way.

2 Thou tookest once our flesh; Thy face
Once on our darkness shone;
Yet through each age new births of grace
Still make Thy glory known.

3 Not only olden ages felt
The presence of the Lord;
Not only with the fathers dwelt
Thy Spirit and Thy word.

4 Doth not the Spirit still descend,
And bring the heavenly fire?
Doth not He still Thy Church extend,
And waiting souls inspire?

5 Come, Holy Ghost, in us arise;
Be this Thy mighty hour;
And make Thy willing people wise
To know Thy day of power.

Thomas Hornblower Gill (1819—   ), 1860. Ab.

LUDWIG. 7. D.

LUDWIG von BEETHOVEN (1770—1827), 1824.

1. Soldiers of the cross, a - rise, Gird you with your ar - mor bright; Might-y are your en - e - mies, Hard the bat - tle ye must fight. O'er a faith - less, fall - en world, Raise your ban-ner in the sky, Let it float there, wide un - furled, Bear it on-ward, lift it high.

645 *"Soldiers of the Cross, arise."*

2 'Mid the homes of want and woe,
　　Strangers to the living Word,
　Let the Saviour's herald go,
　　Let the voice of hope be heard.
　Where the shadows deepest lie,
　　Carry truth's unsullied ray;
　Where are crimes of blackest dye,
　　There the saving sign display.

3 To the weary and the worn
　　Tell of realms where sorrows cease;
　To the outcast and forlorn
　　Speak of mercy and of peace.
　Guard the helpless, seek the strayed,
　　Comfort trouble, banish grief;
　With the Spirit's sword arrayed,
　　Scatter sin and unbelief.

4 Be the banner still unfurled,
　　Bear it bravely still abroad,
　Till the kingdoms of the world
　　Are the kingdoms of the Lord;

Praise with songs of holy glee,
　　Saints of earth and heavenly Host,
　Godhead One in persons Three,
　　Father, Son, and Holy Ghost.

Bp. William Walsham How (1823—), 1854.

646 *"Go, ye Messengers of God."*

1 Go, ye messengers of God,
　　Like the beams of morning fly,
　Take the wonder-working rod,
　　Wave the banner-cross on high,
　Where the lofty minaret
　　Gleams along the morning skies,
　Wave it till the crescent set,
　　And the "Star of Jacob" rise.

2 Go to many a tropic isle,
　　In the bosom of the deep,
　Where the skies for ever smile,
　　And th' oppressed for ever weep.
　O'er the negro's night of care
　　Pour the living light of Heaven;
　Chase away the fiend despair,
　　Bid him hope to be forgiven.

3 Where the golden gates of day
　Open on the palmy East,
Wide the bleeding cross display,
　Spread the gospel's richest feast.

Bear the tidings round the ball,
　Visit every soil and sea;
Preach the cross of Christ to all,
　Christ, whose love is full and free.
Rev. Joshua Marsden (1777—1837), 1812.

ONIDO. 7. D.

IGNACE PLEYEL (1757—1831).
Arr. by LOWELL MASON (1792—1872), 1840.

1. HAS-TEN, Lord, the glo-rious time, When, be-neath Mes-si-ah's sway, Ev-'ry na-tion, ev-'ry clime, Shall the gos-pel call o-bey. Mightiest kings His power shall own, Heathen tribes His Name a-dore; Sa-tan and his host o'erthrown, Bound in chains, shall hurt no more.

647　*The Victory anticipated.*
Ps. lxxii.

2 Then shall wars and tumults cease,
　Then be banished grief and pain;
Righteousness, and joy, and peace,
　Undisturbed shall ever reign.
Time shall sun and moon obscure,
　Seas be dried, and rocks be riven,
But His reign shall still endure,
　Endless as the days of Heaven.
Miss Harriet Auber (1773—1862), 1829. Ab.

648　*"The Song of Jubilee."*

1 HARK, the song of jubilee,
　Loud as mighty thunders roar,
Or the fulness of the sea,
　When it breaks upon the shore:
Hallelujah! for the Lord
　God Omnipotent shall reign;
Hallelujah! let the word
　Echo round the earth and main.

2 Hallelujah! hark, the sound,
　From the centre to the skies,
Wakes above, beneath, around,
　All creation's harmonies.
See Jehovah's banners furled,
　Sheathed His sword: He speaks; 'tis done,
And the kingdoms of this world
　Are the kingdoms of His Son.

3 He shall reign from pole to pole
　With illimitable sway;
He shall reign, when like a scroll
　Yonder heavens have passed away.
Then the end; beneath His rod
　Man's last enemy shall fall:
Hallelujah! Christ in God,
　God in Christ, is All in all.
James Montgomery (1771—1854), 1819, 1825. 1717.

WESLEY. 8.7.D.

JOHN ZUNDEL (1815—1882), 1870.

1. SAV-IOUR, sprink-le ma-ny na-tions, Fruit-ful let Thy sor-rows be;

By Thy pains and con-so-la-tions, Draw the Gen-tiles un-to Thee:

D.S. Let them see Thee in Thy glo-ry, And Thy mer-cy man-i-fold.

Of Thy cross the won-drous sto-ry, Be it to the na-tions told;

649

"So shall He sprinkle many Nations."
Is. lii. 15.

2 Far and wide, though all unknowing,
 Pants for Thee each mortal breast;
Human tears for Thee are flowing,
 Human hearts in Thee would rest,
Thirsting, as for dews of even,
 As the new-mown grass for rain;
Thee, they seek, as God of Heaven,
 Thee as Man for sinners slain.

3 Saviour, lo, the isles are waiting,
 Stretched the hand, and strained the
For Thy Spirit, new creating [sight,
 Love's pure flame and wisdom's light;
Give the word, and of the preacher
 Speed the foot, and touch the tongue,
Till on earth by every creature
 Glory to the Lamb be sung.

Bp. Arthur Cleveland Coxe (1818—), 1851.

650

"Come over and help us."
Acts xvi. 9.

1 HARK, what mean those lamentations,
 Rolling sadly through the sky?
'Tis the cry of heathen nations,
 "Come and help us, or we die."
Lost and helpless and desponding,
 Wrapt in error's night they lie;
To their cries your hearts responding,
 Haste to help them ere they die.

2 Hark, again those lamentations
 Rolling sadly through the sky;
Louder cry the heathen nations,
 "Come and help us, or we die."
Hear the heathen's sad complaining;
 Christians, hear their dying cry;
And the love of Christ constraining,
 Join to help them ere they die.

Rev. John Cawood (1775—1852), 1819. Alt.

BAVARIA. 8.7.D.

German Melody.

VISION. 11.10.

LOWELL MASON (1792—1872), 1830.

1. HAIL to the brightness of Zi - on's glad morn-ing; Joy to the lands that in dark-ness have lain;

Hush'd be the ac - cents of sor - row and mourning; Zi - on in tri-umph be - gins her mild reign.

651   *The Latter Day.*

2 Hail to the brightness of Zion's glad morning,
    Long by the prophets of Israel foretold;
    Hail to the millions from bondage returning;
    Gentiles and Jews the blest vision behold.

3 Lo, in the desert rich flowers are springing;
    Streams ever copious are gliding along;
    Loud from the mountain-tops echoes are ringing;
    Wastes rise in verdure, and mingle in song.

4 See, from all lands, from the isles of the ocean,
    Praise to Jehovah ascending on high;
    Fallen are the engines of war and commotion;
    Shouts of salvation are rending the sky.

Thomas Hastings (1784—1872), 1831.

652   *The Church victorious.*

1 DAUGHTER of Zion, awake from thy sadness;
    Wake, for thy foes shall oppress thee no more:
    Bright o'er thy hills dawns the day-star of gladness;
    Rise, for the night of thy sorrow is o'er.

2 Strong were thy foes; but the arm that subdued them,
    And scattered their legions, was mightier far:
    They fled, like the chaff, from the scourge that pursued them;
    Vain were their steeds and their chariots of war.

3 Daughter of Zion, the power that hath saved thee
    Extolled with the harp and the timbrel should be;
    Shout, for the foe is destroyed that enslaved thee;
    Th' oppressor is vanquished, and Zion is free.

Fitzgerald's Collection, 1830.

BLACKBURN. C. M.

HENRY SMART (1813—1879), 1872.

1. DAUGH-TER of Zi - on, from the dust Ex - alt thy fall - en head;

A - gain in thy Re - deem - er trust: He calls thee from the dead.

653 *The Restoration of Israel.*
Is. lii. 1—10.

2 Awake, awake, put on thy strength,
  Thy beautiful array;
  The day of freedom dawns at length,
  The Lord's appointed day.

3 Rebuild thy walls, thy bounds enlarge,
  And send thy heralds forth;
  Say to the South, "Give up thy charge,
  And keep not back, O North."

4 They come, they come; thine exiled bands,
  Where'er they rest or roam,
  Have heard Thy voice in distant lands,
  And hasten to their home.

James Montgomery (1771—1854), 1825, 1853. Ab.

654 *The Martyr-Spirit.*

1 THE Son of God goes forth to war,
  A kingly crown to gain;
  His blood-red banner streams afar:
  Who follows in His train?

2 Who best can drink His cup of woe,
  Triumphant over pain,

Who patient bears His cross below,
  He follows in His train.

3 The martyr first, whose eagle eye
  Could pierce beyond the grave,
  Who saw his Master in the sky,
  And called on Him to save:

4 Like Him, with pardon on His tongue,
  In midst of mortal pain,
  He prayed for them that did the wrong:
  Who follows in his train?

5 A glorious band, the chosen few
  On whom the Spirit came,
  Twelve valiant saints, their hope they knew,
  And mocked the cross and flame.

6 They climbed the steep ascent of Heaven
  Through peril, toil, and pain:
  O God, to us may grace be given
  To follow in their train.

Bp. Reginald Heber (1783—1826), 1827. Ab.

HERMON. C. M.

LOWELL MASON (1792—1872), 1832.

ST. PETER. C. M.   ALEXANDER ROBERT REINAGLE (1799—1877), 1826.

1. LET Zi - on and her sons re - joice; Be - hold the prom - ised hour:

Her God hath heard her mourn - ing voice, And comes t' ex - alt His pow'r.

655 *Prayer heard, and Zion restored.*
Ps. cii. 13—21.

2 The Lord will raise Jerusalem,
  And stand in glory there;
Nations shall bow before His Name,
  And kings attend with fear.

3 He sits a Sovereign on His throne,
  With pity in His eyes;
He hears the dying prisoners groan,
  And sees their sighs arise.

4 He frees the souls condemned to death,
  Nor when His saints complain,
Shall it be said, that praying breath
  Was ever spent in vain.
    Rev. Isaac Watts (1674—1748), 1719. Ab.

656 *The Millennium.*
Micah. iv. 1, 2. Is. ii. 1—4.

1 BEHOLD, the Mountain of the Lord
  In latter days shall rise,
Above the mountains and the hills,
  And draw the wondering eyes.

2 The beam that shines on Zion's hill
  Shall lighten every land;
The King who reigns in Zion's towers
  Shall all the world command.

3 No strife shall vex Messiah's reign,
  Or mar the peaceful years;   [swords,
To ploughshares soon they beat their
  To pruning-hooks their spears.

4 No longer hosts encountering hosts
  Their millions slain deplore;
They hang the trumpet in the hall,
  And study war no more.

5 Come, then, O come from every land,
  To worship at His shrine;
And, walking in the light of God,
  With holy beauties shine.
    Michael Bruce (1746—1767), 1781. Ab.

657 *Mustering the Host.*
Isa. xiii. 4.

1 LIFT up your heads, ye gates of brass,
  Ye bars of iron, yield;
And let the King of glory pass:
  The cross is in the field.

2 That banner, brighter than the star
  That leads the train of night,
Shines on their march, and guides from far
  His servants to the fight.

3 Ye armies of the living God,
  His sacramental host,
Where hallowed footsteps never trod,
  Take your appointed post.

4 Uplifted are the gates of brass,
  The bars of iron yield;
Behold the King of glory pass:
  The cross hath won the field.
    James Montgomery, 1854? Ab.

MOSCOW. 10s.

Arr. from ALEXIS THEODORE LWOFF (1799—1870).

1. Rise, crown'd with light, im-pe-rial Sa-lem, rise: Ex-alt thy tow'ring head, and lift thine eyes;

See Heav'n its sparkling por-tals wide dis-play, And break up-on thee in a flood of day.

658   *Gentiles coming into the Church.*

2 See a long race thy spacious courts adorn,
    See future sons and daughters yet unborn
    In crowding ranks on every side arise,
    Demanding life, impatient for the skies.

3 See barbarous nations at thy gates attend,
    Walk in thy light, and in thy temple bend;
    See thy bright altars thronged with prostrate kings,
    While every land its joyful tribute brings.

4 The seas shall waste, the skies to smoke decay,
    Rocks fall to dust, and mountains melt away;
    But fixed His Word, His saving power remains;
    Thy realm shall last, thy own Messiah reigns.

                         Alexander Pope (1688—1744), 1712. Ab. and alt.

DOWNS. C. M.

LOWELL MASON (1792—1872), 1832.

1. On Zi-on and on Leb-an-on, On Car-mel's bloom-ing height,

On Sha-ron's fer-tile plains, once shone The glo-ry, pure and bright.

659 *Home Missions.*

2 From thence its mild and cheering ray
  Streamed forth from land to land;
And empires now behold its day;
  And still its beams expand.

3 But ah, our deserts deep and wild
  See not this heavenly light;

No sacred beams, no radiance mild,
  Dispel their dreary night.

4 Thou, who didst lighten Zion's hill,
  On Carmel who didst shine,
Our deserts let Thy glory fill,
  Thy excellence divine.

Bp. Henry Ustick Onderdonk (1789—1853), 1826. Ab.

LANCASHIRE. 7.6.D.

HENRY SMART (1812—1879), 1836?

1. A-WAKE, a-wake, O Zi-on, Put on thy strength di-vine, Thy garments bright in beau-ty, The brid-al dress be thine: Je-ru-sa-lem the ho-ly, To pur-i-ty re-stored; Meek Bride, all fair and low-ly, Go forth and meet thy Lord.

660 *Meeting the Bridegroom.*

2 The Lamb who bore our sorrows
  Comes down to earth again;
No sufferer now, but Victor,
  For evermore to reign;
To reign in every nation,
  To rule in every zone:
O wide-world coronation,
  In every heart a throne.

3 Awake, awake, O Zion,
  The bridal day draws nigh,
The day of signs and wonders,
  And marvels from on high:
Thy sun uprises slowly,
  But keep thou watch and ward;
Fair Bride, all pure and lowly,
  Go forth to meet thy Lord.

Benjamin Gough (1805—), 1865. Ab.

661 *"Mighty to save."*
Is. lxiii. 1.

1 HE comes in blood-stained garments;
  Upon His brow a crown;
The gates of brass fly open,
  The iron bands drop down;
From off the fettered captive
  The chains of Satan fall,
While angels shout triumphant,
  That Christ is Lord of all.

2 O Christ, His love is mighty,
  Long-suffering is His grace;
And glorious is the splendor
  That beameth from His face.
Our hearts up-leap in gladness
  When we behold that love,
As we go singing onward
  To dwell with Him above.

Mrs. Charitie Lees Bancroft (1841—), 1860. Ab.

PILGRIM. 8.7.D.

GEORGE KINGSLEY (1811–1884), 1838.

1. Toss'd up - on life's rag-ing bil - low, Sweet it is, O Lord, to know, Thou didst press a sail - or's

pil - low, And canst feel a sail - or's woe. Nev - er slumb'ring, nev - er sleep - ing, Though the

night be dark and drear, Thou the faithful watch art keep - ing, "All, all's well," Thy con - stant cheer.

662

Christ on the Lake of Galilee.
Mark iv. 38.

2 And though loud the wind is howling,
    Fierce though flash the lightnings red,
Darkly though the storm-cloud's scowling
    O'er the sailor's anxious head;
Thou canst calm the raging ocean,
    All its noise and tumult still,
Hush the tempest's wild commotion,
    At the bidding of Thy will.

3 Thus my heart the hope will cherish,
    While to Thee I lift mine eye,
Thou wilt save me ere I perish,
    Thou wilt hear the sailor's cry;
And though mast and sail be riven,
    Life's short voyage will soon be o'er;
Safely moored in Heaven's wide haven,
    Storms and tempests vex no more.

Rev. George Washington Bethune (1805–1862), 1847. Alt.

KEARNS. L. M.

HENRY SMART (1812–1879), 1872.

1. O GOD, who met - est in Thy hand The wa - ters of the might - y sea,

And bar - rest o - cean with the sand By Thy per - pet - u - al de - cree:

663   *For Seamen.*
Ps. cvii. 23—30.

2 When they who to the sea go down,
   And in the waters ply their toil,
   Are lifted on the surge's crown,
   And plunged where seething eddies boil;

3 Rule then, O Lord, the ocean's wrath,
   And bind the tempest with Thy will;
   Tread, as of old, the water's path, [still."
   And speak Thy bidding, "Peace, be

4 And when there shall be sea no more,
   Save that of mingled flame and glass,
   Where goes no galley sped by oar,
   Where gallant ships no longer pass;

5 When dawns the Resurrection morn,
   Upon that shore, O Jesus, stand,
   And give Thy pilgrims, faint and worn,
   Their welcome to the Happy Land.

Rev. Richard Frederick Littledale (1833—   ). 1867. Ab.

664   *Prayer for Mariners.*

1 While o'er the deep Thy servants sail,
   Send Thou, O Lord, the prosperous gale;
   And on their hearts, where'er they go,
   O let Thy heavenly breezes blow.

2 If on the morning's wings they fly,
   They will not pass beyond Thine eye:
   The wanderer's prayer Thou bend'st to
   And faith exults to know Thee near. [hear,

3 When tempests rock the groaning bark,
   O hide them safe in Jesus' ark;
   When in the tempting port they ride,
   O keep them safe at Jesus' side.

4 If life's wide ocean smile or roar,
   Still guide them to the heavenly shore;
   And grant their dust in Christ may sleep,
   Abroad, at home, or in the deep.

Bp. George Burgess (1809—1866), 1840.

DOMINE SALVA. 12.   Sir Arthur Sullivan (1842—   ). 1869.

1. When through the torn sail the wild tem-pest is streaming, When o'er the dark wave the red light-ning is gleam-ing, Nor hope lends a ray the poor sea-man to cher-ish, They fly to their Mas-ter, "Save, Lord, or we per-ish!"

665   *"Save, Lord, or we perish."*
Mark viii. 25.

2 O Jesus, once rocked on the breast of the billow,
   Aroused by the shriek of despair from Thy pillow,
   Now seated in glory, the poor sinner cherish,
   Who cries in his anguish, "Save, Lord, or we perish!"

Bp. Reginald Heber (1783—1826), 1820. Ab. and alt.

WAVE. 8.7.4.

Arr. by WILLIAM BATCHELDER BRADBURY (1816—1868), 1844.

1. STAR of peace, to wand'rers wea-ry, Bright the beams that smile on me; Cheer the pi-lot's vis-ion dreary, Far, far at sea; Cheer the pi-lot's vis-ion dreary, Far, far at sea.

666   *The guiding Star.*

2 Star of hope, gleam on the billow,
    Bless the soul that sighs for Thee ;
Bless the sailor's lonely pillow,
    Far, far at sea.

3 Star of faith, when winds are mocking
    All his toil, he flies to Thee ;

Save him on the billows rocking,
    Far, far at sea.

4 Star divine, O safely guide him,
    Bring the wanderer home to Thee :
Sore temptations long have tried him,
    Far, far at sea.

Mrs. Jane Bell Cross Simpson, 1830. Ab

COOLING. C. M.

ALONZO JUDSON ABBEY (1825—   ). 1868.

1. WHEN lan-guor and dis-ease in-vade This trem-bling house of clay, 'Tis sweet to look be-yond the cage, And long to fly a-way.

667   *In Sickness.*

2 Sweet on His faithfulness to rest,
    Whose love can never end ;
Sweet on His covenant of grace
    For all things to depend ;

3 Sweet, in the confidence of faith,
    To trust His firm decrees ;

Sweet to lie passive in His hands,
    And know no will but His ;

4 Sweet to rejoice in lively hope,
    That, when my change shall come,
Angels will hover round my bed,
    And waft my spirit home.

Rev. Augustus Montague Toplady (1740—1778), 1776. Ab

DAWN. S. M.

Rev. EDWIN POND PARKER (1836—). 1611.

1. ONE sweet - ly sol - emn thought Comes to me o'er and o'er,

Near - er my part - ing hour am I Than e'er I was be - fore.

668 *Nearing Home.*

2 Nearer my Father's house,
   Where many mansions be ;
   Nearer the throne where Jesus reigns,
   Nearer the crystal sea ;

3 Nearer my going home,
   Laying my burden down,
   Leaving my cross of heavy grief,
   Wearing my starry crown.

4 Nearer that hidden stream,
   Winding through shades of night,
   Rolling its cold, dark waves between
   Me and the world of light.

5 Jesus, to Thee I cling :
   Strengthen my arm of faith ;
   Stay near me while my way-worn feet
   Press through the stream of death.

Miss Phœbe Cary (1825—1871), 1852. Ab. and alt.

669 *"The Death of the Righteous."*

1 O FOR the death of those
   Who slumber in the Lord :
   O be like theirs my last repose,
   Like theirs my last reward.

2 Their bodies in the ground,
   In silent hope may lie,
   Till the last trumpet's joyful sound
   Shall call them to the sky.

3 Their ransomed spirits soar,
   On wings of faith and love,
   To meet the Saviour they adore,
   And reign with Him above.

4 With us their names shall live
   Through long-succeeding years,
   Embalmed with all our hearts can give,
   Our praises and our tears.

James Montgomery (1771—1854), 1804. Ab. and much alt.

670 *Resting in Hope.*

1 REST for the toiling hand,
   Rest for the anxious brow,
   Rest for the weary, way-sore feet,
   Rest from all labor now.

2 Rest for the fevered brain,
   Rest for the throbbing eye ; [more
   Through these parched lips of thine no
   Shall pass the moan or sigh.

3 Soon shall the trump of God
   Give out the welcome sound,
   That shakes thy silent chamber-walls,
   And breaks the turf-sealed ground.

4 Ye dwellers in the dust,
   Awake, come forth and sing ;
   Sharp has your frost of winter been,
   But bright shall be your spring.

5 'Twas sown in weakness here,
   'Twill then be raised in power :
   That which was sown an earthly seed,
   Shall rise a heavenly flower.

Rev. Horatius Bonar (1808—), 1857. Ab.

MAGDALENE. 6.5.D.   Rev. JOHN BACCHUS DYKES (1823—1876), 1861.

1. In the hour of tri - al, Je - sus, pray for me; Lest by base de-
-ni - al I de - part from Thee: When Thou seest me wa - ver,
With a look re - call, Nor for fear or fa - vor, Suf - fer me to fall.

671   *The Hour of Trial.*

2 If with sore affliction
    Thou in love chastise,
Pour Thy benediction
    On the sacrifice:
Then, upon Thine altar
    Freely offered up,
Though the flesh may falter,
    Faith shall drain the cup.

3 When in dust and ashes
    To the grave I sink,
While Heaven's glory flashes
    O'er the shelving brink,
On Thy truth relying
    Through that mortal strife,
Lord, receive me, dying,
    To eternal life.

James Montgomery (1771—1854), 1835. Ab.

VESPER. 8.7.   Arr. from FRIEDRICH FREIHERR von FLOTOW (1812—1883), 1847.

1. This is not my place of rest - ing; Mine's a cit - y yet to come;
On - ward to it I am hast - ing, On to my e - ter - nal home.

672 *"This is not your Rest."*
MICAH. ii. 10.

2 In it all is light and glory;
O'er it shines a nightless day·
Every trace of sin's sad story,
All the curse, hath passed away.

3 There the Lamb, our Shepherd, leads us,
By the streams of life along,

On the freshest pastures feeds us,
Turns our sighing into song.

4 Soon we pass this desert dreary,
Soon we bid farewell to pain;
Never more are sad or weary,
Never, never sin again.

Rev. Horatius Bonar (1808—), 1845.

GREENWOOD. S. M.
JOSEPH EMERSON SWEETSER (1825—1873), 1849.

1. FAR from my heav'n-ly home, Far from my Fa-ther's breast,
Faint-ing I cry, "Blest Spir-it, come, And speed me to my rest."

673 *Far from Home.*
Ps. cxxxvii.

2 Upon the willows long
My harp has silent hung:
How should I sing a cheerful song
Till Thou inspire my tongue?

3 My spirit homeward turns,
And fain would thither flee;
My heart, O Zion, droops and yearns,
When I remember thee.

4 To thee, to thee, I press,
A dark and toilsome road:
When shall I pass the wilderness,
And reach the saints' abode?

5 God of my life, be near:
On Thee my hopes I cast;
O guide me through the desert here
And bring me home at last.

Rev. Henry Francis Lyte (1793—1847), 1834.

674 *"For ever with the Lord."*

1 FOR ever with the Lord:
Amen, so let it be;

Life from the dead is in that word,
'Tis immortality.

2 Here in the body pent,
Absent from Him I roam,
Yet nightly pitch my moving tent
A day's march nearer home.

3 My Father's house on high,
Home of my soul, how near,
At times, to faith's foreseeing eye,
Thy golden gates appear.

4 Ah, then my spirit faints
To reach the land I love,
The bright inheritance of saints,
Jerusalem above.

5 "Forever with the Lord;"
Father, if 'tis Thy will,
The promise of that faithful word
E'en here to me fulfil.

James Montgomery (1771—1854), 1835. Ab.

THE BETTER LIFE.

FREDERICK. 11.

GEORGE KINGSLEY (1811—1884). 1838.

1. I WOULD not live alway; I ask not to stay Where storm aft-er storm ris-es dark o'er the way;

The few lu-rid mornings,that dawn on us here, Are enough for life's woes, full e-nough for its cheer.

675   *"I would not live alway."*

2 I would not live alway, thus fettered by sin,
  Temptation without and corruption
    within;
  E'en the rapture of pardon is mingled with
    fears,
  And the cup of thanksgiving with penitent
    tears.

3 I would not live alway; no, welcome the
    tomb;
  Since Jesus hath lain there, I dread not its
    gloom;
  There sweet be my rest, till He bid me
    arise,
  To hail Him in triumph descending the
    skies.

4 Who, who would live alway, away from
    his God;
  Away from yon Heaven, that blissful
    abode,
  Where the rivers of pleasure flow o'er the
    bright plains,
  And the noontide of glory eternally reigns?

5 Where the saints of all ages in harmony
    meet,
  Their Saviour and brethren transported
    to greet;
  While the anthems of rapture unceasingly
    roll,
  And the smile of the Lord is the feast of the
    soul.

Rev. William Augustus Muhlenberg (1796—1877), 1823.

THE LAST SLEEP. 4.6.D.

JOSEPH BARNBY (1838—). 1868.

1. SLEEP thy last sleep! Free from care and sor-row; Rest,where none weep,Till th'e-ter-nal mor-row:

Though dark waves roll O'er the si-lent riv-er, Thy fainting soul Je-sus can de-liv-er.

676

The Last Sleep.

2 Life's dream is past;
  All its sin, and sadness;
  Brightly, at last,
  Dawns the day of gladness:
Under thy sod,
  Earth, receive our treasure,
  To rest in God,
  Waiting all His pleasure.

3 Though we may mourn
  Those in life the dearest,
  They shall return,
  Christ, when Thou appearest:
Soon shall Thy voice
  Comfort those now weeping,
  Bidding rejoice
  All in Jesus sleeping.

Rev. Edward Arthur Dayman (1807—   ), 1868.

TRIUMPH. 13.11.

JOSEPH BARNBY, 1867.

1. Thou art gone to the grave; but we will not de-plore thee, Though sor-rows and dark-ness en-com-pass the tomb: The Sav-iour has pass'd through its por-tal be-fore thee, And the lamp of His love is thy guide through the gloom.

677

"Gone to the Grave."

2 Thou art gone to the grave; we no longer behold thee,
  Nor tread the rough path of the world by thy side;
  But the wide arms of mercy are spread to enfold thee,
  And sinners may die, for the Sinless hath died.

3 Thou art gone to the grave; and, its mansion forsaking,
  Perchance thy weak spirit in fear lingered long;
  But the mild rays of Paradise beamed on thy waking,
  And the sound which thou heardst was the seraphim's song.

4 Thou art gone to the grave; but we will not deplore thee;
  Whose God was thy Ransom, thy Guardian and Guide:
  He gave thee, He took thee, and He will restore thee;
  And death has no sting, for the Saviour has died.

Bp. Reginald Heber (1783—1826), 1812.

CHALVEY. S. M. D.

Rev LEIGHTON GEORGE HAYNE (1836—), 1868.

1. A few more years shall roll, A few more sea-sons come, And we shall be with those that rest A-sleep with-in the tomb.

CHORUS.

Then, O my Lord, pre-pare My soul for that great day; O wash me in Thy precious blood, And take my sins a-way.

678

"The Time is short."
1 Cor. vii. 29.

2 A few more storms shall beat
   On this wild, rocky shore;
   And we shall be where tempests cease,
   And surges swell no more.—Cho.

3 A few more struggles here,
   A few more partings o'er,

A few more toils, a few more tears,
   And we shall weep no more.—Cho.

4 'Tis but a little while,
   And He shall come again,
   Who died that we might live, who lives
   That we with Him may reign.—Cho.

Rev. Horatius Bonar (1808—), 1857. Ab.

RUTHERFORD. P. M.

CHARLES D'URBAN, 1845.

1. The sands of time are sink-ing, The dawn of Heav-en breaks; The sum-mer morn I've sigh'd for, The fair, sweet morn a-wakes Dark, dark hath been the mid-night, But

day-spring is at hand, And glo - ry, glo - ry dwell - eth In Im - man - uel's land.

679 *"Immanuel's Land."*

2 O Christ, He is the fountain,
The deep, sweet well of love;
The streams of earth I've tasted,
More deep I'll drink above.
There to an ocean fulness
His mercy doth expand,
And glory, glory dwelleth
In Immanuel's land.

3 The bride eyes not her garment,
But her dear bridegroom's face ·
I will not gaze at glory,
But on my King of grace;
Not at the crown He giveth,
But on His piercéd hand :
The Lamb is all the glory
Of Immanuel's land.

Mrs. Annie Ross Cousin, 1857. Ab.

REST. L. M. WILLIAM BATCHELDER BRADBURY (1816—1868), 1843.

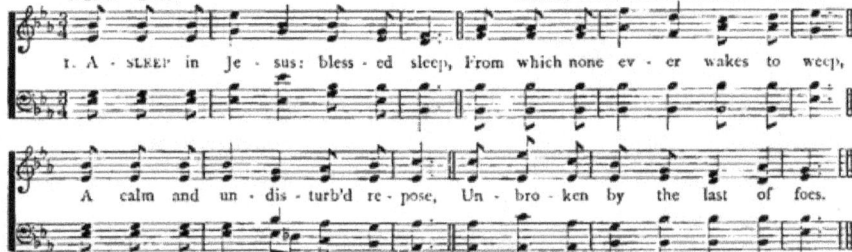

1. A - sleep in Je - sus: bless - ed sleep, From which none ev - er wakes to weep,

A calm and un - dis - turb'd re - pose, Un - bro - ken by the last of foes.

680 *"Asleep in Jesus."*

2 Asleep in Jesus: O how sweet
To be for such a slumber meet;
With holy confidence to sing,
That death hath lost his venomed sting.

3 Asleep in Jesus: peaceful rest,
Whose waking is supremely blest;
No fear, no woe, shall dim that hour
That manifests the Saviour's power.

4 Asleep in Jesus: O for me
May such a blissful refuge be;
Securely shall my ashes lie,
Waiting the summons from on high.

5 Asleep in Jesus: far from thee
Thy kindred and their graves may be;
But thine is still a blessed sleep,
From which none ever wakes to weep.

Mrs. Margaret Mackay (1801—), 1832. Ab.

681 The Death of the Righteous.
Num. xxiii. 10.

1 How blest the righteous, when he dies,
When sinks a weary soul to rest:
How mildly beam the closing eyes,
How gently heaves th' expiring breast.

2 So fades a summer cloud away;
So sinks the gale, when storms are o'er;
So gently shuts the eye of day;
So dies a wave along the shore.

3 A holy quiet reigns around,
A calm which life nor death destroys;
And naught disturbs that peace profound,
Which his unfettered soul enjoys.

4 Life's labor done, as sinks the clay,
Light from its load the spirit flies;
While Heaven and earth combine to say,
"How blest the righteous when he dies!"

Mrs. Anna Lætitia Barbauld (1743—1825), 1773. Ab. and alt.

RESIGNATION. 6. 6. 4. 6. 6. 6. 4.   JOHN HENRY CORNELL (1828—). 1872.

1. Low - ly and sol - emn be Thy children's cry to Thee, Fa - ther di - vine: A hymn of

suppliant breath; Own - ing that life and death, Own - ing that life and death A - like are Thine.

682   *Resignation.*

2 O Father, in that hour,
  When earth all succoring power
    Shall disavow ;
  When spear, and shield, and crown,
  In faintness are cast down ;
    Sustain us, Thou.

3 By Him who bowed to take
  The death-cup for our sake,
    The thorn, the rod ;

From whom the last dismay
Was not to pass away ;
  Aid us, O God.

4 Tremblers beside the grave,
  We call on Thee to save,
    Father divine :
Hear, hear our suppliant breath ;
Keep us in life and death,
  Thine, only Thine.

Mrs. Felicia Dorothea Hemans (1794—1835), 1832. Ab.

SAUL. L. M. 6 l.   From GEORGE FREDERICK HANDEL (1685—1759). 1740.

1. Un - veil thy bo - som, faith - ful tomb; Take this new treas - ure to thy trust,

And give these sa - cred rel - ics room, To seek a slum - ber in the dust;

And give these sa - cred rel - ics room, To seek a slum - ber in the dust.

683 *Peaceful Sleep.*

2 Nor pain, nor grief, nor anxious fear
  Invade thy bounds. No mortal woes
Can reach the peaceful sleeper here,
  While angels watch the soft repose.

3 So Jesus slept: God's dying Son [bed;
  Passed through the grave, and blest the

Rest here, blest saint, till from His throne
  The morning break, and pierce the shade.

4 Break from His throne, illustrious morn;
  Attend, O earth, His sovereign word;
Restore thy trust: a glorious form
  Shall then ascend to meet the Lord.
                    Rev. Isaac Watts (1674—1748), 1731. Alt.

LEOMINSTER. S. M. D.   Arr. by SIR ARTHUR SULLIVAN (1842—).

1. SERVANT of God, well done, Rest from thy lov'd em - ploy; The bat - tle fought, the vic - t'ry won, En - ter thy Mas - ter's joy. The voice at mid - night came, He start - ed up to hear; A mor - tal ar - row pierc'd his frame, He fell, but felt no fear.

684 *On the Death of a Minister.*

2 At midnight came the cry,
  "To meet thy God prepare!"
He woke, and caught his Captain's eye;
  Then, strong in faith and prayer,
His spirit with a bound
Left its encumbering clay;
His tent, at sunrise, on the ground,
A darkened ruin lay.

3 The pains of death are past,
  Labor and sorrow cease,
And, life's long warfare closed at last,
  His soul is found in peace.
Soldier of Christ, well done,
  Praise be thy new employ;
And, while eternal ages run,
  Rest in thy Saviour's joy.
        James Montgomery (1771—1854), 1825. Ab.

685 *Signal Consecration and Courage.*

1 O SHEPHERD of the sheep,
  High Priest of things to come,
Who didst in grace Thy servant keep,
  And take him sweetly home:
His heart was Thine alone,
  From selfish longings free;
Thy throne the cross, a cross his throne,
  His life was hid in Thee.

2 So, trusting in Thy might,
  He won a fair renown;
So, waxing valiant in the fight,
  He trod the lion down;
Then rendered up to Thee
  The charge Thy love had given,
And passed away, Thy face to see
  Revealed in highest Heaven.
                V. S. C. Coles, 1868. Ab.

FAITHFUL. C. M.

SAMUEL PARKMAN TUCKERMAN (1819—), 1848.

1. THROUGH sor-row's night and dan-ger's path, A - mid the deep - 'ning gloom,

We, sol - diers of an in - jured King, Are march-ing to the tomb.

686

"Marching to the Tomb."

2 There, when the turmoil is no more,
    And all our powers decay,
Our cold remains in solitude
    Shall sleep the years away.

3 Our labors done, securely laid
    In this our last retreat,
Unheeded, o'er our silent dust
    The storms of life shall beat.

4 Yet not thus lifeless, thus inane,
    The vital spark shall lie;
For o'er life's wreck that spark shall rise
    To seek its kindred sky.

5 These ashes too, this little dust,
    Our Father's care shall keep,
Till the last angel rise and break
    The long and dreary sleep.

6 Then love's soft dew o'er every eye
    Shall shed its mildest rays,
And the long-silent dust shall burst
    With shouts of endless praise.

Henry Kirke White (1785—1806), 1806.

687

"To live is Christ, and to die is Gain."
PHIL. i. 21.

1 LORD, it belongs not to my care
    Whether I die or live;
To love and serve Thee is my share,
    And this Thy grace must give.

2 Christ leads me through no darker rooms
    Than He went through before;
He that unto God's kingdom comes
    Must enter by this door.

3 Come, Lord, when grace hath made me
    Thy blessèd face to see;   [meet
For, if Thy work on earth be sweet,
    What will Thy glory be?

4 Then I shall end my sad complaints,
    And weary sinful days,
And join with the triumphant saints
    That sing Jehovah's praise.

5 My knowledge of that life is small;
    The eye of faith is dim;
But it's enough that Christ knows all,
    And I shall be with Him.

Rev. Richard Baxter (1615—1689), 1681. Ab. and alt.

YORK. C. M.

Scotch Psalter, 1615.

GLEBE FIELD. 7.

Rev. JOHN BACCHUS DYKES (1823—1876), 1874.

1. BROTH - ER, though from yon - der sky Com - eth nei - ther voice nor cry,

Yet we know from thee to - day Ev - 'ry pain hath pass'd a - way.

688 *A Student's Death.*

2 Not for thee shall tears be given,
Child of God and heir of Heaven;
For He gave thee sweet release;
Thine the Christian's death of peace.

3 Well we know thy living faith
Had the power to conquer death;
As a living rose may bloom
By the border of the tomb.

4 Brother, in that solemn trust
We commend thee, dust to dust;
In that faith we wait, till, risen
Thou shalt meet us all in Heaven.

5 While we weep as Jesus wept.
Thou shalt sleep as Jesus slept;
With thy Saviour thou shalt rest,
Crowned, and glorified, and blest.
Rev. James Henry Bancroft (1819—1844), 1842.

689 *Citizenship in Heaven.*
Ps. xv.

1 WHO, O Lord, when life is o'er,
Shall to Heaven's blest mansions soar?
Who, an ever-welcome guest,
In Thy holy place shall rest?

2 He whose heart Thy love has warmed;
He, whose will to Thine conformed,
Bids his life unsullied run;
He whose words and thoughts are one;

3 He who shuns the sinner's road,
Loving those who love their God;
Who, with hope and faith unfeigned,
Treads the path by Thee ordained;

4 He who trusts in Christ alone,
Not in aught himself hath done;
He, great God, shall be Thy care,
And Thy choicest blessings share.
Rev. James Merrick (1720—1769), 1765. Alt.

690 *"The Dead in Christ."*

1 THEY whose course on earth is o'er,
Think they of their brethren more?
They before the Throne who bow,
Feel they for their brethren now?

2 Yea, the dead in Christ have still
Part in all our joy and ill;
Keeping all our steps in view,
Guiding them, it may be, too.

3 We, by enemies distrest,
They, in Paradise at rest;
We the captives, they the freed,
We and they are one indeed.

4 One in all we seek or shun;
One, because our Lord is One;
One in heart, and one in love:
We below, and they above.
Rev. John Mason Neale (1818—1866), 1844.

350

MONMOUTH. 8.,, 8.8.7.

Joseph Klug's Gesangbuch, 1535.

THE Lord of might from Si-nai's brow Gave forth His voice of thun - der;
1. *And Is - rael lay on earth be - low, Outstretch'd in fear and won - der;* Be-neath His feet was

pitch-ly night, And at His left hand and His right The rocks were rent a - sun - der.

691

Earth and Heaven shaken.
Heb. xii. 26.

2 The Lord of love, on Calvary,
 A meek and suffering stranger,
Upraised to Heaven His languid eye
 In nature's hour of danger:
For us He bore the weight of woe,
For us He gave His blood to flow,
 And met His Father's anger.

3 The Lord of love, the Lord of might,
 The King of all created,
Shall back return to claim His right,
 On clouds of glory seated ;
With trumpet-sound, and angel-song,
And hallelujahs loud and long,
 O'er death and hell defeated.

Bp. Reginald Heber (1783—1826), 1827.

FORMOSA. 8.7. D.

Sir ARTHUR SULLIVAN (1842—   ), 1872.

1. HE is com-ing, He is com-ing, Not as once He came be - fore, Wail-ing in - fant, born in

weakness On a low - ly sta - ble floor: But up - on His cloud of glo - ry, In the

crim-son-tint - ed sky, Where we see the gold - en sun - rise In the ro - sy dis-tance lie.

692

"He is coming."

2 He is coming, He is coming,
　Not as once He wandered through
All the hostile land of Judah,
　With His followers poor and few:
But with all the holy angels
　Waiting round His Judgment-seat,
And the chosen twelve Apostles
　Sitting crownéd at His feet.

3 He is coming, He is coming:
　Let His lowly first estate,
And His tender love, so teach us
　That in faith and hope we wait,
Till in glory eastward burning,
　Our redemption draweth near;
And we see the sign in Heaven
　Of our Judge and Saviour dear.

Miss Frances Ridley Havergal (1836—1879), 1874. **Ab.**

ADVENT. P. M.

WILLIAM HENRY MONK (1823—

1. Thou art com-ing, O my Saviour, Thou art com-ing, O my King, In Thy beauty all-resplendent, In Thy glo-ry all-transcend-ent; Well may we re-joice and sing; Com-ing! In the op'ning east Her-ald brightness slow-ly swells; Com-ing! O my glo-rious Priest, Hear we not Thy gol-l-en bells?

693

"Thou art coming."

2 Thou art coming, Thou art coming;
　We shall meet Thee on Thy way,
We shall see Thee, we shall know Thee,
We shall bless Thee, we shall show Thee
　All our hearts could never say;
What an anthem that will be,
Bringing out our love to Thee,
Pouring out our rapture sweet
At Thine own all-glorious feet.

3 O the joy to see Thee reigning,
　Thee, my own belovéd Lord!
Every tongue Thy Name confessing,
Worship, honor, glory, blessing,
　Brought to Thee with one accord;
Thee, my Master and my Friend,
Vindicated and enthroned,
Unto earth's remotest end
Glorified, adored, and owned.

Miss Frances Ridley Havergal, 1874. **Ab.**

VIGIL. P. M.   Har. by JACOB PRAETORIUS (1600—1651).

{ WAKE, a - wake, for night is fly - ing, The watchmen on the heights are cry - ing;
{ Mid-night hears the wel-come voi - ces, And at the thrill-ing cry re - joi - ces:

A - wake, Je - ru - sa - lem, at last! }
Come forth, ye vir - gins, night is past! } The Bridegroom comes, a - wake, Your lamps with gladness take;

Hal - le - lu - jah! And for His mar-riage-feast pre - pare, For ye must go to meet Him there.

694   *The final Joy.*

2 Zion hears the watchmen singing,
  And all her heart with joy is springing,
  She wakes, she rises from her gloom;
  For her Lord comes down all-glorious,
  The strong in grace, in truth victorious,
  Her Star is risen, her Light is come!

Ah, come, Thou blessèd One,
  God's own beloved Son;
  Hallelujah!
We follow till the halls we see,
Where Thou hast bid us sup with Thee.

Rev. Philip Nicolai (1556—1608), 1598.
Tr. by Miss Catherine Winkworth (1829—1878), 1858. Ab.

LUX VITAE. L. M.   From the Psalmodia Nova, 1630.

1. LORD Je - sus Christ, my Life, my Light, My strength by day, my trust by night,

On earth I'm but a pass - ing guest, And sore - ly with my sins op - prest.

695   *"Mein Lebenslicht."*

2 O let Thy sufferings give me power
  To meet the last and darkest hour;
  Thy cross the staff whereon I lean,
  My couch the grave where Thou hast been.

3 Since Thou hast died, the Pure, the Just,
  I take my homeward way in trust;

The gates of Heaven, Lord, open wide,
When here I may no more abide.

4 And when the last great day is come,
  And Thou, our Judge, shalt speak the [doom,
  O sit me then upon Thy right,
  Among the angels pure and bright.

Rev. Martin Behemb (1557—1622), 1608.
Tr. by Miss Catherine Winkworth, 1858. Ab. and sl. alt.

CAERSALEM. 8.7,7,7.   Welsh Melody.

1. On the fount of life e - ter - nal Gaz - ing wist - ful and a - thirst;

Yearn - ing, strain - ing, from the pris - on Of con - fin - ing flesh to burst;

Here the soul an ex - ile sighs For her na - tive Par - a - dise.

696   *"Ad perennis Vitae Fontem."*

2 There the saints of God, resplendent
    As the sun in all its might,
  Evermore rejoice together,
    Crowned with diadems of light;
  And from peril safe at last,
  Count up all their triumphs past.

3 Happy they, who with them seated
    Shall in all their glory share!
  O that we, our days completed,
    Might be but admitted there!
  There with them the praise to sing
  Of our glorious God and King.

Peter Damiani (1007—1072),
Tr. by Rev. Edward Caswall (1814—1878), 1858. Ab. and sl. alt.

697   *"Wer sind die vor Gottes Stuhl?"*

1 WHO are these like stars appearing,
    These, before God's throne who stand?

Each a golden crown is wearing,
  Who are all this glorious band?
Alleluia! hark, they sing,
Praising loud their heavenly King.

2 These, like priests have watched and
    Offering up to Christ their will; [waited,
  Soul and body consecrated,
  Day and night they serve Him still:
  Now, in God's most holy place,
  Blest they stand before His face.

3 Lo, the Lamb Himself now feeds them,
    On Mount Zion's pastures fair;
  From His central throne He leads them
    By the living fountain there:
  Lamb and Shepherd, Good Supreme,
  Free He gives the cooling stream.

Rev. Heinrich Theobald Schenk (—1727),
Tr. by Miss Frances Elizabeth Cox ( ), 1841. Ab.

MIDNIGHT CRY. 14.

GEORGE ALEXANDER MACFARREN (1813—), 1872.

1. BE - HOLD, the Bride - groom com - eth in the mid - dle of the night,

And blest is he whose loins are girt, whose lamp is burn - ing bright;

But woe to that dull serv - ant, whom the Mas - ter shall sur - prise

With lamp un - trimm'd, un - burn - ing, and with slum - ber in his eyes.

698

Ἰδοὺ ὁ Νύμφιος ἔρχεται.

2 Do thou, my soul, beware, beware lest thou in sleep sink down,
Lest thou be given o'er to death, and lose the golden crown;
But see that thou be sober, with watchful eye, and thus
Cry, "Holy, holy, holy God, have mercy upon us."

3 That day, the day of fear, shall come; my soul slack not thy toil,
But light thy lamp, and feed it well, and make it bright with oil;
Who knowest not how soon may sound the cry at eventide,
"Behold the Bridegroom comes.   Arise! Go forth to meet the Bride."

4 Beware, my soul, take thou good heed, lest thou in slumber lie,
And, like the five, remain without, and knock, and vainly cry;
But watch, and bear thy lamp undimmed, and Christ shall gird thee on
His own bright wedding-robe of light, the glory of the Son.

Rev. Gerard Moultrie (1839—   ), 1867. Ab.

CUM NUBIBUS. 8.7.4. HENRY SMART (1812-1879), 1868.

1. Lo! He comes, with clouds de-scend-ing, Once for fa-vor'd sin-ners slain;

Thou-sand thou-sand saints at-tend-ing Swell the tri-umph of His train:

Hal-le-lu-jah! hal-le-lu-jah! God ap-pears, on earth to reign.

699
Christ's Second Coming.

2 Every eye shall now behold Him,
   Robed in dreadful majesty;
Those who set at naught and sold Him,
   Pierced and nailed Him to the tree,
      Deeply wailing,
   Shall the true Messiah see.

3 Now redemption, long expected,
   See in solemn pomp appear:
All His saints, by men rejected,
   Now shall meet Him in the air:
      Hallelujah!
   See the day of God appear.

4 Yea, amen: let all adore Thee,
   High on Thine eternal throne:
Saviour, take the power and glory;
   Claim the kingdom for Thine own:
      O come quickly,
   Hallelujah! come, Lord, come.
      Rev. Charles Wesley (1708—1788), 1758. V. 1, 2, 4.
      Rev. John Cennick (1717—1755), 1752. V. 3.
      Rev. Martin Madan (1726—1790), 1760. Ab.

700
      "Surely I come quickly."
      REV. xxii. 20.

1 O'ER the distant mountains breaking,
   Comes the reddening dawn of day;

Rise, my soul, from sleep awaking,
   Rise, and sing, and watch, and pray:
      'Tis thy Saviour,
   On His bright, returning way.

2 O Thou long-expected, weary
   Waits my anxious soul for Thee;
Life is dark, and earth is dreary
   Where Thy light I do not see:
      O my Saviour,
   When wilt Thou return to me?

3 Nearer is my soul's salvation,
   Spent the night, the day at hand;
Keep me in my lowly station,
   Watching for Thee, till I stand,
      O my Saviour,
   In Thy bright and promised land.

4 With my lamp well-trimmed and burning,
   Swift to hear, and slow to roam,
Watching for Thy glad returning
   To restore me to my home,
      Come, my Saviour,
   O my Saviour, quickly come.
      Rev. John Samuel Bewley Monsell (1811—1875), 1863. Ab.

ST. CROSS. L. M.

Rev. JOHN BACCHUS DYKES (1823—1876), 1860.

1. THAT day of wrath, that dread-ful day, When heav'n and earth shall pass a - way,

What pow'r shall be the sin - ner's stay? How shall he meet that dread - ful day?

701 *"Dies iræ, dies illa."*

2 When, shrivelling like a parchéd scroll,
The flaming heavens together roll;
When louder yet, and yet more dread,
Swells the high trump that wakes the dead;

3 O on that day, that wrathful day,
When man to judgment wakes from clay,
Be Thou the trembling sinner's stay,
Though heaven and earth shall pass away.

Thomas of Celano, c. 1250.
Sir Walter Scott (1771—1832), 1805.

MERIBAH. C. P. M.

LOWELL MASON (1792—1872), 1839.

1. O GOD, mine in - most soul con - vert, And deep - ly on my thoughtful heart E-

- ter - nal things im - press; { Give me to feel their solemn weight, And wake to right-eous - ness.
{ And trem- ble on the brink of fate,

702 *Death and Judgment anticipated.*

2 Before me place, in dread array,
The pomp of that tremendous day,
When Thou with clouds shalt come
To judge the nations at Thy bar;
And tell me, Lord, shall I be there
To meet a joyful doom?

3 Be this my one great business here,
With holy trembling, holy fear,
To make my calling sure,

Thine utmost counsel to fulfil,
And suffer all Thy righteous will,
And to the end endure.

4 Then, Saviour, then my soul receive,
Transported from this vale to live,
And reign with Thee above,
Where faith is sweetly lost in sight,
And hope in full, supreme delight,
And everlasting love.

Rev. Charles Wesley (1708—1788), 1749. Ab. and alt. v. 3.

RHINE. C. M. 5l.   Arr. from FRIEDRICH BURGMÜLLER (1804—   ). c. 1840.

1. JE - RU - SA-LEM, my hap - py home, Name ev - er dear to me, When shall my la - bors have an end In joy, and peace, and thee? In joy, and peace, and thee?

703   *"Jerusalem, my happy Home."*

2 When shall these eyes thy heaven-built
  And pearly gates behold;   [walls
  Thy bulwarks with salvation strong,
  And streets of shining gold?

3 O when, thou city of my God,
  Shall I Thy courts ascend,
  Where congregations ne'er break up,
  And Sabbaths have no end?

4 There happier bowers than Eden's bloom,
  Nor sin nor sorrow know: [scenes
  Blest seats, through rude and stormy
  I onward press to you.

5 Apostles, martyrs, prophets, there,
  Around my Saviour stand;
  And soon my friends in Christ, below,
  Will join the glorious band.

6 Jerusalem, my happy home,
  My soul still pants for thee;
  Then shall my labors have an end,
  When I thy joys shall see.
    Unknown. Williams and Boden's Collection, 1801. Ab.

704   *"O Mother dear, Jerusalem."*

1 O MOTHER dear, Jerusalem,
  When shall I come to thee?
  When shall my sorrows have an end?
  Thy joys when shall I see?

2 O happy harbor of God's saints,
  O sweet and pleasant soil;
  In thee no sorrow can be found,
  Nor grief, nor care, nor toil.

3 No dimming cloud o'ershadows thee,
  Nor gloom, nor darksome night;
  But every soul shines as the sun,
  For God Himself gives light.

4 Thy walls are made of precious stone,
  Thy bulwarks diamond-square,
  Thy gates are all of orient pearl:
  O God, if I were there !

5 Right through thy streets with pleasing
  The flood of life doth flow,   [sound
  And on the banks, on either side,
  The trees of life do grow.

6 Those trees each month yield ripened fruit;
  For evermore they spring,
  And all the nations of the earth
  To thee their honors bring.

7 O mother dear, Jerusalem,
  When shall I come to thee?
  When shall my sorrows have an end?
  Thy joys when shall I see?
    Rev. Francis Baker (   ), 1616. Alt.
    Rev. David Dickson (1583—1663), 1649. Ab.

POSEN. 7. GEORG CHRISTOPH STRATTNER (1650—1705), 1691.

1. Zi - on, at thy shin-ing gates, Lo, the King of glo-ry waits;

Haste thy Mon-arch's pomp to greet, Strew thy palms be - fore His feet.

705 *"Peace within."*

2 Christ, for Thee their triple light,
Faith, and hope, and love unite;
This the beacon we display,
To proclaim Thine advent day.

3 Come, and give us peace within;
Loose us from the bonds of sin;

Give us grace Thy yoke to wear;
Give us strength Thy cross to bear.

4 So, when Thou shalt come again,
Judge of angels and of men,
We, with all Thy saints, shall sing
Hallelujahs to our King.

Rev. Benjamin Hall Kennedy (1804—), 1863. Ab.

ALFORD. 7. 6. 8. 6. D. Rev. JOHN BACCHUS DYKES (1823—1876), 1875.

1. Ten thou-sand times ten thou-sand In spark-ling rai - ment bright, The ar - mies of the

ran-som'd saints Throng up the steeps of light: 'Tis fin - ish'd, all is fin - ish'd, Their

fight with death and sin: Fling o - pen wide the gold - en gates, And let the vic - tors in.

706 *The Saints marching up.*

2 What rush of hallelujahs
  Fills all the earth and sky;
  What ringing of a thousand harps
  Bespeaks the triumph nigh.
  O day, for which creation
  And all its tribes were made;
  O joy, for all its former woes
  A thousand fold repaid.

3 O then what raptured greetings
  On Canaan's happy shore;
  What knitting severed friendships up,
  Where partings are no more.
  Then eyes with joy shall sparkle,
  That brimmed with tears of late:
  Orphans no longer fatherless,
  Nor widows desolate.

  Rev. Henry Alford (1810—1871), 1866.

BEULAH. 7. D.   Irish Melody. Arr. by ELAM IVES, Jr. (1802—1864), 1846.

1. PALMS of glo-ry, raiment bright, Crowns that nev-er fade a-way, Gird and deck the saints in light,
D.S.—And proclaim, in joy-ful psalms,

Priests, and kings, and conqu'rors they. Yet the conqu'rors bring their palms To the Lamb a-midst the throne,
Vic-t'ry through His cross a-lone.

707 *Heaven in Prospect.*
Rev. vii. 9.

2 Kings for harps their crowns resign,
  Crying, as they strike the chords,
  "Take the kingdom, it is Thine,
  King of kings, and Lord of lords."
  Round the altar, priests confess,
  If their robes are white as snow,
  'Twas the Saviour's righteousness,
  And His blood, that made them so.

3 Who were these?—On earth they dwelt,
  Sinners once of Adam's race,
  Guilt, and fear, and suffering felt,
  But were saved by sovereign grace.
  They were mortal, too, like us:
  Ah, when we, like them, shall die,
  May our souls, translated thus,
  Triumph, reign, and shine on high.

  James Montgomery (1771—1854), 1829.

708 *The Song of the Ransomed.*
Rev. v. 13.

1 SEE the ransomed millions stand,
  Palms of conquest in their hand;
  This before the throne their strain,
  "Hell is vanquished, death is slain;
  Blessing, honor, glory, might,
  Are the Conqueror's native right;
  Thrones and powers before Him fall,
  Lamb of God, and Lord of all!"

2 Hasten, Lord, the promised hour;
  Come in glory and in power;
  Still Thy foes are unsubdued;
  Nature sighs to be renewed.
  Time has nearly reached its sum;
  All things, with Thy Bride, say "Come;"
  Jesus, whom all worlds adore,
  Come, and reign for evermore.

  Josiah Conder (1789—1855), 1836.

SAFE HOME. H. M.

Sir ARTHUR SULLIVAN (1842—), 1872.

1. Safe home, safe home in port! Rent cord-age, shatter'd deck, Torn sails, pro-vis-ions short, And on-ly not a wreck: But, O! the joy up-on the shore To tell our voy-age-per-ils o'er!

709   *"Safe Home."*

2 No more the foe can harm :
  No more of leaguered camp,
And cry of night-alarm,
  And need of ready lamp:
And yet how nearly had he failed,
How nearly had that foe prevailed !

3 The lamb is in the fold
  In perfect safety penned :
The lion once had hold,
  And thought to make an end ;
But One came by with wounded side,
And for the sheep the Shepherd died.

Joseph of the Studium (—883),
Rev. John Mason Neale (1818—1866), 1862. Ab.

TAPPAN. C. M. 51.

GEORGE KINGSLEY (1811—1884), 1838.

1. There is a land of pure de-light, Where saints im-mor-tal reign; In-fi-nite day ex-cludes the night, In-fi-nite day excludes the night, And pleasures ban-ish pain.

710   *"Sweet Fields."*

2 There, everlasting spring abides,
  And never-withering flowers:
Death, like a narrow sea, divides
  This heavenly land from ours.

3 Sweet fields, beyond the swelling flood,
  Stand dressed in living green :

So to the Jews old Canaan stood,
  While Jordan rolled between.

4 But timorous mortals start and shrink
  To cross this narrow sea,
And linger, shivering on the brink,
  And fear to launch away.

5 O could we make our doubts remove,
   Those gloomy doubts that rise,
And see the Canaan that we love
   With unbeclouded eyes:

6 Could we but climb where Moses stood,
   And view the landscape o'er, {flood,
Not Jordan's stream, nor death's cold
   Should fright us from the shore.
                 Rev. Isaac Watts (1674—1748), 1709.

711   *The Heavenly Rest.*   C. M. 5 l.

1 THERE is an hour of peaceful rest
   To mourning wanderers given:
There is a joy for souls distressed,
   A balm for every wounded breast:
'Tis found above, in Heaven.

2 There is a home for weary souls
   By sin and sorrow driven;
When tossed on life's tempestuous shoals,
   Where storms arise, and ocean rolls,
And all is drear but Heaven.

3 There, faith lifts up her cheerful eye,
   To brighter propects given;
And views the tempest passing by,
The evening shadows quickly fly,
   And all serene in Heaven.

4 There, fragrant flowers, immortal, bloom,
   And joys supreme are given;
There, rays divine disperse the gloom:
Beyond the confines of the tomb
   Appears the dawn of Heaven.
         Rev. William Bingham Tappan (1794—1849), 1822, 1846. Ab.

LEYDEN. 7. D.
LUDWIG SPOHR (1784—1859).
Arr. by SAMUEL SEBASTIAN WESLEY (1810—1876.).

1. WHAT are these in bright ar - ray, This in - nu - mer - a - ble throng, Round the al - tar,
night and day, Hymn - ing one tri - umph ant song? "Wor - thy is the Lamb, once slain,
Bless - ing, hon - or, glo - ry, pow'r; Wisdom, rich - es, to ob - tain, New do - min - ion ev - 'ry hour."

712   *The Song of the Sealed.*
           Rev. vii. 9—16.

2 These through fiery trials trod;
   These from great afflictions came;
Now, before the throne of God,
   Sealed with His almighty Name;
Clad in raiment pure and white,
   Victor-palms in every hand,
Through their dear Redeemer's might,
   More than conquerors they stand.

3 Hunger, thirst, disease, unknown,
   On immortal fruits they feed;
Them the Lamb amidst the throne,
   Shall to living fountains lead;
Joy and gladness banish sighs,
   Perfect love dispels all fear,
And forever from their eyes
   God shall wipe away the tear.
         James Montgomery (1771—1854), 1819, 1853.

LEONI. 6.6.8.4.D.   Hebrew Melody.

1. The good-ly land I see, With peace and plen-ty blest; A land of sa-cred lib-er-ty, And end-less rest: There milk and hon-ey flow, And oil and wine a-bound, And trees of life for-ev-er grow With mer-cy crown'd.

713   *"The goodly land."*

2 There dwells the Lord, our King,
 The Lord, our Righteousness:
Triumphant o'er the world and sin,
 The Prince of Peace,
On Zion's sacred height,
 His kingdom still maintains,
And glorious, with His saints in light,
 For ever reigns.

3 Before the Saviour's face
 The ransomed nations bow,
O'erwhelmed at His almighty grace,
 For ever new:
He shows His prints of love:
 They kindle to a flame,
And sound, through all the worlds above,
 "The slaughtered Lamb!"

4 The whole triumphant host
 Give thanks to God on high;
"Hail, Father, Son, and Holy Ghost,"
 They ever cry.
Hail, Abr'am's God and mine!
 I join the heavenly lays)
All might and majesty are Thine,
 And endless praise.

Rev. Thomas Olivers (1725—1799), 1770. Ab.

714   *The God of Abr'am praised.*
    Ex. iii. 6. Ps. cxlvi. 2.

1 The God of Abr'am praise,
 Who reigns enthroned above;
Ancient of everlasting days,
 And God of love:
Jehovah, Great I Am!
 By earth and Heaven confest:
I bow and bless the sacred Name,
 For ever blest.

2 The God of Abr'am praise,
 At whose supreme command
From earth I rise, and seek the joys
 At His right hand:
I all on earth forsake,
 Its wisdom, fame, and power;
And Him my only portion make,
 My Shield and Tower.

3 He by Himself hath sworn,
 I on His oath depend;
I shall on eagles' wings upborne
 To Heaven ascend;
I shall behold His face,
 I shall His power adore,
And sing the wonders of His grace
 For evermore.

Rev. Thomas Olivers, 1770. Ab.

ETON. 8.7.D.   JOSEPH BARNBY (185–). 1466.

1. HARK, the sound of ho-ly voi-ces, Chant-ing at the crys-tal sea, Hal-le-lu-jah,

hal-le-lu-jah, Hal-le-lu-jah! Lord, to Thee. Mul-ti-tude, which none can num-ber,

Like the stars in glo-ry stand, Cloth'd in white ap-par-el, hold-ing Palms of vic-t'ry in their hand.

715 *The Multitude before the Throne.*
        REV iv. 6; vii. 9.

2 They have come from tribulation,
    And have washed their robes in blood,
Washed them in the blood of Jesus:
    Tried they were, and firm they stood.
Gladly, Lord, with Thee they suffered,
Gladly, Lord, with Thee they died;
And by death to life immortal
    They were born, and glorified.

3 Now they reign in heavenly glory,
    Now they walk in golden light,
Now they drink, as from a river,
    Holy bliss and infinite.
Love and peace they taste forever,
    And all truth and knowledge see
In the beatific vision
    Of the Blessed Trinity.

Bp. Christopher Wordsworth (1807–1885), 1863. Ab.

OLIVERS. 6.6.8.4.D.   JOHN STAINER (1840–).

364

PEARSALL. 7. 6. D.

Katholisches Gesangbuch. 1868.

1. THE world is ver-y e-vil, The times are wax-ing late; Be so-ber and keep vig-il, The Judge is at the gate; The Judge that comes in mer-cy, The Judge that comes with might, To term-in-ate the e-vil, To di-a-dem the right.

716 *"Hora novissima."*

2 Arise, arise, good Christian,
  Let right to wrong succeed ;
Let penitential sorrow
  To heavenly gladness lead ;
To light that hath no evening,
  That knows no moon nor sun,
The light so new and golden,
  The light that is but one.

3 O Home of fadeless splendor,
  Of flowers that fear no thorn,
Where they shall dwell as children
  Who here as exiles mourn.
'Midst power that knows no limit,
  Where wisdom has no bound,
The beatific vision
  Shall glad the saints around.

Bernard of Cluny, c. 1145.
Tr. by Rev. John Mason Neale (1818—1866), 1858. Ab. and sl. alt.

717 *"O bona Patria."*

1 FOR thee, O dear, dear country,
  Mine eyes their vigils keep ;
For very love, beholding
  Thy happy name, they weep.
The mention of thy glory
  Is unction to the breast,
And medicine in sickness,
  And love, and life, and rest.

2 O one, O only mansion,
  O paradise of joy,
Where tears are ever banished,
  And smiles have no alloy ;
The Lamb is all thy splendor,
  The Crucified thy praise ;
His laud and benediction
  Thy ransomed people raise.

3 With jasper glow thy bulwarks,
  Thy streets with emerald blaze ;
The sardius and the topaz
  Unite in thee their rays ;
Thine ageless walls are bonded
  With amethyst unpriced ;
The saints built up its fabric,
  And the Corner-stone is Christ.

4 Thou hast no shore, fair ocean ;
  Thou hast no time, bright day :
Dear fountain of refreshment
  To pilgrims far away.
Upon the Rock of Ages
  They raise thy holy tower ;
Thine is the victor's laurel,
  And thine the golden dower.

Bernard of Cluny, c. 1145.
Tr. by Rev. John Mason Neale, 1851. Alt.

EWING. 7.6.D.   ALEXANDER EWING (1830—   ), 1853.

1. JE - RU - SA - LEM, the gold - en, With milk and hon - ey blest, Be - neath thy con - tem - pla - tion Sink heart and voice op - prest: I know not, O I know not, What so - cial joys are there; What ra - dian - cy of glo - ry, What light be - yond com - pare.

718   *"Urbs Syon aurea."*

2 They stand, those halls of Zion,
   All jubilant with song,
And bright with many an angel,
   And all the martyr throng:
The Prince is ever in them,
   The daylight is serene;
The pastures of the blessed
   Are decked in glorious sheen.

3 There is the throne of David;
   And there, from care released,
The shout of them that triumph,
   The song of them that feast:
And they who, with their Leader,
   Have conquered in the fight,
Forever, and forever,
   Are clad in robes of white.

Bernard of Cluny, c. 1145
Tr. by Rev. John Mason Neale, 1751. Alt.

719   *"Hic breve vivitur."*

1 BRIEF life is here our portion;
   Brief sorrow, short-lived care;
The life that knows no ending,
   The tearless life, is there.
O happy retribution:
   Short toil, eternal rest;
For mortals and for sinners
   A mansion with the blest.

2 And now we fight the battle,
   But then shall wear the crown
Of full and everlasting
   And passionless renown.
But He whom now we trust in
   Shall then be seen and known;
And they that know and see Him
   Shall have Him for their own.

3 The morning shall awaken,
   The shadows shall decay,
And each true-hearted servant
   Shall shine as doth the day.
There God our King and Portion,
   In fulness of His grace,
Shall we behold forever,
   And worship face to face.

Bernard of Cluny, c. 1145
Tr. by Rev. John Mason Neale, 1851. Alt.

720 *General Ending of the four preceding Hymns.*

1 O SWEET and blessed country,
   The home of God's elect,
O sweet and blessed country
   That eager hearts expect:
Jesus, in mercy bring us
   To that dear land of rest;
Who art with God the Father,
   And Spirit, ever blest.

Bernard of Cluny, c. 1145.
Tr. by Rev. John Mason Neale, 1851.

BLESSED HOME. 6. D.

JOHN STAINER (1840—), 1872.

1. THERE is a bless-ed home Be-yond this land of woe, Where tri-als nev-er come, Nor tears of sor-row flow; Where faith is lost in sight, And pa-tient hope is crown'd, And ev-er-last-ing light Its glo-ry throws a-round.

721

The Rest that remaineth.

2 There is a land of peace,
　Good angels know it well;
Glad songs that never cease
　Within its portals swell;
Around its glorious throne
　Ten thousand saints adore
Christ, with the Father One
　And Spirit, evermore.

3 O joy all joys beyond,
　To see the Lamb who died,
And count each sacred wound
　In hands, and feet, and side;

To give to Him the praise
　Of every triumph won,
And sing, through endless days,
　The great things He hath done.

4 Look up, ye saints of God,
　Nor fear to tread below
The path your Saviour trod
　Of daily toil and woe;
Wait but a little while
　In uncomplaining love,
His own most gracious smile
　Shall welcome you above.

Rev. Sir Henry Williams Baker (1821—1877), 1861.

PARADISE. P. M.

JOSEPH BARNBY (1838—), 1866.

1. O PAR-A-DISE! O Par-a-dise! Who doth not crave for rest? Who would not seek the

Where loy - al hearts and true

CHORUS.

hap - py land Where they that lov'd are blest? Where loy - - - al hearts and true

Stand ev - er in the light, All rapt - ure through and through, In God's most ho - ly sight?

722 *Paradise.*

2 O Paradise! O Paradise!
  The world is growing old;
  Who would not be at rest and free
  Where love is never cold?—CHO.

3 O Paradise! O Paradise!
  'Tis weary waiting here;
  I long to be where Jesus is,
  To feel, to see Him near;—CHO.

4 O Paradise! O Paradise!
  I want to sin no more,

I want to be as pure on earth
  As on Thy spotless shore;—CHO.

5 O Paradise! O Paradise!
  I greatly long to see
  The special place my dearest Lord
  In love prepares for me;—CHO.

6 Lord Jesus, King of Paradise,
  O keep me in Thy love,
  And guide me to that happy land
  Of perfect rest above;—CHO.

Rev. Frederick William Faber (1814—1863), 1854. Ab. and alt.

PARADISE. P. M.

Rev. JOHN BACCHUS DYKES (1823—1876), 1861.

1. O Par - a - dise! O Par - a - dise! Who doth not crave for rest? Who would not seek the

CHORUS.

hap - py land Where they that lov'd are blest? Where loy - al hearts and true Stand

Where loy - al hearts .... and true

ev - er in the light, All rapt - ure through and through, In God's most ho - ly sight?

NELSON. 7.6.D. HENRY JOHN GAUNTLETT (1805—1876), 1872.

1. From all Thy saints in war-fare, For all Thy saints at rest, To Thee, O bless-ed Je-sus, All prais-es be ad-dress'd: Thou, Lord, didst win the bat-tle That they might conqu'rors be; Their crowns of liv-ing glo-ry Are lit with rays from Thee.

723 *"Saints of the most High."*

2 Apostles, prophets, martyrs,
  And all the sacred throng,
Who wear the spotless raiment,
  Who raise the ceaseless song;
For these passed on before us,
  Saviour, we Thee adore,
And walking in their footsteps,
  Would serve Thee more and more.

3 Then praise we God the Father,
  And praise we God the Son,
And God the Holy Spirit,
  Eternal Three in One;
Till all the ransomed number
  Fall down before the throne,
And honor, power, and glory
  Ascribe to God alone.

Earl Horatios Nelson (1823—), 1867. Ab.

GERMANY. L. M. LUDWIG von BEETHOVEN (1770—1827).

1. E-ter-nal Source of ev-'ry joy, Well may Thy praise our lips em-ploy, While in Thy tem-ple we ap-pear, Whose good-ness crowns the cir-cling year.

724 *For New Year's Day.*
Ps. lxv. 11.

2 Wide as the wheels of nature roll,
Thy hand supports and guides the whole;
The sun is taught by Thee to rise,
And darkness when to veil the skies.

3 The flowery spring, at Thy command,
Perfumes the air and paints the land;
The summer rays with vigor shine,
To raise the corn and cheer the vine.

4 Thy hand in autumn richly pours
Through all our coasts redundant stores;
And winters, softened by Thy care,
No more a face of horror wear.

5 Seasons, and months, and weeks, and days,
Demand successive songs of praise;
And be the grateful homage paid,
With morning light and evening shade.

6 Here in Thy house let incense rise,
And circling Sabbaths bless our eyes;

Till to those lofty heights we soar,
Where days and years revolve no more.
Rev. Philip Doddridge (1702–1851), 1755. Ab. and alt.

725 *Help obtained of God.*
Acts xxvi. 22. **L. M.**

1 GREAT God, we sing that mighty hand
By which supported still we stand:
The opening year Thy mercy shows;
Let mercy crown it till it close.

2 By day, by night, at home, abroad,
Still we are guided by our God;
By His incessant bounty fed,
By His unerring counsel led.

3 With grateful hearts the past we own;
The future, all to us unknown,
We to Thy guardian care commit,
And peaceful leave before Thy feet.

4 In scenes exalted or deprest,
Be Thou our joy, and Thou our rest;
Thy goodness all our hopes shall raise,
Adored through all our changing days.
Rev. Philip Doddridge, 1755. Ab. and alt.

DORT. 6.6.4.6.6.6.4.   LOWELL MASON (1792–1872), 1832.

1. THE God of harvest praise, In loud thanksgivings raise Hand, heart, and voice; The valleys laugh and sing, Forests and mountains ring, The plains their tribute bring, The streams rejoice.

726 *Thanksgiving for Harvest.*

2 Yea, bless His holy Name,
And joyous thanks proclaim
Through all the earth;
To glory in your lot
Is comely; but be not
God's benefits forgot
Amidst your mirth.

3 The God of harvest praise;
Hands, hearts, and voices raise
With one accord;
From field to garner throng,
Bearing your sheaves along,
And in your harvest song
Bless ye the Lord.
James Montgomery (1771–1854), 1822. Ab. and alt.

BENEVENTO. 7. D.

SAMUEL WEBBE (1740—1816), c. 1770.

1. WHILE with cease-less course the sun
Hast-ed through the for-mer year,
Ma-ny souls their
D.S.—They have done with all be-low;
We a lit-tle

race have run, Nev-er-more to meet us here: Fix'd in an e-ter-nal state,
lon-ger wait, But how lit-tle, none can know.

727 *The New Year.*

2 As the wingéd arrow flies
Speedily the mark to find ;
As the lightning from the skies
Darts and leaves no trace behind ;
Swiftly thus our fleeting days
Bear us down life's rapid stream :
Upward, Lord, our spirits raise,
All below is but a dream.

3 Thanks for mercies past receive ;
Pardon of our sins renew :
Teach us henceforth how to live
With eternity in view :
Bless Thy word to young and old ;
Fill us with a Saviour's love ;
And when life's short tale is told,
May we dwell with Thee above.
Rev. John Newton (1725—1807), 1779.

CULFORD. 7. D.

EDWARD JOHN HOPKINS (1818—).

1. FOR Thy mer-cy and Thy grace, Faith-ful through an-oth-er year, Hear our songs of

thank-ful-ness, Fa-ther and Re-deem-er, hear. In our weak-ness and dis-tress,

Rock of strength, be Thou our Stay; In the path-less wild-er-ness Be our true and liv-ing Way.

728 *For New Year's Eve.*

2 Who of us death's awful road
In the coming year shall tread?
With Thy rod and staff, O God,
Comfort Thou his dying bed.
Keep us faithful, keep us pure,
Keep us evermore Thine own;
Help Thy servants to endure,
Fit us for the promised crown.

Rev. Henry Downton (1818—), 1839. Ab.

COME, LET US ANEW. 5. 5. 5. 12. D.

Samuel Webbe, c. 1770.

1. COME, let us a-new Our jour-ney pur-sue, Roll round with the year, And nev-er stand still till the Mas-ter ap-pear. His a-dor-a-ble will Let us glad-ly ful-fil, And our tal-ents im-prove { By the patience of hope, and the la-bor of love, } love. { By the patience of hope, and the la-bor of........ }

729 *New Year's Day.*

2 Our life is a dream,
Our time, as a stream,
Glides swiftly away,
And the fugitive moment refuses to stay.
The arrow is flown,
The moment is gone,
The millennial year
Rushes on to our view, and eternity's
here.

3 O that each in the day
Of His coming might say,
"I have fought my way through,
"I have finished the work Thou didst give
me to do."
O that each from his Lord
May receive the glad word,
"Well and faithfully done,
"Enter into My joy, and sit down on My
throne."

Rev. Charles Wesley (1708—1788), 1750.

372

ST. SYLVESTER. P. M.

Rev. JOHN BACCHUS DYKES (1823—1876), 1860.

1. { Days and moments quickly fly - ing Speed us onward to the dead; O how soon shall we be
{ Je - sus, mer - ci - ful Re - deem - er, Rouse dead souls to hear Thy voice; Wake, O wake each i - dle

REFRAIN.

ly - ing Each with-in his nar-row bed! } Life passeth soon; death draweth near: Keep us, good Lord,
dreamer Now to make th'eternal choice. }

till Thou ap-pear: With Thee to live, with Thee to die, With Thee to reign through eter - - ni - ty.

730 *"Life passeth soon."*

2 As a shadow life is fleeting;
  As a vapor so it flies;
For the old year now retreating
  Pardon grant and make us wise:

Soon before the Judge all-glorious
  We with all the dead shall stand;
Saviour over death victorious,
  Place us then on Thy right hand.—REF.

Rev. Edward Caswall (1814—1878), 1849. Ab.

COLUMBA. 7.

JOHN BAPTISTE CALKIN, (1827—), 1872.

1. PRAISE to God, im - mor - tal praise, For the love that crowns our days!

Boun - teous Source of ev - 'ry joy, Let Thy praise our tongues em - ploy.

731 *Thanksgiving.*
Ps. lxv.

2 For the blessings of the field,
  For the stores the gardens yield;
For the fruits in full supply,
  Ripened 'neath the summer sky;

3 Flocks that whiten all the plain;
  Yellow sheaves of ripened grain;
Clouds that drop their fattening dews;
  Suns that temperate warmth diffuse;

4 All that spring with bounteous hand
Scatters o'er the smiling land;
All that liberal autumn pours
From her rich o'erflowing stores:

5 These to Thee, my God, we owe,
Source whence all our blessings flow;
And for these my soul shall raise
Grateful vows and solemn praise.

Mrs. Anna Lætitia Barbauld (1743—1825), 1773. Ab. and alt.

ELLACOMBE. C. M. D.

St. Gall.

1. WITH songs and hon-ors sound-ing loud, Ad-dress the Lord on high: O-ver the heav'ns He spreads His cloud, And wa-ters veil the sky. He sends His show'rs of bless-ings down, To cheer the plains be-low; He makes the grass the mountains crown, And corn in val-leys grow.

---

732   *The revolving Seasons.*
Ps. cxlvii.

2 His steady counsels change the face
Of the declining year;
He bids the sun cut short his race,
And wintry days appear.
His hoary frost, His fleecy snow,
Descend and clothe the ground;
The liquid streams forbear to flow,
In icy fetters bound.

3 He sends His word and melts the snow,
The fields no longer mourn;
He calls the warmer gales to blow,
And bids the spring return.
The changing wind, the flying cloud,
Obey His mighty word:
With songs and honors, sounding loud,
Praise ye the sovereign Lord.

Rev. Isaac Watts (1674—1748), 1719. Ab.

---

733   *"The Voice of Praise."*
Ps. lxvi.

1 LIFT up to God the voice of praise,
Whose breath our souls inspired;
Loud, and more loud, the anthem raise,
With grateful ardor fired.
Lift up to God the voice of praise,
Whose goodness, passing thought,
Loads every moment, as it flies,
With benefits unsought.

2 Lift up to God the voice of praise,
From whom salvation flows;
Who sent His Son our souls to save
From everlasting woes.
Lift up to God the voice of praise,
For hope's transporting ray,   [death,
Which lights, through darkest shades of
To realms of endless day.

Rev. Ralph Wardlaw (1779—1853), 1803. Ab.

CAMBRIDGE. C. M.   JOHN RANDALL (1715—1799), 1790.

1. O Lord, our fa - thers oft have told, In our at - tent - ive ears, Thy wonders in their

days perform'd, And eld - er times than theirs, And eld - er times than theirs And eld - er times than theirs.

734   *God's Dealings with our Fathers.*
Ps. xliv.

2 For not their courage, not their sword,
    To them salvation gave;
Nor strength that from unequal force
    Their fainting troops could save.

3 But Thy right hand and powerful arm,
    Whose succor they implored;
Thy presence with the chosen race,
    Who Thy great Name adored.

4 As Thee their God our fathers owned,
    Thou art our sovereign King:
O therefore, as Thou didst to them,
    To us deliverance bring.

5 To Thee the triumph we ascribe,
    From whom the conquest came;
In God we will rejoice all day,
    And ever bless Thy Name.

              Tate and Brady, 1696. Ab. and alt.

ST. MARTIN'S. C. M.   WILLIAM TANS'UR (1699—1774), 1735.

1. Let chil - dren hear the might - y deeds, Which God per - formed of old;

Which in our young - er years we saw, And which our fa - thers told.

735   *The Story handed down.*
Ps. lxxviii.

2 He bids us make His glories known,
    His works of power and grace;
And we'll convey His wonders down
    Through every rising race.

3 Our lips shall tell them to our sons,
    And they again to theirs,

That generations yet unborn
    May teach them to their heirs.

4 Thus shall they learn, in God alone
    Their hope securely stands;
That they may ne'er forget His works,
    But practise His commands.

              Rev. Isaac Watts (1674—1748), 1719.

ALEXIS. 11. 10. 11. 9.

ALEXIS THEODORE LWOFF (1799—1870), 1833.

1. God, the All-Ter - ri - ble, King who or - dain - est Thun-der Thy clar - ion, and lightning Thy sword;

Show forth Thy pit - y on high where Thou reignest; Give to us peace in our time, O Lord.

736 *Prayer for Peace.*

2 God, the Omnipotent, Mighty Avenger,
Watching invisible, judging unheard;
Save us in mercy, O save us from danger;
Give to us peace in our time, O Lord.

3 God the All-Merciful, earth hath forsaken
Thy ways all holy, and slighted Thy
word.

Let not Thy wrath in its terror awaken;
Give to us pardon and peace, O Lord.

4 So will Thy people, with thankful de-
votion,
Praise Him who saved them from peril [and sword,
Shouting in chorus, from ocean to ocean,
Peace to the nations, and praise to the
Lord.

Henry Fothergill Chorley (1808—1872).

LINCOLN. 8. 8. 8. 6.

JOHN KNOWLES PAINE (1839—), 1873.

1. From foes that would the land de - vour; From guilt - y pride, and lust of pow'r;

From wild se - di - tion's law - less hour; From yoke of slav - er - y;

737 *Prayer for Protection.*

2 From blinded zeal, by faction led;
From giddy change, by fancy bred;
From poisoned error's serpent head,
Good Lord, preserve us free.

3 Defend, O God, with guardian hand,
The laws and rulers of our land,

And grant Thy churches grace to stand
In faith and unity.

4 Thy Spirit's help of Thee we crave,
That Thy Messiah, sent to save,
Returning to the world, might have
A people serving Thee.

Bp. Reginald Heber (1783—1826), 1827. Alt.

376

WITTEMBERG. 6, 7, 6.

JOHANN CRÜGER (1598—1662), 1649.

1. { Now thank we all our God, With heart, and hands, and voic - es, }
   { Who wondrous things hath done, In whom this world re - joic - es; } Who from our mother's

arms Hath bless'd us on our way With count-less gifts of love, And still is ours to-day

738

"Nun danket alle Gott."

2 O may this bounteous God
    Through all our life be near us,
With ever joyful hearts
    And blessed peace to cheer us;
And keep us in His grace,
    And guide us when perplext,
And free us from all ills
    In this world and the next.

Rev. Martin Rinkart (1586—1649), 1644.
Tr. by Miss Catherine Winkworth (1829—1878), 1858. Ab.

739

"Herr Gott, wir danken Dir."

1 LORD God, we worship Thee:
    In loud and happy chorus
We praise Thy love and power,
    Whose goodness reigneth o'er us.
To heaven our song shall soar,
    For ever shall it be

Resounding o'er and o'er,
    Lord God, we worship Thee.

2 Lord God, we worship Thee:
    For Thou our land defendest;
Thou pourest down Thy grace,
    And strife and war Thou endest.
Since golden peace, O Lord,
    Thou grantest us to see,
Our land with one accord,
    Lord God, gives thanks to Thee.

3 Lord God, we worship Thee:
    Thou didst indeed chastise us,
Yet still Thy anger spares,
    And still Thy mercy tries us.
Once more our Father's hand
    Doth bid our sorrows flee,
And peace rejoice our land;
    Lord God, we worship Thee.

Johann Frank (1618—1677), 1653.
Tr. by Miss Catherine Winkworth, 1852. Ab.

OLD HUNDREDTH. L. M.

LOUIS BOURGEOIS, 1531.

1. O GOD, be - neath Thy guid - ing hand, Our ex - iled fa - thers cross'd the sea;

And when they trod the win - try strand, With pray'r and psalm they worshipp'd Thee.

740 *Forefathers' Day.*

2 Thou heard'st, well pleased, the song, the prayer:
Thy blessing came, and still its power
Shall onward through all ages bear
The memory of that holy hour.

3 Laws, freedom, truth, and faith in God
Came with those exiles o'er the waves;
And where their pilgrim feet have trod,
The God they trusted guards their graves.

4 And here Thy Name, O God of love,
Their children's children shall adore,
Till these eternal hills remove,
And spring adorns the earth no more.

Rev. Leonard Bacon (1802—1880; 1838, 1845. Ab.

RUTH. 6.5. D.

SAMUEL SMITH (1804—1873)

1. SUM-MER suns are glow - ing O - ver land and sea; Hap-py light is flow - ing, Boun - ti - ful and free. Ev - 'ry-thing re - joic - es In the mel-low rays; All earth's thou-sand voi - ces Swell the psalm of praise.

741 *A Summer Song.*

2 God's free mercy streameth
Over all the world,
And His banner gleameth,
Everywhere unfurled.
Broad and deep and glorious,
As the heaven above,
Shines in might victorious
His eternal love.

3 Lord, upon our blindness,
Thy pure radiance pour
For Thy loving-kindness
Makes us love Thee more.

And when clouds are drifting
Dark across our sky,
Then, the vail uplifting,
Father, be Thou nigh.

4 We will never doubt Thee,
Though Thou vail Thy light;
Life is dark without Thee,
Death with Thee is bright.
Light of light, shine o'er us
On our pilgrim way,
Go Thou still before us
To the endless day.

Bp. William Walsham How (1823—).

ST. GEORGE'S CHAPEL. 7. D.

Sir GEORGE JOB ELVEY (1816—). 1860.

1. Come, ye thank-ful peo-ple, come, Raise the song of Har-vest-home: All is safe-ly gath-er'd in, Ere the win-ter storms be-gin; God, our Mak-er, doth pro-vide For our wants to be sup-plied: Come to God's own tem-ple, come, Raise the song of Har-vest-home.

742 *Harvest Hymn.*

2 All the world is God's own field,
Fruit unto His praise to yield;
Wheat and tares together sown,
Unto joy or sorrow grown;
First the blade, and then the ear,
Then the full corn shall appear:
Lord of Harvest, grant that we
Wholesome grain and pure may be.

3 For the Lord our God shall come,
And shall take His harvest home;
From His field shall in that day
All offences purge away;
Give His angels charge at last
In the fire the tares to cast;
But the fruitful ears to store
In His garner evermore.

4 Even so, Lord, quickly come
To Thy final Harvest-home;
Gather Thou Thy people in,
Free from sorrow, free from sin;

There, forever purified,
In Thy presence to abide:
Come, with all Thine angels, come,
Raise the glorious Harvest-home.

Rev. Henry Alford (1810—1871), 1845.

743 *Thanksgiving or Fast.*

1 Christ, by heavenly hosts adored,
Gracious, mighty, sovereign Lord,
God of nations, King of kings,
Head of all created things,
By the Church with joy confest,
God o'er all forever blest;
Pleading at Thy throne we stand,
Save Thy people, bless our land.

2 On our fields of grass and grain
Drop, O Lord, the kindly rain;
O'er our wide and goodly land
Crown the labors of each hand
Let Thy kind protection be
O'er our commerce on the sea;
Open, Lord, Thy bounteous hand,
Bless Thy people, bless our land.

3 Let our rulers ever be
  Men that love and honor Thee;
  Let the powers by Thee ordained
  Be in righteousness maintained;

In the people's hearts increase
  Love of piety and peace;
  Thus, united we shall stand
  One wide, free, and happy land.

Rev. Henry Harbaugh (1818—1867), 1860. Ab. and alt

AMERICA. 6. 6. 4. 6. 6. 6. 4.
HENRY CAREY (1693—1743), 1740. Har. 1745.

1. My coun-try, 'tis of thee, Sweet land of lib - er - ty, Of thee I sing; Land where my

fa - thers died, Land of the pilgrim's pride, From ev - 'ry mount-ain side Let free-dom ring.

744   *"My Country."*

2 My native country, thee,
  Land of the noble, free,
    Thy name I love;
  I love thy rocks and rills,
  Thy woods and templed hills;
  My heart with rapture thrills
    Like that above.

3 Let music swell the breeze,
  And ring from all the trees
    Sweet freedom's song:
  Let mortal tongues awake,
  Let all that breathe partake,
  Let rocks their silence break,
    The sound prolong.

4 Our fathers' God, to Thee,
  Author of liberty,
    To Thee we sing;
  Long may our land be bright
  With freedom's holy light;

Protect us by Thy might,
  Great God, our King.

Rev. Samuel Francis Smith (1808—   ), 1832.

745   *"God save the State."*

1 God bless our native land:
  Firm may she ever stand,
    Through storm and night:
  When the wild tempests rave,
  Ruler of wind and wave,
  Do Thou our country save
    By Thy great might.

2 For her our prayer shall rise
  To God, above the skies;
    On Him we wait;
  Thou who art ever nigh,
  Guarding with watchful eye,
  To Thee aloud we cry,
    God save the State.

Rev. Charles Timothy Brooks (1813—1883), 1835.
Alt. by Rev. John Sullivan Dwight (1813—   ), 1844

PLYMOUTH ROCK. S. M. D. Arr. from Miss BROWNE (—).

1. THE break-ing waves dash'd high, On a stern and rock-bound coast,

And the woods a-gainst a storm-y sky Their gi-ant branch-es toss'd;

And the heav-y night hung dark The hills and wa-ters o'er,

When a band of ex-iles moor'd their bark On the wild New Eng-land shore.

746 *The Landing of the Pilgrims.*

2 Not as the conqueror comes,
   They, the true-hearted, came;
Not with the roll of the stirring drums,
   And the trumpet that sings of fame;
Not as the flying come,
   In silence and in fear :—
They shook the depths of the desert gloom
   With their hymns of lofty cheer.

3 Amidst the storm they sang,
   And the stars heard, and the sea :
And the sounding aisles of the dim woods
   rang
      To the anthem of the free.

The ocean eagle soared
   From his nest by the white wave's foam,
And the rocking pines of the forest
   roared—
      This was their welcome home !

4 What sought they thus afar?
   Bright jewels of the mine?
The wealth of seas, the spoils of war?
   They sought a faith's pure shrine !
Ay, call it holy ground,
   The soil where first they trod !
They have left unstained what there they
   found—
      Freedom to worship God.

Mrs. Felicia Dorothea Hemans (1794—1835).

DOXOLOGIES.

1 C. M.
To Father, Son, and Holy Ghost,
  The God whom we adore,
Be glory, as it was, is now,
  And shall be evermore.
Tate and Brady, 1696.

2 S. M.
To God the Father, Son,
  And Spirit, One and Three,
Be glory, as it was, is now,
  And shall forever be.
Rev. John Wesley (1703—1791), 1741.

3 L. M.
PRAISE God, from whom all blessings flow;
Praise Him, all creatures here below;
Praise Him above, ye heavenly host;
Praise Father, Son, and Holy Ghost.
Bp. Thomas Ken (1637—1711), 1697.

4 L. M.
To God the Father, God the Son,
And God the Spirit, Three in One,
Be honor, praise, and glory given,
By all on earth, and all in Heaven.
Rev. Isaac Watts (1674—1748), 1709.

5 L. M. 6l.
To God the Father, God the Son,
And God the Spirit, Three in One,
Be honor, praise, and glory given,
By all on earth, and all in Heaven ;
As was through ages heretofore,
Is now, and shall be evermore.
Rev. Isaac Watts, 1709. First 4 lines.

6 C. P. M.
To Father, Son, and Holy Ghost,
The God whom Heaven's triumphant host
  And saints on earth adore ;
Be glory as in ages past,
As now it is, and so shall last,
  When time shall be no more.
Tate and Brady, 1696. Alt.

7 L. P. M.
Now to the great and sacred Three,
The Father, Son, and Spirit, be
Eternal praise and glory given,
Through all the worlds where God is
      known,
By all the angels near the throne,
And all the saints in earth and Heaven.
Rev. Isaac Watts, 1719.

8 H. M.
O GOD, for ever blest,
  To Thee all praise be given ;
Thy Name Triune confest
  By all in earth and Heaven ;
As heretofore it was, is now,
  And shall be so for evermore.
Rev. Edward Henry Bickersteth (1825—), 1870.

9 8. 7.
PRAISE the Father, earth and Heaven,
  Praise the Son, the Spirit praise,
As it was, and is, be given
  Glory through eternal days.
Unknown Author, 1827.

10 8. 7. D.
WORSHIP, honor, glory, blessing,
  Lord, we offer to Thy Name :
Young and old their praise expressing,
  Join Thy goodness to proclaim.
As the saints in Heaven adore Thee,
  We would bow before Thy throne ;
As the angels serve before Thee,
  So on earth Thy will be done !
Edward Osler (1798—1863), 1836.

11 8. 7. 4.
GLORY be to God the Father,
  Glory be to God the Son,
Glory be to God the Spirit,
  Great Jehovah, Three in One :
    Glory, glory,
  While eternal ages run.
Rev. Horatius Bonar (1808—), 1866.

12   7. 6. D.

FATHER, Son, and Holy Ghost,
    One God whom we adore,
Join we with the heavenly host,
    To praise Thee evermore:
Live, by Heaven and earth adored,
    Three in One, and One in Three,
Holy, holy, holy Lord,
    All glory be to Thee.
                    Rev. Charles Wesley (1708—1788), 1746. Alt.

13   7.

SING we to our God above
Praise eternal as His love:
Praise Him, all ye heavenly host,
Father, Son, and Holy Ghost,
                    Rev. Charles Wesley, 1740.

14   7. 61.

Praise the Name, of God most high,
Praise Him, all below the sky,
Praise Him, all ye heavenly host,
Father, Son, and Holy Ghost;
As through countless ages past,
Evermore His praise shall last.
                    Unknown Author, 1827.

15   7. 61.

GOD the Father, God of grace,
Saviour, born of mortal race,
Comforter, our Life and Light,
One in essence, love and might;
Thee whom all in Heaven adore,
We would worship evermore.
                    Rev. Ray Palmer (1808—   ), 1873.

16   7. D.

PRAISE our glorious King and Lord,
Angels waiting on His word,
Saints that walk with Him in white,
Pilgrims walking in His light:
Glory to the Eternal One,
Glory to His Only Son,
Glory to the Spirit be
Now, and through eternity.
                    Rev. Alexander Ramsay Thompson (1822—   ), 1869.

17   6. 4.

To the great One in Three
The highest praises be,
    Hence evermore;
His sovereign majesty
May we in glory see,
    And to eternity
    Love and adore.
                    Rev. Charles Wesley, 1757.

18   6. 4.

To God the Father, Son,
And Spirit, Three in One,
    All praise be given:
Crown Him in every song;
To Him your hearts belong,
Let all His praise prolong
    On earth, in Heaven.
                    Rev. Edwin Francis Hatfield (1807—1883), 1843.

19   10.

ALL praise and glory to the Father be
And Son and Spirit, undivided Three,
As hath been alway, shall be, and is now,
To Thee, O God, the everlasting Thou.
                    Bp. Edward Henry Bickersteth (1825—   ), 1870.

20   10, 11.

ALL glory to God, the Father and Son,
And Spirit of grace, the great Three in
    One;
Let highest ascriptions forever be given
By all the creation on earth and in
    Heaven.
                    Rippon's Collection, 1778.

21   11.

O FATHER Almighty, to Thee be addrest,
With Christ and the Spirit, One God
    ever blest,
All glory and worship, from earth and
    from Heaven,
As was, and is now, and shall ever be
    given.
                    Unknown Author.

I BELIEVE in GOD THE FATHER Almighty, Maker of Heaven and earth:

And in JESUS CHRIST His only Son our Lord; who was conceived by the Holy Ghost; born of the Virgin Mary; suffered under Pontius Pilate; was crucified, dead, and buried; He descended into Hell; the third day He rose again from the dead; He ascended into Heaven; and sitteth on the right hand of God the Father Almighty; from thence He shall come to judge the quick and the dead.

I believe in the HOLY GHOST; the holy Catholic Church; the Communion of Saints; the Forgiveness of sins; the Resurrection of the body; and the Life everlasting. Amen.

CHANTS.

AFTER THE TEN COMMANDMENTS.

1 LORD, have mer-cy up-on us, and in-cline our hearts to keep Thy law.

LORD, have mer-cy up-on us, and write all these Thy laws in our hearts, we be-seech Thee.

2 LORD, have mer-cy up-on us, and in-cline our hearts to keep Thy law.

LORD, have mer-cy up-on us, and write all these Thy laws in our hearts, we be-seech Thee.

MENDELSSOHN.

3 WILT Thou have mer-cy up-on us, O Lord, and in-cline our hearts to keep these laws.

PATER NOSTER.

1 OUR Father who art in Heaven, | hallow - ed | be Thy | Name ; || Thy kingdom come,
  Thy will be done on | earth ·· as it | is in | Heaven.
2 Give us this | day our | daily | bread ; || And forgive us our trespasses, as we forgive
  them that | trespass ·· a- | gainst— | us.
3 And lead us not into temptation, but de- | liver | us from | evil ; || For Thine is the king-
  dom, and the power, and the glory, for ever. | A- —|— | men.

GLORIA PATRI. No. 1.   HENRY WELLINGTON GREATOREX (1811—1858).

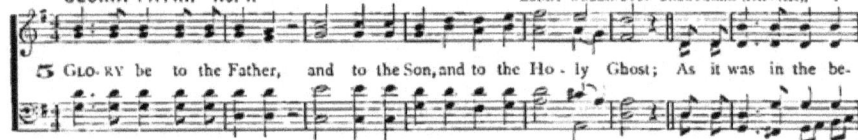

5 GLO- RY be to the Father,   and to the Son, and to the Ho- ly Ghost ; As it was in the be-

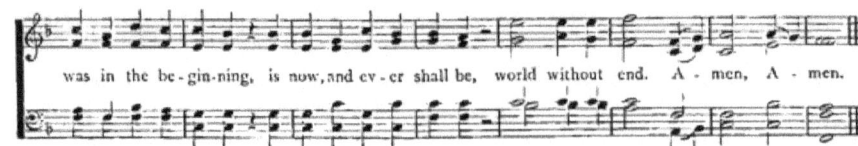

gin - ning,   is now, and ev - er shall be,   world with-out   end...... A- men, A - men.

GLORIA PATRI. No. 2.   HENRY WELLINGTON GREATOREX.

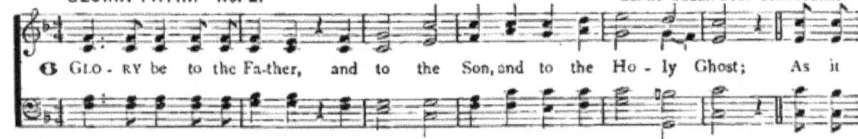

6 GLO- RY be to the Fa-ther,   and to   the   Son, and to the Ho- ly Ghost ;   As it

was in the be - gin-ning, is now, and ev - er shall be,   world without end. A - men, A - men.

GLORIA PATRI. No. 3.   RICHARD FARRANT. (1530-1580; 1570.

7
1 GLORY be to the Father, and | to the | Son, || And to the | Holy | Ghost;
2 As it was in the beginning, is now, and | ever | shall be, || World | without | end.   A- | men.

GLORIA PATRI. No. 4.   LUDWIG SPOHR (1741-1859).

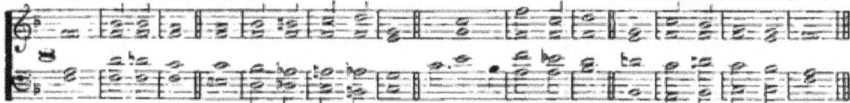

No. 5.   HENRY PURCELL (1658-1695).   No. 6.   P. HUMPHREYS.

GLORIA IN EXCELSIS.

11
1 GLORY be to | God on | high, || And on earth | peace, good- | will · · towards | men.
2 We praise Thee, we bless Thee, we | worship | Thee, || We glorify Thee, we give thanks
    to | Thee for | Thy great | glory.
3 O Lord God, | heavenly | King, | God the | Father | Al- —| mighty.
4 O Lord, the only begotten Son, | Jesus | Christ; || O Lord God, Lamb of God, | Son of
    the | Father,

5 That takest away the | sins · · of the | world, || Have mercy | upon | us.
6 Thou that takest away the | sins . . of the | world, || Have mercy | upon | us.
7 Thou that takest away the | sins . . of the | world, || Re- | ceive our | prayer.
8 Thou that sittest at the right hand of | God the | Father, || Have mercy | upon | us.
9 For Thou | only . . art holy: || Thou | only | art the | Lord:
10 Thou only, O Christ, with the | Holy | Ghost, || Art most high in the | glory . . of |
    God the | Father. | A- | men.

DOMINUS REGIT ME.

12

1 THE Lord is my Shepherd ; I | shall not | want. || He maketh me to lie down in green pastures ; He leadeth me beside the | still— | waters.

2 He restoreth my soul ; He leadeth me in paths of righteousness for His | Name's— | sake. || Yea, though I walk through the valley of the shadow of death, I will fear no evil: for Thou art with me ; Thy rod and Thy staff | they— | comfort me.

3 Thou preparest a table before me in the presence of mine enemies, Thou anointest my head with oil: my | cup ' ' runneth | over. || Surely goodness and mercy shall follow me all the days of my life ; and I will dwell in the house of the | Lord, for | ever. || A- | men.

DEUS MISEREATUR.   LUDWIG SPOHR (1784—1859).

13

1 GOD be merciful unto us, and | bless— | us, || And cause His | face to | shine up- | on us,

2 That Thy way may be known up- | on— | earth, || Thy saving | health a- | mong all | nations.

3 Let the people praise | Thee, O | God ! || Let all the | people | praise— | Thee.

4 O let the nations be glad and | sing for | joy, || For Thou shalt judge the people righteously, and govern the | na - tions up- | on— | earth.

5 Let the people praise | Thee, O | God ! || Let all the | people | praise— | Thee.

6 Then shall the earth | yield her | increase, || And God, even our own | God, shall | bless— | us.

*7 God shall | bless— | us, || And all the ends of the | earth shall | fear— | Him.

QUAM DILECTA.   THOMAS SANDERS DUPUIS (1733—1796).

14

1 How amiable are Thy | taber- | nacles, || O | Lord— | of— | hosts !

2 My soul longeth, yea even fainteth for the | courts ' ' of the | Lord, || My heart and my flesh crieth out | for the | living | God.

3 Yea, the sparrow hath found her an house, and the swallow a nest for herself, where she may | lay her | young || Even Thine altars, O Lord of hosts. my | King— | and my | God.

4 Blessed are they that|dwell in · · Thy|house ‖ They will be|still—|praising|Thee.
5 Blessed is the man whose|strength · · is in|Thee ‖ In whose heart|are the|ways of|them.
6 Who passing through the valley of Baca|make · · it a|well ‖ The rain|also|filleth · · the|pools.
7 They go from|strength to|strength ‖ Every one of them in Zion ap-|peareth · · be-|fore—|God.
8 O Lord God of hosts,|hear my|prayer ‖ Give ear, |O—|God of|Jacob.
9 Behold, O|God our|shield ‖ And look upon the|face of|Thine an-|ointed.
10 For a day in Thy courts is better|than a|thousand ‖ I had rather be a door-keeper in the house of my God, than to dwell in the|tents of|wicked-|ness.
11 For the Lord God is a|sun and|shield ‖ The Lord will give grace and glory; no good thing will He withhold from|them that|walk up-|rightly.
12 O|Lord of|hosts ‖ Blessed is the|man that|trusteth · · in|Thee.

VENITE, EXULTEMUS.

15   Ps. xcv.

1 O COME, let us|sing · · unto the|Lord ‖ Let us heartily rejoice in the|strength of|our sal-|vation.
2 Let us come before His presence with|thanks- —|giving ‖ And show ourselves|glad in|Him with|psalms.
3 For the Lord is a|great—|God ‖ And a great|King a-|bove all|gods.
4 In His hands are all the corners|of the|earth ‖ And the strength of the|hills is|His—|also.
5 The sea is His|and He|made it ‖ And His hands pre-|pared · · the|dry—|land.
6 O come, let us worship|and fall|down ‖ And kneel be-|fore the|Lord our|Maker.
7 For He is the|Lord our|God ‖ And we are the people of His pasture, |and the|sheep · · of His|hand.
8 O worship the Lord in the|beauty · · of|holiness ‖ Let the whole earth|stand in|awe of|Him.
*9 For He cometh, for He cometh to|judge the|earth ‖ And with righteousnes to judge the world, and the|people|with His|truth.

No. 2.   HENRY SMART (1812–1879).

JUBILATE DEO.

Sir GEORGE JOB ELVEY (1816—).

17   Ps. c.

1 MAKE a joyful noise unto the Lord, | all ye | lands || Serve the Lord with gladness; come before His | presence | with— | singing.

2 Know ye that the Lord | He is | God || It is He that hath made us, and not we ourselves; we are His people, | and the | sheep of ·· His | pasture.

3 Enter into His gates with thanksgiving, and into His | courts with | praise || Be thankful unto Him, | and— | bless His | Name.

4 For the Lord is good; His mercy is | ever- | lasting || And His truth endureth to | all— | gene- | rations.

No. 2.

Gregorian.

18

No. 3.

THOMAS ATTWOOD (1761—1858).

19

BENEDIC ANIMA MEA.

CHARLES NORRIS (1740—1790).

20   Ps. ciii.

1 PRAISE the Lord, | O my | soul; || And all that is within me, | praise His | holy | Name.

2 Praise the Lord, | O my | soul; || And for- | get not | all His | benefits.

3 Who forgiveth | all Thy | sin, || And healeth ·· all | thine in- | firmities.

4 Who saveth thy | life ·· from de- | struction; || And crowneth thee with | mercy ·· and | loving- | kindness.

5 O praise the Lord, ye angels of His, ye that ex- | cel in | strength; || Ye that fulfil His commandment, and hearken unto the | voice of | His— | word.

6 O praise the Lord, | all ·· ye His | hosts; || Ye servants of | His that | do His | pleasure.

*7 O speak good of the Lord, all ye works of His, in all places of | His do- | minion. || Praise thou the | Lord, O | —my | soul.

LEVAVI OCULOS.

Dean HENRY ALDRICH (1647—1710).

21

Ps. cxxi.

1 I WILL lift up mine eyes|unto the|hills || From whence|cometh|my—|help.
2 My help cometh|from the|Lord || Which|made—|heaven ·· and|earth.
3 He will not suffer thy|foot ·· to be|moved ; || He that|keepeth ·· thee|will not|slumber.
4 Behold, He that|keepeth|Israel || Shall neither|slumber|nor—|sleep.
5 The Lord|is thy|keeper ; || The Lord is thy shade up-|on thy|right—|hand.
6 The sun shall not|smite thee ·· by|day, || Nor the|moon—|by—|night.
7 The Lord shall preserve thee from|all—|evil ; || He|shall pre-|serve thy|soul.
8 The Lord shall preserve thy going out and thy|coming|in || From this time forth,
   and|even ·· for|ever-|more.

No. 2.

JAMES TURLE (1802—1882), 1862

LÆTATUS SUM.

RICHARD FARRANT (1530—1580), 1570.

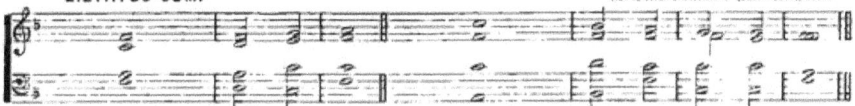

23

Ps. cxxii.

1 I WAS glad when they said|unto|me. || Let us go in-|to the|house ·· of the|Lord.
2 Our feet shall stand with-|in thy|gates, || O —|Je-|rusa-|lem.
3 Jerusalem is builded|as a|city || That|is com-|pact to-|gether:
4 Whither the tribes go up, the|tribes ·· of the|Lord, || Unto the testimony of Israel,
   to give thanks un-|to the|Name ·· of the|Lord.
5 For there are set|thrones of|judgment, || The thrones|of the|house of|David.
6 Pray for the peace of Je-|rusa-|lem ; || They shall|prosper ·· that|love—|thee.
7 Peace be with-|in thy|walls || And prosperi-|ty with-|in thy|palaces.
8 For my brethren and com-|panions'|sakes || I will now say, |Peace—|be with-|in thee.
9 Because of the house of the|Lord our|God || I will|seek—|thy—|good.

No. 2.

Sir GEORGE JOB ELVEY.

LAUDATE DOMINUM.

WILLIAM BOYCE (1710—1779).

25   Ps. cl.

1 PRAISE ye the Lord.   Praise God | in His | sanctuary : || Praise Him in the | firma - ment | of His | power.

2 Praise Him for His | mighty | acts : || Praise Him ac- | cording ·· to His | excel - lent | greatness.

3 Praise Him with the | sound ·· of the | trumpet : || Praise Him | with the | psaltery ·· and | harp.

4 Praise Him with the | timbrel ·· and | dance : || Praise Him with | stringed ·· instru- | ments and | organs.

5 Praise Him upon the | loud— | cymbals : || Praise Him upon the | high— | sounding | cymbals.

6 Let every thing that | hath— | breath, || Praise the | Lord.   Praise | ye the | Lord.

No. 2.

QUAM PULCHRI SUPER MONTES.

WILLIAM CROTCH (1775—1847).

27   ISAIAH lii. 7-9.

1 How beautiful up- | on the | mountains || Are the feet of him that bringeth good | tidings, ·· that | publish - eth | peace ;

2 That bringeth good tidings of good, that publisheth | sal- — | vation ; || That saith unto Zion, | thy— | God— | reigneth !

3 Thy watchmen shall lift | up the | voice ; || With the voice to- | gether | shall they | sing :

4 For they shall see | eye to | eye, || When the Lord shall | bring a- | gain— | Zion.

5 Break forth | into | joy, || Sing together, ye waste places | of Je- | rusa- | lem.

6 For the Lord hath comforted | His— | people, || He hath re- | deemed ·· Je- | rusa- | lem.

*7 The Lord hath made bare His holy arm in the eyes of | all the | nations ; || And all the ends of the earth shall see the sal- | vation | of our | God.

BENEDICTUS DOMINUS.

THOMAS SANDERS DUPUIS (1733—1796).

28

LUKE i. 68—71.

1 BLESSED be the Lord God of | Isra- | el, || For He hath visited | and re- | deemed
His | people;

2 And hath raised up a mighty sal- | vation | for us || In the house | of His | servant | David.

3 As He spake by the mouth of His | holy | prophets, || Which have been | since the |
world be- | gan;

4 That we should be saved | from our | enemies, || And from the | hand of | all that | hate us.

MAGNIFICAT.

Rev. SAMUEL WESLEY (1662—1735).

29

LUKE i. 46—55.

1 My soul doth magni- | fy the | Lord, || And my spirit hath re- | joiced in | God my |
Saviour.

2 For He hath regarded the low estate of | His hand- | maiden; || For behold, from
henceforth all gener- | ations · · shall | call me | blessed.

3 For He that is mighty hath done to me great | things, || And | holy | is His | Name.

4 And His mercy is on | them that | fear Him, || From gener- | ation · · to | gener- | ation.

5 He hath showed strength | with His | arm, || He hath scattered the proud in the
imagi- | nation · of their | hearts.

6 He hath put down the mighty | from their | seats, || And exalted | them of | low de- | gree.

7 He hath filled the hungry | with good | things, || And the rich He | hath sent | empty · ·
a- | way.

8 He hath holpen His servant | Isra- | el, || In re- | membrance | of His | mercy.

*9 As He spake to our fathers, to | Abra- | ham, || And | to His | seed for- | ever.

No. 2.

JOHN RANDALL (1715—1799).

30

No. 3.

From BEETHOVEN, by JOHN GOSS (1800—1880).

31

392

TE DEUM LAUDAMUS.

WILLIAM CROTCH (1775–1847).

392

1 WE praise Thee, | O— | God ; || we acknowledge | Thee to | be the | Lord. || All the earth doth | worship | Thee, || the Father | ever- | last- — | ing.

2 To Thee all Angels | cry a- | loud ; || the Heavens, and | all the | powers ·· there- | in. || To Thee Cherubim, and | Sera- | phim || con- | tin - ual- | ly do | cry,

3 Holy, | Holy, | Holy, || Lord | God of | Saba- | oth ; || Heaven and earth are full of the | Majes- | ty || of | Thy— | glo- — | ry.

4 The glorious company | of the | Apostles || praise | — — | — | — — | Thee ; || The goodly fellowship | of the | Prophets || praise | — — | — — | Thee.

5 The noble army | of— | Martyrs || praise | — — | — | — — | Thee. || The holy Church throughout | all the | world || doth | — ac- | knowledge | Thee,

6 The | Fa- — | ther || of an | in - finite | Majes- | ty || Thine a- | dora - ble, | true, || and | on- — | ly— | Son ;

7 Also the | Holy | Ghost, || the | Com- — | — fort- | er. || Thou art the | King of | Glory, || O | — — | — — | Christ.

8 Thou art the ever- | lasting | Son || of | — the | Fa- — | ther. || When Thou tookest upon Thee to de- | liver | man, || Thou didst humble Thyself to be | born— | of a | Virgin.

9 When Thou hadst overcome the | sharpness ·· of | death, || Thou didst open the Kingdom of Heaven to | all be- | liev- — | ers. || Thou sittest at the right hand | of— | God || in the glory | of the | Fa- — | ther.

10 We believe that | Thou shalt | come || to | be — | our — | Judge. || We therefore pray Thee, | help Thy | servants, || whom Thou hast redeemed | with Thy | precious | blood.

11 Make them to be numbered | with Thy | saints || in glory | ever- | last- — | ing. || O Lord, | save Thy | people, || and | bless Thine | heri- | tage.

12 Gov- | —ern | them || and | lift them | up for- | ever. || Day | by— | day || we | magni- | fy— | Thee.

13 And we worship | Thy —| Name, || ever, | world with- | out —| end. || Vouchsafe, | O— | Lord, || to keep us | this day | without | sin.

14 O Lord, have mercy up- | on — | us, || have | mercy ·· up- | on — | us. || O Lord, let Thy mercy be up- | on — | us, || as our | trust — | is in | Thee.

*15 O Lord, in Thee | have I | trusted, || let me never | be con- | found- — | ed.

BAPTISMAL CHANT.

THOMAS TALLIS (c. 1529—1585). 1575.

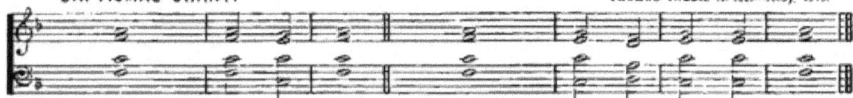

33

Before the Administration.
Ps. ciii. 17, 18.

1 THE mercy of the Lord is from everlasting to everlasting upon|them that|fear
Him, || And His righteousness|unto|children's|children.

2 To such as keep His|cove-|nant; || And to those that remember His com-|mand-
ments to|do —|them.

BAPTISMAL CHANT.

34

MARK x. 14.

1 SUFFER the little children to come unto Me, and for-|bid them|not: || For of|such
· · is the|kingdom · · of|heaven.

ACTS ii. 39.

2 For the promise is unto you, and|to your|children; || And to all that are afar off,
even as many as the|Lord our|God shall|call.

BAPTISMAL CHANT.

35

After the Administration.
EZEK. xxxvi. 25, 26.

1 THEN will I sprinkle clean|water · · up-|on you, || And|ye shall|be —|clean:

2 A new heart also|will I|give you, || And a new spirit|will I|put with-|in you,

3 And I will take away the stony heart|out of · · your|flesh, || And I will|give · · you
a|heart of|flesh.

Is. xliv. 3, 4.

4 I will pour my Spirit up-|on thy|seed, || And my|blessing · · up-|on thine|offspring:

5 And they shall spring up as a-|mong the|grass, || As|willows · · by the|water-|courses.

No. 2.

RICHARD FARRANT (1530—1580). 1570.

36

No. 3.

JOSEPH BARNBY (1538—   ).

37

PASCHA NOSTRUM.

38   1 Cor. v. 7, 8.   Rom. vi. 9-11.   1 Cor. xv. 20-22.

1 CHRIST our passover is sacri-|ficed|for us, || Therefore|let us|keep the|feast.
2 Not with the old leaven, neither with leaven of|malice ˙˙ and|wickedness, || But with the unleavened bread of sin-|ceri - ty|and —|truth.
3 Christ, being raised from the dead,|dieth ˙˙ no|more; || Death hath no more do-|minion|over|Him.
4 For in that He died, He died unto|sin —|once: || But in that He liveth, He|liveth|unto|God.
5 Likewise reckon ye also yourselves to be dead indeed|unto|sin, || But alive unto God through|Jesus|Christ our|Lord.
6 Now is Christ risen|from the|dead, || And become the first-|fruits of|them that|slept.
7 For since by|man came|death, || By man came also the resur-|rection|of the|dead.
8 For as in Adam|all —|die, || Even so in Christ shall|all be|made a-|live.

AUDIVI VOCEM.

39   Rev. xiv. 13; xx. 6; i. 5, 6.

1 I HEARD a voice from Heaven, saying|unto ˙˙ me,|Write, || Blessed are the dead, who die|in the|Lord from|henceforth:
2 Yea, saith the Spirit, that they may rest|from their|labors, || And their|works do|follow|them.
3 Blessed and holy is he that hath part in the first|resur-|rection; || On such the|second ˙˙ death|hath no|power;
4 But they shall be priests of God|and of|Christ, || And shall reign with|Him a|thousand|years.
5 Unto Him that|loved|us, || And washed us from our sins|in His|own —|blood,
6 And hath made us kings and priests to God|and His|Father; || To Him be glory and do-|minion ˙˙ for|ever ˙˙ and|ever.

"THY WILL BE DONE."

LOWELL MASON (1792–1872).

FINE.

D.C.

Close. Thy will be done!

40

1 "THY will be|done!" || In devious way
   The hurrying stream of|life may run; ||
   Yet still our grateful hearts shall say, |
      "Thy will be|done."

2 "Thy will be|done!" || If o'er us shine
   A gladdening and a|prosperous|sun, ||
   This prayer will make it more divine—|
      "Thy will be|done!"

3 "Thy will be|done!" || Though shrouded o'er
   Our|path with|gloom, || one comfort—one
   Is ours:— to breathe, while we adore. |
      "Thy will be|done."

Sir John Bowring (1792—1872), 1825.   Ab.

SANCTUS. Irr.

41 Ho - ly! ho - ly! ho - ly! Lord God of Sa - ba - oth! Heav'n and earth are full, full of Thy

glo - ry; Heav'n and earth are full, are full of Thy glo - ry;   Glo - ry be to   Thee,
                                                                     Glo - ry be to

Glo - ry be to   Thee,   Glo - ry be to Thee, to Thee, O   Lord...... Most High.
Thee,   Glo - ry be   to Thee,

THE MISSIONARY'S CALL.

EDWARD HOWE, Jr.

1 My soul is not at rest. There comes a strange and secret whisper to my|spirit, ||
Like a dream of|night, || That tells me I am on en-|chanted|ground.

2 Why live I here? the vows of God are|on me, || And I may not stop to play with
shadows, or pluck earthly|flowers, || Till I my work have done, and rendered
up ac-|count.

3 And I will|go! || I may no longer doubt to give up friends and idol|hopes, || And
every tie that binds my heart to|thee, my|country!

4 Henceforth, then, it matters not if storm or sunshine be my|earthy lot, || Bitter or
sweet my|cup, || I only pray, "God, make me holy, and my spirit nerve for the
stern|hour of|strife!"

5 And when I come to stretch me for the|last, || In unattended agony, beneath the
cocoa's|shade, || It will be sweet that I have toiled for|other worlds than|this.

6 And if one for whom Satan hath struggled as he hath for|me, || Should ever reach
that blessed|shore — || O how this heart will glow with|gratitude and|love.

CHORUS vv. 1–5.   cres.

The voice of my de-part-ed Lord, "Go, teach all na-tions," Comes on the

CHORUS v. 6.

night-air and a-wakes mine ear. Through a-ges of e-ter-nal years, my spir-it

nev-er shall re-pent That toil and suf-f'ring once were mine be-low.

ALPHABETICAL INDEX OF TUNES.

INDEX OF CHANTS.

METRICAL INDEX OF TUNES.

400

402

METRICAL INDEX OF TUNES.

INDEX OF AUTHORS.

The figures refer to the numbers of the hymns.

INDEX OF COMPOSERS.

The figures refer to the numbers of the pages.

INDEX OF SCRIPTURE TEXTS.

INDEX OF SUBJECTS.

The figures refer to the numbers of the hymns.

418

INDEX OF FIRST LINES.

INDEX TO CHANTS.

www.ingramcontent.com/pod-product-compliance
Lightning Source LLC
Chambersburg PA
CBHW031828270326
41932CB00008B/584